MY
BIBLE
STORY
BOOK

Presented to

_____

From

_____

MY BIBLE STORY BOOK

Dena Korfker

Illustrations
DIRK GRINGHUIS and DON ELLENS

KREGEL PUBLICATIONS
Grand Rapids, Michigan 49501

Library of Congress Cataloging-in-Publication Data

Korfker, Dena, 1908–
  My Bible Story Book.

  Reprint. Originally published: My Picture Story Bible.
Grand Rapids, Mich.: Zondervan Pub. House, ©1960.
  Summary: Retells 270 Bible stories, from Genesis to
Revelation.
  1. Bible stories, English [1. Bible stories]
I. Title.

B551.2.K65 1988   220.9′505   88-7236

ISBN 0-8254-3045-3

Printed on acid-free paper

1 2 3 4 5 6 7 8 Printing/Year 93 92 91 90 89 88

Printed in the United States of America

With all my love,
to my grandnephew
and grandniece, Bill
and Marci Korfker, who
have always been a
joy to me.

CONTENTS

Publisher's Preface 14
Preface 15

Old Testament

1. How God Made the World (*Genesis 1*) 17
2. How God Made Man (*Genesis 1, 2*) 19
3. Man's First Home (*Genesis 2*) 21
4. Adam and Eve Disobey God (*Genesis 3*) 22
5. The First Brothers (*Genesis 4*) 26
6. The World and the Flood (*Genesis 6*) 29
7. The Rainbow of Promise (*Genesis 7–9*) 30
8. The Tower of Babel (*Genesis 11*) 32
9. God Calls Abram (*Genesis 12*) 34
10. Abram's Choice and Lot's Choice (*Genesis 13*) 36
11. God's Promises to Abram (*Genesis 15*) 38
12. "Thou, God, Seest Me" (*Genesis 16*) 40
13. Abraham's Heavenly Visitors (*Genesis 17, 18*) 41
14. The Rain of Fire (*Genesis 19*) 44
15. A Little Boy in the Desert (*Genesis 21*) 46
16. Abraham Obeys God (*Genesis 22*) 48
17. Abraham Finds a Wife for Isaac (*Genesis 24*) 52
18. Esau Sells His Birthright (*Genesis 25*) 56
19. Jacob Gets the Birthright (*Genesis 27*) 57
20. Jacob's Dream (*Genesis 28*) 60
21. Jacob Is Fooled by His Uncle (*Genesis 29*) 62
22. Jacob Runs Away (*Genesis 31*) 65
23. Jacob Wrestles With God (*Genesis 32*) 68
24. Jacob Keeps His Promise (*Genesis 35*) 70
25. Joseph, the Dreamer (*Genesis 37*) 72
26. Joseph Sold by His Brothers (*Genesis 37*) 74
27. Joseph Goes to Prison (*Genesis 39*) 76
28. The Butler and the Baker (*Genesis 40*) 77
29. A Dream Comes True (*Genesis 41*) 79
30. Joseph's Brothers Come to Egypt (*Genesis 42*) 81

8 *Contents*

31. Two Brothers Meet (*Genesis 43*) 83
32. Jacob Meets His Son Joseph (*Genesis 46*). 86
33. The Story of Job (*Job 1; 2, 38–42*) 89
34. The Baby Moses (*Exodus 1, 2*) 92
35. Moses Runs Away (*Exodus 2*) 95
36. The Burning Bush (*Exodus 3, 4*). 96
37. Water Turned to Blood (*Exodus 4–7*) 98
38. "Let My People Go!" (*Exodus 8–10*). 101
39. "Saved by the Blood" (*Exodus 11–13*) 103
40. Through the Red Sea (*Exodus 14*) 106
41. Water and Food for Tired Travelers (*Exodus 15, 16*). 108
42. Water From a Rock (*Exodus 17*) 110
43. Moses Prays for Victory (*Exodus 17*) 111
44. Moses and God on the Mountain (*Exodus 18, 19*). 112
45. The Ten Commandments (*Exodus 20*) 114
46. The Golden Calf (*Exodus 32*) 116
47. Moses' Shining Face (*Exodus 33, 34*) 118
48. God's House and the First Priest (*Exodus 36–40;
    Leviticus 8*) 119
49. The Story of the Feasts (*Leviticus 23; Numbers 9*) 121
50. God Punishes Swearing (*Leviticus 24*) 123
51. God's People Leave the Mountain (*Numbers 10, 11*) 123
52. Miriam Becomes a Leper (*Numbers 12*). 125
53. The Twelve Spies (*Numbers 13*) 128
54. The Earth Swallows the Wicked Men (*Numbers 16*) 129
55. Aaron's Wonderful Rod (*Numbers 17*). 131
56. Moses Disobeys God (*Numbers 20*) 132
57. God Sends Fiery Serpents (*Numbers 21*) 134
58. A Donkey Talks (*Numbers 22–24*) 136
59. God's People Sin Again (*Numbers 25, 26*). 138
60. God Calls Moses Home (*Deuteronomy 34*) 140
61. Rahab Helps God's People (*Joshua 1*) 141
62. A Path Through the River (*Joshua 3–5*) 143
63. The Walls of Jericho (*Joshua 6*) 145
64. God Punishes a Thief (*Joshua 7, 8*) 147
65. Joshua Is Fooled by His Neighbors (*Joshua 9*). 148
66. God Fights for His People (*Joshua 10*) 150
67. Dividing the Land and Joshua's Farewell (*Joshua 13, 14;
    Exodus 23*) 151
68. Israel Ruled by Judges (*Judges 1–3*) 153
69. Ehud and Shamgar Save Israel (*Judges 3*). 154
70. Deborah the Judge, and Barak the Captain (*Judges 4*). 155
71. Gideon and the Angel (*Judges 6*) 157
72. God Wins Through Gideon's Army (*Judges 7*) 159
73. God Gives Samson Super-Strength (*Judges 13, 14*) 161
74. Samson Fights the Philistines (*Judges 15*) 162
75. A Failure That Became a Victory (*Judges 16*) 164
76. Ruth (*Ruth 1*). 166
77. God Blesses Naomi and Ruth (*Ruth 2–4*) 168
78. God Answers Hannah's Prayer (*1 Samuel 1*) 170

79. God Calls Samuel (*1 Samuel 3*) 174
80. The Ark of the Lord Is Stolen (*1 Samuel 4*) 175
81. The Ark of the Lord in Philistia (*1 Samuel 5–7*) 177
82. God Gives His People a King (*1 Samuel 7, 8*) 179
83. God Sends the New King to Samuel (*1 Samuel 9, 10*)...........181
84. Saul Becomes King (*1 Samuel 10*) 183
85. Saul Proves He Is a Good King (*1 Samuel 11*)..................184
86. Saul Disobeys God (*1 Samuel 13*) 186
87. Jonathan's Victory (*1 Samuel 14*) 187
88. Saul Rejected as King (*1 Samuel 15*)...................189
89. God Chooses a New King (*1 Samuel 16*) 191
90. The Sweet Singer of Israel (*1 Samuel 16*)...................193
91. David Kills the Giant (*1 Samuel 17*)...................195
92. Saul Tries to Kill David (*1 Samuel 18, 19*) 197
93. David and Jonathan (*1 Samuel 18–20*) 198
94. Saul Again Tries to Kill David (*1 Samuel 21–23*) 200
95. David Saves Saul's Life (*1 Samuel 24*) 202
96. David and Abigail (*1 Samuel 25*)...................204
97. David Again Saves Saul's Life (*1 Samuel 26*) 205
98. King Saul and the Witch (*1 Samuel 28*) 207
99. David at Ziklag (*1 Samuel 30*) 209
100. The Death of Saul and Jonathan (*1 Samuel 31; 2 Samuel 1; 1 Chronicles 10*)...................211
101. David Becomes King (*2 Samuel 2–6; 1 Chronicles 11*)...........213
102. David Brings the Ark to Jerusalem (*2 Samuel 6; 1 Chronicles 13, 15*)...................215
103. David Plans to Build a House for God (*2 Samuel 7; 1 Chronicles 17, 22*)...................216
104. The Little Lame Prince (*2 Samuel 4, 9*) 218
105. The Little Ewe Lamb (*2 Samuel 11, 12*)...................219
106. Trouble in the King's Palace (*2 Samuel 13–16*) 221
107. A King's Son Dies (*2 Samuel 17–19*)...................223
108. Solomon Becomes King (*1 Kings 1; 1 Chronicles 23*) 225
109. Solomon's Wise Choice (*1 Kings 2, 3; 1 Chronicles 22, 28; 2 Chronicles 1*) 227
110. Solomon's Great Kingdom (*1 Kings 3, 4, 10; 2 Chronicles 8, 9*) 229
111. Solomon Builds the Lord's House (*1 Kings 6, 8, 9; 2 Chronicles 2–7*) 231
112. King Solomon Forgets His Promise (*1 Kings 11*) 233
113. The Kingdom Is Divided (*1 Kings 12; 2 Chronicles 10, 11*)......235
114. Jeroboam Makes Israel Sin (*1 Kings 12, 13*)...................236
115. Jeroboam's Wife Visits Ahijah (*1 Kings 14*)...................238
116. War Between Israel and Judah (*1 Kings 14–16; 2 Chronicles 12–16*)...................240
117. Bad Times for the Kingdom of Israel (*1 Kings 15, 16*)...........242
118. Elijah Fed by the Ravens (*1 Kings 17*)...................243
119. Elijah and the Widow (*1 Kings 17*) 245
120. Elijah Prays for Fire (*1 Kings 18*) 247
121. God Comforts Elijah (*1 Kings 19*) 250

122. Ahab and His Enemies (*1 Kings 20*) 252
123. King Ahab Becomes a Thief (*1 Kings 21*) 254
124. God Punishes King Ahab (*1 Kings 22; 2 Chronicles 18*) 256
125. Elijah and King Ahaziah (*2 Kings 1*) 258
126. Elijah and the Fiery Chariot (*2 Kings 2, 3*) 260
127. Two Boys Saved From Slavery (*2 Kings 4*) 263
128. Elisha and the Shunammite Woman (*2 Kings 4*) 264
129. Elisha and the Leper (*2 Kings 5*) 266
130. Elisha and the Army of God (*2 Kings 6*) 269
131. Elisha and the Starving City (*2 Kings 7*) 272
132. The Servant Who Killed His Master (*2 Kings 8*) 274
133. The End of Ahab's Family (*2 Kings 9, 10;*
     2 Chronicles 21, 22) 275
134. A Little Boy Becomes King (*2 Kings 11;*
     2 Chronicles 22, 23) 278
135. Joash's Treasure Chest (*2 Kings 12; 2 Chronicles 24*) 280
136. The Death of Elisha (*2 Kings 13*) 281
137. Jonah Disobeys God (*Jonah 1, 2*) 283
138. Jonah Is Unhappy Because of God's Kindness
     (*Jonah 3, 4*) 285
139. A King Who Became a Leper (*2 Kings 14, 15;*
     2 Chronicles 26) 287
140. The Brave Prophet Isaiah (*Isaiah 6, 7, 9, 53*) 289
141. The Ten Lost Tribes of Israel (*2 Kings 17;*
     2 Chronicles 28) 291
142. Hezekiah Brings His People Back to God (*2 Kings 18;*
     2 Chronicles 29, 30) 293
143. God Destroys Israel's Enemy (*2 Kings 18, 19;*
     2 Chronicles 32; Isaiah 36, 37) 295
144. God Answers Hezekiah's Prayer (*2 Kings 20;*
     2 Chronicles 32; Isaiah 38, 39) 296
145. Wicked Manasseh Turns to God (*2 Kings 21;*
     2 Chronicles 33) 298
146. Josiah and God's Lost Book (*2 Kings 22, 23;*
     2 Chronicles 34, 35) 299
147. God Chooses a New Prophet (*Jeremiah 1, 2, 36–40;*
     2 Chronicles 36) 301
148. God's People Taken to Babylon (*2 Kings 25;*
     2 Chronicles 36; Jeremiah 39) 303
149. Daniel Refuses the King's Food (*Daniel 1*) 305
150. Daniel Explains the King's Dream (*Daniel 2*) 306
151. The Fiery Furnace (*Daniel 3*) 308
152. A Proud King Humbled (*Daniel 4*) 310
153. The Writing on the Wall (*Daniel 5*) 312
154. Daniel Safe in the Lions' Den (*Daniel 6*) .314
155. God Brings Back His People (*Ezra 1–8*) 316
156. Jerusalem Rebuilt (*Ezra 4–6*) 318
157. Beautiful Queen Esther (*Esther 1, 2*) 320
158. Esther Saves God's People (*Esther 3–10*) .322
159. Ezra Helps God's People (*Ezra 7–10*) 325

160. Nehemiah Goes to Help Ezra (*Nehemiah 1–6*) 326
161. "If I Forget Thee, O Jerusalem" (*Nehemiah 8–13*) 328

New Testament

162. The Promise God Had Made (*Luke 1*) 331
163. An Angel Visits Zacharias (*Luke 1*) 332
164. Mary and the Angel (*Luke 1*) 334
165. John the Baptist Is Born (*Luke 1*) 335
166. The Saviour Is Born (*Luke 2*) 337
167. Anna and Simeon Meet Jesus (*Luke 2*) 338
168. A Wonderful Star (*Matthew 2*) 340
169. God Takes Care of His Son (*Matthew 2*) 341
170. A Visit to the Temple (*Luke 2*) 343
171. Jesus Is Baptized by John (*Matthew 3; Mark 1; Luke 3; John 1*)...345
172. Jesus Is Tempted by Satan (*Matthew 4; Mark 1; Luke 4*)........347
173. Followers of Jesus (*Matthew 9: Mark 3; John 1*)..............349
174. Jesus Helps at a Wedding Feast (*John 2*)......................350
175. "My Father's House" (*John 2*) 352
176. A Ruler Visits Jesus (*John 3*)..............................353
177. "No, Never Thirst Again" (*John 4*)..........................354
178. Jesus Helps a Believing Father (*John 4*) 356
179. The Cripple at the Pool of Bethesda (*John 5*) 357
180. Not Wanted by His Own People (*Luke 4*) 360
181. A Wonderful Catch of Fish (*Luke 5*) 361
182. A Busy Sabbath Day for Jesus (*Matthew 8; Mark 1; Luke 4*) 363
183. Jesus Heals a Leper (*Matthew 8; Mark 1; Luke 5*) 365
184. Through the Roof (*Matthew 9; Mark 2; Luke 5*) 366
185. The Lord of the Sabbath (*Matthew 12; Mark 2, 3; Luke 6*) 367
186. Jesus Teaches on the Mountain Side (*Matthew 5; Luke 6*) 368
187. Jesus Teaches His People to Pray (*Matthew 6*)..................370
188. Jesus Shows the Way of Heaven (*Matthew 7*)..................372
189. Jesus Heals a Servant and Gives Life to a Son (*Matthew 8; Luke 7*) 373
190. A Sinful Woman Shows Her Love for Jesus (*Luke 7*)...........374
191. The Farmer Who Planted His Seed (*Matthew 13; Mark 4; Luke 8*) 376
192. Jesus Teaches About His Kingdom (*Matthew 13*)..............377
193. More Stories Which Jesus Told (*Matthew 13; Mark 4*) 379
194. Jesus Rules the Wind and the Waves (*Matthew 8; Mark 4; Luke 8*) 380
195. Jesus Heals a Wild Man (*Matthew 8; Mark 5; Luke 8*) 381
196. Jesus Gives Life to the Dead (*Matthew 9; Mark 5; Luke 8*) 383
197. The Death of John the Baptist (*Matthew 14; Mark 6; Luke 3*) 384

198. Jesus Feeds Five Thousand People (*Matthew 14; Mark 6;*
    Luke 9; John 6) 386
199. Jesus Walks on the Water (*Matthew 14; Mark 6; John 6*) 387
200. Jesus Answers Prayer (*Matthew 15; Mark 7*) 389
201. Jesus Feeds the Hungry People Again (*Matthew 15;*
    Mark 8) 391
202. The Blind Man of Bethsaida (*Mark 8*) 392
203. Jesus Asks, "Who Am I?" (*Matthew 16; Mark 8; Luke 9*) 393
204. Jesus' Face Shines as the Sun (*Matthew 17; Mark 9;*
    Luke 9) 394
205. Who Is First With Jesus? (*Matthew 17, 18; Mark 9; Luke 9*) 396
206. Jesus Teaches About Forgiveness (*Matthew 18*) 398
207. I Am the Light of the World (*John 8*) 400
208. The Man Born Blind (*John 9*) 401
209. "I Am the Good Shepherd" (*John 10*) 403
210. The Good Samaritan (*Luke 10*) 404
211. Jesus in the Home of Friends (*Luke 10, 11*) 406
212. The Rich Fool (*Luke 12*) 407
213. The Lost Is Found (*Luke 15*) 408
214. The Rich Man and Lazarus (*Luke 16*) 411
215. Jesus Makes Lazarus Live (*John 11*) 413
216. A Lesson in Thankfulness (*Luke 17*) 415
217. Lessons on Prayer (*Luke 18*) 416
218. Jesus Loves Little Children (*Matthew 19; Mark 10;*
    Luke 18) 418
219. The Rich Young Ruler (*Matthew 19; Mark 10; Luke 18*) 419
220. The Workers in the Vineyard (*Matthew 20*) 420
221. Jesus Teaches His Friends to Be Humble (*Matthew 20*) 422
222. Blind Bartimaeus (*Matthew 20; Mark 10; Luke 18*) 423
223. Zacchaeus (*Luke 19*) 424
224. Mary Shows Her Love for Jesus (*John 12*) 426
225. Jesus, the King (*Matthew 21; Mark 11; Luke 19; John 12*) 427
226. Chasing the Wicked From the Temple (*Matthew 21;*
    Mark 11; Luke 19) 429
227. A Day in the Last Week (*Matthew 21; Mark 12;*
    Luke 20) 431
228. The Wedding of the King's Son (*Matthew 22*) 433
229. A Widow's Gift (*Mark 12; Luke 21; John 12*) 434
230. Ten Girls and Their Lamps (*Matthew 25*) .436
231. The Story of the Talents (*Matthew 25*) 437
232. The Last Supper (*Matthew 26; Mark 14; Luke 22;*
    John 13) 439
✗ 233. The Lord's Supper (*Matthew 26; Mark 14; Luke 22; John 13;*
    1 Corinthians 11) 441
234. Jesus Prays in the Garden (*Matthew 26; Mark 14; Luke 22;*
    John 13–18) 443
235. Jesus Sold by His Friend (*Matthew 26; Mark 14; Luke 22;*
    John 18) 445
236. Peter's Great Sin (*Matthew 26; Mark 14; Luke 22;*
    John 18) 446

237. Jesus Must Die (*Matthew 27; Mark 15; Luke 23; John 18*)...448
238. Jesus Dies on the Cross (*Matthew 27; Mark 15; Luke 23; John 19*)...450
239. Jesus Is Buried (*Matthew 27; Mark 15; Luke 23; John 19*)........453
240. Jesus Is Alive Again (*Matthew 28; Mark 16; Luke 24; John 20*)...455
241. Mary Magdalene (*John 20*)...................................457
242. Jesus Comes to His Friends (*Mark 16; Luke 24; John 20; 1 Corinthians 15*)...459
243. Thomas (*John 21*)...461
244. By the Sea of Galilee (*John 21*)............................462
245. Jesus Goes Back to Heaven (*Mark 16; Luke 24; Acts 1*).........464
246. Jesus Sends His Spirit (*Acts 1, 2*).........................466
247. The Lame Man Healed (*Acts 3*)..............................467
248. "Thou Shalt Not Lie" (*Acts 5*).............................470
249. The Apostles Persecuted for Doing Good (*Acts 5*).............471
250. Stephen Gives His Life for Jesus (*Acts 7*)..................473
251. The Magician Who Tries to Buy God's Power (*Acts 8*)..........474
252. Philip Helps the Ethiopian (*Acts 8*)........................476
253. Saul Turns to Jesus (*Acts 9*)...............................478
254. Peter Works Miracles for Jesus (*Acts 9*)....................480
255. Peter Is Sent to Help the Roman Soldier (*Acts 10*)...........481
256. An Angel Saves Peter (*Acts 11, 12*).........................483
257. Paul Goes on a Missionary Journey (*Acts 13*)................485
258. Paul Stoned at Lystra (*Acts 14*)............................486
259. Paul's Second Missionary Journey (*Acts 15, 16*).............489
260. Paul Suffers for Jesus (*Acts 16*)...........................490
261. "The Unknown God" (*Acts 17*)...............................493
262. A Great Bonfire (*Acts 19*).................................495
263. A Riot in Ephesus (*Acts 19*)...............................496
264. Eutychus Falls From a Window (*Acts 20*).....................498
265. Paul a Prisoner in Jerusalem (*Acts 23*).....................500
266. Paul Saved by His Nephew (*Acts 23*).........................502
267. Paul on Trial (*Acts 24–26*)................................503
268. Paul Shipwrecked (*Acts 27*)................................505
269. Paul Reaches Rome (*Acts 28*)...............................508
270. Jesus Shows Himself to John (*Revelation 1*).................510

PUBLISHER'S PREFACE

Although there have been many Bible story books written throughout the years, the author and the publishers take great pleasure in presenting to you *My Bible Story Book*.

There is always room for a retelling of these wonderful stories from God's Holy Word. We feel that both the parents and the children, no matter what age, will enjoy reading these stories. The author knows how to reach the minds and hearts of children, for she has told these stories daily for more than thirty years—to pre-schoolers in Sunday school, to kindergartners in the Christian day school, to older children in catechism classes, in Sunday schools, and in daily vacation Bible schools.

Each story is short enough to be read at one sitting. A few of the longer stories are broken up into two parts for your convenience. Another feature you will like is the list of questions at the end of each story, to be asked of the children after the story has been read. This should help the children remember what has been read.

PREFACE

After I had been teaching for almost twenty years, parents were aware of the fact that God had given me a special gift for story-telling. In fact, when I now meet former pupils, who are grand-parents and almost ready to retire, their first comment about my teaching is not the many excursions, programs and fun times we enjoyed, but rather: "I remember your Bible Stories."

Parents suggested that I have my stories published. When it finally materialized in 1960, I did not have the faintest idea of the wide-spread audience it would have. Almost a quarter of a million copies are in circulation. And since the spring of 1985, when it was no longer in print, I have had constant calls for new copies. Their old copies are completely worn out, and they want new ones for their grandchildren.

The stories have also been published in Brazil, in the Portugese language. And requests have come for many copies, new or used, from New Zealand. So, I am very grateful to Kregel Publications for putting this book back into print.

This book has been circulated in all parts of our country and far beyond. It has been read in my ancestral homeland, the Nether-lands, in Germany, in Korea, in Africa, and even in Jesus' own birthplace.

In all these places, as a "Thank You" to God, I have tried to help orphans.

May the Holy Spirit continue to open the hearts of young lis-teners wherever they will be, and gather them into our Master's fold. And I look forward to the day when I shall meet them all in our eternal home, where we shall join with the angels in praising our great Redeemer and King!

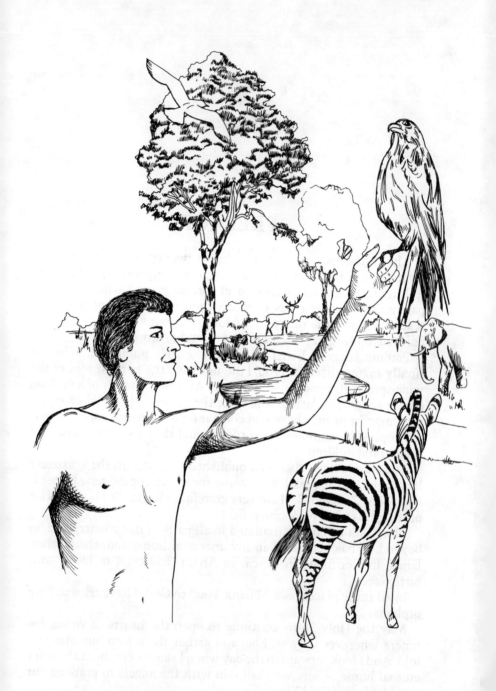

How God Made the World

Genesis 1

The world is full of many beautiful things, isn't it? There are tall trees, lovely flowers, and pretty birds everywhere. There are majestic mountains, powerful waterfalls, and huge oceans of water in many places. There are many lakes and rivers and streams. Where did all these wonderful things come from? Were they always here, and are they always going to be here just as they are now?

No, they were not always here. Long, long ago there were no trees or flowers or birds. There were no people. There wasn't even a world. There was nothing at all but God. And where did God come from? God did not come from anywhere, because He was always there. God did not have to be made. And He never changes, He is always the same. We cannot understand about God, because we are only creatures who had to be made. But we can believe what God tells us, and we are happy that we have a God who is so great.

In that long-ago time when there was only God, God decided He wanted to make a world. The three Persons in God worked together. God the Father thought about what He wanted to make. God the Son, whom we call Jesus, was the Word

*Everything in the world God made
was beautiful and wonderful*

through which everything was made. And God the Holy Spirit gave life to the things that were made.

When God decided to make a world, He did not need any tools or any material with which to work. Because He is God, He could *create*. To create means to make something out of nothing. God simply said that the world should be, and the world was there.

At first the world was nothing but a huge dark ball. The water and sky and land were all mixed through each other. Then God said, "Let there be light." At once it was light. God called the light day, and He called the darkness night. That was when time began. Before that there was no time, but when God made light, that was the first day.

God said next that there should be a sky over the earth. And at once it was there. That was the second day. On the third day God said that the water should be in one place, and the land in another. So God separated the land from the water. He made the brooks, the lakes, and the rivers, and the great, wide oceans. He made the dry land with its fields and meadows, with its hills and mountains reaching up towards the clouds. And God called the dry land earth.

Next God covered the earth with grass. Everywhere flowers began to grow. God made shade trees, and fruit trees covered with fruit. He made wheat and oats and corn and vegetables of every kind to grow in the fields. And all these things had their own fruits and seeds so that new ones could grow from the old. All that was done on the third day.

Then God made the sky more beautiful. He made the big, bright sun to give light and heat during the day, and the moon to shine at night. He also made thousands of stars to shine in the night sky. That was the fourth day.

The earth was now a lovely place, but it was very quiet. That was because there were no living things. So God made fish of all kinds to swim in the waters. He made the tiny little minnows that swim in the creeks as well as the giant whales that live in the oceans. He made hundreds of kinds of fish of every color and size. And He made the birds to fly through the air. He made hundreds of kinds of birds too. He made the bright, flaming cardinal with its cheery song and the tiny little humming bird with its ruby-colored throat. He also made the huge eagle that soars through the air like an airplane. That was the fifth day.

But something was missing. There were no animals. So when the sixth day came, God said that the earth should bring forth all kinds of animals and creeping things. He made the little kittens and the white bunnies, the big elephants and the strong lions, the butterflies and the bugs and the worms. God made many different kinds of animals to show His glory in many different ways.

Yes, God made everything that was ever made. And when the sixth day was over, God looked at everything He had made, and He said, "It is very good."

Were you listening? Where did God come from? Who made the world? Can you name the things that were made on each of the six days? What did God think about the world He had made?

Story 2

How God Made Man

Genesis 1 and 2

Everything in the world God made was beautiful and wonderful. But there was one creature that was more beautiful and wonderful than anything else. That was man.

On the sixth day, when God made the animals, He also made man. But He made man different from all other things. All the rest of the world was made out of nothing. When God decided to make man, He took some dust from the ground. With this dust He formed a man. Then God breathed into the man the breath of life, and the man became a living soul.

This man was different in another way too. He was different because God made him like Himself in some ways. Man was like God because he had a soul. He could think and speak, and he could know God. None of the other things God made had a soul. The animals do not have souls. But man was greater than all other creatures. God made him to be ruler over the animals, over the fish, the birds, and over all the earth.

Yes, all the beautiful things God made He gave to the man. "It is all yours to rule and to enjoy," God said. God gave him all the plants and fruit for food. And God called the man Adam.

But Adam was lonely at times in that beautiful world, for he was the only living soul. The birds and the animals could not talk to him. They could only make sounds.

God knew that Adam was lonely. He said, "It is not good that the man should be alone. I will make him a helper."

So one day God caused Adam to fall into a deep sleep. While Adam was asleep, God took out one of his bones. It was a rib. And God closed up the hole and put flesh there instead. Then, out of this rib, God made a woman. He breathed into the woman and made her a living soul too, just as Adam was. Then God brought the woman to Adam. He called her Eve.

When Adam awoke, there was Eve.

"I shall call her woman, because she was taken from man," said Adam when he saw Eve. "She really belongs to me, because she is bone of my bone and flesh of my flesh."

So God made Adam and Eve as a man and woman to live together. They were to be a family. And God promised that He would give them many children. The woman was called Eve because she would be the first mother.

Adam and Eve were wonderfully happy in the beautiful world God had made for them. They were happy because they were without sin. They were perfect. They loved only the good, and they did not even know what sin was.

When God finished all His work of creation, He rested. God called the seventh day "a day of rest." And He made His "rest day" a holy day. He said that the people He made should always remember to keep the Sabbath Day holy. One day out of every week is God's "rest day." We call this the Sabbath day. We worship God in His house on the Sabbath day.

Were you listening? What was the most wonderful thing God made? Why was this the most wonderful thing God made? Why did God make Eve?

Story 3

Man's First Home

Genesis 2

At the beginning of the world, when God made all things, He made a special home for the people He had made. It was a garden — the Garden of Eden.

No garden that has ever been made since was half so beautiful as the garden God planted for Adam and Eve. This garden was filled with many different kinds of trees and plants and flowers. Because God knew that His people would need food to eat, He planted many tiny seeds in the garden. Some grew to be great trees with every kind of fruit on their branches —apples, dates, pears, peaches, cherries, and many more. Some of the seeds grew into little plants bearing all kinds of good things to eat — carrots, potatoes, corn, wheat, and every other kind of food you can think of.

And because God wanted His people to have beautiful things in their homes, too, some of the seeds grew into lovely flowers, and some into tall palm trees with great shady leaves. Oh, God's first garden was a wonderful place! In it was every thing any one could wish for! Not a thing was forgotten. There were many animals too. These animals were given to Adam and Eve for friends. There was the friendly dog to live with them, and the strong horse to work for them. There were the lion, the deer, the sheep, and many more — too many to count! And there were beautiful birds that filled the air with their songs.

There was a beautiful river running through the Garden of Eden. It watered the trees, the plants, and the flowers so they would grow. Here the animals and the birds could drink, too.

God gave everything in this lovely garden to Adam and Eve. They took care of the garden. They gave names to all the animals and the birds. God taught them how to rule the garden. He showed Adam how to care for the animals and birds. And God said, "I made all these fruit trees and food plants for you and for the animals who live in the garden with you. These fruits and plants shall be to you for food."

Adam and Eve were filled with happiness in their beautiful garden home. They were happy because of the beauty all around them. They were happy because of the many good things to eat. They were happy because of their many animal and bird friends who were there to keep them company and to help them. And they were happy because they had each other. But they were happiest of all because each day Jehovah, their God, came into the garden to walk with them and to talk with them in the cool of the evening.

If you love Jesus, and have been washed in His blood, you will some day go to live in a garden as beautiful as the Garden of Eden. It is called Paradise. It is the garden where Jesus will live with His people.

> *Were you listening?* What kind of home did God make for Adam and Eve? What was in this home? Why were Adam and Eve so happy there? What is Paradise?

Story 4

Adam and Eve Disobey God

Genesis 3

When God made the first people, Adam and Eve, He made them perfect, without any sin. He gave them the beautiful Garden of Eden for a home, and He filled the garden with everything they could possibly want to keep them happy.

God wanted to find out if Adam and Eve really loved Him best of all. If we truly love God, we obey Him, don't we? God knew that if Adam and Eve truly loved Him, they would obey Him. So He said to Adam, "You may eat freely of every tree in your garden, except one. You must not eat of the tree in the middle of your garden. If you disobey Me and eat of that tree, you will surely die."

When God first made the world, He also made angels. He made them to live with Him in heaven. Angels are bright, shining creatures, who serve God night and day. They are different from people. They can do things man cannot do. Angels have wings, and they can fly to the earth whenever God sends them there. Angels are always happy. They spend their time loving and praising God and carrying out His wishes. There are thousands and thousands of angels — too many to count.

At one time there were some angels in heaven who turned away from God. They no longer loved Him, they hated Him instead. The leader of these wicked angels was Satan. When Satan and his followers no longer wanted to serve God and obey Him, God sent them out of heaven. Ever since that time Satan and his wicked helpers have been trying to work against God.

When Satan saw that God was testing Adam and Eve's love, he decided to see if he could get them to obey him instead of God. He went into the beautiful garden where Adam and Eve lived. He saw Eve sitting alone close to the tree from which they might not eat. Satan did not want Eve to see who he was, so he hid in a snake and made the snake talk for him.

The snake came close to Eve and said, "God said you could not eat from *any* of the trees of the garden, didn't He?"

Eve answered, "We may eat the fruit of the trees in this garden, but not from the *middle* tree. God says we must not eat from that tree, nor even touch it. If we do, we shall surely die."

"You will not die," Satan sneered. "God knows that if you eat from that tree you will be just as wise as He is. That is why God doesn't want you to eat from it." Then Satan showed Eve how beautiful the tree was, and how good the fruit looked.

When Eve saw the good fruit, and thought that she might become wise like God, she reached out her hand and took some of the fruit. She ate it. When Adam came to her a little later, she gave him some of the fruit too. And Adam ate it. The fruit was good.

Adam and Eve had disobeyed the Heavenly Father! They had sinned. And because they had sinned, they were afraid and ashamed. Before this time, when Adam and Eve had been perfect, they did not wear any clothing. They did not have to cover their bodies because their hearts were perfect. But now they were ashamed of their nakedness. They knew they were not perfect anymore. They were sinners. Their hearts were wicked.

So Adam and Eve sewed fig leaves together and made themselves aprons for a covering.

Soon evening came. And with evening, God came to walk with His people in the garden, as He often did. But when Adam and Eve heard God coming, they were afraid. They ran. They hid themselves among the trees of the garden.

God called and said, "Adam, where are you?"

Adam knew he could not hide from God. At last Adam answered, "I heard your voice in the garden, and I was afraid because I was naked. So I hid myself."

"Who told you that you were naked?" God asked. And then came the terrible question, "Did you eat from the middle tree?"

Adam did not want to take the blame, so he said, "The woman You gave me, she gave me some of the fruit, and so I did eat."

God turned to Eve and said, "What is this that you have done?"

Eve wanted to pass the blame to someone else too. So she answered, "The snake told me to take the fruit. And so I ate it."

Then God turned to the snake. "Because you have done this," God said, "from now on you are cursed above all animals. You shall always have to crawl instead of walk, and you shall have to eat dust all the days of your life. You and the woman shall always be enemies. Some day one of her children shall crush your head, and you shall hurt his heel."

God also punished Eve. "From now on," He said, "you shall have much sorrow and pain and sickness. And your husband shall rule over you."

Finally, God turned to Adam. He said, "Because you listened to your wife, and ate from the forbidden tree, all the earth shall be cursed for your sake. Instead of growing good food, the earth shall grow thorns and thistles. To make the food grow, you shall have to work until the sweat pours from your body. And when you are old, you shall die and your

body shall go back to the ground it came from. For you were made out of dust, and now you shall turn back into dust again."

If Adam and Eve had obeyed God and had not eaten from the forbidden tree, they would have lived forever in their beautiful garden. They would never have died. But now they had disobeyed God. When they disobeyed God, sin entered the world. And sinners must die. All the children that would be born of Adam and Eve would be sinners, just as their parents were. So from now on, all people would have to die.

Adam and Eve were not allowed to live in their lovely garden any longer. God sent them out of His garden. He put an angel with a big, flaming sword at the gate of the garden. The angel turned the sword this way and that way to guard the gate, so that Adam and Eve could not go back into the garden.

But God still loved the people He had made. He gave them a wonderful promise. He promised that someday He would send His own Son, Jesus Christ, to be their Saviour. He died for our sins on the Cross. Satan, the serpent, harmed Jesus for a little while. But in the end Jesus was the victor when He rose from the dead. What a wonderful promise God made to Adam and Eve!

> *Were you listening?* What did God do to test Adam and Eve's love? Who got Eve to disobey God? How did God punish Adam and Eve? What great promise did God give?

Story 5

The First Brothers

Genesis 4

Adam and Eve had to make a new home for themselves. They had to work hard each day in order to make food grow in their fields. Without food they could not live. But because God still loved Adam and Eve, God sent them sunshine and rain so their food would grow. He gave them many children too. When their first baby boy was born, they named him Cain. The second little boy was named Abel.

When Cain and Abel grew up, they had to work hard too. Cain became a farmer like his father. He raised crops of grain and fruits and vegetables. Abel liked to watch the sheep and care for the little lambs. So he became a shepherd. God was kind to Cain and Abel. He made many good things grow in the fields for Cain. And He gave Abel many little lambs, so that soon he had a large flock of sheep.

Abel was a good man. He loved God and was happy to serve Him. But Cain was not a good man. He did not love God, and he did not really want to serve Him.

One day Cain and Abel brought offerings to God. These offerings were gifts for the heavenly Father to say "thank you" for His kindness to them. Cain and Abel made an altar of stones. The altar was like a high table. They put wood and fire on the altar. Cain brought some of his best food to lay on the altar and burn to God for his "thank you." Abel brought his best lambs for his "thank you" offering.

The Heavenly Father was pleased with Abel and his offering,

because Abel loved God and tried to serve Him well. But God was not pleased with Cain and his offering, because Cain's heart was filled with sin.

Cain was angry because he knew that God was not pleased with him. He was angry with God.

So God came to Cain and said, "Why are you angry, Cain? If you did well, I would be pleased with you, wouldn't I? But if I am not pleased with you, that is because you do not love Me. You love sin instead. Cain, you must turn away from sin."

But Cain would not listen to God. He was still angry with God. Now he became jealous of his brother, because Abel's offering had been pleasing to God. He began to hate his brother.

One day when Cain and Abel were alone in the field, Cain suddenly rose up and killed his brother.

God saw what Cain did. God sees and knows everything.

Soon God came to Cain. "Where is your brother?" He asked.

"I don't know," Cain answered. "Am I my brother's keeper?"

"I saw what you did, Cain," said God. "I saw your brother's blood on the ground. Because of your sin, the ground shall not give you good food to eat. And I shall send you away from your father's house and from your family. You shall wander around the earth without a home."

When Cain heard God's words, he cried out, "My punishment is harder than I can bear. If I must wander around the earth, everyone who sees me will want to kill me."

But God answered that He would set a mark on Cain, so that people who found him would not kill him.

Cain had to go far away from his father and his mother. He had no home. He was never really happy again, because he had hated his brother and had killed him.

Were you listening? Who was the first baby ever born? How did Cain and Abel say "thank you" to God? Why was God not pleased with Cain's "thank you"? Why did Cain kill Abel?

The World and the Flood

Adam and Eve had many children. When these children grew up, they also had many children. Soon the world was full of people. But all the people were sinful. Most of them, like Cain, did not love God. They would not obey Him. Each day they became more and more wicked, until finally the wickedness in the world was very great. The hearts of men were filled with evil.

When God saw the people doing so many evil things, He was grieved in His heart. "I will destroy man whom I have made," said God. "I will wipe them off the earth. And I will destroy the beasts, the creeping things, and the birds of the heavens. But there is one man and his family whom I will save. That man is Noah. I will save Noah because He alone loves Me."

Noah had a wife and three sons—Shem, Ham, and Japheth. The three sons had wives too. All the eight people in this family loved God. They obeyed Him and served Him.

One day God said to Noah, "The world is very wicked. The people do not obey Me. So I am going to send a big flood. I will destroy all the people and the things I have made. But I will not destroy you and your family."

Then God told Noah to build an ark, a big wooden boat that would float on the water. He told Noah exactly how to build the ark. It would be a very large boat. It would have three floors, and it would have a roof on the top. There would be windows in the boat, and a large door that would reach to the third floor. There would be room in this boat for stalls for all the different kinds of animals, and cages for all the birds. For God was also going to save some of every kind of bird and animal.

Noah obeyed God. He began at once to build the ark. But

it took a long time to build such a huge boat. It took one hundred and twenty years! And during all those years, while Noah was working on the ark, he preached to the wicked people. He warned them of the great flood that was coming. But the people only laughed. They thought Noah was foolish for building such a huge boat when there was no flood. They did not believe God's word. And they kept on being wicked.

> *Were you listening?* How did the world become full of people? Why did God decide to destroy the world? How many people who loved God were left in the world? How would God save the people who loved Him?

Story 7

The Rainbow of Promise

Genesis 7, 8 and 9

Noah spent many long years building the ark, as God had commanded him. When the ark was finally finished, God told Noah to gather together all the different kinds of animals and birds. For the next week Noah worked hard getting all the animals and birds together. He brought them into the ark. There were two—a father and a mother—of certain kinds of animals. And there were seven of all the other kinds of animals, and seven of all the kinds of birds.

When all the animals and birds were given a place in the ark, and there was enough food stored away to last a whole year, Noah and his family went into the ark too. Then God shut the door.

Soon it began to rain. It rained for forty days and forty nights. At first the people thought Noah was very foolish to lock himself up in a watertight boat with so many animals and birds. But soon they saw that the water was beginning to cover everything on the earth. Not only did the rain pour down from the sky, but all the water hidden underneath the ground sprang up too, in huge fountains.

Now the people were filled with fear. They climbed to their housetops. They climbed into trees. They climbed hills and mountains. But no matter how high they climbed, the water reached their hiding place. Soon all the people were drowned. All the birds and animals were drowned too, except those in the ark. When the forty days and nights were over, there was nothing at all left on the earth.

But God remembered Noah and his family in the ark. As the water rose higher and higher, the ark floated above the water. It floated for many months.

At last God sent a strong wind to dry up the water. Slowly the water began to go down. Finally, the ark rested on the top of a mountain called Mount Ararat.

Noah waited forty more days. Then he opened a window and let out a big black bird, called a raven. The raven did not come back to the ark. It found a place to rest. But a raven can fly a long time without stopping to rest, so Noah still did not know if the water had gone down below the treetops.

After seven more days, Noah sent out a little dove. The dove could not find a place to rest. It soon grew tired and came back to the ark. Noah put out his hand and took the little dove back into the ark.

A week later Noah sent the dove out again. This time the dove came back with an olive leaf in its mouth. Then Noah knew that the treetops were beginning to show.

After another week Noah sent out the little dove again. This time it did not come back. It found a resting place, for the waters had dried up.

Then Noah lifted the cover of the ark and saw that the water was gone. Soon God called Noah and his family to come out of the ark. They quickly obeyed. Noah and his wife, and their three sons and their wives left the ark and stood on the dry ground. And all the animals and the birds came out too.

The first thing Noah did after he left the ark was to build an altar. He burned many animals on the altar as a sacrifice to God to say "thank you" for saving him and his family from the great flood.

God was pleased with Noah's offering. God said, "I will never again destroy the whole world with a flood. From this time on, as long as the world lasts, there shall always be springtime and summer, fall and winter. And there shall always be day and night."

God came down and talked with Noah and his family. God blessed them, and He promised them that they would have many children, so that the world would again be filled with people. As a sign of His promise that He would never again destroy the world with a flood, God used the beautiful rainbow in the sky. Every time Noah and his family saw the rainbow, they remembered God's promise and knew that God was remembering it too.

> *Were you listening?* Did it take Noah long to build the ark? Who went into the ark? What happened to everything on the earth? What is the rainbow a sign of?

Story 8

The Tower of Babel

Genesis 11

It was not long after God had destroyed the world with the flood that the world again began to be filled with people. And all the people who lived in the world at that time lived together in one place. They all spoke the same language. We do not know what language that was, but we do know that everyone talked alike, and they could all understand each other.

It happened one day that they all traveled together eastward until they came to a place called Shinar. Here they decided to live. There was a large plain in Shinar, and the people decided to build themselves a city there, with a great tower. They wanted the tower to be so high that it would reach to heaven.

Although these people knew the story of the terrible flood, and knew that Jehovah was a righteous God who wanted His children to obey Him, they were already forgetting to serve the Lord. They were filled with pride. They thought more of themselves than they did of God. And so they wanted to build this tower. "Let us make a name for ourselves," they said, "so that we shall not be scattered over the face of the whole earth."

They began to work very hard. They used brick for stone and slime for mortar. They burned their bricks in the fire until they were strong. Little by little the tower began to grow. Higher and higher it reached into the open sky.

But God saw what the people were doing. God sees all things and He knows all things. God knew that the people were building the tower because they wanted to do without God. He knew that they wanted to be strong for themselves. They did not want to trust God for strength. They did not want to obey Him.

God said, "The people are all one and they speak one language. And this is what they do. If I do not stop them, they will become more and more wicked and godless."

So God stopped the people from building their tower. Do you know how God did this? He did this by changing their language. After that, some of the people spoke one language and some another. They could not understand each other. Because the people could not understand each other, they could not go on with their tower.

The building of the tower was stopped.

Soon the people who spoke one language lived together in one country. The people who spoke another language moved to another country. After a while the people were scattered over all the earth. The tower was left unfinished.

The people called the unfinished tower the Tower of Babel. Babel means "noise" or "confusion." When God changed the

language of the people, there was truly a babel or confusion of languages.

Today the people from different countries still speak different languages.

Were you listening? What is a language? What language do you speak? When did all people have the same language? Why did God change their language? Why didn't God want the people to finish the Tower of Babel?

Story 9

God Calls Abram

Genesis 12

After the Tower of Babel, the world was still filled with wickedness. But just as Noah loved God in the days before the flood, when all the world was wicked, so now there was one man who loved and feared God. His name was Abram.

Abram and his father, Terah, lived in a land called Ur of the Chaldees. Ur was one of the cities of Babylonia, and the people of Babylonia were all idol-worshipers. They had many gods. They worshiped the sun, the moon, the stars, and other things in nature. Terah, Abram's father, worshiped idols too. But Abram worshiped the true God.

One day God came to Abram and said, "Abram, I want you to leave your country and your home, and I want you to go to a land that I will show you."

At that time many people were moving from Ur. Terah was the leader of such a group. So Abram joined the group. He took with him his wife Sarai, and his nephew Lot, and all their possessions.

Terah planned to go as far as Canaan, but when the people he led came to Haran, they settled there instead. After they had been in Haran fifteen years, Terah, Abram's father died.

The city of Haran was no better than Ur, for the people here were also idolaters. They worshiped what they called the god of the moon. After Terah died, God came to Abram again.

"Abram," God said, "I want you to go away from these wicked people. I want you to say good-by to your family and to all your friends. I want you to go to a land far away. I will show you where to go."

God said something more to Abram. God gave him a beautiful promise. You see, Abram did not have any children, and he was already seventy-five years old. This is what God said:

"Abram, I will give you many children. I will make of you a great nation. I will bless you and make your name great."

Yes, the Saviour who was promised to Adam and Eve in the Garden of Eden would some day come from Abram's family!

Abram did as God told him. He left all his friends and his family and began to travel. He took with him his wife Sarai and his nephew Lot, with his family, with all their servants and all their animals. Abram was a rich man. He had more than three hundred servants and thousands of animals. Lot also had many servants and animals. So it was not easy for Abram to travel with such a large group. Besides, there were many dangers along the way, and Abram was no longer a young man. He was growing old.

But Abram was not afraid. He knew that his Heavenly Father was leading him.

After a long, long time Abram and his family came to the land of Canaan. Here they saw rich fields of grain, and trees loaded with fruit. There were green pastures for the animals.

Then God spoke again to Abram. "Some day," God promised, "I will give all this land to your children."

Abram built an altar and burned sacrifices to God to thank Him for bringing him to this beautiful land. And he never forgot God's wonderful promises.

Were you listening? Who was Abram? Why did God send him away from his homeland? What beautiful promise did God give Abram? How can you tell from this story that Abram loved God?

Abram's Choice and Lot's Choice

Story 10

Genesis 13

Abram and Lot lived together in the beautiful land of Canaan. God made Abram very rich. He gave him gold and silver, sheep and cows, and many servants. Lot had many animals and servants too. Abram loved Lot and was kind to him. They would have been happy living together, but Lot's servants and Abram's servants were always quarreling over the grass and the water for their animals.

"We are going to feed our sheep here," Lot's servants would say.

"No, we were here first. We are going to feed our sheep here. You go away," Abram's servants would answer.

When Abram's servants were giving water to their sheep, Lot's servants would come for water too. Then they would fight again and say unkind words to each other. And the servants would tell their troubles to their masters.

Abram was a friendly man. He knew the Heavenly Father was not pleased when the servants quarreled together. And he was afraid that soon he and Lot would begin to quarrel too.

So Abram talked to Lot. He said, "Our servants are always quarreling. Pretty soon they will make us quarrel too. So let us not live together any more."

Then Abram took Lot to a place where they could look over all the land about them. "You choose first," Abram said. "If you want to go to the left, then I will go to the right." God had given all this land to Abram, but Abram was kind to his nephew Lot. He was so kind that he let Lot choose first.

Lot looked at all the land. Below him he could see the river Jordan. All around the river there was plenty of green grass for his sheep and cows. Lot was selfish. He chose the best land for himself. He said, "I will go there." And he pointed to the lovely land around the river. It was a beautiful land. It seemed almost as beautiful as the Garden of Eden.

So Lot chose the rich land around the river, and Abram took what was left. Lot put up his tent near the wicked cities of Sodom and Gomorrah. Later he moved right into the wicked cities.

But Abram stayed in the fields by himself.

God was pleased with Abram. He came to Abram again and said, "Lift up your eyes, Abram, and look all around you. All this land that you see, I will give to your children forever. And I will give you as many children as the dust of the earth."

Abram believed God, and worshiped Him.

Not long after Lot moved into Sodom, there was a great war in the land. Four kings left their cities and came up to fight against the kings of five other cities. The four kings came to fight in Sodom too, where Lot lived. They ran off with all the riches of Sodom, and all the food, and they took many of the people with them as captives. They took Lot too.

Soon one of the men who had escaped ran to tell Abram what had happened.

When Abram heard that Lot was a prisoner, he quickly gave weapons to a great number of his servants and went after the enemy. These servants of Abram were trained as soldiers. There were three hundred and eighteen of them.

Soon Abram and his servants found the enemy kings and fought against them. Abram's men won the battle. They brought back all the goods that had been stolen, and all the people. They rescued Lot too.

As Abram was coming back from the battle, the king of Sodom came out to meet him. The king of Sodom said, "Give me the people, and you can keep all the goods that you brought back."

But Abram said, "No, I shall not take anything, not even a shoelace. For God alone will make me rich."

Then Abram went back to his tents. And God blessed Abram again. Once more God repeated to him His promises.

Were you listening? Why did Abram and Lot separate? How do you know that Lot was a selfish man? What did Abram do for Lot when Lot was living in Sodom? What things did God promise Abram?

Story 11

God's Promises to Abram

Genesis 15

One day God came to Abram again. God said, "Don't be afraid, Abram. I am your shield, and your great reward."

But Abram answered, "Dear God, how can I ever receive all Your promises? I am old and I still have no children. Can Eliezer, my servant, become my son? He was born in my house, and he belongs to me."

"No, Abram," God said, "Eliezer cannot be your son. You are still going to have a son of your own."

Then God took Abram outside his tent.

"Look up at the sky, Abram," God said. "Tell me how many stars there are up there. Count them if you can."

But Abram could not count them. There were too many.

"That is how many children you are going to have," God said. "You will have as many children as the stars of heaven —a countless number."

And Abram believed God.

God kept on talking with Abram. He said, "Remember, I am the Lord who brought you out of your old home, the Ur of the Chaldees, to give you this land."

"But how shall I know that I shall really get all this land?" Abram asked.

"Take Me a three-year-old cow," God answered, "and a three-year-old mother goat, a three-year-old ram, a turtle dove, and a young pigeon."

Abram did as God said. He divided each animal in half and laid the parts in two rows, each half opposite the other. Then he laid the slain turtle-dove and the pigeon in the rows too, but left them whole.

Abram watched over this sacrifice all day. When the birds tried to eat the meat, he chased them away.

As the sun was going down, Abram fell into a deep sleep. In his sleep a terrible darkness came over him. Through the darkness he heard God's voice saying, "Abram, know for certain that these children I promised you will be strangers in a strange land for four hundred years. They will be slaves and will suffer greatly. But I will punish their enemies. Finally, they will all come back to this land."

The sun had now gone down. It was night. Suddenly a smoking furnace from which torch-like flames shot out passed between the rows of meat and burned Abram's sacrifice. Then God gave His wonderful promise to Abram once more. And Abram awoke.

God spoke to Abram about His promise many times. He did not want Abram to forget it. But He waited until Abram was an old, old man before He kept His promise. God wanted to test Abram's faith. He knew that Abram's faith would become stronger if it was tested, just as our muscles become stronger when we use them. And only by trusting God could Abram prove that he loved Him.

Abram did not fail God's test, as Adam had done. Abram showed that he loved God by believing God's word.

Were you listening? What promise did God give Abram again and again? Why did God wait so long to fulfill His promise? How did Abram show that he loved God?

Story 12

"Thou, God, Seest Me"

Genesis 16

Abram and Sarai waited and waited for God to keep His promise and give them a son. Finally, one day, Sarai said to Abram, "Look now, it doesn't seem as if God is going to give me a son. I am much too old to have children. Perhaps you had better marry my maid, Hagar. She is younger than I am. Perhaps God will give you and Hagar a son."

Abram thought Sarai's idea was a good one, so he married Hagar. He felt that perhaps God would give him the long-promised son that way.

At first Sarai was pleased with what she had done. But she was not pleased very long. As soon as Hagar realized that she was going to be the mother of Abraham's child instead of Sarai, she looked down on her mistress. She felt that she was an important lady now, and she would not obey Sarai as her maid.

Sarai was greatly distressed. She went to Abram. "I was wrong," she said, "when I gave you my maid as your wife. Now Hagar despises me. What shall I do?"

"She is your servant," Abram answered. "You may do as you please with her."

So Sarai punished Hagar and treated her harshly. Hagar did not like this. She ran away. She ran far, far away into the wilderness. Finally she sat down to rest near a fountain of water.

Although Hagar had run far into the wilderness, she could not run away from God. God saw her there. He sent His angel to talk to her. The angel found Hagar at the fountain.

"Hagar, Sarai's maid, where did you come from?" the angel asked. "And where are you going?"

"I'm running away from my mistress, Sarai," Hagar answered.

Then the angel said to her, "You must not run away from your mistress, Hagar. You must go back to Sarai and do what she tells you. Remember, the Lord sees you and will take care of you wherever you are. When your baby comes, you must call him Ishmael, because the Lord has heard you in your trouble."

Then the angel went away, and Hagar stood up to go home. She was not afraid to go back to Sarai now, for she knew that God could see her and would take care of her. "Thou, God, seest me," she said.

So Hagar went back to her mistress. Soon her little boy was born. She called him Ishmael, as the angel had commanded. Hagar was happy with her little baby. And Abram thought that God had finally given him the long-promised son.

Were you listening? Who was Hagar? Why did she run away? Why did she say, "Thou, God, seest me"?

Story 13

Abraham's Heavenly Visitors
Genesis 17 and 18

When Abram was ninety-nine years old, God came to him once more. "I am the Almighty God," He said. "Walk before Me, and be perfect. And I will make a covenant between Me and you, and I will give you a great many children. I will make nations out of you, and kings shall come from your family. And I will be a God to you and to your children after you."

Then God changed Abram's name. "You shall no more be called Abram," God said, "I shall now call you Abraham, because I have made you a father of many nations. And you must change Sarai's name to Sarah, for she shall be a mother of many nations and of kings."

Abraham fell on his face before God, and laughed. He said to himself, "Shall a child be born to him that is a hundred years old, and shall Sarah, who is ninety, still have a baby?" He did not think God's words were possible any more. He thought God had given him Ishmael as the promised son. So he turned to God and said, "O God, please let Ishmael be the promised son!"

"No," God answered, "Sarah is really going to have a son, and you must call him Isaac. And as for Ishmael, I have blessed him too. I will also make of him a great nation. But I will make My covenant with Isaac, who shall be born next year at this time." Then God left Abraham, and once more Abraham believed God's words.

AT MAMRE

✝ One day, not long after this, Abraham was sitting at the door of his tent. He suddenly looked up and saw three men coming towards him. He quickly ran to meet them. Now two of the men were angels, and the other one was God. Abraham bowed himself to the earth before his visitors and said, "Please stop and rest yourselves under my tree. And let me get you something to eat before you go on your way."

"Do as you have said," God answered.

So Abraham hastened into his tent to Sarah and said, "Quickly, Sarah, make cakes and prepare dinner. For we have guests."

Abraham ran to the fields and fetched a tender calf and gave it to his servant to prepare for meat. When all was ready, Abraham took butter and milk and the cakes and the meat and set it before his three visitors under the tree. Then Abraham stood by them, while the men did eat.

After a while the men said to Abraham, "Where is Sarah, your wife?"

"Behold in the tent," Abraham answered.

Then one of the three men said, "Before another year is over, Sarah shall have a son." It was God speaking.

Sarah, in the tent door behind them, heard God's words. She laughed to herself and said, "What, after we are both old, are we still going to have a baby?"

Then God said to Abraham, "Why did Sarah laugh? Is anything too hard for God? Sarah shall have her son!"

Now Sarah was afraid and quickly said, "I laughed not."

But God said, "That is an untruth. You did laugh, Sarah."

After that the three men rose to go. They went towards the cities of Sodom and Gomorrah, where Lot and his family lived. Abraham went with them for a little way.

Then God said, "Shall I hide from Abraham what I am going to do, seeing I have chosen to bless him and his family?" He turned to Abraham. "I have heard the cry of the wicked cities of Sodom and Gomorrah," God said. "I am going there to prove their wickedness. Then I am going to destroy them."

After God had spoken, the two angels went on to Sodom, but Abraham stood alone before God. Abraham was worried about what would happen to Lot and his family.

"Oh, Lord," Abraham said, "will You destroy the good people with the wicked? What if there are fifty good people in the city, will You destroy it then? Far be it from You to kill the good with the wicked! Shall not the Judge of all the earth do right?"

And God answered, "I will save the city for fifty good people."

"Behold now," Abraham went on, "I am being very bold to dare to speak to the Lord, when I am but dust and ashes. But what if there are only forty-five good people in the city? Oh, Lord, will You destroy it then?"

And God said, "If I find forty-five good people, I will not destroy it."

"And what if there are only forty?"

"I will not do it for forty's sake."

"Oh, let not the Lord be angry," said Abraham. "But what if there are only thirty?"

"I will not do it if I find thirty there."

"Behold now," Abraham repeated—for he was very worried

about Lot—"I have been bold enough to speak to the Lord these many times. But what if there are only twenty there?"

"I will not destroy it for twenty's sake."

"Oh, let not the Lord be angry, and I will speak just once more!" said Abraham. "What if there are only ten good people in the city?"

"I will not destroy the city for ten's sake."

Then the Lord went His way, and Abraham stopped pleading for the city. He went back to the door of his tent.

> *Were you listening?* What special visitors came to Abraham one day? Why did Sarah laugh? Why was God going to Sodom and Gomorrah? What did Abraham do when God told him why He was going to Sodom and Gomorrah? Why did Abraham plead with **God so long?**

The Rain of Fire

While God and Abraham had been talking about the good people who might be left in the wicked cities of Sodom and Gomorrah, the two angels went on to Sodom. It was evening when the angels arrived at the city. Lot was sitting at the gate. When Lot saw the angels, he rose to meet them.

Lot bowed himself to the ground and said, "Please, my lords, come to your servant's house for the night. In the morning you can go your way."

But the angels answered, "No, we will stay in the street all night." The street was an open space in the city where strangers often lay down to sleep, if they had no friends in the city.

Lot knew that the men of Sodom were extremely wicked and that it would not be safe for these visitors to stay in the street all night. So he persuaded them to come into his home. The angels went with Lot. Lot made them a feast, and they ate together.

Before it was time to go to bed, some wicked men from

Sodom came to the door. They called to Lot, "We want those men who came to your house tonight."

Lot went outdoors to talk to them. "Please don't be so wicked," he pleaded. "You may have my daughters, but don't take my visitors."

"Stand back!" the men shouted. They pushed against the door, trying to get in. They would have broken the door, but the angels pulled Lot back into the house. Then the angels made the wicked men blind so they could not see the door nor find their way.

"Go quickly and gather your family," said the angels to Lot. "You must leave this city at once, for God is going to send fire from heaven to burn this wicked place."

So Lot went out to find his family. Some of Lot's daughters were married and lived with their husbands. They would not listen to Lot. They laughed at him and refused to come along. They did not believe that the city would be destroyed by fire.

As the morning began to dawn, the angels hastened Lot saying, "Go quickly, or you will burn with the rest of the city."

But Lot held back. He hated to leave his home.

At last the angels took Lot and his wife and the two daughters who lived at home. They took them by the hand and brought them outside the city. For the Heavenly Father loved them, and was kind to them.

"Now, run for your life," the angels said, "and don't look back! Run to the mountains, or you will be destroyed!"

But Lot said, "Oh, please, my lord, not to the mountains! I will die there. Let us go to the little city of Zoar not far from here." So the angels said they could go to Zoar.

When Lot reached Zoar, the sun was already up. Then God rained fire and brimstone upon Sodom and Gomorrah. The two cities were completely destroyed, and all the people that lived there perished.

But Lot's wife had not run on, as the angels had commanded.

She went more slowly than Lot and his two daughters. She loved the wicked city of Sodom. At last she disobeyed the angels and stopped running. She turned to look back. Suddenly the burning-hot brimstone that was raining down on the wicked cities covered her also, and she was left standing as a tall pillar of salt.

When Abraham arose early that morning he went to the place in the road where he had talked with God. He looked toward Sodom and Gomorrah, and he saw the smoke rise up into the sky as the smoke of a furnace.

Then Abraham knew that God had not found even ten good people in that city. But God remembered Lot and his family, and brought them out in safety.

> *Were you listening?* Where did the angels visit in Sodom? What happened to Sodom and Gomorrah? What happened to Lot and his two daughters? What happened to Lot's wife? Why did this happen to her?

Story 15

A Little Boy in the Desert

Genesis 21

When God told Abraham that Sarah was going to have a child, Sarah had laughed. She thought, "I am too old to have a baby now!"

But God kept His promise. Before another year had passed, God gave Sarah a little boy. She and Abraham called the baby's name Isaac, for Sarah said, "God has made me laugh with happiness, and everyone who hears about it will laugh with me." Abraham was a hundred years old when Isaac was born.

Yes, Abraham and Sarah were very happy with their little boy. They loved him with all their heart. And they taught Isaac to love God and to serve Him.

But there was another little boy in Abraham's household, you remember. He was Abraham's son, too, but Sarah was not his mother. His mother was the servant-girl, Hagar, Sarah's maid. Hagar's little boy was called Ishmael. Ishmael was older than Isaac.

Ishmael was not always kind to his little brother Isaac. He was jealous of him and often teased him. One day Abraham and Sarah had a party for their son Isaac. It was like a birthday party. Ishmael was at the party too. While Sarah was watching the children, she saw Ishmael teasing and mocking Isaac. This made her very angry. She told Abraham about it that night.

"I don't want Hagar and her son to live here any more," Sarah said. "Send them away!"

Abraham did not know what to do. He did not want Ishmael to mock his son Isaac, but he did not want to send his son Ishmael away either. That night, God talked to Abraham.

"Do not be afraid to send the lad away," God said. "Do as Sarah asks, for her son Isaac is to be the son of promise. But I will take care of Ishmael too, because he is also your son."

Early the next morning Abraham took some bread and a bottle of water and gave it to Hagar, putting it on her shoulder. Then he gave her the lad, Ishmael, and sent them both away.

Hagar and Ishmael walked for a long time. They wandered about in the wilderness of Beer-sheba. When they were hungry they ate the bread, and when they were thirsty they drank the

water. But at last all the water was gone. Ishmael was thirsty. He cried for water, but there was none.

Soon Ishmael was too thirsty to go on. He became very ill. He was so ill that he was about to die. His mother laid him under one of the bushes. She did not want to see him die. Then she went to sit on a stone, not far away. Hagar cried and cried. Ishmael, lying under the bush, cried too. God heard him cry. He sent His angel to Hagar.

"What is the matter, Hagar?" the angel said. "Do not be afraid. God has heard the voice of the lad. Go, lift up the boy. God will make a great nation of him."

Then God opened Hagar's eyes. She saw a well of water near her.

Quickly she brought water to Ishmael. Ishmael drank, and soon he was better. After that, Hagar and Ishmael always lived in the wilderness. God took care of them. And Ishmael's family became a great nation just as God had promised.

> *Were you listening?* Why did Sarah call her baby Isaac? Why did Abraham send Hagar and Ishmael away? How did God take care of Ishmael and Hagar?

Story 16

Abraham Obeys God

Genesis 22

After Hagar and Ishmael moved away, Isaac was the only son in Abraham's house. Abraham and Sarah were very happy with their son. They were happy because the child for whom they had waited so long had come at last. They were happier still because out of him was to come a great nation. But they were happiest of all because God had promised that out of this nation was to be born the Saviour of the world. Yes, Jesus, God's Son, was some day going to be born into the world as a little baby, out of Isaac's line.

God had given a wonderful promise to Abraham. But God wanted Abraham to trust Him, to trust His word. So one day

God came to Abraham to test him. He wanted to prove Abraham's faith.

"Abraham," God said. "I want you to take your son, your only son Isaac, whom you love, and go to the top of one of the mountains in Moriah. I will show you where to go. I want you to offer him there for a burnt offering."

Abraham was filled with sorrow. How was he going to take his only son, whom he loved so much, and lay him on a burning altar? And if he slew his only son, how then could Isaac become a great nation?

But Abraham loved God best of all. He trusted God. He knew that God never makes mistakes. He believed that God would keep His promises to him. God had said Isaac was going to be a great nation. If God said so, it was true. "Even if Isaac dies," thought Abraham, "I know that God will raise him from the dead."

So Abraham left the rest up to God. He knew that all he had to do was obey.

Early the next morning Abraham made ready to go. He saddled his donkey, took Isaac and two young servants, and started out. They brought with them the wood and the fire for the altar.

For three days they traveled. Finally they came to the place God had told them. Abraham left his servants at the foot of the mountain.

"Wait here with the donkey," Abraham said, "while my son and I go up this mountain to worship God. When we have finished, we shall come back to you."

Abraham did not say, *"I* shall come back to you." No, he said, *"We* shall come back to you." So sure Abraham was that God would keep His word.

Then Abraham gave Isaac the wood, and he took the fire in his one hand (it was in an iron pot) and a knife in the other hand. Together they walked up the mountainside.

As they were walking, Isaac suddenly turned to his father. "My father," he said.

"Here I am, my son," Abraham answered.

"Look, father," Isaac went on, "you have the fire and I have the wood, but where is the lamb for a burnt offering?"

"My son," Abraham answered, "God will provide Himself a lamb for a burnt offering."

So they both went on.

Finally they reached the place God had pointed out. Abraham built an altar. He laid the wood in order. Then he bound Isaac, his son, with a rope.

Now Isaac knew that he was to be the offering on the altar. He thought he would have to die.

But Isaac knew also that God had promised to make a great nation out of him. Both Abraham and Isaac knew that what God says is always the truth.

Abraham laid Isaac on the altar. He took the knife. He raised his hand to slay his son.

At that very moment God called to Abraham out of heaven. "Abraham, Abraham!"

"Here am I," Abraham answered.

"Do not hurt your son," God said. "Now you have proved that you love Me best. You are even willing to give Me your only son."

Then Abraham looked about him and saw a ram caught by his horns in the bushes. God had provided the ram as an offering.

Abraham quickly took his son off the altar. How happy he was to offer the ram for a burnt offering instead of his son!

God was pleased with Abraham because Abraham trusted Him. And there on the mountain top God repeated His wonderful promise that some day the Saviour would come from Isaac's line. Yes, some day God the Father was going to send His only Son to die on the cross as a sacrifice for our sins.

God was teaching us all, through Abraham, how great is the love of our Heavenly Father for lost sinners.

At last Abraham and Isaac went back to the young servants. Soon they set out together on their homeward journey. Abraham was no longer sad. He was filled with joy because he had obeyed God, and because God was pleased with him.

> *Were you listening?* Did God want Abraham to offer his son for a burnt sacrifice? Why did God ask Abraham to do this? In this story of Abraham and Isaac, what does God teach us about His great love as a Heavenly Father?

Story 17

Abraham Finds a Wife for Isaac

Genesis 24

Abraham and Sarah lived with their son Isaac in the land of promise for many years. Isaac grew to be a young man. Then one day Sarah died, when she was a hundred and twenty-seven years old. Abraham was now a very old man. He loved his son Isaac more than anything else in the world. But Isaac was lonely. He had no brothers or sisters, and now his mother was gone too.

One day Abraham called his faithful servant Eliezer to him. "Eliezer," said Abraham, "I want you to go back to my people where I used to live, and find a wife there for Isaac. Promise me that you will not get a wife from this land of Canaan, for the young women of Canaan do not know and love God."

"What if the young woman I find will not come back with me?" Eliezer asked. "Shall I bring Isaac to her country then?"

"No," Abraham answered, "you must not bring Isaac back to that country. But God will find you a young woman who will come here to live."

So the faithful old servant took ten camels and many beautiful gifts and started out. He rode for many days until he came to the far-away land where Abraham once lived. He stopped at a well to rest. He was thirsty. His camels were thirsty too. It was evening, and at that time many young women

came to the well to fill their jars with water. As the old servant rested at the well, he prayed to God.

"Dear Lord of my master Abraham," he said. "Please help
me find the right young woman to be Isaac's wife. For a sign
to me, please let it be the young woman who gives me a drink
and gives my camels a drink."

Before Eliezer had finished his prayer, a beautiful girl named
Rebekah came to the well.

"Give me, I pray, a little water from your pitcher," the
servant asked.

"Drink, my lord," Rebekah answered, and she let down her
pitcher to give him a drink.

"I will draw water for your camels too," she added. She
quickly did so.

The faithful servant watched Rebekah as she drew the water
for his camels. "This must surely be the young woman God
has chosen," he thought.

When Rebekah had finished drawing water, Eliezer gave her
a beautiful gold ring and two beautiful bracelets, as a reward
for her kindness. Then he asked her if there was room in her
father's house for him to lodge. For in those days there were
not many inns, and no hotels or motels as we have now.

"Yes, we have room," Rebekah said, "and also feed and
straw for your camels."

When Eliezer saw how quickly God answered his prayer,
he bowed his head and worshiped God, thanking Him for His
help.

Rebekah ran home to tell her family about the stranger at
the well. Her brother, whose name was Laban, ran back to
the well and brought the old servant to their home.

Rebekah's family treated Eliezer, and the other servants he
had brought with him, with great kindness. "Come in, thou
blessed of the Lord," they said. "Why do you stand outside
the door? See, we have everything ready for you. And we
have a place for your camels too."

They quickly invited Eliezer to sit down at the table to eat.

But the old servant would not eat until he had told them his errand.

"The Lord has blessed my master Abraham greatly," Eliezer began. "He is a rich man. He has many flocks of sheep and herds of cattle. He has many camels and donkeys. He has much silver and gold, and many men servants and women servants. But Abraham has only one son, Isaac, who was born when he and his wife, Sarah, were very old. All that Abraham has will belong to his son Isaac. I have come here to find a wife for Isaac."

Then Eliezer told Rebekah and her family about his prayer at the well, and how he knew that Rebekah was the young woman God had chosen.

"Will Rebekah come with me to be Isaac's wife?" he asked.

Then Laban and his father said, "The thing comes from God, so what can we say? Here is Rebekah, take her, and let her be Isaac's wife, as the Lord has said."

When Eliezer heard these words, he bowed himself to the ground and worshiped God. Then he brought out many more beautiful gifts — gold and silver, jewels and expensive clothing. He gave them to Rebekah. He gave gifts to Rebekah's brother Laban and to her mother too. Then they all sat down to eat.

The next morning Eliezer said, "Now let me go back to my master."

But Rebekah's mother and brother said, "Don't go so soon. Wait at least ten days; then we will let Rebekah go."

"Do not make me wait," Eliezer answered. "Seeing the Lord has found me a wife for Isaac so soon, let me go at once to my master."

"We will call Rebekah," they answered, "and see what she has to say." So they called her and asked if she was willing to go that very day.

"Yes, I will go," said Rebekah.

So Rebekah quickly gathered all her belongings, and took her nurse, and went with Abraham's servant.

It was a long journey back to the land of Canaan. As they neared Abraham's home one evening, Isaac was walking alone in the fields, thinking. He saw the camels coming and ran to meet them.

"Who is that man coming to meet us?" Rebekah asked.

"It is Isaac," Eliezer answered.

Rebekah quickly came down from her camel and covered her face with a veil, as was the custom in those days. Eliezer told Isaac all about his journey. Isaac loved Rebekah at once. He took her into his mother's tent, and she became his wife. Isaac was no longer lonely. He and Rebekah were very happy together.

Were you listening? Why was Isaac lonely? What important errand did Abraham give Eliezer to do? How did God help Eliezer? Who became Isaac's wife?

Esau Sells His Birthright

Isaac and Rebekah lived together in the land of Canaan for many years. For a long time they had no children. But Isaac prayed to God again and again for a son.

God heard Isaac's prayer. He gave Isaac and Rebekah two sons—twin boys. Their names were Jacob and Esau. Although the boys were twins, they did not look at all alike. Jacob's skin was smooth and soft. Esau's skin was red and covered with hair. The boys did not act alike either. Jacob liked to live at home, close to his mother's tent. Esau was a brave hunter who lived in the fields, hunting for wild animals. Isaac loved Esau best because he ate the meat Esau brought him. But Rebekah loved Jacob best.

In those days the oldest son in the family had a special right that none of the other children in the family had. It was called the birthright. The son who had the birthright would take his father's place as the head of the family, after the father died. He would also receive much more of his father's possessions than would the other children in the family.

In Abraham's family it had been Isaac, and not the oldest son Ishmael, who had received the birthright. That is because God wanted it so. The great blessings of God were now Isaac's. And Isaac would in turn give them to one of his sons. The son who received the birthright would be the one who would become a great nation. And from his nation would come the Saviour.

Esau was the oldest son in Isaac's family, because he was born first, before his twin brother Jacob. So the birthright would be Esau's. But Esau was not much interested in the birthright. He did not care for the blessings of God that would come to him some day. Jacob, however, was sorry he was not the older of the two, for he wanted the birthright badly.

One day Esau came home from hunting. He had been in the open country for a long time, and he was very hungry. As he came close to his mother's tent, he saw Jacob cooking himself some red pottage. Pottage was a kind of vegetable, something like our beans. It smelled delicious.

When Esau smelled the pottage, it made him still more hungry. He said to his brother, "Let me have some of your pottage, for I am faint with hunger."

Jacob thought this would be a good chance to get the birthright away from his brother. So he said, "You may have the pottage, if you will first sell me your birthright."

"What good will my birthright do me, if I die of hunger?" Esau said. "You may have the birthright."

"Swear to me that you will surely give it to me," Jacob said.

So Esau swore. Then Jacob gave him the pottage and some bread. Esau quickly ate it. As soon as he had finished, he went back to his hunting. He forgot all about his birthright. He did not care for it anyway. He did not care much about the promises of God.

But Jacob did not forget. He would see to it that he kept the birthright!

> *Were you listening?* How many children did Isaac have? Why did Isaac love Esau best? Who wanted the birthright? How did he get it?

Story 19

Jacob Gets the Birthright

Genesis 27

Isaac and Rebekah were now old. Isaac was becoming weak and feeble. He could no longer see. He did not think he would live much longer. One day he called his older son, Esau.

"Esau," said Isaac, "I am old, and I do not know how long I shall live. Take your bow and arrow and go into the fields and find a deer. Make a tasty dish of venison for me, such as I love. Then I shall eat and give you the birthright blessing."

Esau took his bow and arrows and went out to find a deer. He paid no attention to his promise to Jacob. But Rebekah remembered. She heard Isaac's words to Esau. She wanted Jacob to have the blessing. She quickly called Jacob, and together they planned to deceive the blind old father.

Rebekah sent Jacob into the field to get two young kids of the goats. She prepared the meat for Isaac, in the way he loved best. But Jacob said to his mother, "Esau is a hairy man, and my skin is smooth. If my father touches me, he will know that I am not Esau. Then he will curse me instead of bless me."

Rebekah answered, "Leave that to me. Only do as I say."

When the delicious food was ready, Rebekah dressed Jacob in Esau's hunting clothes, so that he would smell like Esau. Then she put goat's skin on his arms and neck so that he would feel like Esau. Then Jacob took the dish into his father's tent.

"My father," Jacob said.

"Here am I," Isaac answered. "Who are you, my son?"

"I am Esau, your first-born," Jacob lied. "I did what you told me to do. Come, I pray you, sit and eat of my venison, so that your soul may bless me."

"How is it that you are back so soon?" Isaac asked.

"God helped me find the deer," Jacob lied again.

"Come here," Isaac commanded, "and let me feel you." So Jacob knelt at his father's knee. Isaac touched the goat skin on his arms and neck.

"The voice is Jacob's," Isaac said, "but your hands feel like the hands of Esau." So Isaac did not discover that it was Jacob. "Are you sure you are my very son, Esau?" he asked.

"I am," said Jacob.

Then Isaac ate of the venison and the food and drink Jacob had brought him.

When he had finished, he said, "Come here, my son, and kiss me."

Jacob knelt at his father's knees and kissed him. Isaac smelled the smell of the woods on Esau's hunting coat and was satisfied. "See, the smell of my son is as the smell of a field that the Lord has blessed," said Isaac.

Then Isaac laid his hands on Jacob's bowed head and gave him the wonderful promises of God that he had received from Abraham, his father. "God will give you great riches and honor," he said. "People will serve you, and nations will bow down to you. Even your own brothers will bow down to you."

As soon as Isaac finished blessing Jacob, Jacob hurried out of his father's tent. He did not want Esau to find him there. No sooner had he gone than Esau came in from the fields with his deer. He quickly prepared the meat and brought it in to his father.

"Let my father arise," he said, "and eat of his son's venison, so that his soul may bless me."

"Who are you?" Isaac asked in surprise.

"I am your son, your first-born, Esau."

Isaac trembled from shock and said, "Who then was just here and brought me the venison? I have already eaten and given away the birthright. Your brother Jacob has received the blessing."

When Esau heard his father's words, he cried loud and bitterly, "Oh my father, bless me, even me too!"

But Isaac answered, "Now it is too late! Your brother came and deceived me, and he has taken away your blessing."

"Jacob is a good name for him!" said Esau angrily. For

Esau knew that the word Jacob means "a deceiver." "Twice he has deceived me. First he took away my birthright, and now he has stolen the birthright blessing! But, father, have you not kept some blessing for me?"

"Behold," said Isaac sadly, "I have made him your master, and I have given him all his brethren for servants. And I have blessed him with all the good things of this earth. What is there left for you, my son?"

"Have you not one little blessing, my father? Bless me, even me too, oh my father!" Esau pleaded, weeping bitter tears.

"Yes," said Isaac, "God will cause the land to yield rich food to you. You must serve your brother, but the day will come when you will no longer have to serve him."

Then Esau left his father's tent. He was very angry with Jacob. He was so angry that he hated him and wanted to kill him.

"My father will not live much longer," said Esau to himself. "As soon as he is dead, I will kill my brother."

Were you listening? How did Jacob and his mother deceive Isaac? What promises did Isaac give to Jacob in the birthright blessing? What blessings did Isaac promise to Esau? How did Esau plan to get back at his brother?

Story 20

Jacob's Dream

Genesis 28

Rebekah heard about Esau's wicked plan to kill Jacob. She quickly called Jacob aside. "Your brother is planning to kill you," she said. "Obey my voice now, and flee to Laban, my brother, in Haran. Stay with him a few days, until Esau's anger has left him. Then I will send for you to come home."

Then Rebekah went into Isaac's tent to ask his permission to send Jacob away. She did not tell Isaac the real reason why she wanted to send Jacob away. Instead she said, "If Jacob is to be the head of a great nation, he must not get himself a wife from these heathen people who live around here. Send him to my people back in Haran to find a wife who loves God."

Isaac saw that Rebekah was right. So he sent for Jacob and told him to go to his uncle Laban's home in Haran to find himself a wife. Once more he blessed Jacob and let him go.

It was a long journey from Canaan to Haran. It must have been very lonely for Jacob as he started out walking all by himself. All day long he walked. When evening came he found himself a resting place. He lay down on the ground to sleep and used a stone for a pillow. And he threw his coat over himself for a blanket.

As Jacob lay all alone under the stars, he must have thought about his father Isaac and how he had deceived him, and about his mother Rebekah and his brother Esau. He must have been happy to have finally received the wonderful birthright. He knew God had wanted him to have it, because God had told his mother so at the time of Jacob's birth. But he must have been sorry that he had cheated his father in order to get it. He should have trusted God and let Him plan the way to give it to him. Finally Jacob fell asleep.

As Jacob slept, God came to him in a dream. In the dream Jacob saw a ladder set up on the ground in front of him. It was a high ladder. The top of it reached to heaven. He saw the angels of God going up the ladder and coming down. And he saw God at the top of the ladder. God was speaking to him.

"I am the Lord God of Abraham and of Isaac," God said. "The land on which you are lying will some day be yours and your children's. And you will have as many children as the dust of the earth. Your family will spread out across all this land, to the east, to the west, to the north, and to the south. And in you and your family shall all the families of the earth be blessed. And behold, I am with you, and I will take care of you wherever you go. I will bring you back again to this land."

Then Jacob woke up. "Surely the Lord is in this place, and

I did not know it!" he said. "This is the house of God. This is the gate of heaven!"

Now Jacob knew that the birthright promises were really for him. God, Himself, had told him! In spite of Jacob's sins, God would bless him. For God forgives all who are truly sorry for their sins.

To express his thankfulness to God, Jacob took the stone that had been his pillow and set it up for a pillar. Then he poured oil on it and called the place Bethel, which means, "House of God." And Jacob made a promise to God. He said, "If God will be with me and take care of me on my journey, and bring me safely back again to my father's house, then He shall be my God. And this stone I have set up as a pillar shall be God's House. And I promise that of everything that God gives me, I shall give back one tenth to Him."

Then Jacob went on with his journey. He was happy because he had seen God, and because he knew that God would be with him.

> *Were you listening?* Why did Jacob have to leave home? What did Jacob see in his dream? What did God tell him? What did Jacob promise God?

Story 21

Jacob Is Fooled by His Uncle

Genesis 29

When Jacob came at last to his uncle's house in Haran, he rested at the well, just as the old servant of Abraham had done many years before. While he rested, his uncle Laban's younger daughter, Rachel, came to the well with her sheep. When Jacob found out that she was his cousin, he rolled away the stone from the well and watered her flock of sheep for her. Then Jacob kissed Rachel and cried for joy.

Rachel quickly told her father that Jacob had come. And Laban welcomed Jacob into his home. Jacob lived with his

Uncle Laban for many years. He became a shepherd. Each day he went out into the fields to care for his uncle's sheep.

When Jacob had worked for his uncle about a month, Laban said to him, "Just because you are my nephew, you should not work for me for nothing. Tell me, what shall I give you for working for me?" In those days people did not work for money. They were usually given things instead of money.

Now Laban had two daughters, Leah and Rachel. The younger daughter, Rachel, was very beautiful, and Jacob loved her with all his heart. So he said to Laban, "I will work for you for seven years if you will give me Rachel for my wife."

Laban was pleased with Jacob's offer. So Jacob took care of his uncle's sheep for seven years. The seven long years seemed as short as a few days to Jacob because he loved Rachel so much.

When the seven years were over, Laban made ready a wedding feast for Jacob. In those days when a young woman became a bride she wore a heavy veil over her face, so that her husband would not be able to see her face until after they were married. At this wedding feast Laban tricked Jacob. He gave him Leah for a wife instead of Rachel. But Jacob did not love Leah. It was Rachel he loved.

The next morning, when Jacob found out that he had married Leah instead of his beautiful Rachel, he was very angry.

"What is this that you have done to me?" he said to his uncle. "Did I not work seven years for Rachel? Then why did you trick me and give me Leah?"

Laban answered, "In our country we cannot give the younger daughter in marriage before her older sisters. Live with Leah for one week, and then we will have another wedding feast. Then I will give you Rachel also. But you will have to work seven more years to pay for Rachel."

So, after one week, Jacob married Rachel too. Then he worked seven more years to pay for her. During all those years Jacob loved Rachel more than he did Leah. When God saw that Jacob did not love Leah, He gave her several children. But He gave none to Rachel. Rachel and Leah were jealous of each other. They often quarreled. God did not intend that a man should have more than one wife, and Jacob's home was often unhappy because of all the quarreling.

In those days a wife wanted children more than she wanted anything else, and when Leah received four little baby boys right after each other, she was filled with joy.

"Perhaps Jacob will now love me better than he loves Rachel," Leah thought. She called her boys Reuben, Simeon, Levi, and Judah.

Rachel was most unhappy because she had no children. Finally she decided to do the same thing Sarah, Abraham's wife, had once done. She gave her servant girl, Bilhah, to Jacob as a wife. If Bilhah had any babies, Rachel could call them hers. In time Bilhah bare Jacob two sons. Rachel said the children were hers because Bilhah was her servant. Rachel called the children Dan and Naphtali.

When Leah saw what Rachel had done, she gave Jacob her servant girl, Zilpah, for a wife. She wanted more children too. And Zilpah got two little boys. Leah named them Gad and Asher. After that Leah had two more little boys of her own. She named them Issachar and Zebulun. Now Leah had eight boys altogether. God also gave her one little girl. She called her Dinah.

After many years, God remembered Rachel and answered her prayers and gave her a little son. She called him Joseph. Rachel was filled with joy to have a baby of her own. Jacob still loved Rachel more than he did Leah, and because Joseph was Rachel's boy, he loved Joseph more than he did all his other children. Joseph was born when Jacob was already old. He brought much joy to his old father.

> *Were you listening?* Where did Jacob go to live when he ran away from his brother Esau? Whom did Jacob want to marry? Why did he have to work fourteen years for his uncle Laban? Why was there much quarreling in Jacob's home? Why was Joseph Jacob's favorite son?

Jacob Runs Away

Jacob lived with his Uncle Laban for twenty years. During all that time he worked for his uncle, taking care of his many cattle and sheep. After he had worked fourteen years to pay for both of his wives, he stayed six more years. During those years Laban paid him by letting him have some of the cattle for his own. At first it was decided that Jacob should have all the speckled and spotted cattle, all the brown sheep, and all the speckled and spotted goats.

God blessed Jacob and saw to it that Jacob soon had more cattle than Laban. More of the speckled and spotted animals got young ones than did the plain colored.

When Laban saw that Jacob had more cattle than he had, he wanted the spotted ones for himself. He gave Jacob the plain ones. But when Jacob had the plain cattle, then God gave more young to the plain animals. Then Laban would change back again and take the plain-colored cattle for his own. Ten times Laban changed Jacob's wages. Jacob was no longer happy in his uncle's home.

One day Jacob heard his cousins complaining. They said that Jacob had taken all their father's cattle. Then Jacob called his two wives to come to him in the field.

"I see that your father is no longer pleased with me," he said. "But God has been with me. He came to me in a dream and told me to go back to my own family and to my own country."

Rachel and Leah answered, "We will go with you, Jacob. Our father does not love us anymore either. He treats us as strangers."

Then Jacob gathered together his large family of children and servants and cattle, and made ready to flee, with all his possessions. As soon as Laban left home for a few days to shear his sheep, Jacob and his family set off on camels, and hurried away as fast as they could.

Jacob had been gone for three days before Laban heard about it. When the news reached him, he quickly went after Jacob. He traveled seven days before he found him in a place called Mount Gilead. There Jacob had pitched his tent.

Laban was very angry with Jacob. He wanted to harm him, but God would not permit him to do this. God came to Laban in a dream and said, "Be careful, Laban, that you do Jacob no harm."

So when Laban came to Jacob he only said, "Why did you flee from me in secret? Why did you not tell me you were leaving, so I could have given you a farewell feast, and have kissed my children good-by?"

"Because I was afraid," Jacob answered. "I knew you would not let me go, and I was afraid you might take your daughters away from me."

Then Laban said, "All right, if you want to go back to your home, then go. But you did not have to steal my gods from me." Laban was talking about his little household idols, made of wood or stone. Although Laban knew the real God, he also worshiped these idols. Laban's daughters worshiped idols too, and as they were getting ready to leave their home, Rachel had taken her father's idols. But Jacob did not know this.

"Whoever has taken your idols shall not live," Jacob answered. "You may look through all our belongings."

So Laban went into Jacob's tent, then into Leah's tent and into the two tents of the servant girls, Bilhah and Zilpah. But he did not find his idols. Last of all, he went into Rachel's tent. Now Rachel had taken the idols and had put them in the pocket of her camel's saddle. She had the saddle on the floor of her tent, and she was sitting on it. As Laban came into her tent, Rachel said, "Please excuse me, father, for not getting up. I do not feel very well." So Laban searched the tent, but he did not find his idols. And he did not find anything else that belonged to him anywhere.

Then Jacob was angry and scolded his uncle. "See, we did not take anything that was yours," he said. "Why did you come after us as if we were thieves?"

Then Jacob added, "Twenty years I worked for you, Laban. I took good care of your cattle. If any were stolen or killed, I gave you mine instead. I was often thirsty in the daytime, and at night I was so cold I could not sleep. Yet you have not been kind to me. If God had not been with me, surely you would have sent me away empty. God has seen my troubles and has punished you, Uncle Laban."

Then Laban was no longer angry. He and Jacob made a pledge together. They built an altar and burned a sacrifice to God. And Laban said, "The Lord watch between me and thee, when we are absent one from another." And they promised never to harm one another.

Early the next morning Laban kissed his children good-by and blessed them. Then Laban went back to his home in Haran, and Jacob went on with his journey.

Were you listening? How long did Jacob live with his uncle? Why did Laban keep changing Jacob's wages? Why did Jacob run away? Why did Laban not harm Jacob? What wrong things had Rachel done?

Jacob Wrestles with God

After Jacob's Uncle Laban had gone back to his home, Jacob and his large family went on their way toward Canaan. Jacob sent servants on ahead to see if they could find his brother Esau.

"When you find him," Jacob said, "tell him that I am coming to meet him, and that I have much cattle and many servants. Tell him that I have been with my Uncle Laban all these years. Tell him that I want to be friends with him."

So the servants went to find Esau. Soon they came back. "We have found your brother," they said. "He is coming to meet you. He has four hundred men with him!"

Jacob was filled with fear when he heard this. He quickly divided all his people and cattle into two groups. Then if Esau should fall upon the one group, the other group could escape.

Jacob prayed to God for help. He cried, "O God of my fathers, You told me to go back to my country and to my people, and You promised to take care of me. I am not worthy of the least of all the lovingkindnesses You have given me. When I passed this way before, all I had was a staff in my hands. And now all my animals and all my people are in two big companies. Please do not let my brother harm us."

When Jacob had finished praying, he made things ready to camp for the night. He sent several servants with many presents to his brother Esau. He sent goats and camels and cows and calves and donkeys. He sent about five hundred animals. He sent each servant with one kind of animal, and he told them each to go separately, one behind the other. He hoped his brother would be pleased with the animals and be kind to him because of these large gifts.

As soon as the servants had gone, Jacob brought his entire family and all his possessions across the brook Jabbok. Then he went back to the other side of the brook. There he spent the night alone.

During the night a man stood before Jacob. The man wrestled with Jacob until morning. Jacob did not know it, but it was the Angel of the Lord who had come to wrestle with him. The Angel of the Lord is really the Lord Jesus before He came to this earth as a man. When the Angel saw that Jacob did not give in, he touched Jacob's hip and put it out of joint. Ever after that Jacob limped on one leg.

When it began to be light the Angel said, "Let me go, for the day is almost here."

By this time Jacob had guessed that his visitor was the Angel of the Lord, so he answered, "I will not let You go, unless You bless me."

"What is your name?" the Angel asked.

"My name is Jacob."

"Your name shall no longer be Jacob," said the Angel. "I will change your name to Israel, because you have wrestled with God and with men, and have won." The name Israel means "a prince of God."

Then Jacob said, "Tell me, I pray, what is Your name?"

"Why do you ask my name?" the Angel answered. Then the Angel blessed Jacob and went back to heaven.

Jacob called the name of the place Peniel. "Because I have seen God face to face," he said, "and He has spared my life."

When it was morning, Jacob crossed the Jabbok and returned to his family. Soon he saw Esau with his four hundred men coming to meet him. Jacob went ahead of his family to meet Esau. He bowed himself to the ground seven times before his brother.

But Esau was no longer angry. He ran to meet Jacob and embraced him and kissed him. They both wept for joy to see one another again.

Esau noticed all the people with Jacob. "Who are all these with you?" he asked.

"These are my wives and the children God has given me,"

Jacob answered. Then Jacob's family came near and bowed to Esau.

"What did you mean by sending all these animals to me?" Esau asked Jacob.

"They are my gift to you," Jacob answered.

"I have enough, my brother. You may keep your cattle."

"Please take them," Jacob urged him, "for God has been kind to me, and I have more than enough."

So at last Esau took them. Then Esau offered to have his men help Jacob on the rest of their journey. But Jacob said, "You and your men had better go on ahead, and we shall follow slowly. For I have many little children, and my sheep and cattle have little ones too. If we should go too fast for them, they would all die."

So Esau and his men went ahead, and Jacob followed with his family. And the brothers were friends once more.

> *Were you listening?* Why was Jacob afraid of Esau? How did he try to make friends with him? Who wrestled with Jacob? What does the name Israel mean? What happened when the two brothers met?

Story 24

Jacob Keeps His Promise

Genesis 35

Jacob had returned to the land of Canaan. He had made friends with his brother Esau. And Jacob had bought some land and pitched his tent in Canaan.

But he had forgotten something. He had forgotten the promise he had made to God. So one day God came to Jacob.

"Get up, Jacob," God said, "and go back to Bethel where you saw God on the top of the heavenly ladder, the day you were running away from your brother Esau."

Then Jacob remembered. After that wonderful dream he had promised God that he would go back to Bethel and offer a sacrifice there. He had promised to give God one tenth of everything God would give him.

Jacob quickly called all the members of his large family together. "Get ready," he said. "We are going on a journey to Bethel. But you must put away the strange gods that you took with you from Haran. And you must wash yourselves and put on clean clothing. For we must go to Bethel to make an altar to God who answered me when I was in trouble, and who was with me wherever I went."

Jacob's children and servants brought him all their idols, for they had learned to worship idols in Laban's home. Jacob buried the idols under an oak tree.

Soon Jacob and his family were ready to begin their journey. In order to get to Bethel they had to travel through many cities belonging to other people. In those days a man was not allowed to travel with a large group through other people's cities. They would have to fight their way through. But when Jacob traveled from one city to the next, God made the people of the cities afraid. They did not pursue after Jacob and his sons, nor fight against them.

Finally Jacob came to Bethel. He built an altar there and offered sacrifices to God, as he had promised. Then God came and spoke to Jacob again.

"Your name shall not be called anymore Jacob," God repeated, "but your name shall be Israel. I am God Almighty. I will make a great nation out of you, and kings shall come from you. All this land that I promised to your fathers I will give to you and your children."

Then God went up from Jacob in the place where he spoke with him. And Jacob set up a pillar of stone and poured an offering and oil on it. Perhaps this stone was the same one he had used for a pillow twenty years before. And Jacob again called the place Bethel—the House of God.

While they were still at Bethel, Rebekah's nurse, Deborah, died. They buried her under an oak tree in Bethel. Then another sad thing happened. A very sad thing. They had not gone far from Bethel on their homeward journey when Rachel

became very sick. She became so sick, when a second baby boy
was born to her, that she died. As she was dying she gave her
new baby a sad name. She called him, Benoni, which means,
"son of my sorrow." But his father called him Benjamin, which
means, "son of the right hand."

Jacob buried Rachel in Bethlehem, the place where they were.
And Jacob set up a large pillar over Rachel's grave. That pillar
is still in Bethlehem today, even though it is more than three
thousand years old.

> *Were you listening?* What promise had Jacob forgotten to keep?
> What did Jacob do just before he went to Bethel? What happened
> to Rachel? Who was Benjamin?

Story 25

Joseph, the Dreamer

Genesis 37

Jacob now had twelve sons, besides daughters. But of all
his sons he loved Joseph best, because Joseph was Rachel's first-
born. And Rachel had been the wife whom Jacob loved.

Joseph's brothers were jealous of him because Jacob their
father loved Joseph best. They hated Joseph and would not
speak kindly to him.

One day Jacob gave his son Joseph a beautiful new coat. It
was made of many colors. The brothers did not receive a new
coat. This made them angry. They became even more jealous
of Joseph. Sometimes Joseph would work in the fields with his
brothers. He would see his brothers doing wrong things. Then
he would tell his father what the brothers had done. This made
the brothers still more angry.

One day Joseph dreamed a dream. He went to his brothers
and said, "Listen to the dream I had. We were all in the field
binding the grain into big sheaves. Suddenly my sheaf stood
up straight. Your sheaves came and stood around my sheaf.
They bowed down to my sheaf as if it were a king."

The brothers said, "Do you think you are going to be a king

some day and rule over us?" Then they hated Joseph still more because of his dream and his words.

Not long after this, Joseph dreamed another dream. He told it to his father and his brothers. Joseph said, "This time I dreamed that I and all my brothers were stars. My father and my mother were the sun and moon. Suddenly the sun and the moon and the eleven stars all bowed down to my star."

Joseph's father rebuked him and said, "What? Do you think that I and your mother and all your brothers shall bow down to you some day?"

The brothers envied Joseph and hated him more and more. They called him "Joseph, the dreamer." But Jacob remembered the dreams in his heart and wondered what they meant. Jacob and his son Joseph did not know that God had sent these dreams to Joseph for a special reason. God had a great work planned for Joseph, and He was getting him ready for it.

Were you listening? Why did Jacob love Joseph best? Why did the brothers hate Joseph? Can you think of three reasons? What did Joseph dream? What did the brothers call Joseph?

Story 26

Joseph Sold by His Brothers

Genesis 37

One day Joseph's brothers took their flocks of sheep to Shechem. Joseph did not go along. The brothers were gone for a long time. Jacob was worried about them. He called his son Joseph to him and said, "Joseph, I want you to go to Shechem to see what has happened to your brothers. Then come back and tell me."

Joseph did not like to go to find his brothers. He knew they hated him. But he was an obedient and God-fearing boy. So he did as his father asked. He put on his beautiful coat of many colors, and started out. He walked a long way, but he could not find his brothers.

As Joseph was wandering in the fields, a man found him. "What are you looking for?" the man asked.

"I am looking for my brothers," Joseph answered. "Have you seen them feeding their flocks?"

"Yes, I saw them," the man answered. "I heard them say that they were going to feed their flocks in Dothan."

So Joseph went down to Dothan. Soon he saw his brothers sitting with their flocks in the fields. Joseph was glad to see his brothers. But when the brothers saw Joseph coming, they were not glad to see him. They said, "Here comes Joseph, the dreamer. Let us do away with him! Let us slay him!"

"No, let us not take his life," said Reuben, the oldest brother. "Let us not shed blood, brothers. But let us cast him into this pit in the wilderness."

Reuben wanted to save Joseph and get him out of the pit later.

As soon as Joseph reached them, the brothers took off his beautiful coat and threw Joseph into the pit. The pit was empty. There was no water in it.

How frightened Joseph was! He begged his brothers to take him out of the well and send him back home to his father. But the brothers sat down to eat and would not listen to his cries.

While the brothers were eating and Reuben had gone off to take care of the sheep, some merchantmen came along, riding on camels. These men were on their way to Egypt to sell salves, called myrrh, and precious spices.

Then Judah, one of Joseph's brothers, said, "Let us sell Joseph to these men. That is better than slaying our own brother."

So the brothers sold Joseph to the merchantmen for twenty pieces of silver.

After a while Reuben went alone to the well. He went quietly, because he wanted to send Joseph back to his father when the other brothers were not looking.

But the well was empty.

Then Reuben cried to his brothers, "Oh, what shall I do! Joseph is gone! What shall I tell our father!"

But the brothers thought up a plan. They killed a goat, and they took Joseph's coat of many colors and dipped the coat into the blood of the goat. Then they took the coat home and brought it to their father.

"Look, father," they said, "this we have found. Is this Joseph's coat or not?"

And Jacob said, "It is my son's coat. An evil beast has torn him. Joseph is dead."

And Jacob tore his clothes and wept for his son. He wept many days. His sons and daughters tried to comfort him, but Jacob would not be comforted. "I will go down to the grave mourning for my son," Jacob said.

But all this time Joseph was riding down to Egypt with the merchantmen.

Were you listening? How do we know that Joseph was an obedient boy? What did Joseph's brothers do to him? How did the brothers deceive their father? Where was Joseph when his brothers told Jacob that Joseph was dead?

Story 27

Joseph Goes to Prison

Genesis 39

The merchantmen to whom Joseph's brothers had sold him were Ishmaelites. The Ishmaelites were grandchildren of Ishmael, the son of Hagar, Sarah's maid. Ishmael had grown up in the wilderness after Abraham sent him and Hagar away.

When these Ishmaelites came to Egypt they took their spices and myrrh to the market place in the city to be sold there. They took Joseph to the market place too, and put him up for sale as a slave.

An important man bought Joseph. He was the captain of the guard and an officer of King Pharaoh of Egypt. His name was Potiphar.

Potiphar took Joseph to his home and made him his servant. God was with Joseph and helped him do his work well. Potiphar soon noticed what a good servant Joseph was. He made him the chief servant in his house. Joseph had charge of everything that belonged to his master. He even took care of all his money and all his property. Potiphar did not even know how much he had. God blessed Joseph in his work. He blessed Potiphar too, because of Joseph.

But after a while something very sad happened. Potiphar's wife became angry with Joseph and told her husband a lie about him.

Potiphar believed his wife instead of Joseph. He threw Joseph into prison. He threw him into the prison where the king's prisoners were kept.

But God was with Joseph even in prison. The prison keeper soon saw that Joseph was a good man. He gave him charge over all the prisoners. And God blessed Joseph while he was in prison.

> *Were you listening?* What happened to Joseph when he arrived in Egypt? Why did Potiphar like him? Why did Potiphar throw Joseph into prison?

Story 28

The Butler and the Baker

Genesis 40

Joseph was in prison, but he was not chained to the wall as the other prisoners were. He was given work to do. Each day he went into the rooms of the other prisoners to bring them their food. He also took care of the other prisoners for the prison keeper. He had complete charge of them.

One day the king became angry with his chief butler and with his chief baker. He threw them into the prison. Joseph had charge of these men too. One morning, as Joseph came to see the butler and the baker, he noticed that they were filled with sadness. "Why do you look so sad today?" he asked.

"We have both dreamed a dream," they answered, "and we do not know what the dreams mean." In those days God often spoke to men in dreams.

"Is not God the only one who can tell the meaning of dreams?" Joseph answered. "Tell me your dreams, I pray you."

Then the butler said, "I dreamed about a vine with three branches. First there were buds, then there were flowers, and then there were grapes on the vines. I had King Pharaoh's cup in my hand. And I squeezed the juice from the grapes into the cup and gave it to the king."

Joseph said, "This is the meaning of your dream. The three branches are three days. In three days the king will come to the prison and take you back to the palace and make you the king's butler again. You will give him his wine as you did before."

When the baker saw that the butler's dream was good, he was eager to tell his dream too. He said, "In my dream I had three white baskets on my head, one on top of the other. In the top basket were all kinds of baked goods for the king. But the birds came and ate the food from the basket on my head."

Then Joseph said, "This is the meaning of your dream. The three baskets are three days. In three days the king will come to the prison to take you out and hang you on a tree. And the birds will come and eat the flesh from your body."

Joseph turned to the butler. "When you go back to the palace, he said, "be so kind as to remember me and tell the king about me. Tell him that I have done nothing wrong that they should put me in prison."

Three days later it was the king's birthday. He made a great feast for all his servants. And he took the butler and the baker out of prison. He brought the butler back to the palace to work for him, just as Joseph had said. And he hanged the baker on a tree, according to the dream.

Joseph waited and waited for the king to take him out of prison. But the king did not find out about Joseph. The butler had forgotten to tell him.

> *Were you listening?* Why were the butler and the baker so sad? What did the three branches and the three baskets mean? What happened to the butler and the baker? Why did Joseph stay in prison?

Story 29

A Dream Comes True

Genesis 41

It took two whole years before the butler finally remembered his promise to Joseph. The reason he finally remembered it was this: One night King Pharaoh had two strange dreams. When he awoke in the morning he was so troubled that he called all his magicians and all his wise men and told them the dreams. But there was no one who could tell the king what the dreams meant.

Then the butler, who was always with the king to serve him, spoke up. He said, "All this time I have forgotten to tell the king something. Do you remember, O King, when you were angry and sent both me and the baker to prison? While we were in prison, we both had a dream. There was a young man in prison who was a servant of the guard. He told us the meaning of our dreams. And it happened just as he said."

The king quickly sent to the prison for Joseph. Soon Joseph stood before the king and listened to the king's dreams.

The king said, "In my dream I stood on the banks of the river. I saw seven well-fed, healthy cows come up out of the water to eat in the meadow. Then I saw seven thin, sickly cows come up out of the water. The sickly cows ate the healthy cows, but yet they were just as thin as they had been before. Then I woke up."

Then Pharaoh told his second dream. "After a while I fell asleep again," said Pharaoh. "I had another dream. I saw a stalk of corn with seven good, fat ears on it. As I looked, seven poor ears of corn sprang up on that same stalk and ate the good ears. But the poor ears were still poor. Then I awoke. And none of my wise men could tell me the meaning of these dreams."

Then Joseph answered the king, "It is not in me, O king, to give the meaning of your dreams. God gives me the answer. The two dreams you have had mean the same thing. God has given you these dreams to show you what is going to happen. The seven cows and the seven ears of corn mean seven years. There are going to be seven good years when there will be plenty of food for everyone. Then there will be seven bad years of famine when everyone will go hungry. There will be a great famine in your land, O king."

Then Joseph gave the king some good advice. "Let the king find a very wise man," he said. "And let the people bring him one fifth of all their food during the seven good years. Then when the bad years come there will be food for everyone."

The king was pleased with Joseph's suggestion. "Where could I find a man who is as wise as Joseph?" he asked. So the king chose Joseph to be ruler under him, and to store up food for the days of famine.

Then the king put his ring upon Joseph's finger and dressed him in fine clothing and put a gold chain about his neck. He made Joseph to ride through the city in the king's own chariot. Everyone bowed down to Joseph.

Joseph was thirty years old when he became a ruler. The king gave him a beautiful home to live in, and he gave him the daughter of the priest of On to be his wife. And God gave them two baby boys. Joseph called the first one Manasseh. This name means, "God has made me to forget all my troubles." And he called the second one Ephraim which means, "God has caused me to have children in the land of my trouble."

Were you listening? What made the butler finally remember his promise to Joseph? What did the king dream? What did the king's dreams mean? What did the king do for Joseph?

Story 30

Joseph's Brothers Come to Egypt

Genesis 42

Next to the king, Joseph was now the greatest man in Egypt. He ruled over the king's house and over all the king's people. Only on the throne was the king greater than Joseph.

Joseph worked hard. During the seven years of plenty, he gathered up much food and stored it in the cities. Soon the storehouses were filled to overflowing. Then, when the seven years of famine began and the people had no food, they came to Joseph to buy the food he had saved.

In the land of Canaan where Jacob lived with his eleven sons, there was also a famine. Jacob and his sons were hungry. Their little children were hungry too. One day Jacob said to his sons, "Why do you stand there looking at one another? I have heard that there is corn in Egypt. Go there and buy us some corn, so that we may live and not die."

Then Joseph's ten brothers went down to Egypt to buy corn. But Benjamin, Joseph's youngest brother, stayed at home with his father. For Jacob did not want any harm to come to him. Once he had sent Joseph away from home, and he never came back. He did not want that to happen to Rachel's other son too.

Each brother took with him an empty sack for the food, and a bag of money. When they reached Egypt, they were directed to the home of Joseph, their brother. But they did not know it was Joseph. They bowed themselves down before Joseph with their faces to the ground.

Joseph saw at once that it was his brothers who had come to him. As they bowed before him, Joseph remembered the dreams he had dreamed when he was a boy. He did not tell his brothers who he was. He wanted to see if they were still wicked as they had once been. So he spoke roughly to them. "Where do you come from?" Joseph asked.

"From the land of Canaan to buy food," they answered.

"You are spies!" said Joseph. "You have come to see how poor our land is."

"No, we are not spies. We are all the sons of one man. One of our brothers is dead, and the youngest one is at home with his father."

But Joseph said again, "No, you are spies." And he put them all in prison for three days.

After the third day Joseph said to his brothers, "This will I do, for I fear God. If you are honest men, let one of the brothers stay here in prison. The rest of you go and take grain to your families. When you come again, bring your youngest brother with you. Then I will know that you have not lied to me."

Joseph took Simeon and put him in prison. Then he told his servants to fill the brothers' sacks with corn and to put their money bags back into the sacks. He did not want their money. He wanted to give them the food.

So the brothers went home to the land of Canaan. On the way they stopped to give their donkeys food. One of the brothers found his money bag in his sack. They were all filled with fear. They were afraid the ruler would think he had stolen it.

The brothers hurried home. They told their father Jacob

all that had happened. They were glad to have the food, but they were afraid of the great ruler in Egypt. They were still more afraid when they opened their sacks and each man found his money bag in his sack.

Then Jacob said, "My son Benjamin shall not go with you to Egypt, for his brother Joseph is dead, and he only is left. If harm should come to him, you will bring down my gray hairs with sorrow to the grave. Benjamin shall not go."

Were you listening? Who was the new ruler in Egypt? Who came to him to buy food? Why did Joseph treat them roughly? Why did Joseph put the money bags back into his brothers' sacks?

Story 31

Two Brothers Meet

Genesis 43

But the famine continued in the land of Canaan. And the time came when Jacob and his large family of children and grandchildren were hungry once more. They had eaten all the grain the brothers had brought from Egypt. At last Jacob said to his sons, "Go again to Egypt and buy us a little food."

Judah said, "We cannot go to Egypt, father, unless we take our youngest brother, Benjamin, with us. The great ruler has ordered it."

"Oh, why did you tell the man you had a younger brother?" Jacob cried. "Why did you treat me so unkindly?"

"The man asked us about our family," Judah answered, "so what could we do? Please, father, let Benjamin go with us so that we and our little ones may live and not die. I promise to bring Benjamin back to you. If I bring him not back, let me have the blame forever."

Finally Jacob let Benjamin go. He sent with his sons some of his best fruit and some nuts and honey and spices to give to the ruler as a present. And they took two bags of money for each sack of food, since they had found their money in their sacks the first time. Then they rose up and went down to Egypt for the second time.

Joseph saw his brothers coming. When he saw that Benjamin was with them, he said to the steward of the house, "Have the men brought into the house. And make ready a feast, for they shall all have dinner with me at noon."

And the man did as Joseph said.

But the brothers were terrified when the steward took them over to Joseph's house. "Oh, my lord," they said to the steward. "The first time we came to buy food, we afterwards found our money in our sacks, as we were on our way home. We do not know how this happened."

They tried to explain about the money in their sacks, and each man gave back what he had found. They were afraid Joseph was going to punish them.

Then the steward said, "Be not afraid. Your God must have given you the money in your sacks. For I had your money." Then he brought Simeon to them. And he brought the men into Joseph's house.

The brothers anxiously waited for Joseph to come home. They knew they were going to have dinner at noon with the great ruler of Egypt, and they were afraid.

When at last Joseph came in they gave him their father's present and bowed to the earth.

Joseph asked about their families and about his father. "The old man about whom you told me, is he well? Is he still alive?"

The brothers bowed again and said, "Your servant, our father, is in good health. He is still alive."

Then Joseph looked at Benjamin. "Is this your younger brother?" he asked. He turned to Benjamin and added, "God be gracious to you, my son." Joseph was so happy to see his young brother that he was ready to cry. He quickly went into his own room so his brothers would not see him weeping.

After he had cried a long time, Joseph washed his face and went back to his brothers. He invited them to his feast. He placed the brothers around the table according to their ages, the oldest first and Benjamin at the end. The brothers were amazed. How could the ruler know their ages, they thought. And Joseph gave Benjamin five times as much food as the other brothers. He wanted to see if the brothers would be jealous of Benjamin as they had always been of him. But the brothers were glad that the ruler was kind to their youngest brother.

Joseph wanted to test his brothers once more to make sure that they were no longer wicked as they had been when he was a boy. He told his servants to fill the brothers' sacks with corn and to put both the bags of money on the top of each sack. Then he had them put his own silver cup in Benjamin's sack to make it look as if Benjamin had stolen it.

Soon the brothers were ready to return home. No sooner had they left the city than they noticed Joseph's servant running after them. They stopped at once. The servant accused them of stealing Joseph's silver cup. He looked in all their sacks. He found the cup in Benjamin's sack.

The brothers were filled with fear and grief. They all returned to the city to Joseph's house and fell before him on the ground.

"What is this that you have done?" asked Joseph.

"Oh, my lord!" said Judah. "What shall we say? How shall we explain? God has found out our wickedness. We all are your servants."

Then Joseph told them they could go home in peace, but only Benjamin, with whom the cup was found, should stay behind.

Judah pleaded and pleaded. He told Joseph all about their father, how greatly he had sorrowed when he lost his son Joseph, and how he could not bear to let Joseph's only brother, Benjamin, go.

"Oh, please, my lord," Judah said at last. "Let *me* stay here in prison instead of Benjamin. My old father will die of sorrow if we do not bring Benjamin back."

Then Joseph could not keep back the tears. He wept aloud and cried out, "Do you not know me? I am Joseph, your brother, whom you sold into Egypt. Is our father yet alive?"

The brothers could not answer. They shook with fear.

But Joseph said, "Do not be afraid. You meant it for evil, to get rid of me. But God meant it for good. He sent me to Egypt ahead of you so that I could save you and your families during this famine."

Then Joseph embraced his brothers and kissed them, and wept over them. And everyone was happy.

> *Were you listening?* Why did the brothers take Benjamin with them? Why did Joseph put his silver cup in Benjamin's sack? What did Joseph mean when he said, "You meant it for evil, but God meant it for good"?

Story 32

Jacob Meets His Son Joseph

Genesis 46

After Joseph made himself known to his brothers, King Pharaoh heard that Joseph's brothers had come. Pharaoh was pleased and sent a message to Joseph.

"Send your brothers home with plenty of the good things of Egypt," said Pharaoh. "Have them take wagons along for their wives and little children, and let them come back with their families to live with you in Egypt."

So Joseph did as the king commanded. He gave many gifts to all his brothers and much goods for his father Jacob. When they were ready to leave he said, "Do not stop along the way. But hurry to bring my father to me."

Jacob was anxiously waiting for the brothers to come home. He was happy to see them. He was especially happy to see that Benjamin and Simeon were with them. The brothers were greatly excited because of their wonderful news.

"Joseph is alive!" they cried. "He is ruler over all the land of Egypt!"

Jacob could not believe that Joseph was still alive. Then the brothers told him everything that had happened. They showed him the wagons and all the gifts Joseph had sent. At last, Jacob believed them.

"It is enough," Jacob said. "Joseph my son is yet alive. I will go and see him before I die."

So Jacob, whose name was now Israel, took all his possessions and all his children and traveled to Egypt. On the way they stopped at Beer-sheba to offer sacrifices to God. Here God talked to Israel in a dream. God called, "Jacob, Jacob."

"Here am I," said Jacob.

"I am the God of your father Isaac. Do not be afraid to take your family down to Egypt. I will go with you to Egypt. Some day I will bring you back to your own land again."

Then Israel and his family started out on their journey. They

took their wives and their little ones, their cattle, and all their possessions.

When Joseph heard that his father was nearing Egypt, he made ready his chariot and went out to meet him. He fell on his father's neck and wept for a long time.

As soon as they entered Egypt, Joseph took five of his brothers and went to see the King. King Pharaoh asked the men what they did. Joseph's brothers told him they were shepherds.

King Pharaoh was kind to Joseph and his brothers. He gave them the best of the land in a place called Goshen. Here they could keep their sheep and cattle. And he gave them his own animals to take care of too.

One day Joseph brought his father Jacob to see the king. Jacob stood before the king and blessed him. King Pharaoh asked, "How old are you?"

Jacob answered, "The days of my life are one hundred and thirty years. Few and evil have been the days of my life. I am not as old as my fathers lived to be."

So Israel and all his family lived in Egypt in the land of Goshen. There were seventy people in Jacob's family at this time, not counting the sons' wives. They were called the Israelites because they were all children of Jacob whose new name was Israel. And God was with His people and blessed the Israelites in Egypt.

There were still many years of famine in Egypt. Each day the people came to Joseph and bought food from his storehouses in the cities. When their money was gone, they gave Joseph their animals. And when their animals were gone, they gave Joseph their farms. Soon everything in Egypt belonged to the king. Then Joseph gave the people seed to plant, and they promised to give the king one fifth of all their food.

Jacob lived in Egypt seventeen years. Before he died he called all his sons to him and gave them each a blessing. When he blessed Judah he said, "From your family shall come the Saviour of the world."

When Jacob died the brothers carried his body back to Canaan and buried him in the same cave where Abraham and Isaac were buried. Then they went back to live in Egypt.

Were you listening? Where did Jacob and his family go to live? What happened in Beer-sheba? How large was Jacob's family when they came to live in Egypt with Joseph? What work did Joseph's brothers do?

Story 33

The Story of Job

Job 1, 2, 38 through 42

Many, many years ago, there was a good man whose name was Job. Job lived in the land of Uz. Job loved God and served Him with his whole heart. And Job always turned away from evil.

God had given Job great possessions. He had ten children —seven sons and three daughters. He had many, many servants. He also had seven thousand sheep, three thousand camels, five hundred yoke of oxen, and five hundred donkeys. He was the richest man in the east country.

But Job was also a godly man. Whenever his sons and daughters came together for a feast, Job would get up early in the morning and sacrifice for them to God. "For it may be," said he, "that my children have sinned against God in their hearts."

Now it happened one day, when the angels came to show themselves before God in heaven, that Satan came too. Satan is sometimes called the devil. He is the leader of the wicked angels whom God cast out of heaven.

God said to Satan that day, "From where do you come?"

And Satan answered, "From going back and forth in the earth, and from walking up and down in it."

"Have you taken notice of my servant Job?" God said. "For there is no one like him in all the earth. He is a perfect man who fears God and turns away from all evil."

Satan answered, "Oh, yes. But does Job fear You for nothing? No wonder he fears God. You have blessed him with riches and given him everything a man could want! But take away all these things, and he will turn his face from You!"

So God said to Satan, "I will permit you to take away all that Job has. But do not touch Job himself."

Then Satan quickly left God and went back to the earth.

Not long after this it happened one day that a servant came running to Job and said, "Master! Master! While we were working in the field, enemies came and stole all your oxen and donkeys, and they killed all the servants in the field with a sword. I alone am escaped to tell you."

Before he was finished speaking, another servant came running and said, "Master! Master! Fire came from heaven and burned all your sheep and the servants. I alone am escaped to tell you."

Before he was finished, a third servant came. "The Chaldeans came and took your camels and killed your servants," he said. "And I alone am escaped to tell you."

Before he was finished, a fourth servant came and said, "Master! Master! A terrible thing happened while all your children were feasting in your oldest son's house, a wind storm came and blew down the house. All your children and servants are killed. I alone am escaped to tell you."

When Job heard all this, he tore his robe, and went and shaved the hair off his head. Then he fell down to the ground, and worshiped God. He said, "Naked was I born, and naked shall I die. Jehovah gave and Jehovah hath taken away. Blessed be the name of Jehovah!"

In all this Job did not sin.

After that, it happened that Satan went again to show himself before God with all the angels. Again God asked him what he thought of Job. And Satan said, "A man's life is his most important treasure. Make Job sick and he will no longer serve you."

So God allowed Satan to make Job sick. Soon Job had sore boils all over his skin, from his head to his feet.

Job was miserable. He went out and sat on an ash pile and scraped his body with a piece of broken earthen pot. Three friends of Job came to comfort him. When they saw Job, they sat down and cried. They tore their clothing and put dust on their heads. They sat on the ground with Job for seven whole days without talking, so great was their grief.

Then they tried to comfort Job with long speeches. But they blamed Job for all his trouble. "You must be a great sinner," they said.

But Job answered, "I have always served God, and I know He will deliver me from all this trouble."

Job's own wife turned against him. "Why do you not curse God and die?" she said.

"What!" Job answered. "Shall we receive good things from God when He sends them to us, and shall we not be willing to receive the evil? You speak as a foolish woman."

After everyone had spoken his mind, God came to Job in a whirlwind. God showed Job what a wonderful God He really is, so wonderful that man cannot understand Him. He told Job about all the wonders He had made.

Then Job said, "Before this I heard of Thee by the hearing of the ear. But now my eyes have seen Thee. Therefore I hate myself, and repent in dust and ashes."

Then God healed Job. He gave him twice as much of everything as he had had before. And He gave him ten more children

too. So Job's last days were even better than at the beginning. And Job lived to be an hundred and forty years old. He lived to see his great, great grandchildren!

Were you listening? What did Satan say to God? What happened to Job? What good things did Job's suffering teach him? Name things that show how great God is. Why can't we understand all that God does?

Story 34

The Baby Moses

Exodus 1 and 2

After Jacob died, the children of Israel remained living in Egypt for many, many years. Even though there was no longer a famine in the land, they stayed in Goshen. They liked to live with their brother Joseph who was the great ruler of the land. In time there were many grandchildren and great grandchildren who were born in Egypt, and Joseph's older brothers died.

When Joseph also became old and was ready to die, he told his brothers' children not to make a special trip back to Canaan to bury him. He told them to ask the Egyptians to embalm his body so it would keep for a long time. Then, when they were ready to leave Egypt, they could take his body with them.

The Israelites did as Joseph said. So when Joseph died, his body was embalmed and kept in a coffin, ready to be taken back to Canaan.

But the Israelites did not go back to Canaan very soon. There arose a new king who did not know about Joseph. He was also called King Pharaoh. This king was not kind to Joseph's people in the land of Goshen. He was jealous of them. God had blessed the Israelites in Egypt, and each family had received many children. By this time there were thousands of Israelites, and the people were strong and healthy.

This new King Pharaoh hated the Israelites. He made them his slaves. He set them to work making bricks and building cities for him. But God was with His people. He made them stronger

all the time. The harder the king made them work, the stronger God made them grow. The Israelites were now becoming a great nation, as God had promised Abraham so many times.

When the king saw that the Israelites were becoming greater in spite of the hard work, he became afraid of them. He was afraid they would some day fight against him. King Pharaoh spoke to the two women nurses who helped the Israelite mothers when they had new babies. He commanded these nurses to kill all the boy babies that were born. Then they would not grow up to be strong soldiers. But the nurses feared God and disobeyed the king. They did not kill the boy babies.

Then the king thought of another plan. He made a rule that all the new-born baby boys should be thrown into the river Nile.

One day God sent a new little baby boy to one of the Israelite families. The parents did not want their little boy to be drowned, so they hid him for three months.

When the baby became too big to hide, the mother took some reeds, called bulrushes, from the water's edge and made a little ark or basket-boat. It was like a boat on the outside, and like a little cradle on the inside. When it was finished, the mother put her baby in it and carried him down to the river Nile. She carefully placed the tiny boat in the water among the blue flags growing near the water's edge. Then the mother went home. But the baby's sister, Miriam, hid in the reeds to see what would happen.

After a while a beautiful princess, the daughter of King Pharaoh, came down to bathe in the river. Her servant girls were with her. The princess saw the little ark among the flags. She sent one of her maids to fetch it. The princess opened the ark to see what was in it, and there she saw a beautiful little baby boy. The baby began to cry. At once the princess felt sorry for him and wanted him for her own.

"This must be one of the babies of the Israelites," she said. She loved the little baby and decided to keep him.

When Miriam saw what was happening, she came out of hiding and stepped up to the princess. "Shall I go and call a nurse for you from the Israelite women, so she can nurse the baby for you?" she asked.

"Yes, go!" the princess answered.

Miriam ran home to her mother. "The princess found our baby," she cried, "and she needs a nurse!"

So the mother went back with Miriam. The princess gave the baby to the mother. "Take this baby," she said, "and nurse it for me. I will pay you wages."

So the mother took her baby back home with her. She thanked God for saving her child and letting her take care of him. When he grew up to be a big boy, she brought him to the palace and he became the princess' son. The princess called him Moses because, she said, "I drew him out of the water."

Were you listening? Why did the Israelites stay in Egypt? What happened to Joseph's body? Why did the king want to kill all the baby boys? How did God take care of the baby Moses?

Moses Runs Away

Moses grew up in the palace as a king's son. The princess had taken him as her own child. Although Moses was an Israelite, he was treated as an Egyptian. He went to school with the other Egyptian boys. He became a great prince in Pharaoh's palace.

But Moses still loved his own people. And he still remembered to serve God as his own mother had taught him when he was a little boy. It bothered him to see his foster grandfather, King Pharaoh, treat the Israelites so cruelly. One day Moses went to Goshen to visit his own people. He wanted to see how hard they had to work and how cruel their masters were.

As Moses walked along he noticed one of the Egyptian masters beating one of the Israelites. He was suddenly filled with anger. He quickly looked around to see if anyone was watching him. When he saw no one, he killed the Egyptian master. Then he dug a hole in the sand and buried him.

The next day Moses went to Goshen again. Once more he watched his people at work. This time he saw two of his own men fighting together. He said to the man who was hurting his partner, "Why are you hurting your brother?"

The man answered with an angry sneer, "Who made you a judge and a prince over us? Do you think you are going to kill me as you did the Egyptian yesterday?"

Moses was afraid when he heard the man's words. "People know what I have done," he thought. Soon King Pharaoh heard about it too. He tried to find Moses so he could kill him. But Moses fled from King Pharaoh and from Egypt. He fled far away to the land of Midian.

At last Moses was tired. He sat down by a well. As he sat there alone, it happened that seven young women came along to draw water from the well, for their father's sheep. These seven young women were daughters of the priest of Midian. They came to the well every day. But other shepherds came to this well also, and they were not kind to the young women. They often chased them away.

Moses saw this. So he stood up and helped the young women and watered all their sheep. They thanked the stranger kindly for helping them. Then they went back home.

"What?" said their father when they came home. "How is it that you are home so soon today?"

Then the young women said, "A stranger, an Egyptian, was sitting at the well. He chased the shepherds away and helped us water our sheep."

"Why did you leave the man there?" asked their father, whose name was Jethro. "Go back and invite the man to the house."

So Moses came back with the young women to Jethro's house. He stayed and lived with the priest of Midian and his seven daughters. He took care of the sheep for them and later he married Zipporah, one of Jethro's daughters.

> *Were you listening?* Why was Moses called a prince? Why didn't Moses stay in King Pharaoh's palace? Who was Jethro, and why did he invite Moses to his house? Who was Zipporah?

Story 36

The Burning Bush

Exodus 3 and 4

Moses stayed in the land of Midian with Jethro for forty years. Each day he led the sheep to find green grass and fresh water. One day he led his flock toward the back of the wilderness until he came to the mountain of God, called Horeb.

Suddenly Moses noticed a fire on the mountain side. As he came closer, he noticed that it was a bush burning with fire. But the bush did not burn up; it remained a living bush.

Moses said to himself, "I shall go up to this bush to see this strange sight. I want to see why the bush does not turn into ashes."

God was in the burning bush. That is why the bush did not burn into ashes.

"Moses, Moses!" God called, as Moses neared the burning bush.

"Here am I," Moses answered.

"Do not come any nearer," God said. "Take the shoes from off your feet, for the place where you are standing is holy ground."

Moses quickly took off his shoes and worshiped God. Then he stood still and listened to what God had to tell him.

"Moses," God went on, "I am the God of your father Abraham, and the God of Isaac, and the God of Jacob."

Moses hid his face, for he feared to look at God.

"I have surely seen the sorrows of my people, Israel, in Egypt," God said. "I am going to deliver them out of Egypt and bring them back to the land of Canaan. Come now therefore, and I will send you to King Pharaoh, so that you may bring my people out of Egypt."

Moses was afraid.

So Moses said, "Who am I, that I should go to Pharaoh, and that I should bring the Israelites out of Egypt?"

And God answered, "Certainly I will be with you."

But Moses was still afraid. "When the Israelites ask me who sent me, what shall I tell them?" he asked.

"Tell them," God said, "I AM THAT I AM has sent you. Tell them that Jehovah, the God of your fathers, the God of Abraham, Isaac, and Jacob has sent you. I AM is my name."

But Moses said, "What if they will not believe me? What if they will not listen to me?"

Then God said, "What is that in your hand?"

It was a rod.

God told Moses to throw the rod on the ground. Moses did so, and immediately the rod became a snake, and Moses ran away from it.

"Now put out your hand," God said, "and take it by the tail."

Moses put out his hand and caught the snake by the tail. And immediately it became a rod again.

"Put now your hand into your bosom," God said to Moses.

And Moses did as God told him. When he took it out again, behold, his hand was as white as snow. It was covered with a terrible disease called leprosy.

"Put your hand back into your bosom," God said.

And Moses put his hand back into his bosom. This time, when he took it out, his hand was as healthy as before.

"Show these signs to your people," God said, "then they will believe that I have sent you."

Once more Moses objected. "Oh, Lord," he complained, "I cannot speak very well. I speak so slowly, and I do not know what to say!"

Then God was angry with Moses. "Who made man's mouth?" God asked him. "Or who makes a man dumb or deaf or seeing or blind? Is it not I, the Lord God Almighty? Now go, and I will be with your mouth and teach you what to say. And I will send Aaron, your brother, to go with you."

So Moses brought his sheep back to Jethro. He asked his father-in-law to let him go back to Egypt. Jethro said, "Go in peace."

And God said to Moses, "All the men are dead who wanted to take your life."

Then Moses took his wife and his two sons and put them on a donkey, and they started out for Egypt. And Moses took the rod of God in his hand.

> *Were you listening?* Why didn't the bush burn to ashes? What did God want Moses to do? What excuses did Moses give? What did Moses take with him?

Story 37

Water Turned to Blood

Exodus 4 through 7

As Moses was on his way to Egypt, he met his brother Aaron in the wilderness. God had sent Aaron to meet him.

"Aaron can do the talking for you," God had promised. So

Aaron went with Moses. But Zipporah, Moses' wife, went back to her father Jethro with Moses' two sons.

As soon as Moses and Aaron reached Egypt they gathered all the elders or leaders of the Israelites together. They told them all the things God had said. The Israelites believed Moses' words. When they heard that God had seen their troubles and was going to help them, they bowed their heads and worshiped.

Then Moses and Aaron went to the palace to speak to Pharaoh. When they were brought before the king, Aaron said, "We have come because Jehovah, the God of Israel, sent us and He commanded us to say to you: 'Let my people go, that they may hold a feast unto Me in the wilderness.'"

But Pharaoh said, "Who is Jehovah that I should listen to him? I do not know Jehovah. Neither will I let Israel go!"

Then Pharaoh made the Israelites work still harder. He said, "If the Israelites have time to think about having a feast in the wilderness, they must not be working hard enough." So he would not give them any more straw for their brick-making. Now they had to find their own straw. And they had to make just as many bricks as before.

The Israelites were more unhappy than ever. They blamed Moses. He felt badly to hear his people complain so bitterly. He cried to God. "Oh, Lord, why did You send me?" he asked. "Why did You let this evil happen to Your people? Things have been worse ever since I came here! And Pharaoh has not listened to me at all."

But God answered, "Now you will see what I am going to do to Pharaoh. I will keep my promises. I will take my people out of Egypt. I will bring them back again to the land of Canaan. And I will make of them a great nation."

Moses went back to his own people and tried to comfort them. But they would not listen to him. They still blamed him for their new troubles.

Then God said, "Go back to Pharaoh, Moses, and ask him again to let my people go."

But Moses said, "How will Pharaoh listen to me, when my own people will not even listen?"

"Pharaoh will not listen at first," God answered, "but I will punish him with many powerful signs. Then Pharaoh will let my people go."

So Moses and Aaron did as the Lord commanded them. They went back to King Pharaoh.

"What miracle can you do, to prove that your God sent you?" asked Pharaoh.

Then Aaron cast down his rod before Pharaoh, and it turned into a snake.

Pharaoh called in his wise men and magicians. Each of them could turn his rod into a snake too. But behold, the snake of Aaron's rod swallowed up the snakes of the magicians' rods. Then Aaron picked up his snake and it turned into a rod again.

Pharaoh would not listen to Moses.

The next morning God sent Moses and Aaron to meet King Pharaoh as he walked along the river Nile. Again they said to him, "Jehovah says, 'Let my people go, that they may serve me in the wilderness.'" But Pharaoh still would not listen.

Then Moses and Aaron went to the river's edge. Aaron struck the water with his rod. All the water turned to blood. All the fish in the water died, and the river stank. All the water in Egypt turned to blood. There was no water to drink.

But King Pharaoh would not let the people go. His magicians could turn water into blood too. So Pharaoh only turned away from Moses and Aaron and went into his palace.

The people had to dig new wells for their drinking water. For seven days the river was blood.

Were you listening? Who went with Moses to Egypt? Why were the Israelites angry with Moses? What happened to the magicians' rods? What happened to the water in Egypt?

"Let My People Go!"

Again and again Moses and Aaron came to Pharaoh in the palace and said, "Jehovah says, 'Let my people go!' " Each time Pharaoh hardened his heart and would not let the people go. Day after day the Israelites gathered straw and made their bricks. If they did not make enough bricks they were whipped by their masters. Each day they cried to God to save them from the cruel Egyptians who made their lives so miserable.

Each time the king said "No!", God sent another plague to the land of Egypt. First it was the water changed into blood. Next God sent them frogs that covered the whole land. Frogs got into the houses. Frogs got into the beds. Frogs got into the food. There were frogs everywhere.

He turned the dust of the earth into lice which settled on all the people and the animals. Then He sent swarms of flies among the Egyptians. The flies were bad, and Pharaoh promised to let the people go if Moses would take away the flies. But when the flies were gone, he changed his mind.

So God sent a bad sickness on all the animals. Many of them died. But when the sickness was taken away, Pharaoh changed his mind again.

The most wonderful part of all this was that none of these plagues bothered the Israelites in Goshen where they lived. God delivered them from all these terrible things.

Then Moses took some ashes out of the furnace and sprinkled them up towards heaven. When the ashes came down as dust it settled on all the people and on all the animals. It gave them bad sores, called boils.

Next there came a terrible hailstorm. In fact, there was fire mixed with the hail. The Egyptians had never seen such a storm before. All the animals which were outdoors were killed. This time the king was really afraid. "I have sinned," he said. "God is righteous, and I and my people are wicked. Please ask God to take away this storm. Then I will let your people go." But when the storm was over, he changed his mind once more.

So God sent locusts. The whole land was dark with them. They covered the ground from one end of Egypt to the other. The locusts were a certain kind of grasshopper. They ate all the food that was growing in the fields. The hailstorm had killed the flax and the barley. Now the locusts ate the wheat and the rye. There was nothing left for the Egyptians to eat.

Remember, none of these plagues were felt in Goshen where the Israelites lived.

One day Pharaoh's servants said to him, "How long are you going to let this man bother us? Let his people go as he asks before his God destroys us all!" So they called Moses and Aaron. "You may go," Pharaoh said, "but you must leave your children here."

Of course Moses would not leave the children behind. So the king made Moses and Aaron leave the palace. Then God sent a thick darkness which lasted three days. It was so dark the people could see nothing! This time King Pharaoh was really afraid. He called Moses. "Go," he said, "and serve your God, but leave your animals here."

"No," Moses said. "We must take our animals with us. We must use them for sacrifices for our God. Not one animal must stay behind!"

"Go away from me!" Pharaoh shouted in anger. "Don't let me ever see your face again! If you do, you will surely die!"

"You are right," Moses answered. "I shall not see your face again." Then Moses left the palace.

Were you listening? How many plagues did God send to King Pharaoh? How many plagues were felt in Goshen too? What did the king finally do?

"Saved by the Blood"

The Israelites were still living in Egypt. Moses and Aaron had gone to Pharaoh nine times. Each time God had sent a plague to punish the king. After the plague was taken away, however, the king had changed his mind and would not let the people go. Finally Pharaoh said he would kill Moses if he ever came back to the palace.

Moses left the king's palace. God talked to him. He listened to God for a long time. God told him what to tell the Israelites so they would be ready when the time came to leave Egypt. Then Moses went to Goshen. He gathered all his people together. "Tonight we are leaving Egypt," he said.

"Tonight at midnight," Moses said, "God will send the Angel of Death into Egypt. He will kill the oldest child in every family —in the king's family, in all the Egyptians' families, and the servants' families. He will even kill the oldest in all the animals' families.

"Each Israelite family must kill a lamb. Catch the blood in a basin and smear it on the doorposts of your houses. Then, when the Angel of Death goes through Egypt tonight, he will pass by your door. Roast the lamb whole. Then, just before you leave, eat the lamb with flat bread (which has not yeast in it to make it rise) and bitter herbs. You must eat this meal with your wraps on, standing up, with your staff in your hand. For as soon as I call, you must follow."

The Israelites were all excited. Quickly they followed Moses' instructions and made ready to leave. They killed the lambs and smeared the blood across their doorposts. They prepared their meals as Moses had commanded.

At midnight the Angel of Death came and walked through all the streets of Egypt. He went into every home. He killed the oldest child in each one. Pharaoh got up in the middle of the night, he and all his servants and all his people. There was great crying in Egypt for all their dead. But in the land of Goshen, where the Israelites lived, there was no death. For the Angel of the Lord saw the blood on the doors and passed by.

Then Pharaoh sent word to Moses. "Go leave Egypt! Go at once!" he commanded. "Take your children and your animals, and go serve your God as you wish!"

All the Egyptians begged the Israelites to leave. They hurried them away while it was still night. They gave them jewels and silver and gold. They gave them beautiful clothing.

When all was ready, Moses called to his people and they all came out to him. Moses quickly led the way through the streets of Egypt and out into the country. And God went with them, too. He went ahead of them to show them the way. He led them in a great cloud. At night the cloud was like fire. In the daytime it was a white cloud.

After four hundred years, God had kept His promise. He led His people out of Egypt on the way back to their own home in the land of Canaan. The Israelites remembered to take the body of Joseph with them, too, as they had promised.

The Israelites called this night the "Passover" because the Angel of Death passed over their houses. Each year since this happened they have had a feast to remember the Passover. They eat the roasted lamb and the bread without yeast, and they eat the bitter herbs. And they remember how God took them out of Egypt.

Today Christians do not celebrate the Passover. They have a new feast. When Jesus died on the Cross, His blood saved His people, just as the lamb's blood saved the Israelites. Jesus became our Passover. So today our Passover feast is the Lord's Supper, Communion. We remember how Jesus' body was broken and how His blood was shed for us on the Cross in this service.

Were you listening? What was the tenth plague? What is the Passover? What is our Passover today? Who led the Israelites out of Egypt?

Through the Red Sea

Pharaoh and all his people were happy to see the Israelites leave Egypt. The Egyptians were afraid of the Israelites' powerful God. There was great mourning and weeping in Egypt. In every family there was a funeral, for the oldest child was dead.

The funerals were over. The people had gone back to their everyday living. Now Pharaoh missed the Israelites. He was sorry he had let them go. Who was going to make bricks and build cities for him?

He quickly called his soldiers. "Get ready!" he commanded. "Take your horses and your chariots. We're going after the Israelites and bring them back to Egypt!" The soldiers hurried to obey their king. Soon the army was hurrying after Moses and the Israelites.

There were so many Israelites that they could not travel very fast. Four hundred years before, when Jacob had come to Egypt, there had been about eighty people. Now there were about a million grown-up people. There were children and babies besides. There were old people. And there were thousands of animals with their young ones.

The Israelites did not go the shortest way to their home. That way led through the land of the Philistines. If the people had gone through that land, they would have had to fight the Philistines. God knew they would be afraid of war and would want to go back to Egypt instead. So He led them another way. He led them through the wilderness. When they came to the Red Sea, they rested.

All at once, in the distance the people saw Pharaoh and his army coming towards them. They were filled with fear. There was no place to hide. There were hills on either side, and in front of them was the Red Sea. The people began to cry out to the Lord. They complained to Moses.

"Weren't there enough graves in Egypt?" they scolded. "Did

you bring us into the wilderness to die? Didn't we ask you to leave us alone so that we could serve the Egyptians? It is better to be slaves than to die here!"

But Moses was not afraid. God had told him that this would happen. And he knew that God would take care of His people. "Don't be afraid," he said. "God will fight for you."

Suddenly God moved the big cloud behind His people. It shone brightly on the Israelites, but it was as black as night for the Egyptians. Then Moses stretched out his rod over the water. God sent a strong wind which blew all that night. It blew a path right through the sea. The water stood up like a high wall. on both sides. Quickly and quietly Moses led the people through the Red Sea. They walked on the dry path.

As it began to get light the next morning, the king and his soldiers saw what was happening. They jumped into their chariots and followed after the Israelites, right down into the Red Sea. That was exactly what God wanted. He told Moses to hold his stick over the water again. At once the waters came together. The dry path was gone. The chariots were stuck in the mud. The king and his soldiers tried to escape on foot, but they got stuck too. Soon the water covered them all. Every one of them drowned.

On the other side of the Red Sea the Israelites stood watching. Moses led them in songs thanking their Heavenly Father for saving them. Moses' sister Miriam took her musical instrument and called all the women to bring theirs. They sang and danced for joy, praising the Lord for His goodness.

Were you listening? Where did God lead the Israelites? What did King Pharaoh do? How did God save His people? What happened to the king and his soldiers? How did the Israelites thank God?

Water and Food for Tired Travelers

Exodus 15 and 16

Moses led his people away from the Red Sea into the wilderness of Shur. It was not a good place to travel. It was hot, dry and sandy. There was no water there—nor any food.

The Israelites traveled through the wilderness for three days. They were hot, tired, and thirsty. But there was no water to drink. Finally, they came to a place called Marah. There was water in Marah. They rushed to the water to get a drink. But when they tasted the water, they found it too bitter to drink.

The people were angry with Moses for leading them into this wilderness. They complained and they scolded. "What are we going to drink?" they cried.

Moses was thirsty, too, but he cried to the Lord. He knew that God was leading them and would take care of them.

God showed Moses a tree. "Cut it down," God said, "and throw it into the bitter water. Then you will be able to drink the water."

Moses did just as God said. He cut down the tree and threw it into the water. The people drank again. Now the water was sweet instead of bitter. The people drank and drank until they were satisfied.

Then God said, "If you people will listen carefully to what I say, and will do what I tell you to do—then I will never send any of those dreadful sicknesses to you which I sent to the Egyptians. For I am the Lord who heals you."

Then the Israelites went on with their journey. They came to a place called Elim. It was a good resting-place. There were twelve wells of water and seventy palm trees in Elim. Here the people rested for a while, camping under the palm trees by the water.

But the Israelites forgot their promise to God at Marah. They forgot how wonderfully God was taking care of them. They forgot to trust in Him. Instead of telling God they were hungry and asking Him to help them, they complained to Moses, "Why did you bring us here? We wish we had stayed in Egypt. At least we had good things to eat there!"

Moses was sorry to hear their cross words. He told God about it. But God loved His people, even though they were angry and unfair. "I will take care of them," He said. "I will send them food from heaven." Then God told Moses what the people should do.

Moses talked to the people. "God will take care of you," he said. "Tomorrow morning He will send you bread from heaven."

The next morning the people hurried out of their tents to see this bread which God had promised. The ground was covered with small round objects. They looked like white seeds. The people cried, "Manna, manna?" The word, "manna," means "what is it?" Since they didn't know what it was, the people called the food "Manna." But Moses said, "This is the bread which the Lord has given you!"

The people gathered the manna in baskets. It tasted sweet like honey. Every day the manna came from heaven, and every day the people ate it. When the people had gathered all they needed for the day, the sun melted the rest and it was gone.

Moses told the people to take just enough manna for each day. God wanted His people to trust Him for their daily food. But some people did not listen to Moses. They gathered more than enough and saved some for the next day. When they wanted to eat it, they found worms in it. It was spoiled.

On the sixth day each family gathered enough for two days. The seventh day was the Sabbath Day. No manna fell on that day. There were no worms in the manna which was saved for the Sabbath Day. Again there were those who did not listen to Moses. They did not gather enough for two days. When the Sabbath Day came, they went out with their baskets as usual, but there was no manna. Those people went hungry that day. For those who listened, however, there was manna to eat every day for forty years!

Moses saved one extra basket of manna. Then when the Israelites reached their homeland, they would be able to show their children God's heavenly bread.

Were you listening? Why were the people disappointed at Marah? What did God do for them there? How did God feed all His people? Why did some of the manna spoil? How long did the Israelites eat manna?

Story 42

Water from a Rock

Exodus 17

The Israelites were still on their long journey. Moses was leading them to their beautiful homeland. God was taking care of them all the way. He sent them manna from heaven to eat. He gave them birds for meat.

They walked and walked until they were tired. Always they could see the big white cloud ahead of them. God was in the cloud to show them the way. At night the cloud was changed into a cloud of fire. When the cloud stopped, the Israelites stopped and put up their tents. Then they rested a while.

One day the Israelites rested at a place called Rephidim. But there was no water there for the people to drink. The people forgot again to trust in God. They forgot that God was feeding them every day. They forgot that He was leading them all the way. They did just as they had done when they were hungry. They became cross and angry.

"We want water to drink!" they said to Moses. "Give us water! We're thirsty!" they shouted. "Why did you bring us up out of Egypt? Did you bring us here so that we and our children and our animals could all die here of thirst?" What foolish people they were!

Moses was troubled. He prayed, "O God, what shall I do with this people? They are almost ready to stone me."

God said to Moses, "Take your rod, Moses, the one you used when you hit the waters of Egypt. And take My people to Mount Horeb. I will be there and I will give you water to drink."

So Moses led the people to Mount Horeb. God stood before the Israelites on the rock. But the people were still angry. They said, "Is God here among us, or isn't He?"

Then Moses took his rod in his hand and went right up to the rock where God was. He hit the rock with his rod. Water came gushing out of the rock. The rock turned into a pool of water. The very stones became a fountain of water. The people all stooped down to drink. There was enough water for all the thirsty people and their animals, enough for all the days that they stayed in Rephidim.

> *Were you listening?* Why did the Israelites become cross again? What happened at the rock? Why did God take such good care of His people?

Story 43

Moses Prays for Victory

Exodus 17

The Israelites had to have more food and water on their journey. God had to protect them from their enemies, too. People from other countries did not like to have a million people walking across their land.

One day a mighty warrior, named Amalek, came with his army to fight the Israelites. The Israelites were still in Rephidim, where God brought water from the rock. They were afraid of Amalek. They did not know what to do. But Moses knew what to do. He chose a young man, Joshua, to lead the Israelites.

"Choose some men to be your soldiers," Moses told Joshua, "and go out to fight this Amalek. Tomorrow I will stand on top of the mountain with the rod of God in my hand. I will pray for you."

Joshua did as Moses told him. He took an army with him and fought with Amalek and his army. While the armies were fighting, Moses went up to the top of the mountain. Aaron and Hur (Hur was one of the leaders of Israel) went along with him. Moses had the rod in his right hand and stood on the mountain top with both his hands raised to God. He prayed to God for victory. When Moses held his hands up towards God, Israel's soldiers won. But when he let his hands down, Amalek and his soldiers won.

Soon Moses became tired. He could no longer hold up his hands. Then Aaron and Hur found a big stone. They made Moses sit on the stone. Then they each held up one of Moses' hands. They kept Moses' hands lifted up towards God until the sun went down in the evening. All day long Moses prayed for victory.

Joshua and his army won over Amalek and his army. They chased them away with the edge of the sword. Then God said, "Write what happened this day in your book, Moses. I want you always to remember it." So Moses did as God commanded. Then he built an altar and made a sacrifice, to say "thank You" to God for all His kindness.

> *Were you listening?* Why did the Israelites have to fight? Who fought against Amalek? What did Moses do?

Story 44

Moses and God on the Mountain

Exodus 18 and 19

Moses and the Israelites were resting in Rephidim. One day Moses' father-in-law, Jethro, came to visit. He brought Moses' wife, Zipporah, and Moses' two sons with him. Jethro had heard about all the wonderful things God had done for Moses and his people. Moses was glad to see his family again. He told them everything that had happened in Egypt and on the journey.

Jethro was filled with joy to hear how good God had been to them. He said, "Blessed be the Lord who has delivered you. Now I know that the Lord is greater than all gods." Then Jethro built an altar and burned sacrifices to God to thank Him for His wonderful care.

While Jethro was with Moses he saw how hard Moses had to work to take care of so many people. He suggested that Moses choose some men from each of the twelve families (now called tribes) to help him rule the people. Moses did as Jethro suggested. Then Jethro went back to Midian, but Zipporah and the two boys stayed with Moses.

Soon the special cloud which was leading the Israelites began to move again. Moses and the people picked up their tents and followed the cloud. This time they walked until they came to another wilderness. It was at the foot of Mount Sinai. Here the cloud stopped and the people rested once more.

God was on the top of Mount Sinai. Moses went up on the mountain to talk with God. God said to him, "Go tell my people these words. You saw what I did to the Egyptians when I drowned them in the Red Sea. And you know that I took care of you as a mother eagle takes care of her babies. (A mother eagle flies under her baby birds when they are learning to fly. She spreads her wings wide so she can catch her babies should they fall.) And now I have brought you here to Me. If you will remember to obey Me, then you shall be My special people. I will always take care of you."

Moses went down to the people. He told them what God had said. And the people answered, "All that God has spoken, we will do."

The next day Moses went up to see God again. "I am going to come down the mountain a little way," God said. "I shall be in a thick cloud so the people will hear my voice when I talk with you. Tell the people to wash carefully and to put on clean clothes. Then bring them to the edge of the mountain. Do not let any one touch the mountain while I am on it, for it will be holy. Anyone who touches it, animal or man, you must kill at once."

Moses went down to the people again. The people made themselves ready. Moses built a fence around the mountain so no one could touch it. Then, on the morning of the third day, the mountain began to smoke like a huge furnace. Thunderings and lightnings came out of it. The whole mountain shook.

The people stood at the foot of the mountain. Moses went

up to talk with God. The people heard God's voice and they were afraid. But Moses wasn't afraid. He listened to God.

The people were still afraid. They said to Moses, "You talk to us, Moses. But don't let God talk to us, lest we die." So the people backed away from the mountain, and Moses went into the thick darkness where God was.

Were you listening? Who was on the top of Mount Sinai? How does a mother eagle take care of her babies? Why did Moses build a fence around the mountain? Why were the people afraid of God's voice?

Story 45

The Ten Commandments

Exodus 20

Moses stayed on the mountain with God a long time. He talked with God for forty days and forty nights. God gave Moses a great many special rules which the people should obey. There were rules for servants, and for the fathers and mothers, and for the children. There were rules for the Sabbath Day. There were rules for punishing wicked people.

God told Moses to bring with him two large flat stones when he came up to see Him. God wrote on these two flat stones or tablets. He wrote ten important rules on the stones. We call them the Ten Commandments. Many of the rules which God gave Moses were for the Israelites alone, but these Ten Commandments were for all the people of the world as long as the world will last.

These are the Ten Commandments:

1. Thou shalt have no other gods before Me.

(There is only one true God. He does not want His people to worship other gods.)

2. Thou shalt not make any graven image. Thou shalt not bow down thyself to serve them.

(Sometimes people make gods out of wood or stone, or gold or silver. They make gods that look like animals, or stars, or people. God does not want His people to make these images.

He wants them to pray only to Him. God will punish those who sin against Him, but He will be kind to those who love Him and keep His commandments.)

3. Thou shalt not take the name of the Lord thy God in vain.

(God does not want His people to use His name unless they are talking to Him or about Him. Some people use God's name when they are angry. That is called swearing or cursing. It is very wicked.)

4. Remember the Sabbath Day to keep it holy.

(God does not want us to work on the Sabbath Day. He wants us to worship Him in His House. He wants us to go to Sunday school. He wants us to be careful how we spend the rest of the day, too. You are too small to do much work, but you can rest from your noisy play. You should play quietly on the Sabbath, which is our Sunday. You could take a walk, or look at books. Sunday should be the happiest day of the week for you, for it is the Lord's Day. And you are His child.)

5. Honor thy father and thy mother.

(God wants you to love and obey your parents.)

6. Thou shalt not kill.

(We must not kill anyone. If we hate them so much that we would like to kill them, in God's sight that is the same as killing them.)

7. Thou shalt not commit adultery.

(God does not want any man to live with another man's wife or any wife to live with another woman's husband. A man and his wife must love each other and always live together.)

8. Thou shalt not steal.

(We must not take anything that belongs to someone else. We should not even take a cookie unless we first ask mother if we may.)

9. Thou shalt not bear false witness against thy neighbor.

(We must always tell the truth. We may not tell lies about other people or about ourselves.)

10. Thou shalt not covet.

(To covet means to want something that belongs to someone else. We should not want anything that belongs to someone else. We should be content with what God has given us.)

Were you listening? How long was Moses on the mountain with God? What did God give Moses? What are the Ten Commandments?

The Golden Calf

Exodus 32

The Israelites grew tired of waiting for Moses to come down from the mountain. One day the people came to Aaron. They said, "Make us a god like the Egyptians had. We want a god that we can see. We want him to go ahead of us to lead us. We don't know what became of Moses. He went into the mountain and never came back. So, come on, Aaron, make us a god!"

Aaron knew that it would be sin to make a god. But he said, "All right. Give me your gold earrings and I'll make you a god."

The people took the gold earrings out of their ears and brought them to Aaron. Aaron made a golden calf. The Egyptians had worshiped a calf as a god. That's what the Israelites wanted.

When the people saw the golden calf, they said, "This is the god who brought us up out of the land of Egypt." When Aaron heard the people and saw how pleased they were, he built an altar in front of the calf.

"Tomorrow we shall have a feast," Aaron said. "We shall burn sacrifices on this altar to the Lord."

The next morning the people gathered around the golden calf. They burned sacrifices on the altar. They bowed down and worshiped the golden calf. They danced wildly around the altar. That was what they had seen the Egyptians do.

All this time Moses was talking with God. Suddenly God said, "Hurry and go down, Moses. This people which I have

loved so much are being very wicked. They have already turned away from Me. They are worshiping a golden calf!"

God was very angry with His people. "Get out of my way, Moses," He cried, "and I will kill all my people!" But Moses pleaded for his people. He begged God to be kind once more. God listened to Moses.

Then Moses picked up the two tables of stone on which God had written. He went down the mountain. As he came closer to the people he heard the shouting and the dancing. When he saw the golden calf, he, too, became angry. He threw down the tables of stone and broke them into pieces. Then he ground the golden calf into powder. He put the powder into the water and made the people drink it.

Moses went to his brother and said, "Why did you lead this people into such great sin?"

But Aaron blamed the people. Then Moses stood in front of the people. "Who is on the Lord's side?" he cried. Many people came to stand by him. He sent them out with their swords to kill those who had worshiped the golden calf. About three thousand people were killed that day.

Were you listening? Why did the people want Aaron to make them a god? What did Aaron make? What did God want to do to all His people? How did Moses punish the wicked people who worshiped the golden calf?

Moses' Shining Face

God's people, the Israelites, had sinned terribly when they worshiped the golden calf. They had been punished. About three thousand people were killed. The next day Moses said to the people, "You have sinned greatly against God. Now I shall go back up the mountain to God. I shall ask God to forgive you."

So Moses went back up the mountain. The people waited at the bottom of the mountain. Moses fell down before God and said, "O God, this people have sinned a great sin, but please forgive them. If their sin is too great, do not punish them. Instead, blot my name out of Thy Book of Life."

But God said, "Whoever has sinned against Me, him will I blot out of My Book." Then He said, "Go now and lead the people to their home in Canaan. I will send an angel to go with you. But I shall not go with you any longer. My people are so stubborn that I am afraid I might destroy them on the way."

When the people heard this bad news, they were filled with sorrow. They mourned for their sins. They took off their pretty clothing and their jewelry. They showed God that they were really sorry for their sins. Moses went into the tent where he met with God. The people all stood at their own tent-doors and worshiped.

Moses talked with God in the tent-house. Moses said, "See, Lord, Thou hast commanded me to take this people to their homeland. But who will go with me? You have told me that I am Your friend, so please be kind to me and remember that this nation is Your people. If You do not go with me, then I do not want to go either. Please go with me!"

God loved Moses. He said, "All right, Moses. I will go with you."

Moses loved God, too. He wished he could really see God in all His glory. He said to God, "Please let me see Thy glory, O Lord." So God put Moses at the opening of a cave. He then let His glory pass by. But Moses did not see God's face. No man can see God and live. As God came by, He covered the opening of the cave with His hand so Moses could not see His face. When God took away His hand, Moses saw God's back as He passed by.

The next day Moses brought God two new tables of stone. God wrote on them. He wrote the Ten Commandments once more. God told Moses many more things which he should tell the people. Again Moses stayed with God for forty days and forty nights. But this time the mountain did not smoke and there were no terrible lightnings and thunderings. This time God did not show His power. He showed His lovingkindness and mercy instead. God forgave His people. Moses bowed himself to the ground and worshiped his loving God.

This time the people did not sin as they waited for Moses. When Moses finally came to them, they were afraid to come near. Moses' face was shining like the sun because he had talked with God for such a long time. God's glory lit up his face, too. Moses did not know that his face was shining.

When Moses finally learned why the people were afraid to come close to him, he covered his face with a veil. He wore the veil whenever he talked to the people. When he went up to talk with God, he took off the veil.

> *Were you listening?* Why did Moses go back up the mountain a second time? What did Moses offer to do for his wicked people? What did God let Moses see? Why were the people afraid to come close to Moses?

Story 48

God's House and the First Priest

Exodus 36 through 40; Leviticus 8

While Moses was up in the mountain with God the second time, God showed him how to build a new church. He showed him exactly how it was to be made. He told him what should be put into it. Moses told the people at the foot of the mountain about the new church.

"This is what God wants you to do," he said. "He wants you to build a new House for your God."

The Israelites were traveling from place to place. They could not build a big church out of bricks or stone. They had to make a tent-church which could be moved from place to place. It was called a tabernacle.

"Whoever would like to bring a gift for the new church, bring it to me," Moses said.

The people were happy to give. They wanted to show how thankful they were that God had forgiven them once more and loved them. They soon came to Moses loaded down with their gifts. They brought gold and silver, and jewels and precious stones. They brought beautiful wood and lovely cloth. Every morning the people came with more and more gifts. They brought much more than could be used. They brought so much that finally Moses had to tell them to stop.

Then they built the tabernacle according to the plans God had given Moses. It took a long time to build it. Every man who was a good builder came and helped with the work. They were careful to use only the best material. They did their best work. It was God's House they were making!

As soon as the tabernacle was put up, Moses lit the lamps. Then the special cloud covered the tent and the glory of the Lord filled the tabernacle. From that time on the special pillar of cloud which was leading them always rested on the new tabernacle, just above the Holy of Holies where the Mercy Seat was. So the people knew that their God was in His tabernacle.

One day God told Moses to tell the people to come to the door of the tabernacle. Now that they had a church, they needed a minister. "This is what God wants to be done," Moses said. Then he brought his brother, Aaron, and the sons of Aaron together in front of the people. First he washed them with water. Then he dressed them in beautiful new clothing which had been made especially for the minister and his helpers. In those days ministers were called priests because they burned sacrifices to God for the people. Now the sons of Aaron were to be the priests. Aaron was to be the high priest. They were to have special clothes.

When Moses finished dressing Aaron and his sons, he poured oil on the tabernacle and on the altar. He poured oil on Aaron's head, too, until it streamed down his beard and down on his robe. He also sprinkled it on the coats of Aaron's sons.

Then they killed many animals and sacrificed them to God. This was to show that they were sorry for their sins, that they would serve God faithfully, and that they were thankful to God for His care. Moses also put blood on Aaron and his sons. He put it on the tips of their right ears, on their right thumbs, and on the big toe of their right feet.

Moses gave Aaron and his sons many rules which they should obey when they served God in His house. But two of the sons did not obey God. They put the wrong kind of fire in their little lamps and burned them before God. God did not like their "prayer." He sent fire and burned them up. Only Aaron and his other two sons were left. You can be sure that they remembered to obey God and to do everything the way God wanted them to.

> *Were you listening?* Why did the people bring gifts to Moses? What was God's new house called? Why did the Israelites have priests instead of ministers? What happened to two of Aaron's sons?

Story 49

The Story of the Feasts

Leviticus 23; Numbers 9

One day while the Israelites were still at Mount Sinai, God called Moses to come to the Tabernacle.

"It is now a year since the Israelites left Egypt," God said. "Tell them to keep the Passover on the fourteenth day of this month."

Moses gave his people God's message. They quickly made ready to celebrate the Feast of the Passover as God had commanded. Each family killed a lamb and the father spread the blood of the lamb on the door-posts of their tents. Then they dressed as if they were going to travel. They ate their Passover meal just as they had done it in Egypt. They ate the roasted lamb and bread without yeast. They drank bitter herbs.

For one whole week the Israelites kept the Passover Feast. They were told to celebrate this feast every year to help them remember what God had done for them.

God commanded His people to celebrate two other feasts every year. First, there was to be the Feast of Weeks, also called Pentecost. This feast was to last one day, and it was to be held fifty days after the Passover Feast. It was a "thank-you" feast. By it the Israelites thanked God for giving them a good harvest of grain. It was on this feast day, more than a thousand years later, that Jesus sent His Holy Spirit to His apostles and the new Christian Church was born. We still call it Pentecost today.

The Passover Feast and the Feast of Weeks both took place in the spring of the year. Late in the year, after the harvest had been gathered in, the Israelites were to have another feast. It was called the Feast of Tabernacles. It was to last one week.

The Feast of Tabernacles was a "thank-you" feast to which the people brought many sacrifices to God to thank Him for giving them food for another year. It was also a "remembering" feast. The people would always remember their journey through the desert or wilderness. To help them remember, they were told to cut down branches of palm trees and willow trees and make little tents or booths of them. They were to live in these booths for the entire week.

All week long the people burned sacrifices on the altar to God. Hundreds of animals were burned. Each day the people came with gifts for God to thank Him for His care. They also brought gifts to the poor.

When it was time for a feast day, Aaron's sons, the priests, would blow a beautiful silver trumpet. There were two trumpets. When both trumpets were blown all the people were to come to the door of the Tabernacle. When only one was blown just the elders of the people came. Every Sabbath morning the trumpets sounded to call the people for worship. There was one special day each year when the trumpets were blown all day long. This was the Day of the Blowing of Trumpets. This was a day when the people were to get ready for the great Day of Atonement. It was also the first day of their new year. It was to remind the people of the great day when God finished creating the world.

> *Were you listening?* How long had the Israelites been on their journey? Why did they celebrate the Feast of the Passover? What was the Feast of Weeks?

God Punishes Swearing

Leviticus 24

While the Israelites were still at Mount Sinai, a terrible thing happened. There was a man whose mother was an Israelite but whose father was an Egyptian. One day this man began to quarrel with another Israelite in the camp. As he quarreled, he swore against God and cursed.

Some of the people heard this man swear and curse. They brought him to Moses. Moses put him in jail until it could be decided how to punish him. Moses asked the Lord what he should do with the man who swore.

The Lord said to Moses, "Take the man who cursed outside the camp. Let everyone who heard him swear throw stones at him until he is dead. Let the people remember that anyone who curses God shall pay for his sin. He that swears against God shall surely be put to death!"

Moses told his people all that God had said. Then they brought the man who had cursed outside the camp. They threw stones at him until he was dead.

It is still a great sin to swear and curse. God does not punish those who swear and curse by having them killed today. But God is just as displeased with swearing and cursing as He was in the days of Israel. He will punish those who do it. Those who love God want to honor His name. They use His great name only in a loving way. Those who swear and curse surely cannot love God. They will never go to live with Him in heaven if they do not love Him.

> *Were you listening?* What happened to the man who swore and cursed? What will happen to those who do not love God today?

God's People Leave the Mountain

Numbers 10 and 11

All the work of the new Tabernacle was finished. All the laws for the priests and for the people had been given. Now it was time to move on. They had been at Mount Sinai one year. One day the special cloud of God rose up from the Tabernacle and began to move. The priests sounded the silver trumpets. Then all the people packed their things and followed the cloud.

Moses' brother-in-law from Midian was visiting Moses at the time. Moses invited him to come along with them to their new home. But the man said, "No, I will go back to my own people in Midian."

"Please don't leave us," Moses asked. "You know this country so well and can help us on our trip. Whatsoever God gives His people, He will also give you." So the brother-in-law went along.

From that time on, whenever the Israelites moved, the Tabernacle had to be taken down and packed, too. This was the task of the priests and Levites. The Levites were the sons of Jacob's son, Levi. They had been chosen to work in the Tabernacle. Before the Levites could begin, Aaron and his sons had to take down the veil which hung in front of the Holy of Holies. They covered the golden Ark of the Covenant with it. A beautiful blue cloth was put over the veil. The Table of Showbread was covered with a scarlet cloth, the Golden Candlestick with a blue cloth, and the golden Altar with a purple cloth. After these holy things had been covered, they were placed on the shoulders of some of the Levites. Their shoulders were also covered with cloth. The Levites carried these things all the way.

The rest of the Tabernacle — the curtains, the golden dishes, the pillars, the altar for burnt-offerings, and the laver — was put into six covered wagons. Twelve oxen pulled the wagons.

The cloud moved for three days. Then the people rested again. They were no longer used to traveling. They did not like it and complained bitterly. God heard His people complain. He sent fire among them. Those whose tents were at the edge of the camp were burned to death. The people cried to Moses and Moses quickly prayed to God. And God stopped the fire.

But the people still complained. They wanted different food to eat. They were tired of manna. "Who will give us meat to eat?" they said.

Moses heard the people crying in their tents. He was angry with them. God was angry, too. Moses cried to God, "Why do

I have to take care of all these people? Am I their father that I must carry them in my arms all the way to their new home like a father carries his baby? Where would I get enough meat for all this people? I cannot take care of them all alone any more. It is too much!"

God was kind to Moses. He chose seventy men from the people to help Moses. He said, "Tell them they will have meat to eat. Tell them I will give them meat not for one day, nor two, nor five, nor ten, nor twenty days. But for a whole month, until it comes out of their noses and they are sick of it."

Moses did not think God could get so much meat for His people. He thought they would have to kill their own sheep and cows. But God sent a wind from the sea and it blew thousands of birds to their camp. The people worked for two days and a night to catch all the birds. They spread them out on the ground to dry in the sun. But while they were eating the birds, God punished them for their complaining. The meat made them sick. Many of the bad people died.

> *Were you listening?* How did the Israelites know it was time to travel again? How did they carry the Tabernacle? Why did God send fire in the camp? Why did some of the people die of the meat?

Story 52

Miriam Becomes a Leper

Numbers 12

Moses was the great leader of his people. He had a brother and a sister. His brother, Aaron, was the high priest who did the work in God's House. His sister Miriam also helped Moses. When Moses was a baby it was Miriam who watched his little basket-boat as it floated among the flags in the river Nile. After Moses had led the Israelites across the Red Sea, Miriam took her timbrel and with the other women played and sang and danced to show her thankfulness to God. Miriam helped Moses by teaching the people, too. She was a prophetess.

While Moses was leading the Israelites through the wilderness to their new home, his wife, Zipporah, died. Then Miriam helped

Moses still more. One day Moses found himself a new wife. She was a dark-skinned woman from the country of Ethiopia.

Miriam and Aaron heard about their brother's new wife. They did not want Moses to marry again. So they talked against Moses. They said, "Is Moses the only leader in Israel? Does God speak only through Moses? Hasn't God spoken through us, too? Aren't we His leaders just as well as Moses?"

God heard what Miriam and Aaron were saying. Moses knew what they were saying, too. But Moses was a very meek man. He would not stand up for his own rights. He just let them talk. Suddenly God came down to the Tabernacle. He called Moses and Miriam and Aaron to come to Him.

God came down in the pillar of cloud and stood at the door of the Tabernacle. Moses and Miriam and Aaron stood before Him. God said, "Listen to My words. Whenever there is a prophet in Israel I speak to him in a dream. But not so with Moses. I talk to him face to face as with a friend. Then how is it that you were not afraid to speak against my servant Moses?"

God showed His anger to them and then left. The cloud moved away from the Tabernacle. Miriam looked down at her hands. They were as white as snow! She was covered with the horrible disease called leprosy!

Now Aaron and Miriam were sorry for what they had done. Aaron said to Moses, "We have been very foolish, Moses. We have sinned against you and against God. Please forgive us. Please do not let Miriam keep this dreadful leprosy. It is worse than death. Her body will be eaten away."

Moses felt sorry for his sister. He prayed to God. "Please make her better now, dear Lord," he said.

And God answered, "Send her outside the camp for seven days. Then I will make her better."

So Miriam was sent away from the camp for seven days. The people did not travel at all that week. They waited for Miriam. As soon as Miriam was well again, they went on with their journey.

Were you listening? What work did Aaron and Miriam do? Why did they complain against Moses? What did God do?

The Twelve Spies

God's people had been traveling toward their new home for a long, long time. It had been more than a year since they had left Egypt. Now they were coming close to the Promised Land. First, they came to the river Jordan. Just across the river was the land of Canaan, where Jacob and his sons lived so many years before.

While the people were resting at the river, Moses chose twelve men — one from each tribe — to go across the river to look over the land. He called these men spies. They were to see what the land looked like. They were to find out what kind of people lived there and how it would be best to fight against them. Moses also told them to bring back some of the fruit of the land.

The twelve spies crossed the river and went into Canaan. They started at the south and traveled all through the land. They walked for forty days. Then they came back. The Israelites all gathered around to see what they had brought with them.

First the spies showed the people the wonderful fruit they had brought. There were grapes and pomegranates and figs. The grapes were so large that they had to hang the bunch on a long pole. Two men carried the pole on their shoulders. The spies said, "Surely it is a wonderful country. It is a land flowing with milk and honey."

"But," ten of the spies said, "we cannot go into that land. The cities are too large. They have high walls around them. And the people are too strong!"

Joshua and Caleb, the other two spies, said, "Yes, we can go into Canaan. Let's go up right away. We'll be able to take it."

"No, we can't go up," the other ten spies answered. "The men are huge giants. We were like little grasshoppers next to them."

When the people of Israel heard the words of the spies, they began to cry. They complained against Moses. "We wish we had died in Egypt or in the wilderness," they said.

Joshua and Caleb tried to stop them. "It's a wonderful land," they said. "We can go there. God took care of us this far. He'll take us into the land, too." But the people would not listen to Joshua and Caleb. Instead, they tried to kill them with stones.

Then the Lord called Moses and said, "How long will My people sin against Me? How long before they trust Me? I am going to kill them all!" Moses pleaded with God once more for his wicked people. Once more God listened to Moses and let the people live.

Yes, the Lord forgave His people. But He punished them for not trusting Him. "Turn around," He said, "and go back into the wilderness. You were afraid to go into your land. Now you will never go in! Now you will have to live in the wilderness forty years until all your men and women have grown old and died. When your little children have grown up I will try it again. They shall live in your home land, but not you!"

So the Israelites could not go into Canaan.

Were you listening? Where did the twelve spies go? What report did the ten spies bring? Which spies did the people believe? How did God punish His people?

Story 54

The Earth Swallows the Wicked Men

Numbers 16

The Israelites were afraid to go into the land of Canaan. They were afraid of the giants. So God punished them. He told them to go into the wilderness again. The people went back into their tents and cried all night. In the morning they arose early and said, "We have sinned. We have changed our minds. Now we will go into the land which God has promised us."

Moses warned them, "Don't go now. It is too late. God will not go with you now."

The people would not listen to Moses. They tried to go into the land anyway. But the people of Canaan fought against them and turned them back. They could not capture the land without God's help.

Back into the wilderness went the Israelites. Three men, a minister and two other leaders, rose up against Moses. They gathered two hundred and fifty men and fought against Moses. They said, "You take too much upon yourself, Moses. You aren't the only leader in Israel. We are holy, too, every one of us!"

Moses was shocked to hear such words. He fell on his face. He said to the men, "God will show you who are His and who are holy. You take too much upon you, you sons of Levi. Do you think it is a small thing that God chose you to be leaders?" Then Moses told the minister, whose name was Korah, to bring his two hundred and fifty leaders to the door of the Tabernacle.

The next morning, the men came to the door of the Tabernacle with their burning lamps. Then Moses sent for the other two trouble-makers to come to the church, too. They were Dathan and Abiram. They were from the tribe of Reuben, Jacob's oldest son. But they would not come. They stood at the door of their tents and said, "Is it a small thing that you brought us away from our wonderful new homeland to die in this wilderness? No, we will not come!" They stayed at the door of their tents with all their families and watched Moses.

"Do not listen to these men, O Lord," Moses cried. "I have never hurt them."

Then God said, "Separate yourself from these people, Moses, and I shall kill them all."

Moses pleaded for his people once more. "Do not kill all the people for one man's sin," he said.

God listened to Moses. "Move the people away from the tents of these wicked men," God said, "lest they be killed, too." So the people backed away.

"Now you shall know if the Lord has chosen me to be your leader," Moses said. "If these men die in a strange way, then you shall know that I am your leader."

Suddenly the earth opened up and swallowed Dathan and Abiram with their families and their tents and all that they had. No trace of them was left. All the other people fled lest they be swallowed up, too.

The minister, Korah, and his two hundred and fifty followers were still standing at the door of the Tabernacle. These men were all Levites who were supposed to work in the Tabernacle. They were not priests and they were not supposed to burn incense. But they had been doing it. Now they stood at the door of the Tabernacle with their incense lamps burning in their hands. God suddenly sent a fire upon them and burned them all up. Then He told Aaron's son to gather all the gold lamps from the fire. A gold plate was made from them. Aaron fastened the plate to the altar so that the people would always remember that no one but the priests were allowed to burn incense or offer sacrifices.

> *Were you listening?* Why were the Israelites turned back into the wilderness? What happened when they tried to go into Canaan? What did Korah, Dathan and Abiram do? How did God punish them?

Story 55

Aaron's Wonderful Rod

Numbers 17

The next morning the people began to complain again to Moses and Aaron. "You have killed the people of the Lord," they said.

Just then they looked toward the Tabernacle. It was covered with the pillar of cloud and the glory of the Lord was there. Moses and Aaron quickly went to the door. They heard God's voice. "Get away from this people," God said. "I want to get rid of them all in a moment."

The two men fell on their faces before the Lord. Then Moses said to Aaron, "Take your little incense lamp as fast as you can. Put fire in it from off the altar. Put incense on it. Then run to the people, praying as you run. There is great danger going out from God. The people are beginning to die."

Aaron did just as he was told. He took his burning lamp and ran in among the people. He prayed to God for them. He stood between the living and the dead. God heard his prayer and stopped the killing. But fourteen thousand and seven hundred people were killed. Then Aaron went back to Moses at the door of the Tabernacle.

God told Moses to have each of the twelve tribes of Israel bring a long stick — a piece of a tree branch called a rod. They were to write the name of their tribe on their stick. Moses was to place these twelve rods in the inner room of the Tabernacle, in front of the little gold Ark. Then the rods were to be taken out of the church again. The one which would be growing like a tree, with blossoms on it, would show who was the real priest in Israel. God wanted His people to know once for all who His leaders were.

So the princes of the tribes brought their rods to Moses. Moses put their names on each one. Then he laid them in front of the golden Ark in the Tabernacle. Aaron's rod was there, too. The next day Moses went back to get the rods. Eleven of the rods were just as they had been when Moses put them there. They were still dead sticks. But Aaron's rod had changed. It was like a tree. It not only had blossoms on it, but it had leaves and buds and flowers. It even had ripe almond nuts.

Moses brought the rods out to the people. Each man took his own rod. The people saw that Aaron was the only one who was God's chosen priest. They were afraid and worshiped God. Then Moses brought Aaron's rod back into the Tabernacle. It was always to be kept in the Ark.

Were you listening? Why was God angry with His people again? How did Aaron save them? Why did Aaron's rod blossom?

Story 56

Moses Disobeys God

Numbers 20

God's people, the Israelites, traveled from Egypt to Canaan, but they did not go into their homeland. They did not trust in God, even though He had led them all the way. Instead, they sinned against God and complained. They refused to go in. So God sent them back into the wilderness. For forty years they wandered around in the wilderness. For forty years God took care of them. He gave them manna for food. He kept their clothing from wearing out. Their feet did not swell.

When the forty years were over, most of the men and women had died. Their children were now fathers and mothers who had children of their own. One day the cloud which had rested over the Tabernacle for all those years now rose up into the sky and began to move. The people packed their things and followed. They started once more on the long journey to Canaan.

Finally they came to the wilderness of Zin where they rested. Here Miriam died, and they buried her. Because there was no water in this wilderness, the people could find nothing to drink. These men and women were just as bad as their parents had been forty years before. Instead of asking Moses to ask God for water, they complained. They said, "Would to God we had died in the wilderness as our fathers did. Why did you bring us into this wilderness where there is no water? Do you want us and our cattle to die here?"

Moses and Aaron left the people. They went to the door of the Tabernacle and fell on their faces. Suddenly, the glory of the Lord came to them. And God said, "Take your rod, Moses. Gather all your people together. Then you and your brother Aaron speak to the rock and it will give you water. Then your people will have water for themselves and for their animals."

Moses did as God said. He went into the Tabernacle and got his rod. Then he and Aaron brought all the people together in front of the rock. But Moses was angry with the people for complaining. He did not feel like speaking quietly to the rock, asking it for water. Instead, he shouted at the people. He cried, "Hear now, you rebels! Must we fetch water for you out of this rock?"

Then Moses hit the rock twice with his rod. The water came streaming out of the rock. There was enough water for everyone, for all the people and all their animals.

But the Lord did not like what Moses and Aaron had done. He came to them and said, "Because you did not believe Me, and did not speak to the rock for water in front of all My people, now you shall not bring this people into their new homeland. You, too, will have to die in the wilderness."

Then they journeyed on to Mount Hor. God called Moses and Aaron and Eleazar, Aaron's son, to come up to Him on the mountain. There He commanded Moses to take Aaron's special priestly clothing off from him. He told Moses to put it on Eleazar.

Then Aaron died there on the mountain-top. Moses and Eleazar came down to the people. So Eleazar became the high priest and took Aaron's place.

> *Were you listening?* How long were the Israelites in the wilderness? What happened when they started their journey again? How did Moses sin against God? How did God punish him?

Story 57

God Sends Fiery Serpents

Numbers 21

The Israelites were once more traveling towards the land of Canaan. For forty years they had lived in the wilderness. It wasn't easy to carry all their belongings and to walk day after day through hot, dry country.

Arad, one of the kings of the southern part of Canaan, heard that the Israelites were coming his way. He came out with his army to fight them. He took some of them as prisoners. But the Israelites asked God to help them. They promised God that if He gave them the victory, they would completely destroy the king's cities. God was kind to His people. He gave them the victory and they kept their promise. They completely destroyed the cities

It wasn't long, however, before the people became tired of traveling. They were cross and dissatisfied again. They forgot what had happened to their parents for complaining against God. They did the same thing. They scolded Moses. They said, "Why did you bring us up out of Egypt to die in this wilderness? There is no bread and no water here. And we hate this manna!"

God saw that His people had forgotten His kindness to them so soon. He was filled with anger. He sent fiery snakes into the camp. These snakes crawled in and out among the tents. They bit the children playing on the ground. They bit the grown-ups, too. Those who were bitten became sick. Their bodies burned with fever, as if they were on fire. They became very thirsty. Many people died.

Now the people were sorry they had sinned. They said to Moses, "We have sinned against you and against God. Please pray to God for us and ask Him to take away these terrible snakes."

Then Moses prayed to God for his people. Once more God listened to Moses. God said, "Make a fiery snake out of brass and set it up on a pole. When the people who were bitten look up at the brass snake, they shall live."

Moses quickly made a fiery snake out of brass and set it up on a pole. "Look," he cried, "look at this snake, and you will all be better!"

The people hurried out of their tents to look at Moses' snake. All those who looked became well again. Once more God was kind to His ungrateful people.

Do you know who the brass snake should make us think of? It should remind us of Jesus. One day Jesus was talking to His people. He said, "Just as Moses lifted up his snake in the wilderness, so must I be lifted up on the cross." Moses' snake saved the Israelites from death. All those who looked were saved. Jesus said, "Look unto Me, and be ye saved." All those who look to Jesus in faith will also be saved. When Jesus died on the cross, He saved all those who would believe on Him.

Were you listening? Why did the Israelites complain this time? How did God punish them? What saved them from death? What saves us from death today?

A Donkey Talks

God's people were on the way to their homeland. They had been walking for many, many days. Now they were resting in the fields of Moab. The people of Moab were afraid. They had heard about all the wonderful things God had done for His people on their long journey.

Now Balak, who was the king of Moab, knew a prophet of God whose name was Balaam. So he sent messengers to Balaam. He wanted Balaam to come to Moab to curse God's people. To curse someone means to ask God to have all sorts of bad things happen to that person. If Balaam succeeded in cursing Israel, then the Israelites would not be able to win against their enemies.

King Balak's servants took along many beautiful gifts for Balaam. They came to Balaam's house and gave him the king's message. Balaam loved money and beautiful gifts. He really wanted the king's gifts. But he couldn't curse anyone unless God told him to. So he asked the men to stay over night. He wanted to find out God's will.

During the night God came to Balaam. "Who are those men with you?" God asked. "What do they want?"

Balaam told God what the king wanted.

"You shall not go with them," God said. "You cannot curse the Israelites for they are blessed."

So, when morning came, Balaam sent the men away. He did not go with them.

King Balak would not give up so easily, however. He sent more servants to Balaam. This time he picked out better servants. He thought they might perhaps be able to persuade Balaam to come. They took along many more beautiful gifts. The king promised to give Balaam anything he wanted.

Balaam listened to the king's servants. He wanted those presents so badly that he asked the men to stay once more. He would ask God again. He said to the men, "Even if Balak would give me his house full of silver and gold, I couldn't do anything that God will not let me do."

God came to Balaam again. He was angry with Balaam. "All right," God said, "go with the men. But remember, you may say only what I tell you to say."

So Balaam went with the servants towards Moab. God sent His angel to stand in the way. Balaam did not see the angel, but his donkey did. The donkey ran into a field. Balaam hit the donkey and drove her back onto the road. A little farther on, the road ran beside a vineyard. The path was narrow. There was a wall on either side. Then the donkey saw the angel on this path. He did not know which way to turn, so he backed against the wall and crushed Balaam's foot. Then Balaam hit the donkey again.

A third time the angel stood in the donkey's path. This time the road was so narrow there was no way to turn. The donkey did not know where to go. He just laid down under Balaam. Now Balaam was really angry. He hit the donkey again. Then God made it so that the donkey could talk. "What have I done to you that you have hit me these three times?" the donkey asked.

"Because you have disobeyed me," Balaam answered. "If I had a sword in my hand I would kill you."

Then the Lord let Balaam see the angel, too. The angel had a sword in his hand. Then Balaam was afraid. He fell flat on his face and said, "I'll go back home if you want me to."

"If your donkey had not seen me these three times," the angel said, "and turned away from me, you would have been killed. Now go with these men. I will tell you what to say."

So Balaam went to Moab. The king took him up on a high mountain. There were all the Israelites in the valley below. Balaam built seven altars and offered sacrifices to God. Then he waited for God to give him the words he should speak. When the words came, Balaam said, "How shall I curse whom God has not cursed?" And he blessed Israel instead.

Three times the king took Balaam to another place. Three times Balaam blessed instead of cursed. He said many wonderful things about God's people. Finally the king sent him home. Balaam did not receive the wonderful gifts. The Israelites were not cursed.

Were you listening? What did King Balak want Balaam to do? Why did Balaam hit his donkey three times? Why did the donkey talk? Did Balaam curse the Israelites?

Story 59

God's People Sin Again

Numbers 25 and 26

Although he was a prophet of God, Balaam was not a good man. He would much rather have cursed God's people than obey God. He wanted those gifts the king had offered him. Because he was a prophet, he could say only what God told him to say. As a man, though, he did not always obey God.

One day he did a wicked thing. Perhaps he hoped to earn some of those fine gifts King Balak had offered him. We do not know. But this is what he did: He went to the Midianites, who were living in Moab under King Balak. He said, "I will tell you a good way to make the Israelites' God so angry with them that He will kill them. Go make friends with them. Let your sons and daughters marry their young men and women. Then get them to come to your feasts and worship your idol-gods. That will really make their God angry!"

What a wicked man Balaam was! He knew it was sin to worship idols instead of God. But he helped the Midianites make the Israelites to sin. Soon the children of Israel were worshiping the Midianite god, Baal-peor. Then God was angry. He punished His people by sending a terrible plague. Twenty-four thousand people died.

Not long after this Moses led the people into the land of Moab. They set up their tents along the river Jordan. On the other side of the river was the city of Jericho. The twelve spies had gone there forty years before. Soon the Israelites would be ready to try to enter their new homeland once more.

First Moses and Eleazar, the new high priest, were to count all the people. All the men who were 20 years or older were to be counted. Joshua and Caleb were the only two men who had been alive when Moses had counted them 40 years before. All the others who had been counted then, had died.

The people were to be counted for two reasons. First, to see how many strong men they had who would be able to fight. They would have to chase the people out of their country. Second, they needed to know how to divide the land among all the people. Each man was to have a piece of land, except the Levites, who were to work in the Tabernacle.

When they counted all the people — men, women and children — they found that there were more than three million Israelites. God had truly kept His promise to Jacob! He had surely given him as many children as the sand on the seashore and as the stars in the sky! He had really made of them a great nation!

After the people had been counted, God told Moses to go out to fight against the wicked Midianites who had made the Israelites sin. Each of the twelve tribes sent a thousand men. Eleazar's son, Phineas, went along to blow the trumpets. God helped the Israelites win this battle. All the Midianites and their five kings were killed. So was wicked Balaam. And all the cities were burned.

The Israelites came back from the war. They brought with them thousands of cattle and sheep, for the Midianites were shepherds and herdsmen. They also had a great deal of silver, gold, iron, tin and lead. The soldiers shared what they brought with those who had not gone to war. They gave some to the Levites, too.

When the captains counted their soldiers, they found that not one had been killed. How thankful to God they were! He had taken such good care of them. They brought all the jewelry they had taken from the Midianites to the Tabernacle as a gift to the Lord.

The plains of Moab, where the Israelites were camping, was a rich, fertile land. It was a wonderful place to raise cows and sheep.

Three of the tribes — Reuben, Gad and half of Manasseh — liked it so well they wanted to live there instead of going across the river with the rest of the people.

Moses said these tribes might have Moab for their land on one condition. They must promise to help the other tribes fight against the people who lived in the land of Canaan. So these three tribes settled on the opposite side of the river from all the rest of the Israelites.

> *Were you listening?* What wicked thing did Balaam do? How many Israelites were there at this time? What happened to the wicked Midianites? Who wanted to live in Moab?

Story 60

God Calls Moses Home

Deuteronomy 34

Moses had been the leader of God's people for forty years. He had led them out of the land of Egypt to the land of Canaan. Then, because of their sin, he had brought them back into the wilderness. There he had cared for them for forty years. Now they were back at the river Jordan. But Moses was not going to take them across the river. His work was almost done.

Besides leading God's people to Canaan, Moses had completed another great task during his lifetime. He had written the first five books of the Bible. This was a most important work. The Bible is God's Holy Word. Moses had to write only what God wanted him to write. He had to be certain that what he wrote was true. When these five books were finished, Moses gave them to the Levites. They were to be kept in the golden Ark.

One day Moses gathered all the people together. He said, "I am a hundred and twenty years old today. I can no longer go in and out among you. God does not want me to go across the river Jordan. But do not be afraid. God will go with you across the river. He will chase away the enemies from your homeland so that you may live there."

Then Moses chose a new leader for God's people. It was the soldier, Joshua. Joshua had been one of the spies forty years before. He had not been afraid of the giants then, and he was a brave soldier now. Moses said to Joshua, "Be strong and full of courage, Joshua. The Lord will go with you. He will show you what to do. He will help you. You do not have to be afraid, for He will never fail you nor leave you."

Moses talked with the people for a long time. He reminded them of all the wonderful things God had done for them. Then he taught them a new song of praise to God for all His kindness to them.

When Moses finished his song, he said good-by to his people. Then God called him to come up on the top of Mount Nebo. So Moses went up the mountain which was in Moab, at the edge of the river Jordan. Although he was old, Moses was still strong and healthy. His eyes were clear and bright. He could walk like a young man. But his work was finished, so he went up the mountain to meet God.

From the mountain top he could look across the river. He could see the promised land to which he had been leading his people for so many years. God showed him all the land of Canaan from one end to the other. And God said, "This is the land which I promised to Abraham and to Isaac and to Jacob. You may see it with your eyes, but you shall not go into the land."

After Moses had seen the beautiful land which God was to give His people, Moses died up there on the mountain top. God buried Moses' body in a valley in the land of Moab. But no one ever knew where that place was.

The people of Israel wept for Moses in the plains of Moab for thirty days. Then Joshua became their leader.

> *Were you listening?* What two great things did Moses do during his lifetime? Whom did God choose to be the new leader? Where did Moses go?

Story 61

Rahab Helps God's People

Joshua 1

Joshua was now the leader of God's people. One day God came to Joshua and said, "Joshua, Moses is dead. I want you to take these people across the river Jordan into the promised land. Just as I was with Moses, I will be with you. Be strong and full of courage. Do not be afraid, for I will go with you wherever you go."

Joshua told all the people to get ready to cross the river. "In three days," he said, "we shall pass over into our new homeland." First, Joshua wanted to find out just how things were in that new country. He chose two men to go quietly across the river, without anyone seeing them. He told them to sneak into the first city, called Jericho. They were to look around and see how they could best fight against the people of Jericho.

The two men did as Joshua commanded. They swam across the river when no one was looking. They went into the city. They walked around and saw all they wanted to see. Then they went to a woman's house to ask if they might stay there. The woman happened to be a wicked lady. Her name was Rahab. Her house was built on the wall of the city. Rahab invited the men to come into her home.

Rahab talked to the two men. She had heard all about the wonderful things their God had done for them—how He had taken them across the Red Sea and had drowned Egyptians in the sea; how they had destroyed their enemies all along the way. "My people are afraid of the Israelites," she said.

But someone saw the two men go into Rahab's home. They ran and told the king. The king sent his soldiers to Rahab's house. "We want the men who came into your house," they said.

Rahab, even though she was a wicked lady, knew that these men were God's men. She knew now that God was going to take their city away from them. So she protected her visitors. She did not tell the soldiers where they were. She said to the soldiers, "Two men were here, but I did not know them. They have already gone. Just as it was getting dark they hurried to get through the gate before it closed. If you run, you should still be able to catch up with them."

The soldiers ran quickly after the men. They went as far as the river Jordan. But, of course, they did not find them. For the men were still in Rahab's house. She had hidden them on her roof, under some plants she was drying.

When the soldiers were gone, Rahab went up to the men on the roof. She told them what had happened. She begged them to be kind to her as she had been kind to them. "Please promise me that you will save me when you come to take our city," she said.

Then she let the men down from her roof by a red cord. "Go hide in the mountains for three days," she said, "until the soldiers have stopped looking for you."

The two men looked up at Rahab. "If you promise not to tell anyone why we were here," they said, "then we will save you. Bring your father and your mother and all your relatives into your house. Then when we come back with our soldiers, keep the red cord hanging in your window. In that way our men will know which house is yours. We'll save you and your family."

The two men hid in the mountains for three days. Then they swam across the river and went back to Joshua. They told him all the things that had happened.

Joshua was happy to hear their report. He said, "Truly the Lord has delivered all the land into our hands. The people are afraid of us!"

> *Were you listening?* How many spies did Joshua send to Jericho this time? What did Rahab do for the spies? What did they promise her? Why was Joshua happy?

Story 62

A Path through the River

Joshua 3, 4 and 5

God's people were almost home. Just across the river Jordan lay their promised land. They rested at the river for three days. They waited for the two men to come back from Jericho. Then the men came back and told all about Rahab and the people who were so afraid of their God. The people were eager to get started. But how were they going to cross the river? It was spring time. The river was wide and deep. The water was even running over the banks.

God told Joshua how to cross the river. Joshua listened to God. Then he said to the people, "When you see the priests walking toward the river, carrying the Ark on their shoulders, pick up your things and follow after them."

Then the Lord said to Joshua, "This day I will work wonders for you. I will make you great so that all Israel may know that I am with you as I was with Moses."

When all was ready the priests picked up the Ark and carried it down to the river's edge. Picking up their tents and all their belongings, the people followed. The priests walked right into the river. As their feet touched the water, the river stopped flowing. The water coming from above piled up like a high wall several miles back. The rest of the water ran away to the Dead Sea. So the river bed was dry for more than twenty miles. The priests stood with the Ark right in the middle of the dry river bed. All the Israelites crossed over.

Then Joshua chose twelve men to go into the river bed and each carry out a large stone on his shoulders. These men went into the river where the priests were standing and found their stones. They carried the stones with them until they came to Gilgal. This was the place where the Israelites were to camp for the night. There Joshua piled the stones up one on top of the other like a high tower. "This tower will be a sign for you," Joshua said, "so that when your children see it, you can tell them where we crossed the river into our own land, and how God dried up the water for us."

Then Joshua went into the river. He took twelve other stones and piled them up in the middle of the river bed. Then he went back to the river's edge. He called to the priests, "Come ye up now out of the Jordan."

As soon as the priests' feet left the river bed, the waters came back where they belonged. But the pillar of stones could be seen above the water. "Now you can always show your children," Joshua said, "where the Lord took us across the river. Then all the people of the earth will know that your God is mighty!"

The people put up their tents at Gilgal. There they rested. It was the first month of the Jewish year that the Israelites reached Canaan. On the fourteenth day of the month it was time to celebrate the Passover Feast. So the very first thing the Israelites did in their new homeland was to celebrate the Passover Feast. In this way they remembered how God had taken His people out of Egypt more than forty years before.

The next morning, when the women went outside with their baskets to gather manna, there was none. For the first time in forty years there was no manna on the ground! The Israelites were in their promised land. They no longer needed manna. They found corn and other grain, and all kinds of fruit, growing down by the river's edge. The people were filled with joy to be home at last!

Were you listening? How did the Israelites cross the river Jordan? Why did Joshua make two towers? Why did God stop sending manna to His people?

Story 63

The Walls of Jericho

Joshua 6

The Israelites had crossed the river Jordan. Now they were waiting by the river's edge for God to show them what to do. The Israelites camped by the river for more than a year. The women and children and the old men stayed in camp. The young men went out with Joshua to fight against all the people who lived in their land.

Jericho was the first city against which they had to fight. It was close to the river Jordan. From their tents the Israelites could see the huge walls which were built around the city.

The people living in Jericho were afraid of God's people, you remember. When they saw how God took His people across the river, they were even more afraid. They hurried to lock their gates. No one was allowed to go out and no one was allowed to come in.

Joshua was told by the Lord exactly what to do. The orders were very strange. Early in the morning the priests took up God's Ark and carried it on their shoulders. Seven other priests went ahead of the Ark, each carrying a trumpet. Ahead of the trumpet-blowers came the armed soldiers. Each one carried his spear and sword and shield. Behind the Ark came all the other men of Israel. In this order they marched all the way around the city of Jericho. The priests blew their trumpets but no one else made a sound. When they finished marching, they went back to camp.

Every morning for a week the Israelites marched around Jericho as God commanded. The people of Jericho watched from behind their walls. They became more and more afraid. They knew that Israel's God was fighting for His people.

On the seventh day the Israelites arose at dawn. They marched around the city seven times instead of only once. Then the priests blew their trumpets long and loud. And Joshua called to the people, "Shout, for the Lord has given you the city! This first city," he added, "is the Lord's. Keep nothing for yourselves. Kill the people and burn all the things. But bring me all the silver and gold and brass and iron. It is for the Lord."

So the priests blew their trumpets and the people shouted. Suddenly the huge walls of Jericho fell down flat. The people walked over the broken walls right into the city. They killed all the people and burned the city with fire. But Rahab, who had been kind to the two spies, was saved. So was all her family. The two spies found her house and brought her and all her relatives, with all their belongings, to the camp of Israel. From that day on Rahab and her family belonged to the people of God. She married one of the Israelites and became a good woman. Later God chose her to be one of the relatives of His own Son, Jesus Christ.

After Rahab was saved, the people of Israel completely destroyed the city of Jericho. They brought the gold and silver and brass and iron to Joshua. He put it in the Lord's House. When all was finished, Joshua warned the people, "No one must ever try to rebuild this city. If you do, when you begin your oldest child will die. And when you get it finished, your youngest child will die."

So the Lord was with Joshua. The people of all the cities round about heard about his greatness.

Were you listening? How did the Israelites fight against Jericho? What made the walls fall down? What happened to Rahab?

God Punishes a Thief

After the Israelites had taken the city of Jericho, the soldiers came back to the camp to rest. While they were resting, Joshua sent some men to the little city of Ai to look around. They were to see how they should fight against Ai. When the men came back they said, "It is a small city. All the soldiers will not have to go. We can easily take the city."

So Joshua sent three thousand men to fight against Ai. But the men of Ai won the battle. They chased the Israelites away and killed thirty-six of them. When Joshua heard what had happened, he was very sad. He tore his clothes and lay on his face on the ground in front of the Ark of the Lord until evening. All the elders of Israel lay with him. They put dust on their heads.

Joshua cried to God, "Why did you let me bring this people across the Jordan to be killed by their enemies?"

But God answered Joshua, "Get up, Joshua! Why are you lying there in the dust? You didn't win at Ai because one of your soldiers sinned against Me. Find him and kill him. Then I will give you Ai."

Joshua quickly gathered the people together. He made all the tribes of Israel pass by him. God chose the tribe of Judah. Then all the families of Judah went by. One man was taken. Finally, all his children went by, and Achan was taken.

Then Joshua said to Achan, "My son, give glory to God. Tell us what you did."

Achan answered, "When we were fighting in Jericho, I didn't burn up everything as God commanded. I found a beautiful robe and some gold and silver. I wanted to keep them. So I hid them in a hole under my tent."

Joshua sent messengers to Achan's tent. They found the hidden things and brought them to Joshua. Then Joshua took Achan and his whole family, his animals and his tents, and everything he owned, and brought them to the valley of Achor. Joshua said to Achan, "Why have you troubled us? The Lord will trouble you this day!" All the people threw stones at Achan and his family until they were dead. After that they burned everything with fire. Finally, they heaped a great pile of stones over the ashes.

When sinful Achan had been taken care of, Joshua sent his soldiers to Ai again. This time all the soldiers went. They fooled the people of Ai. During the night about thirty thousand brave soldiers went and hid in the rocks and hills around Ai. The following morning the rest of the soldiers went up to Ai to fight. As soon as the men of Ai came to meet them, the Israelites made believe they were losing the battle. They turned and ran from the city. All the men of Ai chased after them, thinking they were winning the battle. As soon as the others were far enough away from Ai, the hidden soldiers came and burned the city. Then the other Israelites turned around and killed their enemies instead of running away from them. So Israel won the battle.

When the battle was over, Joshua and his men went back to the camp of Israel. They brought with them all the animals and riches they had found in Ai. For God had said they might keep what they found. Then Joshua built an altar to God to thank Him for giving them the victory.

> *Were you listening?* Why couldn't the Israelites win over Ai? How did they punish the man who sinned? How did they finally win over Ai?

Story 65

Joshua Is Fooled by His Neighbors

Joshua 9

The Israelites were now in their promised land of Canaan. They had to do much fighting to take the land from the people who lived there. But God helped them fight their battles. Each time the Israelites won a great victory.

The city of Gibeon was not far from where the Israelites were living. The Gibeonites soon heard what had happened to Jericho and to Ai. They knew that Israel would soon come to their city, too. They were afraid, so they planned a trick to fool Joshua.

They sent several men to Joshua. These men wore old and torn clothing. Their shoes were worn and patched. They tied old sacks on their donkeys' backs. They used old, worn-out wineskins, which had been torn and mended again. They took dry, mouldy bread in their sacks. When they came to Joshua, they acted as if they had been on a long, long journey.

They said to Joshua, "We have come from a faraway country. We would like to make a bargain with you."

"Who are you?" Joshua asked. "What country do you come from?"

The Gibeonites answered, "We are your friends. We have come from a land which is far away. But we have heard about the wonderful things your God has done for you. We have heard how He has destroyed all your enemies along the way. So our people sent us to visit you. We are your servants. We want to make peace with you."

Then the Gibeonites showed Joshua their old things. "Look," they said, "this bread we have with us was fresh when we left home. We took it hot from the oven. Now it is dry and mouldy. These wine-skins were new. Now they are old and torn. And our clothes and our shoes have worn out while we traveled."

Joshua and his men listened to the men of Gibeon and believed their story. Joshua forgot to ask God what he should do. God had told Joshua that all the people in all the cities in Canaan should be destroyed. Now Joshua thought that these men of Gibeon lived in a country far beyond Canaan. So he made peace with the Gibeonites. He promised never to fight against them. So the Gibeonites fooled Joshua. Then they went back to their own city.

Three days later Joshua found out that he had been fooled. He heard that his visitors had been the Gibeonites, who were his neighbors. The Israelites were angry with Joshua for making peace with the men of Gibeon. But Joshua could not break his promise. So he made the Gibeonites his servants, instead. From that day on, the Gibeonites had to cut wood and draw water for the Israelites.

Were you listening? Who were the Gibeonites? How did they fool Joshua? What did Joshua do to the Gibeonites?

God Fights for His People

The people who were still living in the cities of Canaan were becoming more and more afraid of Joshua and his God. The king of Jerusalem had also heard about the things that had happened at Jericho and at Ai. He heard how the Gibeonites had fooled Joshua and made peace with him. Now the king of Jerusalem became even more afraid. He knew that Gibeon was a large city and that the Gibeonites would fight with Joshua.

So the king of Jerusalem sent messengers to the kings of four other cities in Canaan. "Come up and help me fight against Gibeon," he said, "for the Gibeonites have made peace with Joshua."

These four kings listened to the messengers. They came up with their soldiers to help the king of Jerusalem. Soon these five kings began to fight against the Gibeonites.

Right away the Gibeonites sent word to Joshua. "Please come at once to help us," they said. "For all the kings in the hill-country are come to fight against us."

Joshua took all his soldiers and went down to help the Gibeonites. God said to Joshua, "Don't be afraid to go up. I will go with you. I will fight for you. There shall not be one of the enemy left."

So Joshua and his soldiers marched all night. When they came upon the five kings, there was a great battle. God helped Joshua win the battle. Soon the enemies were running away from the Israelites, for God sent huge hailstones from heaven to kill the enemy.

All day long the battle raged. It was almost evening. Still the fighting went on. Knowing they would not be able to fight in the dark, Joshua commanded the sun to stand still until the battle was over. God listened to Joshua. He made the sun stand still where it was for a whole day. Night did not come until the battle was over. There has never been another day like that. God listened to Joshua and stopped the passing of time!

The five kings ran away from the battle and hid in a cave. Some of Joshua's soldiers saw where the kings were hiding. They told Joshua. Joshua told them to go back to the cave and roll a big stone in front of the opening so the kings could not get out. The soldiers obeyed at once.

When the battle was over, Joshua went to the cave and brought out the five kings. He killed the kings and hung their bodies on five trees. The dead kings hung on the trees until evening, so that everyone could see what happened to the men who had fought against God's people.

> *Were you listening?* How did it happen that Joshua fought against five cities in one battle? Who helped him win the battle? What happened that day which never happened before or after? What happened to the five kings?

Story 67

Dividing the Land and Joshua's Farewell
Joshua 13 and 14; Exodus 23

There were still many cities in the land of Canaan which had to be conquered. Joshua and his brave soldiers fought for a long time. They won one city after another. Finally, Joshua stopped fighting. He was an old man by this time. God told him he could now rest from his hard work.

Although all the cities had not been taken, God told Joshua to divide the land among the nine and a half tribes. The other two and a half tribes already had their land on the other side of the river Jordan, you remember. Joshua divided the land by lot. He gave each tribe an equal portion, according to the size of the tribe. The tribe of Levi was not to have any farm-land, for they worked in the Tabernacle with the priests. So the Levites were given forty-eight cities. Each city had enough pasture land around it for the animals.

Joshua also chose six cities which were to be called the Cities of Refuge. Three were on one side of the river Jordan, and three on the other. These cities were safe hiding places for those who had accidentally killed someone. In the Cities of Refuge, no one was allowed to hurt them. These cities were given by God as a sign of Jesus who is our great refuge from sin.

Joshua chose the city of Shiloh for the Tabernacle. All the people of Israel gathered together in Shiloh. They put up the Tabernacle. Here it stood for hundreds of years until the days of King Solomon when the Temple was built.

When all the land was divided, Joshua called the tribes of Reuben and Gad and the half tribe of Manasseh to him. "You have kept your promise," he said, "to come with us across the Jordan. You have helped us fight our enemies. Now you may go back to your homes on the other side of Jordan."

By the time the people were finally settled in Canaan, Joshua was one hundred and ten years old. One day he called all the people together. He talked to them for a long time. He helped them remember how God had helped them win all their battles. He reminded them of God's many promises. He warned them not to turn away from God.

"Don't make friends with your heathen neighbors," Joshua said. "You might learn to serve their gods. You know that God has done everything He promised. Not one thing did He forget! But if you turn away from God, He will also remember to send you all the bad things He has promised. If you serve other gods, God will surely chase you out of this promised land. So choose you this day whom you will serve. If you think it is bad to serve the Lord, then serve the gods of the other nations. But as for me and my house, we will serve the Lord."

The people answered, "Far be it from us to turn away from the Lord. We, too, will serve Him!"

Not long after this Joshua died.

Were you listening? How was the land of Canaan divided? Where was the Tabernacle placed? What was a city of refuge? What did Joshua tell his people before he died? What did the people promise?

Israel Ruled by Judges

God's people, the Israelites, were living in their own land of Canaan. They were happy in their new home. For many years they worshiped God and obeyed Him. They served God during all the days of Joshua, their leader. After Joshua died, the elders who had ruled with Joshua led the people. But after the elders were dead, the Israelites disobeyed God. They made friends with their heathen neighbors and learned to serve idols as they did.

Then God was angry with His people. He punished them by sending their heathen neighbors to fight with them. When they first arrived, the Israelites had not destroyed all the heathen peoples who were living in Canaan. Now God used those very nations to punish them. The king of Mesopotamia came with his army and conquered the Israelites. For eight years this heathen king was their ruler.

All the people did not forget God, however. There were a few who had not worshiped the heathen gods. These good people prayed to God. They asked Him to save them from their enemies.

God heard their prayers. After many years God chose one of the Israelites to be a judge. His name was Othniel. He was the son of Caleb's younger brother. Caleb, you remember, was the other good spy who had gone into Jericho with Joshua.

Othniel became Israel's new leader. He trained an army and went out to fight against the king of Mesopotamia. God helped Othniel win. Then the king and his army went back to Mesopotamia. Israel was free once more.

Othniel judged Israel for forty years. During all that time the people worshiped God and obeyed Him. And there was peace in the land.

> *Were you listening?* What did the Israelites do after Joshua and the elders were dead? How did God punish them? Who was Othniel? What did he do?

Ehud and Shamgar Save Israel

The Israelites remembered to serve God as long as they had a good leader. After Othniel died, the people soon forgot their promises. They would rather serve gods they could see and had made, than serve the great God, Jehovah, who had made them. It was not long before many of the people were worshiping idols again.

God is a kind and loving God. He takes wonderful care of His people. But when those people turn away from Him, God must punish them. This time God allowed another heathen king to come and fight against Israel. King Eglon of Moab led his army across the river Jordan. He brought with him two other heathen armies, too. The soldiers of Ammon and Amalek joined King Eglon in the battle. All three of these nations had fought against Israel when they were traveling through the wilderness. Then God had helped His people win against them.

Now King Eglon and his great army came into Jericho. They captured that city. For eighteen years King Eglon ruled over Israel from Jericho. After all those years the Israelites finally remembered that Jehovah was their God. They turned away from their idol-worship and cried unto the Lord for help.

Once more God heard His people. He chose a new judge to help them. He chose a man from the tribe of Benjamin which lived in Jericho. His name was Ehud. Ehud was a left-handed man.

One day the Israelites sent Ehud to King Eglon with a present. Before Ehud took the present to the king, he made himself a two-edged dagger, eighteen inches long. He hid the dagger under his coat on his right hip. Many servants went with Ehud to carry the large gift.

They found King Eglon sitting in his summer palace. King Eglon was a very fat man. Since it was a hot day, he was trying to keep cool in this summer room with its large windows. The men gave the king the gift. Ehud made a fine speech. Then Ehud sent his men away. He went back to the king alone. "I have a secret message for you, O king," he said.

"Hush," the king said. "Wait until I am alone." Then he sent all his servants out of the room.

Ehud went close to the king. "I have a message from God for you," he said. Then he put his left hand under his coat and pulled out the dagger from his right hip. Before the king knew what was happening, Ehud forced the dagger through the king's body. Then Ehud quietly left the room. He shut the door and locked it. He hurried out of Jericho.

After Ehud had gone, the king's servants came back. When they saw that the door was locked they waited for the king to come out. They waited and waited. Finally they found a key and opened the door. The king lay on the floor, dead.

By this time Ehud had reached the mountain in Ephraim. He blew his trumpet and the soldiers of Israel came to him. "Follow me," he said, "for God has delivered our enemies into our hands."

Ehud led his soldiers to the river Jordan. They guarded the river so no stranger could cross over. Then they fought against the people of Moab and killed ten thousand of their brave men. So Ehud chased away the Moabites from their land. And Israel had peace once more. For eighty years there was no trouble in the land of Canaan.

The next judge to rule Israel was Shamgar. He fought against the Philistines and killed six hundred men with an ox goad. This was a pointed stick used to drive oxen when one wanted them to go. So Shamgar saved Israel from the Philistines.

Were you listening? Who came to live in Jericho? What did Ehud have hanging on his right hip? How did Ehud save Israel? How did Shamgar save Israel?

Story 70

Deborah the Judge, and Barak the Captain
Judges 4

After Shamgar died the Israelites had no leader. Whenever there was no leader in Israel, the people did as they pleased. In a short time heathen idols were brought back into their land. The people once more turned away from God and worshiped idols.

These were not the same people who had worshiped idols before. Those people had become old and had died. These were their children and the grandchildren. They were now grown up to be the men and women of Israel. But they were just as bad as their parents had been.

So once more God punished His people. This time He sent Jabin, the king of Canaan, to make war against them. For twenty years Jabin and his soldiers ruled Israel. The people were filled with fear, for this king was cruel. He had nine hundred chariots of iron. The Israelites could not fight against him.

Finally the people turned away from their heathen gods, and cried unto God. Again God heard His people. He began at once to help them. There was a woman in Israel at that time whose name was Deborah. Deborah was a judge. She sat under a palm tree in the hill-country. The people came to her for help.

Now God told Deborah to send an army to fight against the cruel king. God promised to help them win. So Deborah called her captain, Barak, and gave him God's message. But Barak was afraid. "I'll go," he said, "if you'll go with me."

"All right," Deborah answered, "I'll go with you. But since you are afraid, the honor will go to a woman."

Deborah and Barak soon gathered an army of ten thousand men and went out to fight. Sisera was the captain of Canaan's army. He came up against Israel with all his iron chariots and all his soldiers. Deborah said to Barak, "Don't be afraid. This day the Lord is going to give Sisera and his army into your hand."

So Barak and his army fought against Sisera. God helped them. When they came to the river Kishon God won the battle for them. During the dry season of the year this river is often without water. An old book tells us that when Sisera and his soldiers rode their chariots into this dry river-bed, God sent down a terrific rain storm. The river-bed quickly filled with water and the chariots could not move. Then Barak and his soldiers killed their enemies with their swords.

Sisera, the captain, got out of his chariot and ran away. He ran to a tent in a field near by. Sisera knew the man who lived in this tent. They were supposed to be friends. When the man's wife, Jael, saw Sisera coming, she went out to meet him. "Come, my lord," she said, "come hide in my tent. Don't be afraid."

Sisera went into her tent. He was so tired he laid down on the floor to rest. Jael covered him with a rug. When he asked for a drink of water, she gave him a glass of milk. Then Sisera fell asleep. Jael took a big tent-pin and hammered it through his head into the ground. That was the terrible way Sisera died.

Jael waited for Barak outside her tent. As soon as she saw him she called, "Come and I will show you the man you are looking for."

Barak went in and found Captain Sisera dead on the floor. So the Israelites won the battle that day, and Jael, a woman, received the honor. Then Deborah and Barak sang a song of praise to God for saving them from their enemies.

After that the Israelites had peace for forty years.

Were you listening? How did God help Barak win the battle? How did Jael help? Why did a woman receive the honor for the victory?

Story 71

Gideon and the Angel

Judges 6

Deborah became old and died. The people forgot her teachings. Soon they were serving heathen gods again. Once more they turned away from Jehovah, their God. Then God punished His people again. He sent another king and his army to fight against the Israelites. This time the Midianites came to live in Israel's country.

The Midianites were even more cruel than the Canaanites had been. They helped themselves to the food which the Israelites were growing in their fields. They took away their animals. The Israelites were so afraid they ran away to hide from the Midianites. They found themselves homes in the caves of the mountains. The Midianites took over all the land. There were so many of them they were like a lot of grasshoppers. The men and their animals were too many to count.

Finally the Israelites remembered their God. They cried to Him in their trouble. Once more He heard them.

One day a young man, named Gideon, was threshing his father's wheat. He was doing it by the winepress where he could be hidden from the Midianites. Just then an angel came and sat under an oak tree. He said to Gideon, "God is with you, brave man."

"If God is with us," Gideon answered, "then why has all this happened to us?"

"God is going to help His people now," the angel went on. "And He wants you to be the leader. He wants you to chase away the Midianites from your land."

"Oh, but I'm only a poor farmer," Gideon said. "What could I do?"

But the angel said, "Surely God will be with you. He will help you."

Gideon thought the angel might be hungry. So he brought a basket of meat and a pot of broth with some bread to the angel. The angel told Gideon to put the meat and bread on a rock and to pour the broth over it. After Gideon had obeyed, the angel touched the food with his staff. Fire came out of the rock and burned the food. The angel went away.

Gideon was afraid, but God talked to him. "Don't be afraid," God said. "You will not die." Gideon immediately built an altar to the Lord and worshiped Him there.

That night, Gideon and some of his friends broke down the heathen altars with their heathen gods. He cut down the trees in the park where the idols had stood. He built an altar to the real God in their place.

The next morning the people were angry at Gideon. They came to his father and wanted to kill him. Gideon's father said, "Do you have to fight for your god? Can't Baal take care of himself? If he is a god, let him punish Gideon for breaking down his altar." So the people did not hurt Gideon.

Gideon was still afraid to be the leader. He asked God for a sign. He put a fleece of wool on the ground. "If the fleece is wet with dew and the ground around it is dry, then I'll know that God wants me to save Israel," he said. In the morning the fleece was full of dew and the ground was dry. But Gideon tried it once more just to be sure. This time he wanted the fleece dry and the ground wet. The next morning the fleece was dry and the ground was covered with dew. So Gideon knew that God had chosen him to save his people.

> *Were you listening?* Why were the Israelites afraid of the Midianites? Who came to see Gideon one day? What happened when Gideon brought the visitor food? What sign did Gideon want?

Story 72

God Wins through Gideon's Army

Judges 7

Gideon knew that God wanted him to save his people from the cruel Midianites. So he went out to find himself an army. In a short time he had thirty-two thousand men. But God said, "You have too many soldiers, Gideon. I want Israel to know that I am the One who is going to save them. Tell the soldiers that all those who are afraid may go back home."

Gideon did as God told him. Twenty-two thousand men went home. There were just ten thousand left. Now Gideon was afraid that his army was too small. But God said, "There are still too many soldiers, Gideon. Bring your soldiers down to the water. Watch them as they drink. All those who lap up the water with their tongues, like a dog does, put on one side. Those who get down on their knees to drink, put on the other side."

So Gideon took his soldiers to the water. He watched them drink. Three hundred of them lapped the water with their tongues. All the rest got on their knees to drink. Then God told Gideon to keep those who had lapped the water with their tongues. The rest he was to send home. So Gideon had only three hundred soldiers to fight all those Midianites!

Gideon led his soldiers to the camp of the Midianites. It was night when they reached a hill above the camp. As far as they could see there were enemy tents. There were so many Midianites they couldn't even be counted. "Go down and fight them," God said to Gideon.

But Gideon was afraid.

"Go first with your servant and listen to what they are saying," God said. "Then you won't be afraid."

So Gideon and his servant crept quietly down into the camp. They heard two guards talking. One said, "I had a dream. I saw a loaf of barley bread come tumbling down the hill. It tumbled into our camp and turned the tents upside down."

The other guard answered, "That must be Gideon, the Israelite, into whose hand God has given Midian."

Gideon thanked God and praised Him. Then he quickly went back to his soldiers. "Get up," he cried, "and let's fight! For the Lord has given the Midianites into our hand."

Then Gideon divided his men into three groups. He gave each man an empty pitcher with a lighted torch inside, and a trumpet. They were to hold the pitcher in one hand and the trumpet in the other.

"Follow me," Gideon cried, "and do as I do."

The men went down to the camp of the sleeping Midianites. They crept all around the camp. Suddenly, Gideon broke his pitcher, held up his light, and blew his trumpet. All his soldiers did as Gideon had done. Then Gideon shouted, "The sword of the Lord and of Gideon!"

The Midianites awoke in terror. The great noise fooled them. They thought that a huge army was after them. They stumbled out of their tents and ran away as fast as they could run. They swung their swords wildly, killing each other as they went. Gideon and his men ran after them.

Then Gideon sent messengers to gather all the other soldiers of Israel. Together they chased the Midianites out of their land. When the battle was over, the Israelites made Gideon their ruler. He judged Israel forty years.

Were you listening? Why did God want Gideon to send most of his army home? How did Gideon choose his three hundred soldiers? How did they fool the Midianites?

God Gives Samson Super-Strength

The Israelites had again forgotten God. Once more they worshiped idols. So, once more God punished His people. This time He sent the Philistines to fight against the Israelites. They ruled over Israel for forty years. Finally, the Israelites remembered God. Then they prayed to Him for help. Once again God chose a new leader to help His people.

There was a man named Manoah. He and his wife were old people. They had no children. One day, when Manoah's wife was out in the field, an angel came to her. He said, "Even though you are old, you are going to have a son. He will be very special. When he grows up he's going to be a leader for God to help fight the Philistines. So you must never let him drink strong drink, nor touch a dead body, nor cut his hair."

Manoah's wife told him about the angel's visit. He asked God to send the angel again. He wanted to learn more about the new baby. Not long after, the angel did come again. He told them once more what they should do. Then Manoah invited the angel to stay for something to eat.

"Even though you make food for me," the angel said, "I shall not eat it. You must sacrifice it to the Lord."

Manoah and his wife hurried to prepare some food. They brought it to the angel and laid it on the rock in front of him. They burned the food up to God as an offering. As the flame went up toward heaven from the altar, the angel went up in the flame. Manoah and his wife fell on their faces to the ground. They were afraid they might die since they had seen an angel.

Soon the new baby came as the angel had promised. They called him Samson. As Samson grew, the Lord blessed him. And Samson remembered never to drink strong drink, nor touch a dead body, nor cut his hair. Since Samson obeyed God, God made him stronger than any other man on the earth.

When Samson was grown, he fell in love with a girl in the Philistines' country. One day as he went to visit her, he heard a young lion roaring in the woods. He went after the lion and tore him to pieces. He did not tell anyone what he had done.

Soon Samson wanted to marry this girl. Although his parents did not like it, they went with him to the wedding. As they walked through the woods again, Samson went to see if the lion was still there. He found a swarm of bees making honey in the lion's body. He ate some of the honey and brought some to his parents. At the wedding Samson made a riddle about the honey in the lion's body. "If you guess my riddle," he said, "I'll give you thirty suits of clothing."

The guests could not guess the riddle. All week long they tried. Finally they forced Samson's wife to find out the answer for them. They threatened to burn her and her house if she didn't. So she teased Samson until he told her. She ran and told the men. When Samson asked for the answer, they said, "What is sweeter than honey, and what is stronger than a lion?"

Samson was angry. "If you hadn't asked my wife, you never would have guessed it," he said.

Samson was so angry he went out and killed thirty Philistines. He took their clothing for the men at the wedding. Then in anger Samson left his wife and went home to his father's house.

> *Were you listening?* Who came to see Manoah's wife? What did she have to remember? What made Samson so strong? Why was Samson angry?

Story 74

Samson Fights the Philistines

Judges 15

Later, when Samson was no longer angry because of the riddle, he went back to the land of the Philistines to get his wife. But when he got there he found that she had not waited for him. She had married someone else. This made Samson angry again. He went out into the woods and caught three hundred foxes. He tied them together two by two by their tails. Then he put a piece of burning wood between their tails. He turned the foxes loose in the Philistines' farms. All the corn and the vineyards and the olive trees were burned up.

When the Philistines saw their fields on fire, they said, "Who did this?" They found out that it was Samson and that he was angry with his wife. Then they burned her and her father's house with fire. That made Samson angry once more. He went out and killed a great many Philistines. Then he went down and lived in the top of the rock, called Etam.

Not long after this, the Philistines came into Israel's country and put up their tents there. The men of Israel said, "Why have you come here against us?"

The Philistines answered, "We're looking for Samson. We want to punish him for what he has done to us."

Then three thousand Israelites went to Etam. They said to Samson, "Don't you know that the Philistines are rulers over us? Why do you fight them all the time? Now we are going to tie you up and bring you to them."

Samson said, "All right. You may bring me to the Philistines, but don't kill me yourselves."

The men of Israel promised not to hurt Samson. They tied him up with two new ropes and carried him down to the Philistines. When the Philistines saw Samson they began to shout. Suddenly, the Lord gave Samson super-strength. He broke the ropes and picked up an old jawbone of an ass. With it, he killed a thousand Philistines.

Then Samson went away, singing,

With the jawbone of an ass, heaps upon heaps,

With the jawbone of an ass have I killed a thousand men!

Leaving the field of battle, Samson threw the jawbone to the ground. He became very thirsty. He called to God. He said, "You gave me this great victory over my enemies. Now are you going to let me die of thirst and fall into the hands of these Philistines?" But God helped Samson. He dug a hole in the jawbone and water came running out. So Samson had water to drink.

Not long after this, Samson went to visit a woman in the Philistine city of Gaza. The elders of the city heard that Samson was in their city. They immediately made plans to capture him. They went to sit by the gate to wait for Samson. "We'll wait until he gets ready to go home," they said. "Then, when he comes to the gate, we'll kill him." So they locked the gate and sat down to wait.

But Samson stayed a long time. The men grew tired of waiting and fell asleep. It was about midnight when Samson finally came to the gate. When Samson saw the sleeping men and the locked gate, he pulled the heavy gate and its posts right out of the wall. He carried it away on his shoulders. He left the gate at the top of a high hill.

When the Philistines awoke, Samson was gone. And so was their gate. Samson could easily carry the heavy gate on his shoulders. But the Philistines must have had a hard time finding their gate and dragging it back to their city. Samson was such a strong man because God made him so strong. With his great strength he could destroy Israel's enemy, the Philistines.

Were you listening? What did Samson do with the foxes? What did he do with the jawbone? What did he do with the gate? Why was Samson so strong?

Story 75

A Failure That Became a Victory

Judges 16

Samson was the strongest man that ever lived. He killed a thousand Philistines with the jawbone of an ass. He tore a lion in pieces with his bare hands. The Philistines tried many times to capture him, but he was too strong for them.

One day Samson fell in love with another girl from the Philistines' country. Her name was Delilah. The rulers of the Philistines promised Delilah that they would each give her eleven hundred pieces of silver if she could find out why Samson was so strong. Then they would be able to capture him.

Day after day Delilah begged Samson to tell her his secret. At first Samson did not tell her the truth. He knew that he should not tell anyone the secret of his strength. So he lied to Delilah instead. He told her to tie him with seven green twigs. The Philistines brought her the twigs. They hid in another room. Then when Samson was asleep, she tied his hands and feet with the twigs. After a while she woke Samson, saying, "The Philistines are after you, Samson!" Samson awoke. He broke the twigs as if they had been a piece of string.

Delilah kept on teasing Samson. "Don't lie to me. Tell me the truth," she said. Samson told her to tie him with new ropes. But when she did, he broke the ropes, too. He broke them as easily as if they had been a thread.

After Delilah had pestered him some more, Samson told her to tie his hair in a weaving machine, called a loom. So, when Samson was asleep, Delilah wove his hair in the loom and fastened the loom to the floor with a strong nail. Then Delilah shouted, "Samson, the Philistines are after you!" Samson jumped up. He pulled the loom, nail and all, off the floor. He ran away with the loom hanging from his long hair. So Delilah was fooled again.

Once more Delilah teased Samson. "How can you say you love me when you lie to me all the time?" she asked. She kept on until Samson could no longer keep his secret. He told her the truth. "I am a special man of God," he explained. "God makes me strong. But if I disobey Him and cut my hair, God will take away my strength." Then Delilah knew he had told her the truth. She called the Philistines once more. They came, bringing money for Delilah.

Delilah made Samson fall asleep with his head in her lap. A barber came in and cut off his long hair. Then Samson's strength went from him. Suddenly Delilah called, "Samson, the Philistines are after you!" Samson awoke. He tried to run away as he had the other times, but his strength was gone. The Spirit of God was not with him any more. The Philistines captured Samson. After putting out his eyes, they placed him in their prison house. They tied him with heavy brass chains and made him grind their corn.

While Samson was in prison, he was sorry he had told Delilah his secret. He asked God to forgive him. God heard his prayer. Samson's hair began to grow long again. God made him strong once more. But the Philistines did not know this.

One day the Philistines made a great feast to their stone god, Dagon. It was a "thank-you" feast for having captured Samson. They sacrificed to Dagon. They drank wine and danced and had a good time. While they were feasting, someone said, "Bring Samson here so we may make fun of him."

So they sent a boy to get Samson from the prison-house. He led Samson to the feast. Samson asked to be placed between the pillars which held up the house. The people laughed at him because he looked so helpless. Samson said to the boy, "Put my hands on the pillars so that I may lean on them."

Samson stood with his hands on the pillars. He cried to God, "O God, please make me strong once more so that I may punish these Philistines for taking my two eyes." Then Samson took hold of the two pillars and pulled with all his might. The pillars broke and the house fell upon all the Philistines and upon Samson, too. Three thousand men and women were killed. So Samson killed more Philistines when he died than when he was alive. And the Philistines could no longer rule over Israel.

> *Were you listening?* In which four ways did Delilah try to capture Samson? Why did Samson's strength leave him? What happened at the Philistines' feast?

Story 76

Ruth

Ruth 1

Many, many years ago during the time of the Judges, there was a famine in the land of Bethlehem. For a long time no rain came to water the land. Nothing would grow in the fields and the people had little to eat. The children were often hungry. There was a man in Bethlehem whose name was Elimelech. His wife's name was Naomi. They had two sons. Elimelech and his family were hungry. They needed bread, but there was no bread in Bethlehem. So Elimelech and Naomi and their two boys moved away from Bethlehem. They crossed the river Jordan and went to the heathen country of Moab.

There was plenty to eat in Moab. But the family had many troubles. Although there was plenty of food in Moab, there was no church there where Naomi and her family could go to worship God. When her two boys grew up they married girls from Moab, who did not know God. Their names were Orpah and Ruth. After a while Naomi's husband, Elimelech, died. Then the two young men died. Now Naomi was left alone with Orpah and Ruth.

Naomi's heart was filled with sadness. She was lonely, too. She had been in Moab ten years. One day she heard that there was no longer a famine in Bethlehem. Rain had come and food was again growing in the fields. Naomi decided to go back to her old home in Bethlehem. Orpah and Ruth wanted to go with her. As soon as they could get ready, they left Moab and started to walk toward Bethlehem.

After a while Naomi stopped. She turned to her two daughters-in-law. "Go back home," she said, "and may God be kind to you because you have been kind to me." Then Naomi kissed Ruth and Orpah. Both girls cried.

"Don't send us home," the girls said. "Let us go along with you."

But Naomi answered, "Why should you come with me? I have no more sons for you to marry. Go back to your own mother's house. Find yourselves another husband in your own country."

Orpah and Ruth cried again. Finally, Orpah kissed Naomi good-by and went back home. But Ruth loved Naomi so much, she would not leave her.

Naomi said, "Look, Orpah has gone back to her people and to her gods. Go, follow her."

But Ruth threw her arms around Naomi and said, "Please don't ask me to leave you. For where you go I want to go. Where you live I want to live. Your people shall be my people, and your God, my God. Where you die I want to die, and there will I be buried. I never want to leave you until I die!"

When Naomi heard Ruth's words, she took the girl with her. The two women walked for a long time until they came to Bethlehem. When the women of Bethlehem saw Naomi, they were surprised. Naomi had changed so much they did not know her. "Is this Naomi?" they asked.

Naomi answered, "Don't call me Naomi any more (Naomi means pleasant or happy). Call me Mara (Mara means bitter). For my life has been very bitter. I went away full with a husband and two sons, and I have come back empty."

So Naomi came back home with Ruth, her daughter-in-law. And the fields of Bethlehem were filled with ripened grain, for it was April and spring had come.

> *Were you listening?* Why did Naomi go to Moab? Why did Naomi go back to Bethlehem? Why did Ruth go with her? Why did Naomi want to change her name to Mara?

Story 77

God Blesses Naomi and Ruth

Ruth 2, 3 and 4

Ruth and Naomi were poor. They had no husband to work for them, so they had no money to buy food.

In those days farmers allowed poor people to "glean" in their fields. This meant that they left some of their grain on the ground for the poor people to pick up.

"Let me go and glean for you," Ruth said to Naomi.

Now Naomi's husband had a rich cousin, whose name was Boaz. Boaz owned a large farm. When Ruth went out to glean, she happened to go to the fields of Boaz. So she followed the reapers and began to glean there. While Ruth was gleaning, Boaz came to his fields to watch his men work. He noticed Ruth. "Who is this?" he asked his head servant.

The servant answered, "It is the girl from Moab, who came with Naomi. She asked me if she could glean here. She has been working hard all day."

Boaz liked Ruth. He went to talk with her. "You may come here every day," he said. "Don't go to any other field to glean. I have told my men not to bother you. When you are thirsty, you may drink from the water my men have drawn."

Ruth bowed to the ground in front of Boaz and said, "Why are you so kind to me, seeing I am a stranger?"

Boaz answered, "I have heard how kind you have been to Naomi. May the Lord pay you for your kindness. May the Lord, the God of Israel, under whose wings you have come to take refuge, reward you."

So Ruth gleaned each day in the fields of Boaz. At meal-time she sat beside the reapers and ate from Boaz' table. And when she gleaned, Boaz told his young men to let her glean even among the sheaves. And he told them to pull some extra grain from the bundles and drop it for her, so she would get enough. Ruth gleaned until the harvest was over. Now she and Naomi had plenty to eat.

Then Naomi said to Ruth, "Boaz is your husband's cousin. In our country, when a man dies, one of his relatives must marry his widow. Perhaps Boaz will ask you to marry him."

Naomi sent Ruth to the fields one night when she knew Boaz would be there. And Boaz offered to marry her. Boaz said, "It is true, I am your cousin, but there is another man who is closer to you than I am. Tomorrow I shall ask him. If he can marry you, fine; if not, I shall be happy to marry you." Then he told Ruth to spread out her robe. He filled it with barley for her.

The next day Boaz found out that the other cousin could not marry Ruth. Then Boaz and Ruth were married. They were very happy together. Naomi came to live with them, too. God blessed them and gave them a little boy. His name was Obed. Later Obed became the grandfather of the great King David. And David was a relative of Jesus Christ, the Son of God! So Ruth, the girl from Moab, came to live with God's people and became a relative of Jesus Christ, our Saviour!

Were you listening? How did Ruth get food for Naomi? Why was Boaz kind to Ruth? Why did Boaz marry Ruth? What wonderful Person came from Ruth's family?

Story 78

God Answers Hannah's Prayer

I Samuel 1

Long ago there lived in Israel a good woman whose name was Hannah. She loved the Lord and tried to serve Him. But she was not happy. Her husband, Elkanah, loved her and was kind to her.

But Elkanah had two wives. His other wife had children while Hannah did not. This made Hannah very sad. She wished God would give her just one little boy to love and care for. Often Elkanah's other wife made fun of Hannah because she had no children. Then Hannah cried and would not eat.

Every year Elkanah and his two wives went to the far-away tabernacle in Shiloh to worship God. Here they would pray and bring their yearly offerings. One day when they were in Shiloh Hannah was still filled with sadness. The other wife had laughed at her again because she had no children. Hannah would not eat. She cried instead.

Elkanah said to her, "Hannah, why are you crying? And why don't you eat? Why are you so sad all the time? I love you. Am I not better than ten sons?"

Hannah did not answer. But when the meal was over she went into God's House by herself. She stood in a lonely place and prayed. She felt so sad that she cried and cried while she was praying. She wanted a baby so badly that she made God a promise. She said, "Dear Heavenly Father, if You will give me a baby boy, I will give him back to You. I'll bring him to this tabernacle to live so he may always work for You."

Hannah prayed for a long time. The old minister, Eli, was sitting in his chair near the door. He was watching Hannah. He saw her lips moving, but he couldn't hear her pray. She was praying in her heart. Eli thought Hannah was a drunken woman. He scolded her. "Woman," he said, "you musn't come into God's House when you are drunken!"

But Hannah said, "Oh, my lord, I'm not drunken. I am filled with sadness. I have been pouring out my heart to God. Do not think I am a wicked woman."

Eli was a kind old minister. "Go home," he said. "And may the Heavenly Father give you what you prayed for."

Then Hannah went to find her husband. She was not sad any more, for she believed that God would answer her prayer.

God did answer Hannah's prayer just as Eli had said. He gave her a dear little baby boy. She called him Samuel because she had

asked for him of the Lord. While Samuel was a baby Hannah did not go with her husband to worship at Shiloh. She stayed at home to care for her little boy. But when Samuel was about five years old, Hannah took him to the tabernacle. She brought him to Eli and said, "I am the woman who stood here praying. For this child I prayed. God answered my prayer. Now I have given him back to God. He shall live here with you as long as he lives." Then Hannah sang a beautiful song of praise to God for answering her prayer.

So Samuel stayed with Eli in God's house and Hannah went home with her husband. Every year she came back to Shiloh to worship God. Each time she brought Samuel a new little coat. It was a nice little coat made of wool. It had no seams and reached almost to the ground. It was the kind of coat that priests and kings wore. Samuel also wore a sleeveless cape, called an ephod. It hung from the shoulders, down the back and down the front, and was held together by a beautiful belt. Only priests wore ephods. Samuel was a little priest living in God's house.

God was pleased with Hannah for giving her little boy to live in His house. He gave her five more children, three boys and two girls. Hannah was filled with happiness.

Were you listening? Why was Hannah often sad? What did Hannah do in God's house? How did Hannah keep her promise? What made Hannah happy?

God Calls Samuel

Little Samuel lived with Eli in God's house at Shiloh. He was very happy there. Every day he helped Eli, for Eli was an old man. He took care of the lamps. He opened the doors of the church. He read to Eli, for Eli could no longer see to read. Samuel was a good boy and always obeyed Eli.

Eli had two sons who were priests and who helped in God's house. But they were not like Samuel. They did not obey their father, Eli. They did many wicked things. They even forced the people to give them the food which was supposed to be sacrificed to God. The priests were allowed to eat the food after it had been on the altar. But Eli's sons did not like the sacrificed food. They wanted the raw meat. When Eli scolded his sons, they would not listen.

Little Samuel worked in God's house year after year. At night he slept in a little room next to Eli's room. One night, when Samuel was about twelve years old, Eli and Samuel both lay down to sleep. There was a dim light in God's house, for the golden candlestick with its seven lights always burned until dawn. Some time during the night Samuel awoke. He heard a voice calling, "Samuel! Samuel!"

Samuel arose and ran to Eli. "Here I am, Eli," he said. "You called me, didn't you?"

But Eli said, "I didn't call you, my son. Lie down again." So Samuel went back to his bed.

Soon Samuel heard the voice again. "Samuel! Samuel!" it called.

Again Samuel arose and went to Eli. "Here I am, Eli," he said. "You called me, now, didn't you?"

But Eli answered, "I didn't call you, Samuel. Go back to sleep." So Samuel went back to his bed again.

Not long after, Samuel heard the Voice calling a third time, "Samuel! Samuel!"

A third time he ran to Eli and said, "Here I am, Eli. Surely you called me this time."

Then Eli realized that it must be God who was calling Samuel. God had not spoken to any of His children for a great many years. Samuel did not know the Voice of the Lord. So Eli said, "Go and lie down again, Samuel. God must be calling you. If you hear the Voice again, say, 'Speak, Lord, Your servant is listening.'"

Samuel went back to his room once more. He lay in his bed and listened. Soon God called him again. "Samuel! Samuel!" He called. And Samuel saw the Lord standing before him.

Samuel quickly answered, "Speak, Lord, for Your servant is listening."

Then God talked to Samuel about Eli's wicked sons. He said, "I am going to do something terrible in Israel. It will make the ears of everyone who hears it tingle." He told Samuel how He had sent His prophet to Eli to warn him about his wicked sons. And how Eli had done nothing about it. Now both his sons were to be killed. No relative of Eli's would ever be priest again.

After God had gone, Samuel lay in his bed until morning. He kept thinking about God's words. He was afraid to tell Eli. But in the morning, as he was opening the doors of the church, Eli called him.

"Did the Lord call you again last night, my son?" he asked. "What did He tell you?"

Then Samuel told Eli everything God had said. He kept nothing back.

Eli knew that God was right. He said, "It is the Lord. Let Him do as it seemeth good to Him."

Were you listening? Where did Samuel live? What did he hear one night? What did God tell Samuel?

Story 80

The Ark of the Lord Is Stolen

I Samuel 4

Samuel grew to be a man. God was with him and he often spoke to Samuel. All the Israelites knew that Samuel was to be the next priest in God's house.

But Eli's two sons, Hophni and Phinehas, were still terribly wicked. One day the Israelites were fighting the Philistines. When

God helped the Israelites, they always won their wars. But God was angry with them for being so wicked. God was not helping His people that day. The Philistines killed four thousand soldiers from Israel's army.

Then the Israelites got together. "Why isn't Jehovah helping us today?" they said. "Let's send for the Ark of the Lord from the house of God. Then the Lord will be with us. Then we'll win the battle!"

So they sent some soldiers to get the Ark. Now the Ark belonged to God. It was holy. No one was supposed to touch it. It had to stay in the house of God. The soldiers did not ask Eli for the Ark. They knew he would not give it to them. Nor did they ask Samuel. They asked Hophni and Phinehas. And those two wicked sons of Eli carried the Ark for them to the battle-field.

When the two men came into the camp with the Ark, the soldiers shouted with a great shout. And the Philistines said, "What does all that noise mean in the Israelites' camp?" When they found out that the Ark of the Lord was in the camp, they were afraid. "Woe is us," they cried, "for God is come into the camp!"

But God had not come with His Ark that day. He would not help His wicked people. The Philistine soldiers fought extra hard. They won the battle. They killed thirty thousand Israelites. They killed Hophni and Phinehas, too. They took the Ark of the Lord home with them!

When the battle was over, one of the soldiers ran to Shiloh to tell the news. His clothing was torn and there was dirt on his head. This was to show that he had bad news. When the people in Shiloh heard the bad news, they all cried out.

Now Eli was ninety-eight years old. And he was blind. He was sitting on his chair at the door of God's house waiting for news. He knew that his wicked sons had taken the Ark of the Lord out of God's house. When he heard the people cry out, he said, "Why are the people crying?"

The runner hurried to Eli. "I have news of the battle," he called.

"What has happened, my son?" Eli asked.

"We have lost the battle," the man went on. "Many soldiers are dead. Your two sons are killed. And the Philistines have taken the Ark of the Lord!"

Eli was grieved to hear that his people had lost the battle. He was even more grieved to hear that his two sons were dead. But when he heard that God's Ark was gone, his grief was too much. He fell backwards off his chair. The fall broke his neck and he died.

When Phinehas' wife heard that Eli was dead, and that her husband was dead, and that the Ark of the Lord was gone, she died, too. Just before she died, God gave her a new baby boy. She called him "Ichabod," because, she said, "The glory is departed from Israel."

So the words of God to Samuel in the night had come true. And Samuel became the priest in God's house.

> *Were you listening?* Why were the Philistines winning against Israel? Why didn't it help to bring the Ark to the battlefield? What happened at the end of the battle? What happened to Eli?

Story 81

The Ark of the Lord in Philistia
I Samuel 5, 6 and 7

The Philistines had taken the Ark of God. When the battle was over, they brought the Ark home with them. They set the Ark next to their stone god, Dagon. When the people came into the house of their god the following morning, Dagon was lying on his face on the floor in front of the Ark. So they took their god and set him back in his place again.

The next day, when the people came to worship their god, they found Dagon again on the floor in front of the Ark. This time Dagon's head and hands were broken off and were lying in the doorway. Then the people were afraid. They left Dagon's house. Never again did anyone step over the doorsill of Dagon's house.

God did not like it that the Philistines had His Ark. He sent trouble to the Philistines who were living in the city where His

Ark was. The people became sick with bad sores, called tumors. And the grain in the fields was eaten by mice. The people of the city of Ashdod said to the five rulers of the Philistines, "What shall we do with the Ark? We do not want it in our city!"

So they sent the Ark to another city, called Gath. As soon as the Ark came to Gath, God troubled the people of Gath with tumors and mice. Then they sent the Ark to Ekron. And God troubled the people of Ekron.

The people of Ekron called the five rulers of the Philistines. "Don't leave the Ark here," they said. "Send it back to the Israelites before we all get killed!" The Ark had been in the Philistines' country seven months.

The rulers of the Philistines called their wise men to tell them what to do. They were afraid of God. They did not want Him to be angry with them. The priests and magic men said, "Don't send the Ark back empty. By all means send a present along so the Israelites' God will stop troubling us."

So they made five mice out of gold and five golden tumors. They put these gifts in a box. Then they took a new cart and set the Ark and the gift-box on the cart. They took two mother cows and tied them to the cart. They kept the baby calves at home. Then they let the cows go without leading them. The Philistines followed the cart to see what would happen. Ordinarily, mother cows would go straight home to find their calves. But these cows left the land of the Philistines and took the road toward the land of Israel.

The cows were lowing as they went. They did not stop anywhere until they reached Israel. Then the Philistine rulers went back home. They now knew that God had sent them all their troubles. They had done the right thing in sending the Ark back.

When the Ark reached the land of Israel it was reaping time. The people in the fields saw the Ark coming towards them. They shouted for joy. The Levites of that city lifted the Ark down from the cart. They put the Ark and the gift-box on a big stone. Then they offered sacrifices to God. But the men of the city did a most wicked thing. They took the cover off the holy Ark and looked inside! God wanted to show His people, as well as the Philistines, that His Ark was holy and not to be touched. So He killed all the men who had looked into the Ark. There were a great many of them.

The rest of the people were filled with fear. They asked their neighbors from a city close by to come for the Ark. Here the Ark stayed for twenty long years. They kept it in a man's house. His son became a priest so he could take good care of it.

> *Were you listening?* What happened to the Philistines' god, Dagon? How did God punish the Philistines for keeping His Ark? How did they send it back? How did God punish His people for sinning against the Ark?

Story 82

God Gives His People a King

I Samuel 7 and 8

Samuel was the priest in God's house for many years. He was also a judge and a prophet. He was a good leader. He persuaded the Israelites to put away their strange gods and to worship the Lord. Then he gathered all the people together at Mizpeh. He prayed for them, asking God to forgive their sins. The people prayed, too. And they went without food all that day to show God they were really sorry for their sins.

While the Israelites were at Mizpeh, the Philistines came down to fight against them. The Israelites were afraid. They begged Samuel to pray for them. Samuel did. He burned a whole lamb on the altar to show God that now the people were ready to serve Him with their whole hearts. God answered them at once. He sent a bad thunder storm on the Philistines as they were nearing Mizpeh. They turned and fled with the Israelites right after them. This time the Israelites won. The Philistines did not come again to bother the Israelites during all the days of Samuel.

When the battle was over, Samuel set up a monument near Mizpeh to help the people remember how God saved them from the Philistines. It was just twenty years since the Philistines had won against Israel on that very battlefield. At that time they had taken God's Ark. Samuel called the place Ebenezer, which means, "Up to this time God has helped us."

Samuel judged Israel all the days of his life. When he became old, he made his two sons to be the judges. But they were not good as their father had been. They loved money more than they did God. They cheated the people in God's house and were dishonest.

One day the leaders of Israel came to Samuel. They said, "You are old and your sons are wicked. Make us a king like all the other nations have." Samuel was filled with sadness to hear his people asking for a king. "God is your king," he said.

Then Samuel talked to God about a king for Israel. God saw how badly Samuel felt. God said, "My people have not turned away from you, Samuel. They have turned away from Me. All these many years I have been their King, from the day I took them out of Egypt until now. But I'll give them a king if that is what they want. Go talk to the people and warn them about the foolishness of wanting a king."

So Samuel called the people together. "God will give you people a king," he said, "if that is what you want. But do you know what it will be like to have a king? The king will take your sons to drive his chariots and to go to war for him. Some of them will have to work on his farm or be servants in his palace. He will take your daughters to work for him, too. He will also take your fields and your food and your servants and your money. He will take anything he wants, and you will not like it."

But the people would not listen to Samuel. They said, "We still want a king. We want to be like the other nations. We want a king to rule over us. We want a king to go ahead of our armies and fight our battles for us."

Samuel talked with God once more. He told Him all that the people had said.

"All right," God said, "just do as they ask. Make them a king."

So Samuel sent the people home. And he promised to find a king for them.

Were you listening? Who was Israel's king? Why did the Israelites want a new king? What would an earthly king want from the people?

God Sends the New King to Samuel
I Samuel 9 and 10

Once there was a farmer in the land that belonged to the family of Benjamin. His name was Kish. He had a son whose name was Saul. Saul was a fine-looking young man. He was a good man, too. There wasn't another young man in all of Israel like him. And there was no one as tall. Saul was a head taller than any man in Israel!

One day Kish lost some of his animals. His donkeys, called asses, were gone. Kish told his son Saul to take a servant and go out to find them. Saul and his servant hunted everywhere for the donkeys. They went through all the land of Benjamin. They went up on Mount Ephraim and through all the country around it. But they could not find the donkeys anywhere.

Finally Saul said to his servant, "Come, we had better go back home. Soon my father will stop worrying about the donkeys and think we are lost."

The servant answered, "Look, we are now coming to the city where Samuel lives. He is a great prophet. All that he says always happens. Perhaps he can tell us where the donkeys are."

Saul was afraid to go to see the prophet. He had no gift to bring him. But his servant had some money they could give. So they asked some girls at the well where they could find Samuel. They were told that if they hurried they could catch up with him. The people were waiting for him to offer sacrifices for them on the top of the hill.

The two men hurried toward the city. They met Samuel coming towards them. Now Samuel was looking for Saul. God had told him the day before that He was going to send him the man whom He had chosen to be Israel's first king. As Saul came to meet him, God said to Samuel, "This is the man!"

Before Saul had a chance to ask about his father's donkeys, Samuel said, "I have been waiting for you. You must come with me to sacrifice to God. And don't worry about your father's donkeys, they have been found. But are you not the man God has chosen to be Israel's first king?"

Saul was amazed at Samuel's words. "I'm only a farmer of the smallest tribe of Benjamin," he said. "And my father's family is the least of all the families of Benjamin. Why say such things to me?"

But Samuel took Saul and his servant with him to the sacrifice. Saul was given the seat of honor at the dinner. And the food which was meant for Samuel, the priest, was given to him.

When the sacrifice was over, Samuel took Saul and his servant home with him. Saul and Samuel sat together on the roof of Samuel's house. They talked together for a long time. The next morning, at dawn, Samuel called Saul. "Get up," he said, "so I can send you on your way."

Soon the young men were ready. Samuel walked with them to the edge of the city. Just before they parted, Samuel told Saul to send his servant on ahead. When they were alone, he asked Saul to kneel before him. Then Samuel took his horn of oil and poured oil on Saul's head. He kissed Saul and said, "The Lord has anointed you to be king over all His people!"

Then Samuel gave Saul three signs — things that would happen to him on the way — to show him that he had truly been chosen by God to be king. He also told Saul to wait until he came to him in another week. Then he would tell him what he had to do.

So Saul went on. The three signs came true. God gave him a new heart so that he would be fit to be a king. But when Saul reached home, he did not tell anyone that he had been chosen to be Israel's first king.

Were you listening? What kind of a man was Saul? How did Saul happen to come to Samuel? What did Samuel do to Saul? What did God give Saul?

Story 84

Saul Becomes King

I Samuel 10

The people of Israel were still waiting for a king. God had promised them that He would choose a king for them. God had already sent the man He had chosen to visit the old prophet, Samuel. Samuel had poured oil on his head and had anointed him to be the first king of Israel.

But the people had not heard about the anointing. And the young man, Saul, did not tell anyone what had happened. He did not even tell his uncle when he asked what Samuel had said to him.

Then one day Samuel called all the people together again at Mizpeh. The people often gathered at Mizpeh to hear the Word of the Lord. Samuel stood before his people and said,

"Listen to what the Lord has to say to you. He says, 'I brought My people Israel up out of Egypt. I delivered you out of the hand of the Egyptians, and from all your enemies. But this day you have turned your back on your God who Himself saved you out of all your troubles. And you have said to your God, "No, but give us a king.'"

"Come then," Samuel went on, "and show yourselves to the Lord by your tribes. He will choose you a king."

Then the head man of each tribe of the twelve tribes stood

before Samuel. And the Lord chose the tribe of Benjamin. Benjamin was the youngest son of Jacob, you remember. Then all the families of the tribe of Benjamin were asked to come before Samuel. And the family of Kish was chosen. Finally all the sons of Kish were asked to stand before Samuel. And God chose Saul. But when they looked for him, they could not find him.

So they asked the Lord if there was still another man coming. God said, "Look, he is hiding himself among the baggage."

They quickly sent someone to look for Saul. They brought Saul before the people. He stood next to Samuel and all the people looked to see the man God had chosen to be their first king. As you know, Saul was a handsome young man. He stood a head taller than any other man. He was almost a giant. Saul was a good young man, too. He was not proud. He did not think he was good enough to be Israel's first king.

Samuel pointed to Saul and said, "See the man whom the Lord has chosen. Notice that there is none like him among all the people."

The people were pleased with what they saw. They shouted, "God save the king!"

Then Samuel told the people once more what kind of kingdom they were to have. He wrote it all in a big book. He put the book in God's house for safe-keeping. Then Samuel sent all the people away to their own homes. Saul went to his own home in Gibeah.

Were you listening? Whom did God choose for Israel's first king? Why couldn't the people find Saul? What did the people think of their new king?

Story 85

Saul Proves He Is a Good King

I Samuel 11

When Saul left Samuel and the people at Mizpeh, a band of young men followed him to his home in Gibeah. But there were some men who sneered at him as he went. They shouted, "How can this man save us?" They would not treat him as a king. They would not bring him any presents. But Saul said nothing. He went back to work on his father's farm.

One day the Ammonites, who were enemies of Israel, came to

fight against one of Israel's cities. They came to Jabesh-gilead and set up their tents. The men of Jabesh were afraid of the Ammonites. They went to the captain and pleaded with him.

"Make a bargain with us," they said. "If you will promise not to fight with us, we will all be your servants."

The captain answered, "We'll agree with your bargain on one condition. We will do as you say if you will let us take out the right eye of all your men."

The men of Jabesh were horrified. They did not know what to do. "Give us seven days," they said. "During that time we will send to all the men of Israel to see if any one will help us fight. If no man will come to save us, then we will come to you and you can do as you wish."

Then the men of Jabesh sent messengers to Saul. As soon as they came into Gibeah, they told all the people what had happened. The people cried aloud. As Saul came out of the field with his herd of animals, he heard the crying. "What is the matter? Why are you crying?" he asked. And they told him about the men of Jabesh.

Saul was angry at the Ammonites. He took two of his oxen and cut them in pieces. Then he sent messengers to all the cities of Israel. Each messenger took a piece of an ox. He told them to say, "Whoever does not come after Saul and Samuel to fight against the Ammonites, his oxen will be cut in pieces like this one."

The people of Israel listened to Saul's messengers. They all came out to fight. Soon Saul had three hundred thirty thousand soldiers. And they went out to fight against the Ammonites. All day long they fought against the enemy. By night the battle was over. They had killed a great many of the Ammonites. The rest had run away.

Then the people said to Samuel, "Where are those wicked men who sneered at Saul and didn't think he would make a good king? Let's find them and kill them!"

But Saul said, "No one shall be killed today. For the Lord has given us this victory."

Then Samuel called all the people together once more. And

at Gilgal they made Saul their king before the Lord. They brought sacrifices to God. And they honored the king He had chosen for them.

> *Were you listening?* Why did some young men sneer at Saul? What did Saul do for the men of Jabesh-gilead? How did Saul show that he was a good king?

Story 86

Saul Disobeys God

I Samuel 13

Saul was thirty years old when he became king. He was a good king. He helped the Israelites fight their battles. He was humble — he listened to God and did what God told him to do. The people liked their new king. Whenever they saw him they shouted for him. They sang songs about his victories. This made Saul very happy, but it made him proud, too. Pretty soon he thought he could be a good king without God.

After Saul had been king for two years he did a most wicked thing. It all happened because of a war with the Philistines. Saul had chosen three thousand men of Israel to be his soldiers. One thousand of the men, led by Saul's son, Jonathan, were sent to Gibeah. Saul kept two thousand with him in Michmash and in the mount of Bethel.

Jonathan and his men fought against the Philistines and won the battle. Then Saul blew the trumpet throughout all the land to tell the people that Saul had killed the Philistines in battle.

When the rest of the Philistines heard about the battle, they made ready to fight against Saul. They came up with thirty thousand chariots and six thousand horsemen. There were as many soldiers as the sand on the seashore. They came and camped close to Saul's army.

Now the soldiers of Israel were afraid. They ran away to hide. Some hid in the caves, some in the woods. Others hid behind rocks or in cisterns. Some of the men crossed the Jordan river and went to the land of Gad and Gilead. But Saul was still in Gilgal, and the rest of his men followed him trembling.

Samuel had promised Saul that he would join him in Gilgal

in seven days. Samuel planned to burn an offering on the altar to God. Saul waited and waited, but Samuel did not come. Many of Saul's men left him because they were afraid. Finally, Saul told his servants to bring him the burnt-offering and the peace-offerings. And Saul burned the sacrifices on the altar, himself, instead of waiting for Samuel. This was wrong, for the priests were the only ones who were supposed to burn sacrifices on the altar. Saul was not a priest, he was a king.

Saul had just finished the sacrifice when Samuel came. Saul went out to meet him. Samuel said, "What have you done?"

"You didn't come when you promised," Saul answered. "My men were running away from me. The Philistines were almost upon me, and I hadn't asked God for help. So I forced myself to offer the sacrifice."

"You have done foolishly," Samuel said. "And you have not kept the commandment of the Lord your God. God was going to let men from your family be king in Israel forever. But now your kingdom will not last. Since you have disobeyed God, He is going to look for a man after His own heart. He will appoint him to be prince over His people."

Samuel left Saul at Gilgal. He crossed the river Jordan and went to Gibeah. Saul gathered his men together and went out to fight.

Were you listening? What made Saul change from a good king to a bad king? How did Saul disobey God? What was God going to do because of Saul's disobedience?

Story 87

Jonathan's Victory

I Samuel 14

Saul and his son Jonathan were still fighting the Philistines. One day Jonathan and his young armor-bearer went down to the Philistines' camp. They did not tell King Saul that they were going. They crept between two rocky hills. Jonathan said to his armor-bearer, "Let's go fight those Philistines. It may be the Lord will work for us. He can help a few as well as many."

The armor-bearer said, "Do whatever you think is best. I will go with you."

"When the Philistines see us," Jonathan went on, "we'll wait a moment. If they say, 'Stay there until we come to you,' then we won't go to fight them. But if they say, 'Come up to us,' then we'll know that the Lord will give them into our hands."

So the two men crept up the high hill between the rocks. When the Philistines saw them, they shouted, "Come on up and we'll show you something."

Jonathan and his armor-bearer crawled over the rocks. As soon as they reached the Philistines they began killing them. In a short time they had killed twenty soldiers. Then God made the earth around the Philistines' camp tremble and quake. This made the Philistines afraid. They ran, killing each other as they went.

The other Israelites were amazed to see the Philistines disappear so suddenly. Saul looked over his army to see who was missing. He soon noticed that Jonathan and his armor-bearer were gone. Then he knew that it was Jonathan who had gained the victory.

When Saul and his men saw that the Philistines were running away, they all chased after them. Even the men who had been hiding came, too. Then Saul, not wanting to waste any time, made a vow for his men. He said, "Cursed be the man who eats any food today until evening, so that we may win over the Philistines."

The Israelites fought hard all day. No one tasted any food. But during the day they came through a woods, and the trees were filled with honey. No one dared touch the honey even though he was weak from hunger. Jonathan had not heard his father make the vow, so he put the end of his rod in the honey as he passed it. He ate the honey and felt much better.

The soldiers quickly told Jonathan about his father's vow. But Jonathan said, "My father was foolish to make such a vow. Soldiers can fight much better when they have eaten."

When night came, Saul asked God if he should go down to the Philistines' camp by night. But God did not answer him. Then Saul knew that someone must have disobeyed. He said, "Whoever has sinned must die." He asked God to show him who had sinned. When he found out that it was his own son Jonathan, he still said, "He shall surely die!"

But the soldiers would not let Saul kill his own son. They said, "Would you kill Jonathan who won such a great victory for us? O no, not a hair shall fall from his head, for he has wrought with God this day!" So the soldiers rescued Jonathan, and King Saul did not kill him.

Were you listening? What did Jonathan and his armor-bearer do? How did Jonathan sin? Who saved Jonathan from death?

Story 88

Saul Rejected As King

I Samuel 15

Saul was no longer a good king. He often forgot to ask God to show him what to do. When he did ask God, he did not always obey God's words. Saul was still a brave soldier. He won many battles. But he was no longer a happy king. He disobeyed God again and again. God no longer helped him with his wars.

One day Samuel came to King Saul. He said, "God chose you to be king. Now listen to Him. God wants you to go fight the Amalekites. He still remembers how wicked they were when He led His people out of Egypt." (Perhaps you remember how the Amalekites hid along the way when the Israelites passed through the wilderness. All the people who followed along behind were killed. They were too weak and old to keep up with the others. Then, you remember, Moses stood on the mountain holding his hands up to God in prayer, while Joshua fought the Amalekites. All day long Aaron and Hur held Moses' hands up so Joshua could win. At that time God had said that He would some day completely destroy the Amalekites for their wickedness.) "Now," Samuel went on, "God wants you to fight them. Kill all the people and all the animals. Save nothing! And burn the entire city!"

King Saul gathered his army together and went out to fight the Amalekites. There was a great battle and King Saul won against the Amalekites. But he didn't obey God. He did not kill Agag, the king of Amalek. Instead, Saul took him home with him. And Saul saved the best of the sheep and oxen and cows. He burned only that which he did not want. He saved all that which was good.

God saw what King Saul had done. He said to Samuel, "I am sorry I chose Saul to be king. For he has turned his back on Me and does not obey My commandments."

Samuel was grieved to hear God's words. All night he prayed to God. In the morning he went to find King Saul. Saul came out to meet Samuel. He greeted him and said, "Blessed be thou of the Lord. I have done exactly what you told me to do."

"What is it that I hear then?" Samuel asked. "I hear the bleating of sheep and the lowing of oxen. Where does this come from?"

"Oh that," King Saul answered carelessly, "we saved those animals to burn up to God as a sacrifice. My men took them home, but all the rest we have utterly destroyed."

"Do you think God likes sacrifices better than obedience?" Samuel asked. "Behold, to obey is better than sacrifice, and to listen, than the fat of rams! Since you have turned away from God, God is going to turn away from you. You may not be king any longer."

King Saul was sorry when he heard Samuel's words. He cried, "I have sinned! I listened to the people instead of to God. Please forgive me. Come with me so we may sacrifice together."

But Samuel said, "No, I will not go with you because you have turned away from God. God has taken the kingdom away from you!" Then Samuel turned to go away. King Saul took hold of his robe to keep him there, and the robe tore. Samuel cried, "As you tore my robe, so God is going to tear the kingdom away from you! He is going to give it to a neighbor of yours, who is better than you. It will surely happen! God will not change His mind, for He is not as a man!"

King Saul knew that he had sinned greatly. He said, "I know I have sinned, but please honor me before the elders of my people and before Israel. Please come with me for the sacrifice so I may worship the Lord."

So Samuel went with Saul. And Saul worshiped the Lord with a sacrifice. Then Samuel killed the wicked king Agag. When he had finished, he left Saul and went to his home in Ramah. He never came to see King Saul again.

Were you listening? What did Samuel ask King Saul to do? How did King Saul disobey God? What happened to Samuel's robe? What was going to happen to Saul's kingdom?

Story 89

God Chooses a New King

I Samuel 16

Samuel was sorry about King Saul. It made him sad to see what was happening to God's anointed one. One day God came to Samuel. He said, "How long are you going to be sad for King Saul? I don't want him to be king over Israel any longer. Fill your horn with anointing oil and go to Bethlehem to find a new king."

But Samuel said, "I'm afraid to go. If King Saul hears about it, he will kill me."

"Don't be afraid," God answered, "just take a young cow with you and say, 'I am come to sacrifice to the Lord.' Then call Jesse to the sacrifice, and I will show you what you must do. I will tell you which of Jesse's sons to anoint to be the next king of Israel."

Samuel obeyed God. He took oil in the horn which hung at his belt. He took a young cow, called a heifer, and went to Bethlehem. When the old men of Bethlehem saw Samuel coming, they were afraid. "Why have you come?" they asked. "Are you coming peaceably?"

"Yes," Samuel answered, "I am coming peaceably. I have come to sacrifice to the Lord. Come along with me."

Then Samuel called Jesse and his sons to the sacrifice, too. When they had all gathered around the altar, Samuel asked Jesse's sons to walk past him. Eliab, the oldest son, came first. He was a tall, handsome young man. He looked as if he would make a fine king. "Surely, this must be the one God has chosen to be Israel's new king," Samuel thought.

But God whispered to Samuel, "Don't look at the man's face or how tall he is. This isn't the man I have chosen. I do not see as you see. Man looks at the outside, but God looks at the heart."

Next Jesse called Abinadab and made him pass before Samuel. But God didn't choose that son, either. One by one the seven sons of Jesse passed before Samuel. But God didn't choose any of them. "Are these all the sons you have?" Samuel asked Jesse.

"There is still the youngest," Jesse answered, "but he is only a boy. He is out in the fields taking care of the sheep."

"Send someone to get him," Samuel said. "We shall not sacrifice or sit down to eat until he comes."

So Samuel waited until the youngest boy was found. His name was David. When David came, Samuel saw that he was a fine-looking boy. His cheeks were red. He looked healthy and happy. As David came up to Samuel, the Lord said, "Arise and anoint him. For this is the one I have chosen to be Israel's new king."

Then Samuel anointed the boy David before all his brothers. He poured the oil on David's head. And the Spirit of the Lord came into David's heart.

Then they burned the sacrifice on the altar and all sat down to eat. When they had finished eating, David returned to his sheep. Samuel went back home.

Were you listening? Why did Samuel go to Bethlehem? Why didn't God choose the oldest son? What kind of work did David do? Why did God choose David?

The Sweet Singer of Israel

David did not become the king of Israel for many years. After Samuel had anointed him, he went back to the fields to take care of his father's sheep. But now he had a new heart. The Spirit of God lived in his heart and taught him all the things that he should know. As David sat alone with his sheep in the lonely hills of Bethlehem, he thought about his Heavenly Father. He knew that God watched over His people just as he, David, watched over the sheep. One day David wrote a beautiful song about God being his shepherd. It is now a part of our Bible. It is called "The Shepherd Psalm." It is Psalm 23.

> The Lord is my shepherd; I shall not want.
> He maketh me to lie down in green pastures:
> He leadeth me beside the still waters.
> He restoreth my soul:
> He leadeth me in the paths of righteousness for his name's sake.
> Yea, though I walk through the valley of the shadow of death,
> I will fear no evil: for thou art with me;
> Thy rod and thy staff they comfort me.
> Thou preparest a table before me in the presence of my enemies:
> Thou anointest my head with oil; my cup runneth over.
> Surely goodness and mercy shall follow me all the days of my life:
> And I shall dwell in the house of the Lord forever.

David wrote many songs about God. They are called psalms and all are found in the Bible. David could make beautiful music, too. He played on a harp. Whenever the people of Bethlehem came through the fields where David cared for his sheep, they would hear the sweet music David made as he played and sang. Soon other people began to hear about David's lovely music. They called him "The sweet singer of Israel."

While David was taking care of his father's sheep, King Saul was still ruling God's people. But now the Spirit of God was no longer living in Saul's heart. An evil spirit was living there instead. This made King Saul most unhappy. He felt sad and lonely. At times he acted as if he were not in his right mind.

King Saul's servants noticed how changed their master was. They felt sorry for him. They tried to think of something to help him. They said, "Master, an evil spirit is troubling you. Why don't you let us find a young man who can play sweet music on his harp. When you listen to him play, the evil spirit will leave you."

Saul was so unhappy that he was eager to try his servants' suggestion. "Go find a young man," he said, "who can play the harp well. Then bring him to me."

One of the servants said, "When I was visiting the man Jesse in Bethlehem, I noticed that he had a son who could play beautifully. He is a handsome young man, and brave. He would make a fine soldier. He is a good young man, too. The Lord is with him."

King Saul was pleased. He sent messengers to Bethlehem at once. They went to Jesse and said, "King Saul wants your son David who is with the sheep."

Jesse sent for David. He gave him a donkey, loaded down with food and gifts for the king. David went with the servants to King Saul.

David sat at King Saul's feet and played sweet music for him. Soon King Saul felt better. The evil spirit left him for a time. He was well again. King Saul was so pleased with David that he wanted to keep him in the palace. He made him his armor-bearer. An armor-bearer had to go with the king to war. He had to stand close to the king and protect him with a big shield.

King Saul loved David very much. And David was kind and helpful. Whenever Saul's heart was troubled with the evil spirit, David would play his sweet music. Then Saul would feel better again. David stayed in the palace with King Saul for some time. He learned many things about palace life which would help him later on when he became the king. Later David returned to Bethlehem to care for his father's sheep.

Were you listening? Why was David called "the sweet singer of Israel?" Why did David call the Lord his shepherd? Why did David go to the palace to live with King Saul? What is an armor-bearer?

David Kills the Giant

I Samuel 17

King Saul and his soldiers fought against the Philistines many times during his years as king. After David had gone back to Bethlehem, the Philistines came once more to fight with the Israelites. King Saul gathered his soldiers and went out to fight against his old enemy.

The Philistines camped on a mountain. The Israelites camped on another mountain. There was a valley between them. CALLED ELAH One day, one of the Philistine soldiers came down from his mountain and stood in the valley. His name was Goliath. He was a giant. He was almost ten feet tall. He wore a suit of brass BRONZE which weighed one hundred and fifty-seven TWENTY-FIVE pounds! He wore a brass BRONZE helmet on his head. He held a long spear in his hand. An armor-bearer stood in front of him with a huge shield.

This giant stood in the valley and shouted at the Israelites. "Send a man down to fight with me!" he called, "If he can kill me, we shall be your servants. But if I kill him, then you will have to be our servants."

The giant also said many wicked things about God. Every morning and every evening Goliath came into the valley and shouted at the Israelites. King Saul and his soldiers were filled with fear. ELIAB, ABINADAB & SHAMMAH

David's three oldest brothers were fighting along with King Saul. Father Jesse hadn't heard from them for many days. He was worried about them. He sent David with some food and a gift for their captain. He wanted to find out if everything was all right. EPHAH (22 litres) Roasted Grain, 10 loaves of bread & 10 cheeses for the captain.

As soon as David found his brothers, he heard the shouting of that giant, Goliath. "Why doesn't someone kill that wicked giant?" he asked. But the soldiers were afraid of Goliath. No one dared to fight him, even though King Saul had promised great riches and his own daughter as a wife to anyone who no carius. He pay would try.

David's brother, Eliab, heard David's words. He scolded David. "You shouldn't be here," he said. "You had better go home to your sheep."

But David said, "If no one else will fight this giant, I will!"

The soldiers brought David to King Saul. The king said to David, "You cannot fight this giant. You're only a boy!"

David was not afraid. He answered, "When I was taking care of my father's sheep, I killed a lion and a bear. God saved me from the lion and the bear. He'll save me from this wicked giant, too."

Finally, King Saul said, "Go, and the Lord be with you." He wanted to give David his heavy brass [BRONZE] suit and helmet [& SWORD] to wear. But the armor was too big and too heavy for David. So he wore his own shepherd's clothing. He took his staff with him. He also took his slingshot.

Everyone watched as David went slowly down the mountain-side. When he reached the brook in the valley, he stooped and picked up five smooth stones from the water. The giant saw him coming. He shouted, "Am I a dog that you come to me with sticks? Come here and I'll tear you to pieces and throw you to the birds!"

David was not afraid. He said, "You come to me with a sword and a spear and a shield. But I come in the name of the Lord. God is going to give you to me. Then everyone will know there is a God in Israel!"

The giant started toward David. David ran to meet him. As he was running, he put one of the stones in his slingshot and aimed it at the giant. The stone whizzed through the air and struck Goliath in the forehead. Goliath fell on his face. David ran and stood on top of the giant. He pulled out Goliath's sword and cut off the giant's head. When the Philistines saw that their giant was dead, they turned and fled. The Israelites chased after them until they reached their own country. David had helped his people win against their enemies.

Were you listening? Who was Goliath? What did he do? How could young David kill a giant? Why wasn't David afraid?

Saul Tries to Kill David

1 Samuel 18 and 19

King Saul had promised that anyone who killed the Philistine giant could marry his daughter. The man could also have great riches. But King Saul did not keep his promise. When King Saul saw what a brave soldier David was, he made him a captain in his army. But he did not give David his daughter.

David was a good captain. He helped Israel win the war against the Philistines. Whenever King Saul and his soldiers came home from a war, the women would always come out to meet them. They would sing and dance. They would praise Saul for his brave deeds. When King Saul and his soldiers came home from the war with the Philistines, the women sang, "Saul has killed his thousands and David his ten thousands."

King Saul became extremely jealous of David when he heard the women's song. He was afraid the people might want David for their king instead of himself. This made him cross and ill again. The evil spirit came back into his heart.

Before, David had played sweet music for Saul on his harp to make him feel better. Now David played for him again. But this time the music did not help. As David sat playing, King Saul suddenly took his spear and threw it at David. David dodged aside and the spear went into the wall.

After that King Saul sent David back into the army again to fight the Philistines. While David was gone, he gave his older daughter, Merab, to another man. Saul had promised her to David, you remember. But David loved Saul's other daughter, Michal. When King Saul heard about it, he said that David could have her if he killed a hundred Philistines. He did not think David would be able to do this. He thought that David himself would be killed. Then Saul would be rid of him.

David was pleased with the king's plan. He rushed right out to fight. He killed two hundred Philistines instead of one hundred! King Saul was surprised to hear what David had done. Finally he gave his daughter Michal to be David's wife.

One day, after David had won his second battle against the

Philistines, King Saul tried once more to kill him with his spear. David jumped aside again, and the spear went into the wall. Then David went home to Michal's house.

King Saul was still angry with David. He sent his servants to Michal's house. He told them to bring David to the palace so he could kill him. But Michal let David down through a window, and he ran away. When the servants asked for David, she said, "David cannot come. He is sick in bed."

When the servants told King Saul what Michal had said, he sent them back again. "Bring him to me on his bed," he said.

But Michal fooled her father. She had a stone god that looked like a man. She dressed this stone god to look like David. She put it under the blankets in David's bed. The servants picked up bed and all and carried it to King Saul. When King Saul tried to kill David, he found out that it wasn't David at all. He was determined to kill David. But David had fled, and the king could not find him.

Were you listening? Why did King Saul begin to hate David? How did he try to kill David? How did Michal fool her father?

Story 93

David and Jonathan

I Samuel 18, 19 and 20

All the Israelites loved David because he was such a brave soldier. King Saul had loved him too at first. But when he saw that the people loved David better than they did him, he began to hate David. Several times he tried to kill him. Then David had to run away and hide.

King Saul had a son whose name was Jonathan. Jonathan was a great prince and a brave soldier. He wore a fine coat and a beautiful belt. He had a big sword and a bow with many arrows.

Jonathan loved David right from the start. He loved him because he was brave and trusted in God. But David was not a prince. He was only a shepherd boy. He had no fine clothes. Prince Jonathan loved David so much that he gave him his fine coat and belt. He gave him his sword, and his bow and arrows, too. David and Jonathan loved each other like brothers. They promised to be faithful friends as long as they lived.

When Jonathan saw that his father no longer loved David, he warned David of his father's hatred. He pleaded with King Saul for David's life. "Let not my father sin against David," he said. "He has not done you any harm. He has been good to you. He even risked his own life to save you and your people from that wicked giant. Then why should you want to kill him?"

King Saul listened to his son Jonathan. He promised that he would not hurt David. So Jonathan brought David back to the palace. All went well for a time, but soon King Saul was jealous of David again. Once more he tried to kill him. Once more David fled for his life. He went to live with Samuel in Ramah.

King Saul tried several times to capture David while he was with Samuel. But Saul did not succeed. Finally, one day, David came back to see Jonathan. He asked, "What have I done to make your father want to kill me?"

"You will not die," Jonathan answered. "I'll go to my father and find out why he is angry with you. He tells me everything, so why shouldn't he tell me this?"

But David answered, "Your father knows that you love me. He wouldn't tell you if he were going to kill me, lest he make you sad. But truly, Jonathan, there is only a step between me and death."

"Tell me what I can do then," Jonathan said. "I'll do anything you wish."

"Tomorrow is the time of the new moon," David said. "Your father will be expecting me to eat at his table. I'll stay away. If your father asks about me, you tell him I asked you to let me go to my father's family in Bethlehem. Our family has a sacrifice there every year at this time. If your father is angry because I am not at his table, then I will know that it is not safe for me to come back to the palace."

Then David and Jonathan went out in the fields together. They planned a way for Jonathan to tell David how the king felt. "You hide in the field," Jonathan said. "In three days I shall come into the field with a little boy. I shall shoot arrows from my bow.

Then I shall send the boy to get them. If I say, 'Look, the arrows are on this side of you. Go get them,' then you will know that my father is no longer angry. But if I say, 'Look, the arrows are beyond you,' then do not come. For then you will know that my father is angry, and that the Lord wants you to go away.''

So David hid in the fields. Jonathan went to the palace. King Saul was extremely angry when he saw David's empty place at the dinner table. When Jonathan delivered David's message, Saul became still more angry. He shouted at Jonathan, "Why are you friends with David? Don't you know that you can never be king as long as David is alive? Go find him at once, for he shall surely die!"

Jonathan pleaded for his friend, but his father would not listen. He became so angry that he tried to kill his own son. He threw his spear at Jonathan.

The next morning Jonathan went to the fields with a little boy. He shot his arrows far beyond the boy. "Run, get the arrows," he said. "See, they are far beyond you." As the boy went after the arrows, Jonathan called, "Hurry as fast as you can!" When the boy came back with the arrows, he sent him into the city with the bow and arrows.

Then David came out of his hiding place. He talked with Jonathan for a little while. They talked about the promise they had made. They had promised in the name of the Lord that they would always be good to each other and their children. "We shall always remember our promise," Jonathan said. Then they said good-by to each other and Jonathan went home. But David went to hide in a cave. Jonathan always loved David as his best friend.

Were you listening? Who was David's best friend? What did he give David? Why did they have to part? What did they promise each other?

Story 94

Saul Again Tries to Kill David

I Samuel 21, 22 and 23

King Saul was still angry with David. He and his soldiers went to find him so they might kill him.

Several young men had followed David when he left King

Saul. So David and his men went from place to place, hiding from King Saul. One day they came to Nob, where the Tabernacle was. David went to the priest in the Tabernacle to ask for food. He and his men were very hungry. The priest had no food, but there was the shew bread from the table in the Tabernacle. This bread was supposed to be only for the priests, but the priest gave it to David and his men.

David also asked the priest for a sword. The sword which David had taken from the giant, Goliath, was still kept in the Tabernacle. So the priest gave it to David. From the Tabernacle David and his men left and fled to the Philistine city of Gath. David went to the king to ask for protection from King Saul. Some of the Philistines recognized David. They said to the king, "Is not this the man who killed our giant? Did not his people sing, 'Saul has killed his thousands, but David his ten thousands'?"

David was afraid. He did not want the Philistine king to kill him. He thought of a good plan to get away. He made believe that he was a mad-man, even scratching on the doors with his fingers. His trick worked. The Philistine king said, "Look, this man is mad! Why did you bring him to me? What would I do with a mad-man?" So he let David go.

David ran on to another city. There he hid in a cave. When his brothers and his father heard that he was in the cave, they came to see him. About four hundred soldiers came to follow him.

One day David heard that the Philistines were fighting against the city of Keilah. The Philistines were stealing food from Keilah. God told David to go and fight against the Philistines. David's soldiers were afraid, but God promised He would help them win. So David and his men went to fight the Philistines. They had a great victory and saved the people of Keilah.

King Saul soon heard that David was in Keilah. He hurried to Keilah. By the time he got there, David and his men were hiding in a mountain in the wilderness of Ziph. King Saul looked for David every day, but God would not let Saul find him.

King Saul was angry that he could not find David. He scolded his soldiers. "Are you all against me?" he cried. "Can't you help me find David?"

Then one of his men said, "I saw David at the Tabernacle when I was there. And the priest gave him the shew bread from the Tabernacle. He also gave him Goliath's sword."

King Saul sent for all the priests of Nob. He scolded them for helping David. Then he asked his soldiers to kill the priests. But the soldiers refused. Finally, Doeg, the wicked man who had told on David, offered to do it. He killed eighty-five priests and destroyed the entire city of Nob. But one of the priest's sons escaped and went to tell David. David made him one of his soldiers.

One day Jonathan came to David in the wilderness. He came to comfort and strengthen him. "Don't be afraid," he said, "my father will never find you. You will finally be the king over Israel. King Saul, my father, knows it, too."

While David was staying in Ziph, the men of that city told King Saul where David was hiding. Saul hurried to Ziph, but by this time David and his men were in another place. King Saul followed them. He was on one side of the mountain and David was on the other. Just about that time a messenger came to tell King Saul that the Philistines were coming into his land. So King Saul went to fight the Philistines. And David went to hide in En-gedi.

Were you listening? What happened at the Tabernacle in Nob? What did King Saul do when he heard about it? How did David trick the Philistine king? Why couldn't King Saul capture David?

David Saves Saul's Life

Story 95

I Samuel 24

After King Saul had finished fighting the Philistines, he heard that David was hiding in the wilderness of En-gedi. He took three thousand of his best soldiers and went to find David.

When Saul and his men came to En-gedi they stopped at a cave. King Saul went into the cave to sleep for a while. Now David and his men happened to be hiding in this very cave.

David's men saw King Saul come into the cave. They came

and told David. "This is the day," they said, "which the Lord has promised you. Remember He said, 'I will deliver your enemy into your hand so that you may do with him as you like.' "

But David did not kill King Saul. He crept softly up to the sleeping king and cut off part of his robe. Later, he was even sorry that he had done that. He said to his men, "I should not have done this to my master. I cannot hurt him seeing he is the anointed one of the Lord." David's men wanted to kill the king, but David would not let them.

Later King Saul woke up and left the cave. David followed him out of the cave. He cried after Saul, "My lord, the king!" When King Saul turned around, David bowed himself with his face to the ground. Then he said, "Why do you believe men's words when they say David is trying to hurt you? Today the Lord gave you into my hand in the cave. Some of my men wanted me to kill you, but I said, 'I will not hurt my lord, for he is the Lord's anointed.'

"Besides," David went on, "my father, see the skirt of your robe in my hand. I cut it off, and I did not kill you. I am not going to hurt you, so why should you try to kill me?"

King Saul was ashamed of himself when he heard David's words. "Is that your voice, my son David?" he cried. Saul stood before David and wept. "You are a better man than I am, David," Saul went on. "For you have given me good for evil. I have been trying to kill you all this time. And when the Lord gave you the chance to kill me, you did not even do it! If a man finds his enemy, does he let him go free? I know you are going to be the next king of Israel. Please promise me that you'll be kind to my family."

David was happy to promise the king that he would be kind to his family. Then Saul went home. But David did not go with him. He did not trust King Saul. He and his men went once more to hide in En-gedi.

Were you listening? Who came into the cave where David was hiding? What did David do? Why didn't David kill his enemy?

David and Abigail

David and the six hundred men who followed him had been living in the mountains. They were still hiding from King Saul. At one time, they went down to the wilderness of Paran.

Now there was a man in a nearby town whose name was Nabal. His wife's name was Abigail. Abigail was a beautiful woman. She was a good woman, too. She was wise and kind. But her husband was wicked. He was very rich. He had three thousand sheep and a thousand goats.

One day Nabal and his men were shearing sheep in Carmel. David heard that Nabal was in Carmel so he sent ten young men to visit him. He gave them a message for Nabal. When the young men came to Nabal they said, "Our master sends his greetings. When your shepherds were taking care of your sheep in the wilderness, our master protected them. Not one of their sheep was missing. Now our master would like some food for himself and his men. Will you please give us some food?"

But Nabal was cross. "Who is this David?" he asked. "Why should I take food away from my shepherds and give it to strangers? I do not know David and I am not going to give him any food!"

David's men turned away and went back to David. They told him what Nabal had said. David was angry. He made plans at once to go fight this wicked Nabal. He left two hundred of his men with their baggage and he took the other four hundred men with him. Each man took a sword in his belt and rode off to Carmel to find Nabal.

One of Nabal's young shepherds had run to Abigail to tell her what Nabal had done. He said, "David and his men were good to us when we were taking care of our sheep. They protected us and kept us and our sheep from harm. But when they asked your husband for food, he would not give them anything. As soon as David hears about this, he will come with his soldiers to fight us."

Abigail quickly gathered some food together. She took two

hundred loaves of bread, two bottles of wine, some sheep, and corn, raisins, and figs. She put the food on the backs of donkeys and commanded several servants to lead them. Then she followed on her donkey. So they rode out to meet David. But she did not tell Nabal, her husband.

When David and his men reached her, Abigail knelt before David. She bowed herself to the ground and said, "Don't pay any attention to my husband. He's a wicked man. I'm sorry I didn't see your young men when they came. See, I have brought you some food. Please don't go to fight against my husband and his men. When the Lord makes you king, you will be glad you didn't shed blood for nothing."

David was pleased with Abigail's words. He accepted her gifts and sent her home in peace. When Abigail reached home, she found Nabal having a grand feast in his home, as if he were a king. And he was very drunken. So she waited until morning to tell him what she had done. When Nabal heard of his narrow escape, he became so upset that he had a stroke. Ten days later he died.

When David heard that Nabal was dead, he sent for Abigail. She became his wife. David had not lived with his other wife, Michal, for a long time. King Saul had given her to be another man's wife.

Were you listening? What kind of a man was Nabal? What did David's men want from Nabal? What did Abigail do for David? What happened to Abigail after Nabal died?

Story 97

David Again Saves Saul's Life

I Samuel 26

David and his men were still hiding in Ziph. King Saul had promised not to hurt David any more. But he did not keep his promise. One day the men of Ziph went to Gibeah where Saul lived. They told Saul that David was hiding in their city. King Saul chose three thousand of his best soldiers and went out once more to hunt for David.

King Saul and his men soon came to the wilderness where

David was hiding. David saw Saul set up his camp on a hill. David sent out some spies to see if it was really the king. It was. Then David went as close to Saul's camp as he dared. It was night. Everyone in the camp was asleep. King Saul and Abner, his captain, were both lying on the ground in the center of the camp. All the other soldiers were grouped around them. The wagons and the baggage were placed on the outside of the camp to keep them safe. No guard was on duty to protect his king.

David went back to his men. He told them what he had seen. Then he said, "Who will go with me to Saul's camp?"

Abishai said, "I will go down with you."

So David and Abishai crept softly into King Saul's camp. They saw all the soldiers sleeping on the ground. They saw King Saul, too. He was asleep with his spear stuck into the ground near his head.

Abishai whispered to David, "God has given you your enemy this time. Now let me kill him. I'll push his spear through him into the ground. I'll strike him just once!"

But David said, "Don't kill him. For who can hurt God's anointed king, and not be guilty? God will see to it that he gets killed when the right time comes. God forbid that I should touch His anointed. But go, take the king's spear and his bottle of water. Then we'll go back to our camp." THE SPEAR SYMBOLISED ROYAL AUTHORITY

So they took King Saul's spear and his water bottle. Not one of the soldiers saw them or heard them. All King Saul's men were sound asleep. Then David went up to the top of another hill. He stood on the hill and called to King Saul and his soldiers. He called to Abner, the captain, too. "Why don't you answer me, Abner?" he called.

Abner awoke. "Who are you?" he cried. "Who is it that is crying to the king?"

"Aren't you supposed to be a brave captain?" David asked. "You are the best soldier in all of Israel. Then how did it happen that you were not guarding your king? Someone came into your camp a few moments ago to kill your king. You were asleep. You have been a bad soldier, and you should die for this. For you were not protecting your master, the Lord's anointed king. Now look and see where the king's spear is and his bottle of water, which were at his side." Then David held up the spear and the water bottle for Abner to see.

By this time King Saul was awake. He recognized David's voice. "Is that your voice, my son David?" he asked.

"It is my voice, my lord, O king," David answered. "Why are you always chasing after me as if I were a bird which men like to hunt and kill?"

"I have sinned," King Saul said. "Come back, my son David. I will not hurt you any more since you saved my life this day. I have been a fool. I have made a big mistake."

Then David held up the king's spear. "Look," he said, "here is the king's spear. Let one of your young men come to get it. The Lord gave you into my hands today, but I did not hurt you. Even so may my life be saved by the Lord. And may he help me out of all my troubles."

"Blessed art thou, my son, David," King Saul said. "I know you will do great things in your lifetime. And you will win over your enemies."

So David went on his way. And King Saul went back to his home.

Were you listening? Who told King Saul where David was hiding? What did David do while King Saul slept? Why didn't David allow his servant to kill the king?

Story 98

King Saul and the Witch

I Samuel 28

Although King Saul had always been a brave soldier, he had a bad time being king after God turned away from him. Whenever he went out to fight, God would not go with him. Then he would lose the battle. And there were always enemies to fight. The Philistines came again and again to make war on the Israelites. Now King Saul was afraid of the Philistines. He knew that he could not win against them without God's help.

King Saul did not know which way to turn. He did not know whether he should fight against the Philistines or whether he

should give up and let them rule over his people. He asked God what he should do. But God would not answer him. Saul could not ask Samuel to help him, for Samuel had died.

Finally King Saul said to his servants, "Find me a witch. I shall go ask her what to do."

When Saul was a good king, in the early days, he had sent his soldiers out to kill all the witches. Witches were people who worked with Satan and did many bad things. Not all the witches had been killed, however. There was one witch who had hidden in a cave in a place called Endor. The servants knew about this witch. So King Saul and two of his servants went out one night to visit the witch of Endor. They put on old clothing so that no one would recognize them. When they came to the cave, they knocked at the door.

"Who's there?" called the witch.

"We want you to bring back a man from the dead for us," King Saul answered. "Let us in."

"I am afraid," the witch said. "King Saul will hear about it, and he will kill me."

King Saul said, "Nothing will happen to you. I promise."

Then she let them in. "Whom shall I bring back for you?" asked the witch.

"I want to talk with Samuel," King Saul said.

Then the witch called Samuel back from the dead. When she saw Samuel, she was afraid. "Now I know who you are," she said. "You lied to me. You are King Saul."

King Saul said, "Don't be afraid. I won't hurt you. Tell me, what did you see?"

"I see a god coming up out of the earth."

"What does he look like?"

"He is an old man, and he is covered with a robe."

When Saul knew that it was Samuel, he bowed himself to the ground. Samuel said, "Why did you bring me here?"

King Saul answered, "The Philistines are after us, and I do not know what to do. God would not answer me, so I called you."

"If God will not answer you, neither will I. But I'll tell you this. Tomorrow, you and your sons are going to be killed by the Philistines. And God is going to give your kingdom to David."

King Saul fell on the ground. He was filled with fear because of Samuel's words. He was weak because he had not eaten any food all day or all night. The witch came to Saul and begged him to get up and eat. But he would not. Then his two servants and the woman coaxed him again and again. Finally he listened to them. He got up from the floor and sat on the bed.

The woman quickly prepared some food. She gave it to the king and his servants. As soon as they had eaten, they left the cave and went out into the dark night.

Were you listening? Why would not God answer King Saul? Why did King Saul go to the witch? What did Samuel tell him?

Story 99

David at Ziklag

I Samuel 30

David and his men had spent many months hiding from King Saul. They lived in caves in the mountains. For more than a year they lived with the Philistines. David was a friend of one of the lords of the Philistines. His name was Achish. Achish gave the city of Ziklag to David and his men.

While David was living in the land of the Philistines, he went out to fight against his enemies. He killed them all and took away their animals. When Achish saw how well David and his men could fight, he promised to take them with him the next time he went to war.

Soon the Philistines went out to fight against the Israelites once more. David and his men went along. But the princes of the Philistines were angry with Achish for taking David along. They said, "Is not this the David of whom the Israelites sang, 'Saul slew his thousands and David his ten thousands'?" They were afraid David might help the Israelites instead of fight against them. So Achish sent David and his men back to Ziklag.

When David and his men came to Ziklag they found that their enemies, the Amalekites, had burned their city with fire. All their women and children had been taken captive. David and his men sat down and wept until they were too tired to cry any more.

David's two wives were gone, too. But David was having even greater trouble. His men were blaming him for all their grief. They were so angry they wanted to stone David. David knew what to do when trouble came. He asked God to help him. God told him to go chase after the Amalekites. Then he could bring back the women and children.

So David left two hundred men with their baggage. He and the other four hundred men went to find the Amalekites. David's men found an Egyptian boy lying in a field. He had eaten no food nor drunk any water for three days and three nights. The men brought the boy to David. David gave the boy food and water. As soon as the boy felt better, David asked him who he was and where he had come from.

"I am an Egyptian servant boy," he said. "My master is an Amalekite. We just burned Ziklag with fire."

"Can you bring us down to the Amalekites?" David asked.

"Promise me you will not kill me nor give me back to my master. Then I will bring you to their army," the boy answered.

David promised to protect the boy. So the boy showed David where to find the Amalekites. The Amalekites were spread out in a huge camp. They were eating and drinking and dancing. They were having a fine time because they had stolen so many things from Ziklag. David rushed in and began to fight the Amalekites. He fought from one evening until the next evening. He killed most of the soldiers and brought back all of the wives and children. He also found everything the Amalekites had stolen.

When David and the four hundred men came to the other two hundred men, they began to quarrel. Some of them said, "We'll give you your wives and children, but you can't have any of the things we brought back, because you didn't fight."

But David said, "You shall not act that way with the things the Lord has given us. We shall all share alike." So David divided the spoil with all his men. And he sent some of the goods to the elders of his own people in Judah. He sent gifts to all his friends who had been kind to him and his men when they had been hiding from King Saul.

Were you listening? Why couldn't David and his men fight with the Philistines? What happened to Ziklag? What did the Egyptian boy do for David? How did David divide the goods he brought back from the battle?

Story 100

The Death of Saul and Jonathan
I Samuel 31; II Samuel 1; I Chronicles 10

The Philistines were camped in Shunem. Saul's army was camped in the mountains of Gilboa. When the Israelites saw the Philistines coming, they turned and fled. Many of the soldiers were killed on the Mount of Gilboa. The Philistines followed fast after King Saul and his sons. Soon Jonathan and all the other sons of Saul were killed. Because Saul no longer trusted in God, God was no longer with him in battle.

Then the archers hit King Saul and wounded him severely. King Saul knew that he would not live much longer. He said to his armorbearer, "Take your sword and kill me, before the Philistines kill me."

But the armorbearer was afraid to kill his own king. So King Saul took his own sword and fell on it. When the armorbearer saw that King Saul had killed himself, he fell upon his own sword and died with him. So King Saul and his armorbearer and his three sons all died on the same day.

The next morning the Philistines came through the fields to take the swords and possessions from the dead soldiers. They found the bodies of King Saul and his sons, too. They cut off Saul's head and took his armor. The Philistines sent word through all the land to let the people know that their enemy was dead. They put Saul's armor in the house of their god, Ashtaroth. They hung the bodies of Saul and his sons on the wall of one of their cities.

When the men of Jabesh-gilead heard what had happened, they remembered how Saul had helped them when he had first become king. So they crept to the Philistine city at night and rescued the bodies of Saul and his sons. They brought the bodies home to Jabesh. They burned the bodies and buried the bones under a tree in Jabesh. Then they mourned and fasted for seven days.

While Saul and the Israelites had been fighting the Philistines, David and his men had been fighting the Amalekites. Two days after David had come back to Ziklag, a messenger came to him. He was an Amalekite. He had torn his clothing and put dirt on his head to show that he had bad news. He came and bowed himself to the ground in front of David.

"Who are you?" David asked. "Where do you come from?"

"I came from the camp of Israel," the man answered.

"How did the battle go?" David asked.

"The people ran away from the Philistines. Many of the soldiers are dead. And King Saul and his son Jonathan are also dead."

"How do you know that King Saul and Jonathan are dead?" David asked.

"I happened to pass by on the mount Gilboa and I saw King Saul leaning on his sword. He called me and asked me to kill him with his sword because he was in such pain. I knew he could not live with such pain, so I killed him. And see, I have brought you the crown from his head and the bracelet from his arm."

David and all his men tore their clothing and mourned and wept until evening for Saul and Jonathan and for all the people of the Lord because they had lost the battle. Then David asked the messenger how he had dared to kill the Lord's anointed. Now the messenger probably had not killed King Saul. He had found King Saul lying dead in the field. But he had thought that David would be pleased to hear that his enemy was dead. He thought David would give him a wonderful present for killing the king. So he had lied to David. He told David he had killed the king, so he could get a reward.

But the Amalekite did not receive a reward. David was angry with him for saying that he had killed the king. David ordered one of his young men to kill the Amalekite. He said to the messenger, "You have brought this on yourself. Your own words are against you since you have said, 'I have killed the Lord's anointed.'" Then the young man was killed.

David was filled with sadness for King Saul and Jonathan. He made a beautiful song about his two friends who had been such great soldiers. He taught the song to the people of Judah. He never forgot his dear friend Jonathan who loved him better than a brother.

> *Were you listening?* Why couldn't King Saul win against the Philistines? How did King Saul die? What happened to the bodies of King Saul and his sons? What lie did the Amalekite tell David?

Story 101

David Becomes King

II Samuel 2 through 6; I Chronicles 11

When David had finished mourning for King Saul and Jonathan, he asked the Lord what he should do. God told him to go into Judah to the city of Hebron. So David took his two wives and all his men and went to live in Hebron.

It was not long before the men of Judah heard that David was in Hebron. They came at once and anointed David to be king over their entire tribe. They told David that the men of Jabesh-gilead had buried King Saul. David was pleased to hear of their kindness. He sent word to them and praised them for their good deed. He also told them that he would be kind to them seeing he was now the king.

But David was not the king of all the tribes of Israel. It was only the tribe of Judah which had made him king. King Saul's cousin, whose name was Abner, was the captain of Israel's army. As soon as he heard that King Saul was dead, he made one of Saul's sons the king. His name was Ishbosheth. Ishbosheth reigned over Israel for two years.

One day Abner took his army and went out to meet David's army. Joab was David's captain. While they were fighting, one of Joab's brothers, Asahel, went after Israel's captain. Asahel was a swift runner. He could run like a deer. He followed Abner for a long time. Abner asked him several times to stop following him, but he would not. So Abner took his spear and killed him.

But Joab and David's soldiers finally won. When they counted their soldiers after the battle, they found that David had lost only nineteen men. But Abner had lost three hundred and sixty men. Although the battle was over, Joab and Abner were at war with each other for a long time. David's army kept getting stronger and stronger, but Abner's army became weaker and weaker.

One day Abner and Ishbosheth had a quarrel. Abner decided not to be friends with Saul's son any longer. He sent messengers to David. He wanted to make friends with David instead.

Joab, David's captain, did not like it that Abner was to be friends with David. Without telling David, he sent for Abner. He made believe that he wanted to talk with Abner. But when Abner came, Joab killed him.

David was sorry to hear that Joab had killed Abner. He went to Abner's funeral and stood at the grave and wept. So all the people knew that it was not David's fault that Abner had been killed.

Ishbosheth was still the king of Israel, but he was a weak king without his captain Abner. One day while Ishbosheth was resting on his bed at noon, two men came into his palace. They said they were coming to get food for the soldiers. But they went into the king's bedroom and killed him, thinking David would be happy to have him dead. But David was horrified at the wicked thing they had done. He commanded his soldiers to kill the men at once.

Then all the tribes of Israel came and asked David to be their king. So David became king over all the tribes of Israel, just as God had promised. He was thirty years old when he became the king.

Were you listening? Why didn't David become king of all Israel as soon as Saul died? What happened to Abner? What happened to Saul's son, Ishbosheth? How old was David when he became king over all of Israel?

David Brings the Ark to Jerusalem

II Samuel 6; I Chronicles 13 and 15

Perhaps you remember how Eli's two wicked sons, Hophni and Phinehas, took the gold box, called The Ark of the Lord, out of the Tabernacle. They brought it to the battlefield when the Israelites were fighting against the Philistines. But the Israelites lost that battle, and the Philistines stole the Ark.

The Ark was kept in the Philistines' country for seven months. But God punished the Philistines for keeping His Ark. So they finally sent it back to Israel. But the Ark never got back to Shiloh. The Philistines had completely destroyed Shiloh. They had killed all the priests except Samuel. The Ark stayed in Gibeah at the home of a priest whose name was Abinadab. The Ark was in Abinadab's home for almost eighty years.

Not long after David became king of all Israel, he called his leaders together. There were thirty thousand of them. They went down to Gibeah to bring back the Ark of the Lord. They set the Ark on a new cart. Abinadab's two sons, Uzzah and Ahio, drove the cart. King David and all his men walked along with the Ark, playing music to God. They had harps and timbrels and cornets and many other musical instruments.

As they were walking along, they came to a threshing-floor. The oxen stumbled, and the cart shook. Uzzah was afraid the Ark was going to fall. He took hold of it with his hands. Uzzah should have known better. God did not want Uzzah to touch His Ark. It was too holy. The priests had been taught that the Ark was never to be touched. God punished Uzzah for his sin. He died at once, there beside the Ark.

When King David saw what had happened, he was afraid to take the Ark any farther. He brought it into the house of Obed-edom, who belonged to the family of men who had carried the Ark through the wilderness. Then David and his men went back home.

The Ark stayed in the house of Obed-edom for three months. He took good care of God's Ark, and God blessed him. When David heard that God had blessed Obed-edom, he decided to try

again. Once more King David and his chosen men took their
musical instruments and went up after the Ark. After they had
gone a little way, David made a sacrifice to God. And he danced
before the Lord with all his might.

When they reached Jerusalem, they carried the Ark into the
tent which David had prepared for it. They offered burnt-offerings and peace-offerings before the Lord. Then David turned
and blessed all the people, in the name of the Lord. And he gave
them each a piece of bread, a piece of meat, and some wine.
The people were filled with gladness and King David was happy
to have the Ark of the Lord with him in Jerusalem.

> *Were you listening?* What happened to Uzzah? Where was the Ark
> finally taken?

Story 103

David Plans to Build a House for God

II Samuel 7; I Chronicles 17 and 22

King David lived in a beautiful palace. It was built on Mount
Zion, in Jerusalem. One day as David was sitting in his palace,
he was thinking about his beautiful home. Suddenly, he remembered that his God did not have a beautiful home. The Ark of
the Lord, which was the place where God dwelt," was still in
the tent David had made for it. *The Ark of the Covenant was a large wooden box covered with gold.*

So David spoke to Nathan, the prophet, about it. "Look," he
said, "I live in a beautiful home made out of expensive cedar
wood. My God lives in a tent. I would like to make a house for
God. I would like to make a beautiful temple."

Nathan thought David's idea was fine. "Do all that is in your
heart," he said, "for God is with you."

But that night, after Nathan had gone home, God came to
him. He said, "Nathan, I want you to go back to my servant
David. Tell him that I do not want him to build me a house.
I have not lived in a house since the day I brought Israel out of
Egypt. I have lived in one tent after another. Tell David that
I took care of him and helped him all these years. Now it shall
be that when David is no longer king, I shall make his son a

It was the sign that God was with his people & guiding them king after him. He shall build me a house. And I will establish his throne for ever and ever. I will be his father and he shall be my son."

So Nathan went back to King David and told him all the things which God had said.

And although King David was not allowed to build God's house, he did make all the plans. He chose the spot where it was to be built. It was the threshing-floor of Ornan, where David had once built an altar to God. God had accepted David's offering by sending fire from heaven to burn it up. The threshing-floor was on Mount Moriah. This mount was just across from Mount Zion where David's palace stood.

David also hired some masons to cut stones for the temple. He gathered iron and brass. He gathered a great many cedar trees from the mountains of Lebanon. He collected gold and silver in huge amounts. Finally after many years, he had an abundance of everything. Then David drew up the plans for the temple. He remembered each small detail, for he said, "My son Solomon is very young. This house which is to be built for God must be exceedingly great."

When everything was ready, David called Solomon to him. "My son," he said, "I wanted to build God a house. But God said to me, 'You have been in too many wars. You have shed too much blood. There has been too much blood on your hands, you must not build my house. But your son Solomon, he shall build my house.'"

Then David showed Solomon all his plans and gave him all the things he had gathered. He gave him a hundred thousand talents of gold, a hundred thousand talents of silver, so much brass and iron that it could not be weighed, and all the necessary wood and stone. Then David blessed Solomon. He said, "Seek the Lord, and build his house." And David commanded all the princes of Israel to help his son Solomon build the temple.

Were you listening? What did David want to do for God? Why didn't God want David to do this? Who was to build the temple? How did David help?

The Little Lame Prince

II Samuel 4 and 9

When King Saul was still living, his grandson, Mephibosheth, was a prince. He lived in the palace with his father, Jonathan, and grandfather. Mephibosheth was just five years old when Jonathan and King Saul were killed in battle. His nurse was taking care of him in the palace. A messenger came one day from the battlefield. He brought the news that both King Saul and Jonathan had been killed. When the nurse heard the sad news, she was afraid the enemy might come into the palace to kill the little prince, too. So she took the little boy in her arms and ran away with him. But in her hurry, she dropped him and the little boy's feet were both badly hurt. The little prince never walked again.

When King David found out that one of Jonathan's sons still lived, he sent a messenger for the lame prince, who was now a grown man. Mephibosheth was afraid, thinking that David meant to kill him. As soon as he came to the palace, he fell down on his face at King David's feet. He cried, "Behold, thy servant!"

"Don't be afraid," King David said. "I will surely be kind to you for your father Jonathan's sake. You shall eat at my table

he was looked after by a rich farmer called Makir who lived in Lo Debar

in my palace every day as if you were my son. And I will give you all the land which belonged to your grandfather, King Saul."

So from that day on Mephibosheth, the lame prince who could not walk, lived in a king's palace again and ate at the king's table.

> *Were you listening?* What was one of the first things King David did after he became king? Who was Mephibosheth? How did he become lame? What did King David do for the lame prince?

Story 105

The Little Ewe Lamb

II Samuel 11 and 12

David was a good king. He was the best king Israel ever had. He loved God and usually tried hard to obey Him. God loved David, too. God said David was a man after His own heart. But David was not always good, just as you and I are not always good.

After David and Joab had finished fighting the Ammonites and all their helpers, they had come home from the wars. For the rest of the year they did not go out to fight. But when springtime came David sent his captain Joab and all the soldiers to fight against the Ammonites again. But David did not go with Joab and the army. He stayed at home in Jerusalem.

One night King David could not sleep. He got up from his bed and walked around on the roof of his house. While David was up on his roof he saw a most beautiful woman. David wanted this beautiful woman for his wife. Now King David had a wife of his own. In fact, he had more than one wife. Besides, this woman was someone else's wife. She belonged to Uriah who was one of the brave soldiers in David's army.

To be rid of Uriah, David planned another wicked thing. He sent a letter to his captain Joab. "Put Uriah in the front row of the battle so he will be killed," the letter said. So Joab put Uriah in the front row, and soon Uriah was killed. Then Joab sent word to King David. Then David thought, "Now Bath-sheba is mine."

King David thought that no one knew what he had done. He forgot that God sees everything we do. One day as David was sitting in his palace, God sent the prophet Nathan to him. Nathan came to talk to David. He told David a story. He said,

"There was once a very rich man who lived next door to a very poor man. The rich man had a beautiful home and a lovely big farm. He had many cows and sheep and lambs. The rich man had everything he wanted. But the poor man had nothing at all. He and his wife and his children lived in a tiny little house. They had no farm. They had no animals. All they had was one little lamb. This little lamb was the children's pet. She ate from their table and slept in their house. The whole family loved the little lamb.

"One day the rich man had a visitor in his home. He thought it would be fine to kill a lamb to serve to his guest at dinner. But he did not take any of his lambs to kill for the dinner. No, he went to his poor neighbor and took their little pet ewe lamb and killed it for his guest."

When King David heard what the rich man had done, he was filled with anger. "As the Lord liveth," he cried, "this man shall surely die! And he shall give the poor man four of his lambs for the little pet lamb he killed!"

Then Nathan pointed at David and said, "You are the man! God sent me here to tell you this story. God gave you everything you wanted. And He let you be king over His people. And what did you do? You didn't steal a lamb, you stole another man's wife. And you didn't kill a lamb, you killed a man. Now God is going to punish you. You will always have trouble in your family. And the little baby God gave Bath-sheba and you will die."

King David was sorry for what he had done. "I have sinned against God," he said.

"God will forgive you," Nathan answered. "But He will punish you."

Not long after this, the little baby did become very sick. David did not eat nor sleep for seven days. He just knelt before God and prayed. But the baby died, as God had said. Later God gave David and Bath-sheba a new baby. They called him Solomon. God loved Solomon and promised that some day he would be the next king.

Were you listening? What did King David do one night when he should have been fighting? What two wicked things did David do? What story did Nathan tell David? What wicked thing did the rich man in the story do?

Trouble in the King's Palace

After David had sinned against God, when he stole Bath-sheba and had Uriah killed, there was always much trouble in the king's palace. David had many children. His oldest son was called Ammon. One of his other sons was called Absalom. Absalom was a handsome young man with beautiful, thick, long hair. Once every year he had it cut. And the hair that was cut weighed six pounds. Absalom wore fine clothing and rode in a splendid chariot with fifty men to run ahead of him. The people all loved Absalom and David loved him more than all his other children.

Absalom did not really love his father, however. He wanted to be king instead of his father, so he told lies to all the people. One day Absalom asked King David to let him go away from the palace. He said he wanted to go to Hebron to worship God and burn a sacrifice. But that is not what he did. He went to a place where his father could not see what he was doing. He called many soldiers to come to him until he had a big army. He said to the soldiers, "As soon as you hear the trumpet you must shout, 'Absalom is king.'" Absalom was planning to go to Jerusalem and take his father prisoner.

King David was at home in his palace. He did not know what Absalom was going to do. But a messenger came running to the palace. "Absalom has made himself king," he said, "and the people are following him!"

David was not ready to fight. He immediately made plans to run away. Soon David and all his servants and many of his people left Jerusalem. They crossed the Brook Kidron and went into the wilderness. The priest and his two sons and all the Levites who worked in the church came too. And they carried the Ark of God with them. But David told them to bring the Ark back to Jerusalem where it belonged.

David and his people climbed the Mount of Olives. They walked barefoot. They covered their heads and cried as they went.

All the people who saw them go cried too. What a sad day that was! How unhappy David was. He was running away from his favorite son, Absalom! When they came to the top of the mount, someone told David that Ahithophel, one of his best men, had joined with Absalom. That was another sad disappointment. Soon his other chief helper, Hushai, came to meet him. His coat was torn and he had put dirt on his head to show how sad he was for his king. David was happy to see him. But he sent him back to Jerusalem.

"Go tell Absalom you will be his servant as you are mine," David told him. "Then you can spy on Absalom and find out what he is doing. If you have any news for me, you can send the priests' sons to tell me." So Hushai went back to Jerusalem.

David and his men went on beyond the Mount of Olives. Soon they met Ziba. Ziba was the servant of King Saul who was taking care of Saul's land for the lame prince, Mephibosheth. Ziba brought David some bread and raisins and fruit, and a bottle of wine. This food was loaded on the backs of several donkeys. "These are all for the king," he said.

"Where is your master, Mephibosheth?" David asked.

Ziba lied to David. He said, "Mephibosheth stayed in Jerusalem. He says the people are going to make him king and give him back the kingdom of his grandfather Saul."

"If that is true," David said, "then I shall give you all the land of Saul which I had given to Mephibosheth."

Not long after this, as David and his people went on with their journey, a relative of King Saul met them. His name was Shimei. He stood across from the king on a hill. He threw stones at David and cursed him. "You wicked man," he shouted. "God is punishing you for taking the kingdom away from Saul. Be gone, be gone, you bloody man! You son of the devil!"

One of David's generals wanted to go over and kill Shimei. "Let me go and cut his head off," he said. "Why should this dead dog curse my lord the king?"

But David shook his head sadly. "No," he said, "leave him

alone. If my own son whom I loved wants to kill me, why shouldn't this man?"

So David's life was filled with sorrow.

> *Were you listening?* Why did David have trouble in his family? Why did David have to run away from Jerusalem? What great troubles did he meet on the way?

Story 107

A King's Son Dies

II Samuel 17, 18 and 19

When David's helper, Hushai, went back to Absalom, Absalom was surprised. But he did not guess that he was a spy. He made Hushai one of his head men. Both Ahithophel and Hushai tried to help Absalom plan his war against David. Hushai purposely gave Absalom bad advice. But Absalom thought it was good advice. When he listened to Hushai instead of to Ahithophel, Ahithophel became angry. He left Absalom. He went home and hanged himself.

Then Hushai was Absalom's only helper. He told Absalom exactly how to go against David. Then he sent the priests' sons to warn David. By this time more and more of the people had gone to be with David. So David had a large army. He sent his army out to fight against Absalom. But David still loved Absalom. Before the army went out to fight, he said to the soldiers, "Don't hurt my son, Absalom."

The two armies met in the woods. David's soldiers soon won the battle. When Absalom saw that he was losing, he tried to run away. He was riding on a mule. He urged his mule to go faster. Just then, the mule ran under a low-hanging tree. Absalom's head caught in a thick branch. His long hair wound itself around the branch. And the mule ran on from under him. There Absalom hung in the tree.

Soon one of David's soldiers saw Absalom hanging there. He quickly ran to tell his captain. Joab said, "Why didn't you kill him?"

The soldier answered, "Even if you gave me a thousand pieces of silver, I would not have killed Absalom. For he is the king's son, and I heard the king say, 'Do not hurt my son.'"

Then Joab went himself. He took three darts in his hand. He threw the darts into Absalom's heart and killed him as he hung there in the oak tree. Then Joab blew his trumpet and called all his soldiers together.

The battle was over. Joab sent two messengers to bring the news to David. When David saw them coming he thought it must be good news. But when he heard that his son Absalom was dead, he was filled with sorrow. He went up to his room. He cried and cried. He would not be comforted. He said, "O Absalom, my son, my son, would to God I had died instead of thee."

But God had punished the boy who did not honor his father.

The soldiers were coming back from the battle. They were filled with happiness to know that their king, whom they loved, could now come back to his palace. But when they drew near and heard David crying for his son, their happiness was turned to sadness.

Joab, the captain, ran to David. "You have hurt all your soldiers," he said. "They saved your life and the lives of all your family. It looks as if you love your enemies and hate your friends. If Absalom had lived and all the rest of us had died, then you would have been pleased. Come now, go speak to your people. Show them you are happy to come back to your palace. If you don't speak to them tonight, your people will all leave you."

So King David went and sat outside. The people all came to greet him. As soon as the Israelites heard that Absalom was dead, they came out to bring their king back to Jerusalem. They sent ferry boats to take David and all his followers across the river Jordan. The people shouted with joy as they saw their king coming back to them.

The first man to meet David on the other side of the river was Shimei, the man who had cursed him. He came with a thousand men. He fell at David's feet and begged him to forgive him for the terrible thing he had done. And David forgave him.

Mephibosheth, the lame prince, also came to meet David. He had not washed nor shaved himself all the while David had been gone. David said to him, "Why didn't you go out with me to fight, Mephibosheth?"

Mephibosheth answered, "Because my servant lied to me. He told me he was getting my mule ready and would ride with me, seeing I am lame. But he went without me and told lies about me to my lord the king. But my lord is as kind as an angel. Do with me as you will."

David forgave Mephibosheth, too. He had given Ziba all of Saul's land, you remember. Now he told Mephibosheth to divide the land with Ziba. But Mephibosheth was kind and unselfish like his father Jonathan. He said, "Let Ziba have all the land. It is enough for me to know that my king has come back to his palace in peace."

So David was king once more in Jerusalem.

> *Were you listening?* What happened to Ahithophel? What happened to Absalom? Why did Joab scold King David? Who came out to meet David as he returned to Jerusalem?

Story 108

Solomon Becomes King

I Kings 1; I Chronicles 23

David was the king of Israel for forty years. Finally David became too old to be a king and to rule his people. He spent most of his time in bed. One day one of David's sons, Adonijah, said to the people, "Now I shall be the king!" He got some chariots and some horsemen. He chose fifty men to run ahead of his chariot. Then he killed some sheep and oxen and cattle, and called all his brothers and his father's servants to a big feast. But he did not invite Nathan, the prophet. Nor did he invite his brother Solomon. Solomon was the youngest son of David. God had promised that Solomon was to be the next king.

When King David heard what Adonijah had done, he did nothing about it. Then Nathan, the prophet, went to Bath-sheba, Solomon's mother. He said to Bath-sheba, "Have you heard that Adonijah is reigning as king instead of David? Now you go to David and say to him, 'O king, didn't you promise me that you would make Solomon king? Why then is Adonijah reigning?' Then while you are talking, I will come in also."

So Bath-sheba went to see King David. She bowed before the king and said, "My lord, you promised me that my son, Solomon, would be the king to sit on your throne. And now Adonijah is reigning. He has made a great feast, but he didn't invite Solomon."

While Bath-sheba was still talking, Nathan came in. He bowed before David and said, "O king, did you say that Adonijah should sit at your throne? Behold the people are eating and drinking. And they are shouting, 'God save King Adonijah!'"

Then David said to Bath-sheba, "Surely your son Solomon shall sit on my throne this day!" He gave orders to Nathan, the prophet, and to Zadok, the priest, to have Solomon anointed king that very day.

Zadok and Nathan put Solomon on David's own mule and took him down to Gihon, which was a fountain near Jerusalem. They took a great many people with them. Zadok took his horn of oil out of the Tabernacle and anointed Solomon to be king. They blew the trumpet, and all the people shouted, "God save King Solomon!" The people were so happy that their shouts could be heard for miles around.

Adonijah and his men heard the shouting, too, as they were feasting. They wondered what all the noise was about. As they were listening, the priest's son came up. Adonijah quickly asked the young man to come in, for he thought he would bring good news. But the young man said, "Our lord, the king, has made Solomon king in his place. Zadok and Nathan have anointed him in Gihon. Now they have come back shouting with joy. That is what you have heard."

Then all the guests at Adonijah's feast were afraid. They quickly left the feast and went to their own homes. Adonijah was also afraid. He went to the Tabernacle and caught hold of the horns on the altar. He thought he would be safe there. Soon someone brought the news to Solomon. He said, "Adonijah is afraid of you. He is hanging on the horns of the altar."

Solomon's men wanted to go to the altar and kill Adonijah as he hung there. But the new king said, "If he shows himself to be a good man, no hair of his head shall be hurt. But if he proves to be wicked, he shall be killed." So King Solomon sent his men to take Adonijah down from the altar. Adonijah came and bowed himself before King Solomon. Then Solomon sent him home.

Were you listening? Who was supposed to be the king after David? What did Adonijah do? What did David do then? Why didn't Solomon kill Adonijah?

Story 109

Solomon's Wise Choice

I Kings 2 and 3; I Chronicles 22 and 28; II Chronicles 1

David was now an old man. He had been king for forty years. His work was almost finished. Solomon, his youngest son, was to be the king in his stead. One day, not long before he died, David called a meeting of all the leaders of Israel. He stood before his men and said, "The Lord has chosen my son Solomon to be your new king. And as you all remember, I had it in my heart to build a house for my God. But the Lord said to me, 'You shall not build Me a house. You have been a man of war, and you have had the blood of soldiers on your hands many times. But Solomon, your son, he will build My house and My courts. For I have chosen him to be My son, and I will be his father.'"

Then David urged his men to help the new king. "Don't forget to keep all the commandments of the Lord," he said. "Then you and your children will be able to live in this land forever."

Finally, David turned to his son, Solomon. "And you, Solomon, my son," he said, "know the God of your father. Serve Him with a perfect heart and a willing mind. For the Lord knows all the thoughts of your mind. If you come to Him, He will be your God. But if you turn away from Him, He will cast you off forever." Then, he added, "The Lord be with you, my son. May He give you wisdom and understanding so that you may rule His people well."

Then David gave Solomon the plans which he had made for the building of the temple. He told Solomon about all the materials he had gathered — the gold and the silver, the iron and the brass, the cedar trees and the stones which the masons had cut. David turned once more to the people and said, "God has chosen my son to be the king, but he is still very young. It is a great and difficult task to build a house for the Lord God. I have done all that I could to help him. I have gathered much material for him. Now who will help him build the Lord's house? And who will bring a gift unto the Lord?"

All the people were glad to help. They brought their gold and silver and iron until there was a huge amount. Together with David's share they collected more than two billion dollars worth of material. King David was happy to see the people give so willingly and so generously. The people were filled with joy, too. They all praised the Lord together and worshiped Him for all His goodness. Then they celebrated with a big feast. It was truly a happy time for all.

They placed Solomon in front of all the people and crowned him king for the second time. Solomon promised that he would always keep the commandments of the Lord. Then Solomon and all the people went up to Gibeon where the Tabernacle was. Together they made a great sacrifice. They offered a thousand burnt offerings to God.

That night God came to Solomon in a dream. He said, "Solomon, you may ask Me for anything you wish."

The young king might have asked for many things. He might

have asked for riches and honor and long life. But he did not ask for any of these things. He said, "Dear Lord, You have made me king instead of my father. I feel as if I am only a child. I do not know how to be a good king over so many people. Make me wise and good so that I shall be a good king like my father, David. Then I shall be able to rule Thy great people well."

The Lord was pleased with Solomon's choice. He said, "You did not ask for riches or long life, or for the life of your enemies. You have asked for wisdom instead. I will make you a wise and a good king. I will make you so wise that there will never be another king as wise as you are. I will make you the richest king that ever lived. I will give you great honor. And if you will obey Me, I will give you a long and happy life."

Were you listening? Who became king when David was too old? What did David and Solomon plan to do? Why were the people so happy? What did Solomon ask for in his dream?

Story 110

Solomon's Great Kingdom

I Kings 3, 4 and 10; II Chronicles 8 and 9

Solomon spoke three thousand wise sayings. He composed more than a thousand songs. Three of the books of our Bible were written by him. His writings show that he knew a great deal about all the wonderful things in nature. He wrote about trees and birds and animals. People came from all over the world to listen to the wise words of this great king.

Although Solomon was such a great king, he was willing to help anyone who came to him. One day two women came to see King Solomon. They had quarreled. The one woman carried a baby in her arms. The other woman wanted to get the baby away from her.

The woman without the baby said, "O my lord, please make this woman give me my baby. We live together in the same house. One day I got a new baby. Three days later she got a baby, too. Last night her baby died because she lay on it in her sleep. But at midnight she awoke and noticed that her baby was dead. She came quietly to my bed and took my son out of my bed while I was sleeping. She left her dead baby in my bed with me. This morning when I awoke I picked up my son so I could feed him. He was dead! Then I looked closely and saw that it wasn't my son at all. It was her baby. And she had my baby in bed with her."

The other woman shouted, "Don't listen to her, O king. The living son is my son, and the dead baby is hers!"

"No," the first woman cried, "you are lying! The dead baby is yours, and the living baby is mine!"

So they quarreled before the king. How was the king to know who was the real mother of the baby? But King Solomon was wise. He said to the women, "You both say that the living baby is yours." Then he turned to his soldiers. "Bring me a sword," he commanded.

When they brought the sword, he said, "Divide the living baby in two. Give half to the one mother and half to the other."

As the soldier started to obey the king, the real mother screamed, "O my lord, give her the living baby! Don't kill it!"

But the other woman said, "That's a good idea. Give us each half."

King Solomon knew at once who the real mother was. "Give the baby to the first woman," he said. "She is his mother." So the live baby was given back to his mother who loved him.

Soon all Israel heard about King Solomon's wise decision. They said, "You can see that the wisdom of God is in him."

King Solomon reigned for many years. There was no war during his reign. The people lived in peace and happiness. Not only did God bless the people, He blessed Solomon, too. He gave Solomon great riches and honor. Solomon lived in a beautiful new palace. He wore fine clothing and a golden crown. He sat on a golden throne. He owned many wonderful things.

One day the Queen of Sheba came to visit King Solomon. She had heard about the great wisdom and riches of this wonderful king. She wanted to see if what she had heard was true. She asked King Solomon many hard questions. And he answered them all! Then he showed her all his wonderful treasures. He gave her a fine dinner in his palace. He took her with him as he went into the House of the Lord.

Finally the Queen said, "I did not believe all the things I had heard about you. But now I have seen with my own eyes. They didn't tell me half of it! Your wisdom and your riches are much greater than anyone has said! How happy your men and your servants must be to continually hear your great wisdom! Blessed be the Lord your God who loves you and made you Israel's king."

Then the Queen of Sheba gave King Solomon a great many rich gifts — gold and spices and precious stones. And Solomon gave her all the things she wanted from his treasures. After that, the Queen went back to her own country.

> *Were you listening?* How many books of the Bible did King Solomon write? How did King Solomon find out who the real mother of the live baby was? Who came to visit the great king? What did she say about him?

Story 111

Solomon Builds the Lord's House

I Kings 6, 8 and 9; II Chronicles 2 through 7

The work of building the temple was now begun. David had made the plans, you remember, and had helped Solomon gather all the materials. Now Solomon sent a letter to an old friend of his father's. He was Hiram, the king of Tyre. Solomon told Hiram about the plans he and his father had made to build a great temple for their God. He asked Hiram to send him some of the great cedar trees which grew in the mountains of Lebanon. He promised to pay for the wood by sending food—wheat, barley, wine and oil.

King Hiram was more than willing to help David's son. While Hiram's men cut the trees, King Solomon had other men cut the stones for the foundation of the building. When all the materials were ready, they were to be brought to Jerusalem. The building of the temple was such a great task that it took thousands of men to do the work. And it took seven years before it was finished. Every part of the temple was fitted together without using a hammer or nail. The entire building was covered with pure gold, both inside and out. The walls and the doors were decorated with angels and palm trees and flowers.

The temple stood on the top of Mount Moriah, the spot David had chosen for it many years before. It was on Mount Moriah that

King David had met an angel. And there he had built an altar to God. The great altar of the new temple was built on the same spot. There was a Holy Place and a Holy of Holies, just as in the Tabernacle. But they were larger.

A beautiful curtain hung in front of the Holy of Holies. It was made of fine linen of many colors. Cherubim were embroidered on it. *The holy place could only be entered by Priest, and the Holy of Holies only once a year by High Priest*

There was a large basin made of brass for the priests to wash in. It was held up by twelve brass oxen. There were ten smaller basins, or lavers, for the washing of the animals to be sacrificed.

Ten golden candlesticks gave light for the temple. Hiram made hundreds of golden basins and spoons and censers and bowls and snuffers. All these were to be used in the temple.

Solomon also had two huge pillars of brass made to stand in front of the temple. The pillars were decorated with wreaths of chain work and with lilies and pomegranates, all made out of brass.

There were two large yards outside the Temple. They were called courts. Only the priests were allowed to go into the inside court and into the rooms of the Temple. The Israelites were the only people who were allowed in the outer court.

The great Temple was finally finished. Thirty thousand Israelites and one hundred and fifty thousand Canaanites had worked on it. It was the most expensive and the most magnificent building on the whole earth at that time. As soon as the Temple was finished, King Solomon had the Ark of God brought into the Holy of Holies. *Ark of Covenant contained the stone tablets with 10 commandments written on them.* As soon as the Ark was brought in, the Pillar of Cloud which had led the Israelites through the wilderness, filled the Temple. The people remembered how the cloud had filled the Tabernacle in the olden days. Now they knew that God was pleased with the beautiful House Solomon had built for Him.

All the people gathered together to see the wonderful Temple. King Solomon stood on a high platform in front of all the people. The priests and the Levites sang and played great songs of praise to God. Then King Solomon knelt on the platform and raised his arms toward heaven. He prayed so everyone could hear.

King Solomon knew that God was too great to live only in a house built by man. He knew that God was everywhere. He asked God to hear him as he prayed. He asked God to hear every prayer for forgiveness which would ever be prayed in that Temple. He asked God to bless the Temple and all those who came to worship there. After that, Solomon and his people celebrated for two whole weeks.

> *Were you listening?* Who built the Temple? What was the Temple like? What happened when it was finished? Can you find God only in His House?

Story 112

King Solomon Forgets His Promise

I Kings 11

King Solomon had finished the great Temple and had dedicated it to God. One night God came to him. God said, "I have heard the prayer which you made in the Temple, Solomon. I will bless the House which you have made for Me. My eyes and My heart will be there continually. And if you will obey Me as your father David did, and if you will keep all My commandments, then I will bless you and your children forever.

"But if you and your children turn away from Me and do not obey Me, if you begin to serve and worship other gods, then I will cut off Israel out of this land which I have given them. And I will hate this house which you have built. I will let other nations come and take away this kingdom. And I will let them destroy this palace."

King Solomon ruled over Israel for forty years. He was one of the greatest kings of all times. But, although Solomon was very wise, he did one extremely foolish thing. He married a great many wives and most of them were heathen. Many of them were the daughters of heathen kings. These heathen princesses worshiped idols. When they came to live in Solomon's palace, they brought their idols with them. When they wanted temples for their gods, Solomon built temples for them. He even went with them to their temples and worshiped their idols with them.

King Solomon knew that God had told His people never to marry heathen women. And he also knew that it was sin to worship idols. Even though King Solomon had heard God's own voice speaking to him twice during his life, he still turned his back on God. He listened to his many wives instead. Solomon had a thousand women living in his palaces. Seven hundred of them were his wives.

No wonder God was angry with King Solomon! God came to him and said, "Since you have turned away from Me and have disobeyed Me, I will surely tear the kingdom away from you. And I will give it to your servant. But for your father David's sake, I will not do it while you are the king. I shall wait until your son is the king. Then I shall take all the tribes away from him except one. I will leave him one tribe for David's sake."

While Solomon was the king he had spent great sums of money putting up beautiful palaces and large storehouses for grain and fruit. To get enough money for all these buildings, Solomon had made his people pay heavy taxes each year. He collected taxes from other nations, too. Soon the people began to turn against their king. They were dissatisfied and unhappy.

One of Solomon's servants was a young man named Jeroboam. He was a good worker. Solomon made him leader of one of his building projects. One day Jeroboam left Jerusalem on business. God sent His prophet, Ahijah, to meet Jeroboam. Just outside Jerusalem Ahijah stopped Jeroboam. The prophet was wearing a new coat. He took it off and tore it into twelve pieces. He gave ten pieces to Jeroboam and said, "Take these, for God is going to take the kingdom away from Solomon. He will give you ten tribes. Solomon is going to lose them because he disobeyed God and worshiped idols. Solomon's son will be king over one tribe because his grandfather David obeyed the Lord as long as he lived. You will be king over the Ten Tribes. If you obey God and keep His commandments, He will be with you."

Soon King Solomon found out that Jeroboam was planning to

be the next king. He tried to kill Jeroboam, but the young servant
ran away to Egypt. He stayed there until Solomon was dead.

Were you listening? What did God tell Solomon one night? What
foolish thing did Solomon do? How did this cause him to sin?
What was going to happen to Solomon's kingdom?

Story 113

The Kingdom Is Divided

I Kings 12; II Chronicles 10 and 11

Solomon was king for forty years. After King Solomon died,
Rehoboam, his son, became the king. Rehoboam was only sixteen
years old. All the people of Israel came together at Shechem, to
make him king.

[handwritten: 32 miles from Jerusalem North.]

Solomon's servant, Jeroboam, had been chosen by God to be
king over ten of the tribes of Israel. But Jeroboam had run away
from King Solomon. He was living in Egypt. When his friends
notified him that King Solomon was dead, Jeroboam hurried to
Jerusalem. He went with his friends to visit the new king in
Shechem.

Jeroboam said to the new king, Rehoboam, "Your father was
hard on us. He made us do heavy work and pay extremely high
taxes. Now if you will be easier on us, then we will serve you."

The new king answered, "Give me three days to think it over."
Then come again and I will give you my answer." So all the
people went home.

Rehoboam was not a wise king as his father had been. He did
not try to be a good king as his grandfather David had been. First
he went to the old men who had helped his father when he was
the king. "What shall I answer the people?" he asked.

The old men said, "If you want this people to be happy in
your kingdom, and if you want to serve them aright, then be kind
to them. They will be your servants forever."

But King Rehoboam did not listen to the words of the old men.
He went to some younger men with whom he had played when
he was a boy. They were now his helpers. He asked them what
they would do. The young men said, "Do not listen to the people.
Don't make their life easier. Tell them you'll make their life

harder than your father did. Tell them, 'My father punished you with whips, I shall punish you with scorpions.' "

King Rehoboam liked the advice of his younger friends. On the third day Jeroboam and all the people came again to see their new king. The king answered them roughly. He told them the words of his friends. When the people heard the cross words of their new king, they were angry. They said, "What part do we have in David? If you won't listen to us, then we won't have you for our king."

Then all the Israelites went back to their homes. Only those who lived in the cities of Judah stayed with King Rehoboam. The rest of the Israelites made Jeroboam their king. King Rehoboam made plans to go up to fight against Jeroboam, but God stopped him. So, from that time on, there were two kingdoms in Israel. The one was called The Kingdom of Israel (ten tribes) and the other was called The Kingdom of Judah (it included the small tribe of Benjamin).

> *Were you listening?* Who became the king after Solomon died? What did Jeroboam and the people want him to do? Whose advice did the young king take? What happened to the kingdom?

Story 114

Jeroboam Makes Israel Sin

I Kings 12 and 13

King Jeroboam and the Ten Tribes of Israel chose Shechem for their chief city. But there was no Temple in Shechem. Jeroboam was afraid that if his people went to Jerusalem to worship God in the Temple, they would change their minds and go back to King Rehoboam. Then they would come and kill him. So Jeroboam worked out a clever plan. He did not ask God to help him even though he must have remembered God's promise. God had promised to help him be a good king if he would remember to obey God.

But Jeroboam did not try to be a good king. When he lived in Egypt he had seen the Egyptians worshiping animals instead of God. He had seen the heathen temples in Jerusalem which Solomon had built for his wives. So he decided he would not allow his people to go to Jerusalem to worship. He would make them a place to worship in their own land. He made two golden calves. He showed them to his people. He said, "It is too far for you to go all the way to Jerusalem to worship God. Look, here are your gods. These are the gods that brought you up out of the land of Egypt. I will make two places for you to worship. I will set one of these calves in Dan so that those who live in the north may worship there. And I will set the other calf in Bethel. Those who live in the south may worship there."

Then Jeroboam built houses for the golden calves at Bethel and at Dan. He put altars for sacrifices at both places, too. Since the Levites could not be the priests for idols, he chose new priests to take care of the work. He chose feast days on the same days when God's people had feast days in Jerusalem in the Temple. So Jeroboam made God's people sin. It was most wicked to worship idols instead of the living God.

God was angry with Jeroboam for making the people sin. He sent a prophet to warn King Jeroboam. The prophet found Jeroboam burning incense on the altar. He stood in front of the king and cried, "Some day one of David's family will be king in Judah. He will come and tear down this altar and get rid of your wicked priests. So that you may know that these are God's words, this altar is suddenly going to fall apart and the ashes are going to be scattered on the ground."

Jeroboam did not like the prophet's words. He reached out his hand to grab the prophet and shouted, "Get him!" Suddenly his hand and arm became dried up and stiff so that he could not move it. At the same time the altar broke in pieces and the ashes fell to the ground.

Jeroboam was badly frightened. He turned to the prophet. "Please pray for me," he begged. "Please ask God to make my arm well again.'"

The prophet prayed and God heard him. He made Jeroboam's arm well again. The king was so glad, he asked the prophet to come with him to his home. "I will give you something to eat," he said. "And I'll give you a present, too, for making me better."

But the prophet said, "Even if you would give me half of all that you own, I would not go with you. For God told me not to stop to eat or drink nor to go back the same way I came."

Then the prophet left the king and started for home. On the way another prophet tricked him into coming to his home to eat. He lied to him and said that an angel had told him to give food to the prophet. The prophet disobeyed God and went with the old prophet to eat at his home. But as he went on again to his home, God punished him. A lion came out of the woods and killed him.

Even though King Jeroboam heard what happened to the prophet who disobeyed God, he did not change his wicked ways. He kept right on worshiping the idols. He even chose more men to be priests for his golden calves.

> *Were you listening?* What wicked thing did Jeroboam do? Who came to warn him? What happened to Jeroboam at the altar? What happened to the prophet?

Story 115

Jeroboam's Wife Visits Ahijah

HE LIVED IN SHILOH   *I Kings 14*

King Jeroboam had a son whose name was Abijah. Abijah was the oldest son, so he would be the next king when his father died. But one day Abijah became ill. Although the doctors did everything they could, the young prince became worse instead of better. King Jeroboam was worried about his son.

Finally the king decided to ask the old prophet, Ahijah, about his son. Ahijah was the prophet who had given Jeroboam the ten pieces of his coat to show that he would be king over the Ten Tribes of Israel (see page 234). King Jeroboam had not been friends with the prophet for many years.

Now the king and his wife planned to trick the old prophet. They thought that if the prophet did not know the queen, he might give her good news about the young prince. So the queen dressed herself in old clothing so that no one would know that she was the queen. She took with her ten loaves of bread, some cakes, and a jar of honey as a gift for the prophet. She planned to ask the prophet if her son would get well. The king would not go along for he knew that he had sinned against God. He was afraid to visit the prophet.

The prophet Ahijah was old and blind. He wouldn't have recognized the queen even if she had come in her beautiful clothing. But God knew about the plan. He told the prophet that the queen was on her way to his house. God told him exactly what to tell her. "She will pretend that she is another woman," God said.

Soon Ahijah heard the footsteps of the queen at his door. "Come in, wife of Jeroboam," he called. "Why are you pretending to be someone else? I have bad news for you."

The queen was surprised. She had not fooled the prophet at all. She and her husband had forgotten that the God of Israel knows everything. They had forgotten, too, that God often talked with His prophets. The queen came into the prophet's home. She gave him her gifts and listened to his message.

The prophet said, "Go home and tell your husband that the Lord is angry with him for all his sins. The Lord has honored you above all His people. He took the kingdom away from the house of David and gave it to you. But you have not been like King David who kept God's commandments and served Him with all his heart. You have turned away from Him. You have thrown Him behind your back and have made yourself idols instead.

"Therefore, the Lord is going to take the kingdom away from your family. Get up and go home. The moment you reach your own city your son will die. All the people will mourn for him. And they will bury him. But he will be the only one of Jeroboam's family who will be buried. Those who die in the city will be eaten by the dogs. Those who die in the field will be eaten by the birds. And God will punish His people Israel for worshiping idols. He will send them away from this wonderful land. He will scatter them all over the world."

When the old prophet had finished speaking, Jeroboam's wife went back to her husband. By the time she reached home her son was dead. They buried him, and all Israel mourned for him. Soon after, Jeroboam died, too. Then his son Nadab became the king.

Were you listening? Why did the queen go to visit the old prophet? How did she try to fool him? What did the prophet tell the queen?

War Between Israel and Judah

While Jeroboam was the king of the Ten Tribes of Israel, Rehoboam, Solomon's son, was king of Judah. Although his father had built such a wonderful Temple for Jehovah, the God of Israel, Rehoboam hardly used it. After a few years, he, too, turned to idol worship. He and his people set up idols with their altars on every high hill and under every green tree.

Then God sent trouble to King Rehoboam. The king of Egypt made war with Judah. He came into the city of Jerusalem and ran off with all the golden treasures from the Temple. He also took away many of Solomon's riches from the king's palace.

King Rehoboam had other troubles, too. King Jeroboam came with his armies and fought against Judah. There was war between the two kingdoms until both the kings had died.

When Rehoboam died, his son Abijah became the king of Judah. Abijah did not like having the kingdom divided. King David was his great grandfather from both his mother's and his father's side. His mother was Absalom's daughter and his father was Solomon's son. So Abijah thought that he should be king over all of David's kingdom. He went to fight against Jeroboam. Jeroboam had twice as many soldiers as Abijah had, but Abijah and his soldiers trusted in God. And God gave them the victory. Five hundred thousand soldiers of Israel were killed.

Abijah was king for only three years. After he died, his son Asa became the king. Jeroboam was still king of Israel when Asa became king in Judah. Although Asa's father, Abijah, and his grandfather, Rehoboam, had both been wicked kings, Asa was a good king. From the very beginning of his reign Asa worshiped God and ruled his people well. He knew that the people had sinned when they worshiped idols. He taught them to worship the one true God. He taught them to obey His laws and to keep His commandments as King David had done so many years before.

Asa ordered his servants to get rid of all the idols which his father had made. They destroyed the idols and broke down their altars. They cut down the groves where the people came to worship these idols. One day Asa discovered that his own grandmother, who was still the queen-mother, had an idol in a grove and was worshiping it. He ordered his servants to destroy the idol. They burned it by the brook Kidron. And Asa no longer allowed his grandmother to be the queen.

Since Asa served the Lord, God blessed him and his people. For several years there was no war in Judah. Asa and his men spent their time building up their cities and making them strong with walls and towers and gates. When the Ethiopians came to fight, God helped Asa win the battle.

The people soon realized that God was with Asa. A great many people came back to Jerusalem to worship God in His Holy Temple which Solomon had built. They came from other tribes as well as from Judah. They came from Benjamin and from Ephraim and Manasseh and Simeon. They brought their sacrifices and worshiped the Lord with all their hearts. What a happy time that was for God's people. They came into the Temple with shouting and with singing. They played loud music on their trumpets and on their cornets. For they knew that worshiping God always brings happiness.

Asa was king over Judah for forty-one years. He was a good king but when he became old he trusted in himself instead of God. When Baasha, the King of Israel, came up to fight against him, Asa asked the king of Syria to help him instead of asking God. Then God sent Hanani, the prophet, to Asa to warn him about forgetting God. Asa did not like to hear the prophet's words. It made him angry, so he put the prophet in prison. But God punished Asa. For three years Asa had a bad sickness in his feet. But he did not ask God to help him. He trusted in the doctors instead. And his sickness did not get better. Finally he died.

> *Were you listening?* What happened to Rehoboam after he turned to idol worship? How long did Abijah reign? What good things did Asa do? What happened when Asa became old?

Bad Times for the Kingdom of Israel

I Kings 15 and 16

Jeroboam, the first king of the Kingdom of Israel, led his people into great sin by teaching them to worship idols. After Jeroboam died his son Nadab became the king. Nadab was just as bad as his father had been. God let him reign for only two years.

One day a son of the prophet Ahijah made war against Nadab. Ahijah, you remember, was the prophet who gave Jeroboam ten pieces of his robe, promising him ten tribes of Israel for his kingdom (see page 234). Ahijah's son was called Baasha. Baasha soon killed Nadab. Then he made himself king over Israel. The first thing King Baasha did was to kill every man belonging to the family of Jeroboam. The prophet Ahijah had told Jeroboam's wife that this was to happen because Jeroboam had led Israel into sin. Now that prophecy came true.

Baasha was also a wicked king. He, too, taught the people to pray to idols and to worship the golden calves. It was about this time that the good king Asa of Judah was winning many of the Israelites back to his kingdom. Baasha was jealous of Asa. He didn't like it that some of his people had gone over to Judah. Nor did he like it that many of those who had stayed in his kingdom were traveling to Jerusalem to worship God. He decided to place his soldiers in the city of Ramah which was near the border of Judah. The soldiers were to keep his people from going into Judah and to keep the people of Judah from coming into his country. He did not want the people of Judah to teach his people to worship the true God.

Baasha did not succeed in his wicked plan. King Asa got the Syrians to fight against Baasha. While they were fighting, he and his men tore down the soldiers' fort at Ramah.

God sent a prophet to Baasha to warn him. He said, "Since you have made Israel sin as Jeroboam did, God is going to punish you. Those of your family who die in the city will be eaten by the dogs. Those who die in the country will be eaten by the birds."

Soon after the prophet's visit, Baasha died. His son Elah became the next king of Israel. Baasha had been king for twenty-four years. His son Elah was king for only two years. Elah was an extremely wicked man. One day, while he was drunk, his servant, Zimri, killed him. Zimri then made himself king. He killed all the members of Elah's family. He was king for only seven days, however. The army of Israel heard that Zimri had killed their king, Elah. Then they made their captain, Omri, king right there in the camp. Then King Omri led his army to Tirzah where Zimri was reigning as king.

As soon as Zimri heard that the army was coming for him, he went into the king's palace and set it on fire. And he burned to death in the palace.

Since the palace in Tirzah was burned, the new king Omri made his home in Samaria. Omri was the king for twelve years. Omri was also a wicked king. In fact, he was more wicked than any king before him. Although he was so wicked, he was a capable king. He became such a great man that for a long time after his day Israel was known as "the land of Omri."

When Omri died his son Ahab became the king. During all these years, while Israel was ruled by six wicked kings, Asa was still the king in Judah.

> *Were you listening?* How many wicked kings did Israel have? Why did all those kings have so much trouble? Why was Israel known as the "land of Omri"? Who was king in Judah during all these years?

Story 118

Elijah Fed by the Ravens

I Kings 17

There were still a few priests of God in Israel, however. They tried to keep the people from worshiping idols. But Queen Jezebel (she was a heathen princess who had married Ahab) did not want these priests to teach about God. She tried to kill these good priests. But one of King Ahab's servants, whose name was Obadiah, loved God and would not let the wicked queen kill God's prophets. He hid one hundred of them in a cave. He brought them food each day to keep them alive.

JEZEBEL - THEY WORSHIPPED BAAL

x Although King Ahab and his heathen queen^ were leading Israel farther and farther away from God, God was not forgetting His people. He chose a good man to be His prophet. His name was Elijah. Elijah was a great man. He was one of the greatest prophets that ever lived.

One day God sent Elijah to the king's palace. Elijah was not afraid. He went into wicked King Ahab's palace without being invited. He stood before Ahab as he sat on his throne. Elijah pointed his finger at Ahab and said, "As Jehovah, the God of Israel lives, before whom I stand, there will be no rain or dew on the earth until I send it."

King Ahab glared in anger at this strange man. Who was this man who walked into king's palaces without being invited, and who could stop the rain by his own word? "Get that man for me!" the king commanded. "Bring him to me that I may kill him!"

But the king's soldiers could not find Elijah. They looked everywhere for him. God had sent him away to hide. "Go hide by the brook Cherith," God said. "You can drink from the water in the brook. And I have commanded the birds to feed you there."

So Elijah went to the brook Cherith. Every morning and every evening big black birds, called ravens, brought him bread and meat. When he was thirsty, he drank from the brook.

Back in Samaria where King Ahab lived, there was no rain. Soon all the food in the fields dried up. There was no water for the cows and other animals. The people were hungry. The animals were hungry, too.

King Ahab was becoming worried. He sent his men into every country round about to look for Elijah. He thought that if he could only find Elijah, his troubles would be over. But Elijah was still hiding at the brook. He stayed at the brook until all the water in the little brook was dried up. No rain came there either to fill up the empty brook. But God was taking care of His prophet. When the water was all gone, God came to Elijah and sent him to another hiding place. *A MAN CAN ONLY SURVIVE 3 DAYS WITHOUT WATER*

Were you listening? What wicked things did King Ahab do? Who was Elijah? Why did Elijah go to live at the brook? How did he get his food?

Elijah and the Widow

When there was no longer any water in the brook Cherith, God came to Elijah. "Go to Zarephath," God said, "and live there. I have told a poor widow woman there to take care of you."

Zarephath was not in Israel's country. It was in the heathen country of Zidon. Elijah obeyed God at once. He left the brook and walked to Zarephath. When he reached the city gate he met the widow woman. She was gathering sticks to make a fire.

Elijah called to the poor widow, "Will you please bring me a little water to drink? I am thirsty."

The woman hurried to her house to get the water. As she hurried, Elijah called after her, "Please bring me a piece of bread, too."

But the poor woman had no bread. "I have only a little bit

of flour in my jar," she said, "and a little oil in my bottle. I was getting this wood so I could bake a little bread for me and my son. After that we shall have to die of hunger."

There had been no rain in Zarephath, either. That was why the widow was so poor.

"Don't be afraid," Elijah said to her. "Go make me some bread first. Then make some for you and your son. For God has promised that if you will take care of me, your flour and your oil will not be used up until the rain comes."

The woman believed Elijah's words. She invited him into her home. She baked a little bread for Elijah. When she had finished, there was enough flour and oil left for bread for herself and her son. And each day after that, when she went to bake her bread, there was always a little flour and a little oil left in her jars. So God provided food each day for the widow and her son and for Elijah. *THIS LASTED APPROX 2 YEARS — THEN THE RAINS CAME AGAIN.*

One day, while Elijah was still living in Zarephath, the widow's little boy became sick. He grew steadily worse. There seemed to be no cure for him. Finally he died. The widow woman was filled with grief. She brought her dead boy to Elijah.

"O man of God," she cried, "why did you come here to my home? Did you come to show me my sin and to kill my boy?"

Elijah was grieved for the woman. "Give me your son," he

GOD ALWAYS PROVIDES FOR HIS PEOPLE.

said. He took the boy from her arms and carried him up to his room. He laid him on his bed. Then he cried to God and said, "O Lord my God, have you also sent evil on this woman by killing her son?"

Then Elijah stretched himself on the body of the dead boy. As he did so, he prayed again to God. He said, "O Lord my God, I pray Thee, let this child's soul come into him again." Three times Elijah lay on the boy and prayed to God. And God heard Elijah's prayer. Soon the boy was alive again.

Elijah picked up the boy and brought him down to his mother. "See," he said, "your son is alive once more."

The woman hugged her little boy. She held him close to her heart. Then she looked at Elijah. "Now I know," she said, "that you are a man of God, and that the words that you speak are the truth!"

Were you listening? Where did Elijah go when the brook dried up? How did the woman get enough food to feed Elijah and her own family? What happened to the widow's son? What did Elijah do for him?

Story 120

Elijah Prays for Fire

I Kings 18

No rain came in the land of the Israelites for more than three years. All the food in the fields dried up. There was no grass for the animals. Many people and many of the animals died. Finally, one day, God came to Elijah. "Go," God said, "show yourself to King Ahab. Soon I will send rain on the earth." So Elijah went to find King Ahab.

King Ahab and his good servant, Obadiah, were out looking for grass for their animals. They each went a different way. As Elijah came into Samaria he met Obadiah. Obadiah was surprised to see him. Elijah said to Obadiah, "Go tell King Ahab that I am here."

But Obadiah was afraid. "Not so, my lord," he said. "Please don't ask me to do that. Didn't people tell you how I saved a hundred prophets from wicked Queen Jezebel by hiding them in a cave? Then why do you send me to King Ahab?

"King Ahab has been looking for you. There is not a country in all this land where he has not sent soldiers to look for you. Now, if I tell him I have seen you, God may hide you away again. Then if the king comes here and does not find you, he will surely kill me."

But Elijah said, "As the Lord liveth, before whom I stand, I shall surely show myself to King Ahab today."

So Obadiah went to get King Ahab. When King Ahab saw Elijah, he said, "Is that you, you troubler of Israel?"

Elijah answered, "It is not I who have troubled Israel! It is you, O king! God has kept back the rain because you and your people are praying to Baal instead of to Him. Now, gather all your people and all your prophets of Baal. Meet me on the top of Mount Carmel tomorrow morning."

The next morning Elijah stood before the Israelites on Mount Carmel. He said, "How long will you people have more than one god? if Jehovah be God, follow Him. But if Baal be God, then follow him! I am the only prophet left of Jehovah, but there are four hundred and fifty prophets of Baal."

Then Elijah gave the people a test. He said they should make two altars — one for Baal and one for Jehovah. They were to put ~~a bull~~ an offering on each altar. The god who would send fire from heaven would be the true god. The people thought that was a fair test.

The wicked prophets of Baal tried first. They built their altar and put an offering on it. They prayed all morning and all afternoon to Baal. They even jumped on their altar and cut themselves with knives until the blood ran down their bodies. They shouted, "Baal, hear us!" But there was no answer. No fire came.

When it was noon, Elijah mocked them. He said, "Cry louder. Perhaps your god is gone on a trip. Perhaps he is talking with someone and can't hear you. Or maybe he is asleep." So they cried louder. They became even more wild. But still there was no answer.

When evening came, Elijah said, "Now it is my turn." Then he built up the altar of the true God which had been broken down. He dug a trench around the altar and filled it with water. He

FROM 4 LARGE JARS
poured water on the offering and on the wood, too. Elijah wanted to show the people that his God could burn the offering even though it was covered with water. THE FILLED THE JARS 3 TIMES

When all was ready, Elijah prayed. "Hear me, O Jehovah, hear me!" he cried. "Show this people that You are the true God!" Elijah prayed for only a few moments. As soon as he finished his prayer, the fire of the Lord fell. It burned the offering and the wood. It even burned the stones and the dust, and licked up the water in the trenches.

When all the people saw it, they fell on their faces. They cried, "Jehovah, He is God! Jehovah, He is God!"

Then Elijah killed all the prophets of Baal. He had the men take them down the mountain to the brook Kishon. They killed them there. Then Elijah sent King Ahab home. He said, "Hurry home, for there is a sound of much rain in the air."

Elijah then took his little servant boy and went still higher up the mountain. At the top of the mountain Elijah threw himself down on the ground and put his face between his knees. He prayed for rain. Suddenly he raised himself and said to the boy, "Go up now and look toward the sea."

The boy looked to see if there were any clouds in the sky. He came back and said, "There is nothing. The sky is as brass above us."

Seven times Elijah prayed. Seven times the servant boy went up to look at the sky. Finally he saw a small cloud arising out of the sea. It was as big as a man's hand. Elijah and his servant ran down the mountain. Elijah sent his servant to warn Ahab to hurry into his chariot lest he get caught in the storm. By this time the sky was black with clouds and wind. The rain came in torrents. All of a sudden God gave Elijah special strength. He gathered his robes about him and ran as fast as Ahab's horses. He entered the royal city ahead of the king.

Finally, after three and a half years, God's people had rain.

Were you listening? Why didn't Obadiah want to tell the king that Elijah was there? What test did Elijah give the people? Who was the real God? How many times did Elijah pray for rain?

God Comforts Elijah

I Kings 19

Elijah, the great man of God, was tired. He had worked hard for God on the top of Mount Carmel. He had stood alone against King Ahab and all his people. He had killed the four hundred and fifty prophets of Baal. Then he had prayed for rain.

When King Ahab went home to his palace that night, he told his queen, Jezebel, all that Elijah had done. Jezebel was angry. She sent a messenger hurrying to Elijah. The messenger said to Elijah, "Queen Jezebel is angry with you for killing her prophets. She says, 'Tomorrow about this time I shall kill you as you killed the prophets of Baal!' "

When the tired prophet heard the words of wicked Queen Jezebel, he was afraid. He ran for his life. He ran with his servant to Beersheba. There he left his servant and went on into the wilderness. He walked for a whole day. By that time he was so tired he could go no further. He sat down under a juniper-tree and wished that he might die.

"It is enough now, O Lord," he cried. "Take away my life, for I am not better than my fathers!"

Then Elijah lay down and slept under the juniper-tree. After a while an angel came and touched Elijah. "Get up and eat," the angel said. Elijah sat up and looked around. There near his head was bread and water. Elijah ate and drank and lay down again. Soon the angel came a second time and touched him. Again he said, "Get up and eat." But this time he added, "For the journey will be too great for you." Once more Elijah ate and drank. Then he walked in the strength of that food for forty days and forty nights. He walked until he came to Mount Horeb, which was the mount of God.

Elijah climbed the mountain until he came to a cave. There he rested. While Elijah was resting in the cave, the word of God came to him. God said, "What are you doing here, Elijah?"

Elijah answered, "I have been very jealous for the Lord, the God of Hosts. I have worked so hard for Thee. But the children of Israel have turned away from Thee. They have thrown down Your altars. They have killed Your prophets. I am the only one left, and now they want to kill me!"

Then God said, "Go out of the cave and stand on the mountain before Me." Suddenly a strong wind came up. It tore at the mountain until huge pieces of the mountain were torn off and went dashing down the mountainside. Large rocks were broken into pieces. But God was not in the wind.

Then there came an earthquake. The entire mountain shook and trembled. But God was not in the earthquake.

After the earthquake, there came a big fire. There was a great crackling and a roaring as the huge tongues of fire leaped from tree to tree, destroying everything they touched. But God was not in the fire.

Elijah still stood within the cave as he watched the powerful things his God could do. Surely the Lord was stronger than wicked King Ahab and his heathen queen. Then a gentle stillness settled over the mountain. In the hushed silence Elijah heard a still, small voice. It was the voice of God. As soon as Elijah heard it, he went out and stood at the mouth of the cave. He covered his face with his robe.

Then God said a second time, "Elijah, what are you doing here?"

Elijah gave the same answer he had given before.

Then God comforted Elijah and encouraged him. He said, "Go back to work, Elijah. You are not alone. There are still seven thousand people in Israel who have not bowed their knees to Baal."

Elijah went back to work. And he found a young man named Elisha to help him. Elisha was plowing in his field with twelve yoke of oxen when Elijah came past. Elijah threw his robe over the shoulders of the young farmer. That was his way of saying, "Come and help me." So the young farmer left his work and went with Elijah.

Were you listening? Why was Elijah tired? Why did he run away?
How did God show Elijah His power? How did God comfort Elijah?

Ahab and His Enemies

King Ahab was not only a most wicked king, he was also very foolish. He did not try to make Israel strong as the kings of Judah had done with their kingdom. By this time Judah had a million trained soldiers, but King Ahab had only seven thousand.

One day Ben-hadad, the king of Syria, came with all his soldiers to make war against Israel. Thirty-two other kings came with him. They came to the city of Samaria where Ahab lived. King Ben-hadad sent a message to Ahab. He said, "Listen to the words of the great King Ben-hadad! All your silver and your gold belong to me. All your wives and your children belong to me, too!"

King Ahab was filled with fear. He did not know what to do. He knew that Baal could not help him and he was afraid to ask God for help. His small army would never be able to fight against such a great enemy. There was nothing to do but to agree with the king. He sent back this humble answer, "Yes, my lord, all that I have belongs to you."

Still King Ben-hadad was not satisfied. He sent an even more unkind message to King Ahab. He said, "Tomorrow I shall send my servants to go through your house and the houses of all your servants. They will take away all your treasures."

Then King Ahab called together all the elders of his people and told them what King Ben-hadad wanted to do. The elders said, "Don't listen to him!" So Ahab sent Ben-hadad this message, "I'll agree to your first demand, but I shall never let you carry out your second threat!"

That's exactly what Ben-hadad wanted to happen. Now he had a good excuse to fight against Ahab. He sent word that he and the other kings would come up with their armies and crush Ahab and his soldiers to pieces. "There won't be even enough dust left in Samaria to give each of my soldiers a handful," he boasted.

"Wait until the battle is finished before you do your boasting," Ahab answered.

Then a wonderful thing happened for King Ahab. Even though Ahab had turned his back on God, God still loved His people. He did not want them to be completely destroyed at this time. Besides, God wanted to show the wicked Syrians that Israel's God was greater than all of Israel's enemies. So God sent a prophet to King Ahab to tell him that God would help him win against the Syrians. "Let the young princes do the fighting," the prophet said.

There were only two hundred and thirty-two young princes in Ahab's army. But they were brave, and God helped them. King Ben-hadad and the other kings did not even come out to fight the young princes. They were drinking in their tents. Ben-hadad commanded his soldiers to capture the young princes alive. But the princes were not captured. They killed many of the Syrians and chased the others away. Even King Ben-hadad fled on his horse.

Soon after this battle the prophet came to Ahab again. "King Ben-hadad will come again next year to fight you," he said. "So make your army strong. Then you will be ready for them."

King Ben-hadad did come back the next year. "We made a mistake last year," he said, "when we went to fight the Israelites in Samaria. For Samaria is on a hill, and the god of the Israelites is a god of the hills. This time we shall fight them out in the open on the plains." So the Syrians stayed in the north. They came only as far as the Sea of Galilee, to the city of Aphek.

King Ahab's army was still small. When the army went out to fight the Syrians it looked like two little flocks of kids. But the Syrians filled the country. Once more God came to His people's rescue. He sent His prophet with this message, "Since the Syrians think I am a God of the hills only, and not of the valleys, I shall give this huge army into your hands. Then they will know that I am the God of the whole earth!"

Once more the Israelites won the battle. They killed one hundred thousand Syrian soldiers in one day. The rest of the Syrian soldiers fled into the city of Aphek for safety. But a wall of the city fell down and killed twenty-seven thousand of those that were left.

Soon Ben-hadad sent a messenger to Ahab begging him to let him live. Then Ahab did a foolish thing. "He said, 'Is the king still alive? He is my friend.'" He sent for Ben-hadad and made friends with him. Then he let him go. God was angry with Ahab for his foolishness. Ben-hadad was wicked and should have been killed. God sent His prophet to Ahab once more. "Because you have let this man go," the prophet said, "you shall die in his stead."

Then Ahab went back to his home in Samaria. He was unhappy and displeased. He did not like to have God's prophets come to him. He did not want God to rule his life.

Were you listening? What did Ben-hadad want to do to King Ahab? Why did God help wicked King Ahab in the battle? What foolish thing did Ahab do after he had won the battle? Why was Ahab displeased with God?

Story 123

King Ahab Becomes a Thief

I Kings 21

King Ahab lived in Samaria, you remember. Close to the king's palace there was a lovely garden. It belonged to Naboth. Naboth grew grapes in his garden, so it was called a vineyard. King Ahab liked this vineyard. Every day when he looked at it he would say to himself, "Oh, how I wish I could have that fine vineyard for my garden!"

Then one day King Ahab went to Naboth. "Let me have your vineyard, Naboth," he said. "I will give you a better vineyard for it, or I will pay you for it with money."

But Naboth was not allowed to sell his vineyard. Many years before, Moses had given his people a law about their land. They were not allowed to sell it. It was to be given to their children. When the Israelites first came into their promised land, they were each given a piece of land. This land was to stay in their family forever. So Naboth said to the king, "This vineyard belongs to my family. I cannot let you have it."

King Ahab was angry with Naboth. He went home and pouted because he could not have the vineyard. Turning his face to the wall as he lay on his bed, he would not even eat.

Soon Queen Jezebel came to him. She said, "Why are you so sad? Why haven't you eaten?"

"Naboth won't let me have his vineyard," answered the king.

"Aren't you the king of Israel?" Jezebel said. "Get up and eat bread. I'll see to it that you get the vineyard!"

The wicked queen set out at once to get the vineyard for her husband. She wrote letters to the leaders of the city. She wrote them in Ahab's name. She wrote, "Call all the people to a meeting. Have two wicked men tell lies about Naboth. Then throw stones at him and kill him."

The men of the city obeyed the queen. They held a meeting and made Naboth stand up before all the people. Then two wicked men told lies about Naboth. They said, "This man has cursed God and the king." Naboth was a good man, but the people would not listen to him. They carried him out of the city and threw stones at him until he was dead. Then they sent word to the queen that Naboth was dead.

As soon as the wicked Queen Jezebel heard that Naboth was dead, she hurried to King Ahab. "Get up," she said, "and go take the vineyard. Naboth is dead and the vineyard is yours."

King Ahab got up at once. He hurried to the vineyard to claim it as his own. But God knew what the wicked queen had done. He sent His prophet Elijah to meet the king in the vineyard.

King Ahab saw Elijah coming. "Hast thou found me, O my enemy?" he cried.

"Yes, I have found you," Elijah answered, "because you have sinned greatly against your God. And now God is going to punish you and your people. He is going to send much evil upon you and your people. He will make your house like the house of Jeroboam. You and your wicked queen will both be killed. The dogs which licked up Naboth's blood will also lick up your blood. And the dogs will eat Jezebel by the wall of your city."

When King Ahab heard Elijah's words, he tore his clothes and put sackcloth on his body. He lay in sackcloth and fasted. He went about quietly to show that he was sorry.

Then God said to Elijah, "See how Ahab humbles himself before Me? Since Ahab is sorry for his sins, I shall not send the punishment on his family now. But when his son is king, the evil will come."

Were you listening? Why did King Ahab pout? How did the wicked queen get the vineyard for King Ahab? What did Elijah tell the king? Why didn't God punish the king at once?

God Punishes King Ahab

I Kings 22; II Chronicles 18

King Ahab was king in Israel for twenty-two years. After Ahab had stolen Naboth's vineyard, and had humbled himself before God because of Elijah's warning, there was peace in his land for three years.

Then one day, the king of Judah came to see King Ahab. His name was Jehoshaphat. As they were sitting visiting, King Ahab said, "The city of Ramoth-gilead is ours. Then why do we just sit here and let the king of Syria keep it? Let us go together with our armies and take it away from him."

King Jehoshaphat thought it would be a good idea to go fight against Ramoth-gilead. "But," he added, "let's first ask God if we should go."

So King Ahab called all his prophets — he had about four hundred — and said to them, "Shall I go up against Ramoth-gilead in battle, or not?"

All the prophets answered, "Yes, go up, for the Lord will give the city to you."

But King Jehoshaphat was not satisfied. "Isn't there another prophet whom we could ask?" he said.

"Yes," King Ahab said, "there is Micaiah. But I hate him. He never tells me anything good. He always says bad things about me."

"Let not the king say so," King Jehoshaphat said.

Then King Ahab sent his servant to get Micaiah. Each of the kings was sitting on his own throne, dressed in his royal purple robe. They were sitting at the entrance of the gate of Samaria. All the other prophets stood in front of them. They kept telling King Ahab to go up to fight.

As the servant brought Micaiah, he said to the prophet, "All these other prophets are telling good things to the king. Let your words be like theirs."

But Micaiah said, "As the Lord liveth, I can only say what God tells me to say." Then Micaiah came and stood in front of the two kings.

And King Ahab said, "Micaiah, shall we go to Ramoth-gilead to battle or not?"

At first Micaiah said the same words as the other prophets had said. He did this to mock the king. Then King Ahab asked, "How many times have I told you to tell the truth?"

Micaiah answered, "I saw all Israel scattered upon the mountains as sheep that have no shepherd."

King Ahab turned to King Jehoshaphat. "Didn't I tell you," he said, "that he would tell me evil words?"

But Micaiah wasn't finished. He added, "I saw the Lord sitting on His throne and all the hosts of heaven were standing around Him. And I heard the Lord say, 'Who will tempt King Ahab so that he will go up and get killed at Ramoth-gilead?' And a spirit stood before the Lord and said, 'I will tempt him.' 'How?' the Lord asked. And the spirit said, 'I will make the prophets lie to him.' And the Lord said, 'Go ahead and tempt him.' "

The king was filled with anger at the prophet Micaiah. "Put this fellow in prison," he commanded, "until I come back in peace."

And Micaiah answered, "If you come back at all in peace, then the Lord has not spoken through me."

So the two kings went up to Ramoth-gilead. King Jehoshaphat of Judah wore his royal robe, but King Ahab dressed as an ordinary soldier. He wanted to fool the enemy. Now the king of Syria had commanded his soldiers to watch especially for King Ahab. When the Syrian soldiers saw King Jehoshaphat in his king's robe, they thought he was King Ahab. They chased after him. Soon they found out that they were mistaken and turned back.

But while the battle was still going on, a certain soldier drew his bow for the fun of it, without aiming it at any one. King Ahab was riding by at that very moment. The arrow hit King Ahab between the joints of his armor. Before evening came, the king died in his chariot. His blood ran out of the wound onto the chariot. Later, when they washed the chariot by the pool of

Samaria, the dogs licked up the blood. So the words of Elijah, the man of God, came true.

> *Were you listening?* What did the two kings want to do? Why didn't King Ahab want to send for Micaiah? What did Micaiah tell the king? What happened to King Ahab?

Elijah and King Ahaziah

King Jehoshaphat was a good king as his father had been. He reigned in Jerusalem over Judah for twenty-five years. While good King Jehoshaphat was king in Judah, Ahab's son, Ahaziah, was king in Israel. Ahaziah took after his father and mother. He walked in their wicked ways and worshiped Baal, just as they had done.

While Ahaziah was king, the people of Moab came and fought against Israel. One day King Ahaziah was upstairs in his palace in Samaria. He fell through the lattice of the window to the ground below. He was badly hurt. He wanted to know if he was going to get well. Instead of asking God, he sent his messengers to ask a heathen god. He sent them to Ekron to ask the god, Baal-zebub.

But God sent Elijah to meet King Ahaziah's servants. Elijah said to the messengers, "Isn't there a God in Israel, that you have to go to the heathen god in Ekron for your master, the king? You go back to your king and tell him that God says that he will never leave his bed. He is surely going to die."

So the messengers went back to King Ahaziah. "Why did you come back?" the king asked.

And the messengers said, "A man came to meet us. He said, 'Isn't there a God in Israel that you have to go to Baal-zebub in Ekron? You tell your master he will never leave his bed. He is surely going to die.'"

"What did that man look like?" King Ahaziah asked.

"He was an old man," they said. "He wore a robe made of haircloth and a leather girdle."

"That must be Elijah," the king said. Then he sent a captain with his fifty men to get Elijah.

Elijah was sitting on the top of a hill. The captain called to him and said, "Thou man of God, the king wants you to come down."

Elijah answered, "If I am a man of God, then let fire come down from heaven to burn you and your fifty men." That very moment fire did come down from heaven and burned to death that captain and his fifty men.

When King Ahaziah heard what had happened, he sent another captain with his fifty men. This captain came to Elijah's hill, too. He called, "O man of God, the king says you must come down quickly!"

Again Elijah answered, "If I am a man of God, let fire come down from heaven to kill you and your fifty men." And the fire of God came down a second time and killed the king's captain and his fifty soldiers.

A third time King Ahaziah sent a captain with his fifty soldiers to get Elijah. This captain went up the hill to where Elijah was. He fell down on his knees in front of Elijah. He pleaded with Elijah and said, "O man of God, I pray thee, please let me and my soldiers live! I know that fire has come down and burned both the other captains with their fifty soldiers. But please let us live!"

Then God said to Elijah, "Go down with this captain. Don't be afraid of him." So Elijah went with this captain to see the king. When he came to the king's palace, he said to the king, "This is what the Lord says, 'Since you did not think there was a God in Israel to help you, since you sent to Baal-zebub, the god of Ekron, to ask about your sickness, you will never leave that bed of yours. You will surely die!'"

So King Ahaziah died, just as Elijah said he would. He reigned only two years. And Jehoram became the king of Israel in his place.

Were you listening? Why didn't King Ahaziah go to fight the people of Moab? Where did he send his messengers? Who stopped them on the way? What happened to the captains and their soldiers who went after Elijah?

Elijah and the Fiery Chariot

Elijah, the prophet of God, was now an old man. He had worked in Israel for many years, teaching the people to serve the true God instead of Baal, who was no god. Elijah had many troubles, but God always took care of him. When he was too old to work alone, God gave him a young man, whose name was Elisha, to be his helper. Elisha went everywhere with Elijah. Some day Elisha would have to be the prophet instead of Elijah. So he watched his master closely. He followed him wherever he went.

One day the two prophets went to visit the schools of the prophets. Young men went to these schools to learn how to be prophets, too. Elijah and Elisha went from one school to another. Perhaps Elijah had one more message for these students before he went home to live with God.

First they went to Gilgal. Elijah tried to get Elisha to stay in Gilgal so that he might go on alone. Elijah knew that the time had come for him to go to heaven. He wanted to be alone with God. So he said to Elisha, "You stay here, while I go to Bethel."

But Elisha knew that Elijah was going to heaven. And he did not want to leave his master. So the two men went on to Bethel. As they came to Bethel, the young students said to Elisha, "Do you know that God is going to take away your master today?"

"Yes, I know it," Elisha answered, "but don't talk about it."

At Bethel Elijah tried again to go on alone. Once more Elisha would not leave his master. So they continued to Jericho. As soon as the young men from the school at Jericho saw Elisha, they said, "Do you know that the Lord is going to take away your master today?"

Again Elisha answered, "Yes, I know it. But don't talk about it."

At Jericho, Elijah said, "You stay here, Elisha. The Lord has sent me to the river Jordan." But Elisha would not stay behind. So the two of them went on toward the river. The fifty men from the school stood and watched them go. When they came to the river, there was no bridge. The water was deep. Then Elijah took

his robe. He wrapped it together and hit the water with it. At once the water went apart. There before the two prophets was a path through the river. The two men crossed over on the path.

When they reached the other side, Elijah said, "I am going to leave you now. Ask what you would like to have me do for you before I am taken away."

Elisha answered, "Let me be a good prophet like you were. Let your spirit rest on me."

"You have asked a hard thing," Elijah said. "But if you see me when I am taken away, then your wish will be granted."

All at once the two men saw a fiery chariot drawn by fiery horses. A strong wind began to blow. The chariot came between the two men. It picked up Elijah. And Elijah went up by a whirlwind into heaven. Elisha saw him go up. He cried out, "My father, my father! The chariot of Israel and the horsemen thereof!"

Soon Elijah was gone. Elisha could see him no longer. Elisha stood up. He tore his robe into two pieces. Then he picked up Elijah's robe, which had fallen from him. Elisha went back to the river Jordan. As he stood at the river's edge, he took Elijah's robe and hit the water with it, just as Elijah had done. The dry path came again and Elisha crossed over to the other side.

The fifty young men from the school came to meet Elisha. They said, "The spirit of Elijah now rests on Elisha." So Elisha became the new prophet instead of Elijah. And the young men bowed themselves down before Elisha.

These young men did not believe that Elijah had gone straight to heaven. They thought God might have dropped him on some mountain or in some valley. They wanted to go to look for him. Elisha did not want them to go. He knew that Elijah had gone to heaven. But the young men begged and begged. Finally Elisha let them go. They searched the mountains for three days. But, of course, they did not find Elijah. For God had taken him to heaven.

When Elisha returned to his home in Bethel that day, the children were playing in the street. They saw Elisha coming. They mocked him. They called him names. They said, "Go up, you bald head! Go up, you bald head!" They wanted Elisha to go up to heaven as Elijah had done. That was a most wicked thing for those children to do. They were not only sinning against Elisha, they were sinning against God.

Elisha turned around and looked back at the children. He cursed them in the name of the Lord. When you curse any one, you are asking God to send great harm to him. When Elisha cursed those wicked children of Bethel, God heard Elisha. He sent two mother bears out of the woods. The bears ran after the children. They killed forty-two of them. This lesson from the Bible shows that God wants children to be good to older people.

Were you listening? Why did Elisha want to go with Elijah? What happened at the river Jordan? What happened to Elijah? Why couldn't the young men find Elijah? What happened to the children who made fun of Elisha?

Story 127

Two Boys Saved from Slavery

II Kings 4

Elisha, you remember, had seen his master, Elijah, go up to heaven. He had asked to have a double portion of Elijah's spirit come upon him. And his prayer was truly answered. He was a fine prophet. He went about from day to day helping all who came to him.

One day a widow woman came to him. She was the widow of a prophet. Some think that her husband was the prophet Obadiah who had worked with King Ahab. He was a good prophet, you remember. He had hidden the prophets of the Lord in a cave when King Ahab and his wicked wife Jezebel wanted to kill all of God's prophets. This widow woman said to Elisha, "Please help me. My husband is dead. You know that my husband was a good man who served the Lord. But he owed a man some money and was never able to pay it. Now this man has come to me. He wants me to give him the money. I do not have it, so now he wants to take my two sons as slaves."

Elisha said to the woman, "What do you want me to do for you? Tell me, what do you have in your house?"

"I do not have anything at all except one jar of cooking oil," the woman said. The women in those days used this oil with their flour to make bread.

Then Elisha said, "Go home and borrow as many empty oil jars as you can from all your neighbors. Don't stop until you have a great many. When you have finished, shut the door so no one will see what you are going to do. Then take your jar of oil and pour it into all these empty jars."

The woman obeyed Elisha at once. She ran home and sent her two sons to the neighbors. The boys came home with as many jars as they could carry. Then they went back again for more. They worked hard until their little home was filled with empty oil jars.

Finally, the woman closed the door as Elisha had commanded. Then she took her jar of oil and began to pour the oil into the empty jars. No matter how many jars she filled, her jar was still not empty. God gave her more and more oil until all the jars were filled. When her boy had brought her the last jar, she said, "Now bring me another jar."

"There are no more empty jars," the boy answered. Then the oil stopped increasing. The woman quickly went back to Elisha. She told him what had happened. And Elisha said, "Go sell the oil and pay your debt. Then you and your children can live from the rest."

Once more the woman obeyed Elisha. She sold the oil and paid her debt. There was enough money left for herself and her two boys to live for a long time.

Were you listening? Why did the poor widow woman come to Elisha? What did Elisha tell her to do? How could she fill all those jars with oil? What did she do with the oil?

Story 128

Elisha and the Shunammite Woman

II Kings 4

Elisha was a busy man. He worked hard every day, teaching and helping the people. He often passed the beautiful home of a rich woman and her husband on his way to work. One day the woman asked Elisha to stop and have supper at her home. The woman was kind to Elisha. She invited him to come in any time to eat with them. After that, whenever Elisha passed that way, he had supper with his new friends.

Then, one day, this kind woman asked her husband to build a little room on the roof of their house for Elisha. It was a fine room. It had a bed in it, and a table and a chair, and a candle to give light. Elisha was most happy with his new room. He and his servant, Gehazi, often visited their kind friend's house and stayed in their little room.

One evening Elisha sent for the Shunammite woman. She came and stood in the doorway. "Tell me," Elisha asked, "what can I do for you? You have been so kind to me. Shall I tell the captain of the army about you, or the king, perhaps?"

The kind woman shook her head. "I do not need anything," she said. "I am happy here among my own people." Then she went downstairs.

"What can we do for her?" Elisha asked his servant.

"I know," Gehazi answered. "She has no children, and now she is too old to have a baby."

"Call her again," Elisha said. The woman came back and stood in the doorway. "Next year," Elisha said, "you will hold a little baby boy of your own in your arms."

"Oh, no, my lord, don't lie to thy servant," the woman cried. But the very next year the woman did have a son, a dear little baby boy. She loved her baby with all her heart. The little boy grew and grew. Soon he was old enough to go out into the fields with his father.

One hot summer day the boy was in the fields with his father. He stood for a long time in the hot sunshine. After a while he began to feel sick. "Oh, my head, my head!" he cried. He ran to his father.

"Carry the boy to his mother," the father said. A servant quickly took the sick little boy to his mother. She did everything she could for him, but he only grew worse. She sat with him on her lap and rocked him until noon. Then the little boy died.

The mother carried her little boy to Elisha's room. She laid him on Elisha's bed. Then she hurried to her husband. She asked for a donkey and rode out to find Elisha. A servant went with her. They hurried to Mount Carmel, fifteen miles away. Elisha saw them coming. He sent Gehazi down to meet the woman to ask if everything was all right. But the woman would not tell Gehazi. She came on to Elisha and fell down at his feet. Gehazi was going to push her away, but Elisha said, "Let her alone. There is something wrong, and God has not told me."

Then the woman said, "Did I ask you for a son? Didn't I say to you 'Don't fool me'?" Then Elisha knew that something must be wrong with the little boy. He sent Gehazi back to the Shunammite's home. "Go, lay my staff on the little boy's face," he said. "Don't stop to speak with anyone, just hurry."

Gehazi ran to obey, but the woman begged Elisha to come, too. So Elisha and the woman followed. As they came near the house, Gehazi met them. "I could not awaken him," he said.

Then Elisha went up to his room. The boy was lying on his bed. He was dead. Elisha shut the door and prayed to the Lord. Then he stretched himself over the little boy, putting his mouth on the boy's mouth and his hands on the boy's hands. And the little boy's body became warm.

Then Elisha went downstairs and walked back and forth through the house. He went back again to his room. He lay on the boy a second time. The little boy sneezed seven times and opened his eyes. Elisha called for the mother. She came and fell at Elisha's feet. Then she lifted her little boy in her arms and carried him downstairs. Her heart was filled with gladness, for her little boy was alive again.

Were you listening? What did the Shunammite woman do for Elisha? What did Elisha do for her? What happened to the little boy? How did Elisha help?

Elisha and the Leper

Story 129

II Kings 5

PART ONE

During the time when Elisha was the prophet in Israel, the Syrian army came to fight against Israel. When the Syrian army went back home they took with them a little Jewish girl. She was stolen away from her parents and carried far off to Syria. Naaman, the captain of the Syrian army, took the little girl home with him. She became a slave in Naaman's home. She worked for Naaman's wife. Although the little girl was far from home, she obeyed her mistress. The little girl soon learned to love her mistress.

Naaman and his wife lived in a beautiful home, for they were rich. Naaman was also a good friend of his king. Naaman was a brave captain and had won many battles. But Naaman and his wife were not happy. They were sad because Naaman was a leper. A leper is a man who has a dreadful sickness called leprosy. Lepers have running sores on their bodies. These sores get worse and worse. Finally, fingers and toes rot away and the leper begins to look dreadful. No doctor could cure a leper. No wonder Naaman and his wife were sad.

The little Jewish slave girl loved her master and mistress. She wished she could help them. One day she said to her mistress, "I wish my lord lived in my home country. The prophet Elisha would cure him of his leprosy."

Naaman's wife soon told her husband what the little girl had said. Naaman told his king about it. The king said, "You go to the land of Israel to see if you can get cured from your leprosy. I will send a letter with you to the king of Israel."

So Naaman made plans to visit the king of Israel. He left Syria and traveled to Canaan. He took with him many servants and many costly presents.

When Naaman came to the king of Israel with his letter, the king was angry. He thought the king of Syria was just trying to pick a fight with him. He tore his clothes and said, "Am I a god that I can cure a leper? This man has come to make war with me again."

When Elisha heard about the king's visitor, he sent his servant to the king. The servant said, "Elisha says, 'Why do you tear your clothes? Send the captain to me so that he may know that there is a prophet in Israel!'"

Naaman and his servants went at once to the home of Elisha. Elisha's servant, Gehazi, came to the door. Before Naaman had a chance to ask for Elisha or to tell Gehazi why he had come,

Gehazi said, "Go wash seven times in the river Jordan and you will be well."

Naaman turned away. He was angry. "I thought the prophet would surely come out to see me," he complained. "I thought he would call on his gods and wave his hands over my sores and make me better! Are not the rivers in my own country better than all the waters in Israel? Why can't I wash in them and be clean?" And he turned angrily away.

The servants of Naaman followed him as he turned towards Syria. After a while one of the servants rode alongside his master and dared to speak to him. He said, "If the prophet had asked you to do a hard thing, you would have done it. Why not try such an easy thing as to wash seven times in the river?".

Then Naaman got over his anger. He turned back once more and went to the river Jordan. He obeyed Elisha and washed himself seven times. When he had washed the seventh time, his leprosy was gone. His skin was as smooth and clean as a new baby's!

Naaman hurried back to Elisha to thank him. This time Elisha came to the door. Naaman said, "Now I know that there is no God in all the earth but in Israel. Now, therefore, take a present from thy servant."

"No," Elisha said, "I do not want any gifts." Naaman urged Elisha to take the gifts, but he refused. Finally, Naaman and his servants went on their way. Because the little girl had been faithful, God had healed Naaman. Isn't it wonderful that God used the little girl to tell Naaman about Himself?

PART TWO

Then something sad happened. All the while Naaman had been urging Elisha to take his gifts, Gehazi had been watching. He thought Elisha was foolish for not taking the gifts. He wished he could have them. Suddenly, he had an idea. He ran after Naaman.

Naaman saw Gehazi coming. He jumped down from his chariot and went to meet him. "Is everything all right?" he asked.

"Yes, everything is all right," Gehazi answered. "But my

master sent me to tell you that he has changed his mind. He would like your gifts. He suddenly received two young visitors from Ephraim. He would like to have you give them each a piece of silver and two suits of clothing."

"Gladly," Naaman said. "Here, take two pieces of silver for each." Naaman gave Gehazi four pieces of silver and four suits of clothing. He sent two of his servants along with Gehazi to carry the gifts. But when they came close to Elisha's home, Gehazi took the gifts from the servants and carried them himself. He did not want Elisha to see what he was doing. He sent Naaman's servants back to their master.

Gehazi brought the gifts into his own house and hid them. Then he went about his work as usual. When evening came, he went in and stood before Elisha as he always did.

But Elisha knew what had happened. God had told him. So Elisha said to Gehazi, "Where did you come from, Gehazi?"

Gehazi answered, "I didn't go anywhere."

"Oh, I know what you did," Elisha said. "I know what happened when the man came out of his chariot to meet you. Is this a time to receive money and clothing and all sorts of gifts? It was God who cured Naaman. We did not deserve his gifts. Now, since you did this wicked deed, the leprosy of Naaman is going to come on you and on all your family. You will never be cured from it!"

Gehazi listened to Elisha's dreadful words. Then he turned away and went toward the door. And as he went he became a leper. His skin was as white as snow!

Were you listening? Why was Naaman sad? Who told him about Elisha? Why didn't Naaman want to obey Elisha? Why did Gehazi become a leper?

Story 130

Elisha and the Army of God

II Kings 6

One day the sons of the prophets said to Elisha, "Look, the place where we live is too small for all of us. Please let us go to the Jordan river. There let us each cut down a tree and build us a place where we can live."

Elisha said it would be all right.

"Please come with us," one of them said. So Elisha went with them. When they came to the Jordan river, they all began to cut down the trees. While one of the men was cutting a tree, the head of his axe fell into the water and went down to the bottom.

"Oh, master," the young man cried, "my axe-head is gone. And it didn't even belong to me! I borrowed it from someone else."

"Where did it fall?" Elisha asked.

The young man showed him where it went down. Elisha cut down a stick and threw it into the water. The stick went down and the iron axe-head came up and floated on the top of the water. "Get it," Elisha said. So the young man reached out and took it out of the water.

Not long after this, the king of Syria came again to Israel to make war. He made careful plans for fighting the Israelites. He and his men camped in a certain place where they knew the Israelites would soon pass. Then they planned to capture them.

God told Elisha about these plans and he ran to warn the king of Israel. He said to the king, "Don't go to such a place, for the king of Syria and his men are hiding there, waiting to capture you."

So the king of Syria and his men waited and waited for the Israelites, but they did not come. This happened several times. Every time the Syrians planned to go to a certain place, God would tell Elisha, and Elisha would warn the king of Israel. This made the Syrian king angry and worried. He called his soldiers together. "Come, tell me," he said, "which one of you is a spy and is telling the Israelites our plans?"

One of the soldiers answered, "No, my lord, we are not spies. But I know what is happening. There is a prophet in Israel. His name is Elisha. He knows everything. He tells his king the very words you speak in your own bedroom!"

"Go find out where Elisha is so I may get him," the Syrian king commanded. They soon found out that Elisha was at Dothan.

Now Elisha and a young man, his new servant, were living on the top of a mountain in Dothan. The king of Syria went at once to Dothan. His men came by night with their horses and chariots and surrounded the city.

The next morning Elisha and his servant arose early. They went outside and saw horses and chariots everywhere! They were coming closer and closer. The young servant was filled with fear. "Oh, my master," he cried, "what shall we do?"

Elisha was not afraid. He answered calmly, "Don't be afraid. We have more soldiers with us than they have with them." But the servant saw no one with Elisha. Then Elisha asked God to open the young man's eyes, so that he might see. God opened his eyes, and he saw that the mountain was full of horses and chariots of fire. They were all about Elisha. God had sent His angels to fight for Elisha!

Elisha went to meet the king of Syria and his army. As he went he prayed to God. He said, "Please, God, make these men blind." God heard Elisha's prayer. He made all the Syrians blind. Then Elisha said to them, "This is not the way, neither is this the city you are looking for. You are in the wrong place. Come with me and I will bring you to the man you want."

Then Elisha led the Syrians down the mountain. He brought them to Samaria to the king of Israel and his army. He asked God to open the Syrians' eyes. God opened their eyes and they saw that they were in the midst of the camp of Israel, their enemy.

The king of Israel was surprised to see the Syrians. He turned to Elisha and cried, "My father, shall I kill them? Shall I kill them?"

"No," Elisha answered, "don't kill them. Set food before them instead so that they may eat and go their way."

So they made a great feast for the Syrian king and his army. When they had finished eating, Elisha sent them home. The Syrian army did not bother the Israelites for a long time after that.

Were you listening? What did Elisha do for one of the sons of the prophets? What did Elisha do for the king of Israel's army? Why wasn't Elisha afraid of the Syrians? What did Elisha do with his enemies?

Elisha and the Starving City

II Kings 7

PART ONE

Elisha was still the prophet in Israel. One day, Ben-hadad, the king of Syria, gathered all his soldiers together and came back into Israel's country. They came to the city of Samaria where the king's palace was. Elisha was living in Samaria, too.

Ben-hadad and his soldiers put up their tents around Samaria and wouldn't let anyone go in or out of the city. Day after day, week after week, month after month they stood guard around Samaria. After some time there was no food left in Samaria. The people and the animals were dying of starvation.

The king blamed Elisha for this great trouble which had come to his city. Elisha had often warned him that God would punish him and his people for not serving God. The king said, "I shall cut off Elisha's head today for bringing all this trouble." He sent his servant to Elisha's house to carry out his threat.

Elisha was sitting in his house with the elders of the city. He said to the men, "Here comes the king's servant to cut off my head. Shut the door on him. Isn't his master, the king, coming right behind him?"

Elisha was right. The king had followed his servant to Elisha's house. Elisha let them both in. The king said, "All this trouble is of the Lord. Why should I wait for the Lord any longer?"

And Elisha answered, "Listen to what the Lord says. He says, 'Tomorrow about this time there will be plenty of food at the very gates of Samaria.'"

But the king's servant did not believe Elisha. He laughed at him. "How could such a thing ever be?" he said. "Why, if God should make windows in heaven and pour the food down, there wouldn't be enough for all these starving people!"

Elisha answered, "Since you do not believe me, you will see it happen with your eyes, but you will not taste any of the food."

PART TWO

That night, four starving lepers were prowling around at the gate of Samaria. They knew that it would do no good to go into the city for there was no food there. They knew, too, that if they did not get food soon they would die. Finally they decided to go to the tents of the Syrians to see if they could steal some food. "If they catch us and kill us, it will make no difference," they said. "We are going to die of hunger anyway."

When they came to the Syrian tents, there were no soldiers there. God had frightened the Syrians. He had made a loud noise as if a huge army of horses and chariots was coming after them. The Syrians thought the king of Israel had hired the kings of Egypt and of the Hittites to come after them. So they all arose in the twilight and fled for their lives, leaving everything behind them.

When the lepers found the empty camp, they were greatly excited. They went into one tent and ate and drank all that they could. Then they carried away all that was left — food and clothing and silver and gold. They hid it in their caves. Then they came back for more.

Finally they said to each other, "We aren't doing right. This is a day of good cheer and we are not telling anyone. Let's go into the city and tell the king." So they ran to tell the watchman on the wall. And the watchman told the king. The king wouldn't believe the good news. He said, "The Syrians are trying to fool us. If we

go out to their tents, they will come into our city and burn it."
Finally, however, he sent some soldiers to look. They found that
the lepers were telling the truth.

When morning came, the king allowed the people to go out
to the Syrian tents to help themselves to anything they found. He
appointed his servant to stand guard at the gate to keep the people
from hurting each other in their hurry. But the people paid no
attention to the servant. They crowded past him. They knocked
him down and stepped on him until he was dead.

So the words of Elisha, the prophet, came true. There was
plenty of food for everyone. But the servant who laughed at Elisha
only saw the food. He did not eat of it, for they killed him in
the gate.

> *Were you listening?* What did Ben-hadad and his army do to Sa-
> maria? Whom did the king blame for their trouble? What did
> Elisha promise the king? How did God provide food for all those
> starving people? Why didn't the king's servant eat any of it?

Story 132

The Servant Who Killed His Master

II Kings 8

One day Elisha went to Damascus. Ben-hadad, the king of
Syria, was sick. When Ben-hadad heard that Elisha was in his
town, he sent his servant Hazael to Elisha to ask him if he would
get better from his sickness. He told Hazael to bring Elisha a
present.

Hazael took a gift to Elisha. He brought some of every good
thing of Damascus. It took forty camels to carry his gifts. When
he came to Elisha, he gave him all the lovely presents. Then he
stood before him and said, "Your son, Ben-hadad, wants to know
if he is going to get better from his sickness."

Elisha said, "Go tell him that his sickness is not serious. He
could easily get better. But he is not going to, for the Lord has
told me that he is surely doing to die."

Hazael looked at Elisha for a long time. Elisha looked at
Hazael. Suddenly Elisha began to cry. "Why are you crying?"
Hazael asked.

"I am crying because I know of the terrible things you are going to do to the children of Israel. You are going to burn their cities with fire and kill their young men with the sword. You will kill their mothers and dash their children to pieces."

Hazael did not believe Elisha's words. "What," he cried, "do you think I am a dog that I should do such a terrible thing?"

But Elisha answered, "The Lord has shown me that you are going to be king over Syria."

Then Hazael left Elisha and went back to his master. As soon as Ben-hadad saw him he asked, "What did Elisha say?"

Hazael answered, "Elisha said that you would surely get better."

But Hazael did not tell his master the whole truth. Neither did he tell him that Elisha had said he, the servant, would be the king over Syria. That night Hazael thought and thought about Elisha's words. The more he thought about it, the more he liked the idea that he would be the next king. Then a most wicked thought came into his head. Ben-hadad was old and sick. It would be an easy matter to kill him. Then he could be the king right away.

So Hazael carefully made his plans. When morning came Hazael took a thick cloth and dipped it in water. Then he took this wet cloth into the king's bedroom. The king was still asleep. Hazael quietly spread the wet cloth over the king's face. He covered the king's nose and mouth so tightly that the king could not breathe. In a short time the king died. Then Hazael sat upon the throne and declared himself the king of Syria.

Were you listening? Why did Elisha cry when he talked with Hazael? How did Hazael become the king of Syria?

Story 133

The End of Ahab's Family

II Kings 9 and 10; II Chronicles 21 and 22

PART ONE

While Elisha was the prophet of Israel, Ahaziah was the king of Judah. Ahab's son, Jehoram, was the king of Israel. One day Jehoram was at home sick, and Ahaziah, the king of Judah, came down to Jezreel to visit him.

At the same time Elisha sent one of the young students at the school of the prophets to run an errand. He sent him to Ramoth-gilead with a bottle of oil. "When you get there," Elisha said, "look for Jehu, the son of Jehoshaphat. Take him aside where no one will see you. Anoint him to be the king over Israel. Then open the door and run away as fast as you can."

The young man hurried to Ramoth-gilead. He found all the generals of the army having a meeting. "I have a message for you, O General," he cried.

"Which general?" Jehu asked.

"You, my lord," the young prophet said. Then Jehu took him inside the house. The young prophet quickly poured oil on Jehu's head. "The Lord God of Israel anoints you to be king over His people," he said. "And you shall destroy all the house of your master Ahab because of what his wife Jezebel did to God's servants, the prophets. God wants you to completely destroy all of Ahab's family."

As soon as the young man had finished giving Jehu his message, he opened the door and fled. Then Jehu went back to the other generals. "What's the matter?" they asked. "What did that mad man want with you?"

"Oh, you know how a fellow like that talks," Jehu said.

"You are lying," they said. "Come on, tell us what happened."

Then Jehu told them that he had been anointed king over Israel. As soon as the generals heard it, they rushed up to Jehu and threw their robes on the bare steps for Jehu to walk on. They blew their trumpets and they shouted, "Jehu is king!"

Jehu quickly got into his chariot and drove off to Jezreel where the king of Judah was visiting the sick king of Israel. The other generals went with him. The watchman on the tower caught sight of Jehu's company. He reported it to the king. King Jehoram quickly sent a soldier on horseback to meet them. "Ask them if everything is all right," the king commanded.

The horseman did as his king commanded.

"What have you to do with peace?" Jehu said. "Get behind me."

When the watchman saw that the horseman did not come back,

he told the king. So the king sent a second horseman with the same message. Jehu sent this horseman behind him, too. And he kept on driving furiously.

The watchman told the king about his second messenger, too. And he added, "It looks as if the man is Jehu, for he drives like a madman." Then Jehoram got into his chariot and King Ahaziah got into his. They both rode out to meet Jehu.

"Is all well, Jehu?" Jehoram asked.

"How can things be well, as long as your wicked mother Jezebel keeps on with all her wickedness?" Jehu answered.

Jehoram quickly wheeled his chariot around and shouted, "Flee, Ahaziah, for he is against us!"

But Jehu had his bow ready. He struck Jehoram through the heart. Jehoram sank down in his chariot. "Throw him out into Naboth's field at the side of the road," Jehu commanded his officer. "For I remember when I rode in his father Ahab's army. I stood on this very spot when God's servant Elijah said to Ahab, 'Since you killed Naboth to get this vineyard, I will have you punished in this same place.' "

Then Jehu went after King Ahaziah, too. Ahaziah was wounded as he was going up a hill, but he got away. He rode as far as Megiddo. There he died.

PART TWO

Then Jehu rode into Jezreel. Queen Jezebel heard that Jehu was coming. She dressed in all her finery. She painted her face and put her crown on her head. Then she went to the open window. As Jehu rode through the gateway she called to him, "How are you, you murderer of your master?"

Jehu looked up to the window. He called, "Who is on my side?"

Two or three young men looked out. "Throw her down," Jehu cried.

The men threw Jezebel out of the window. She fell to the ground and was killed. Then Jehu went inside to eat his dinner. When he had finished eating, he said to his servants, "Now go and see to that wicked woman. You had better have her buried, for she was a king's daughter."

But when the servants went to bury her, her body was no longer there. The dogs had eaten her up.

Jehu's work was not yet finished, however. The prophet who had anointed him to be king had commanded that he should kill everyone who belonged to Ahab's family. Now Ahab had many wives and children. His seventy sons were living in Samaria. So Jehu sent letters to the men who had charge of all these sons. "I command you to kill them all," he wrote.

Not long after this Jehu met forty-two young men who were Ahab's grandsons. He ordered his soldiers to kill them all, too. Jehu did not rest until Ahab's family was completely wiped out. So Elijah's words came true. The wicked family of Ahab was destroyed.

> *Were you listening?* What did Elisha want one of the young prophets to do for him? What did Jehu do as soon as he became king? What did Jehu do when he came into Jezreel? How did Elijah's words come true?

Story 134

A Little Boy Becomes King

II Kings 11; II Chronicles 22 and 23

When Ahaziah, the king of Judah, was killed by Jehu, his mother, Athaliah, made plans of her own. Athaliah was the daughter of the wicked Queen Jezebel. She was just as wicked as her mother had been. She had been the queen in Judah's palace for many years, first as King Jehoram's wife and then as King Ahaziah's mother. Now she wanted to be the queen in her own right. She ordered all the members of the royal family killed. She killed her own grandchildren and nieces and nephews, so that she might be the only one left to rule over Judah.

But this wicked queen did not succeed in her evil plans for long. One of her grandchildren had not been killed. King Ahaziah had a little baby boy who was just one year old when his father was killed. When this little boy's grandmother was busy killing all of his relatives, his aunt, who was King Ahaziah's sister, hid him and his nurse in a bedroom. So grandmother Athaliah did not find the baby.

For six years this wicked grandmother, Athaliah, was queen over Judah. During all those six years, the little boy, whose name was Joash, was hidden in the house of the Lord.

One day, when Joash was seven years old, the minister in God's house, Jehoiada, brought a great number of soldiers and captains and guards into the Temple. He showed them the little boy Joash. Then the minister set the soldiers as guards at all the doors of the Temple and at the queen's palace. He brought out all the spears and the shields, which had once belonged to King David, from the Temple. He gave them to the soldiers.

As the soldiers stood guard over the Temple, the minister brought out the young boy, Joash. He placed the king's crown on Joash's head and anointed him to be the king over Judah. Many people had gathered at the Temple to see what was going to happen. When they saw the new young king, they shouted, "God save the king!"

Queen Athaliah heard all the noise. She ran into the temple. There stood the little boy-king, a crown on his head. He was standing by a pillar, as the kings always did. The princes and the trumpeters were standing around him. The people were still shouting for joy and blowing their trumpets. The queen tore her clothing and cried out, "Treason; Treason!" She meant that her people had turned against her.

The minister did not think it was treason. He knew that it was the queen who was the wicked one. He commanded the soldiers to take her outside the Temple and kill her. The soldiers quickly captured the queen. They brought her outside and killed her.

Then all the people brought the little boy-king out of the Temple and into the palace of the king. So the little boy, Joash, sat on the throne of the kings. And he was just seven years old when he began to reign over Judah.

> *Were you listening?* Why did Athaliah try to kill all the royal family? What happened to the baby, Joash? What did the minister do six years later? What happened to Joash's grandmother?

Joash's Treasure Chest

II Kings 12; II Chronicles 24

Joash reigned over Judah for forty years. Jehoiada, the minister, taught him and helped him to be a good king. Although Joash was a good king, he did not take away the places where the people sacrificed to idols.

When Joash's grandmother, the wicked Athaliah, had been the queen, her sons had broken up the beautiful House of God, the Temple. They had taken away the lovely gold and silver vases and plates and cups which King Solomon had made for the Temple. They had used them in their idol worship. Besides this, for many years the people had forgotten to pay their taxes for the church, even though Moses had commanded them to do so. So the Temple was still broken down.

One day Joash told all the ministers again to collect the taxes from all the people so that they might repair the broken-down church. But the ministers did not obey King Joash. Nothing was done.

After Joash had been king for twenty-three years, the Temple was still broken down. The king called for Jehoiada, the minister. "Why haven't you repaired the broken House of the Lord?" he asked.

Then Jehoiada promised to do something about it. He had a large chest made. It had a hole bored in the cover. He put the chest beside the altar, on the right side as one came into the Temple. Then he sent a notice to all the people to come to pay their taxes. The people were asked to drop their money into the big treasure chest.

Day after day the minister collected money in the treasure chest. Whenever the chest was too full, it was emptied and the money brought to the king. Finally, when enough money had been collected, the king and the minister hired carpenters and masons. They set to work at once repairing the House of the Lord. When it was all finished, they brought the rest of the money to the king. Then the king ordered new gold and silver vessels to be made for the Temple.

As long as Jehoiada, the minister lived, King Joash was a good king. But the minister was old. Finally Jehoiada died when he was a hundred and thirty years old. Then the princes of Judah came to help King Joash, and the king listened to these men. Together they left the House of the Lord and worshiped idols. Again and again the Lord sent prophets to the king and his princes to bring them back to the Lord. But they would not listen. Finally the old minister's son, Zechariah, came to warn the king. But the king would not listen to him, either. He had him stoned to death.

Then the Lord sent the Syrian army to fight against Judah. The Syrians won the battle because the people of Judah had turned away from their God. After the war was over and the Syrians had gone, King Joash was sick in bed. His servants were angry with him for killing the minister's son, Zechariah. These servants went into the king's bedroom and killed him as he lay in his bed.

Were you listening? How long did the little boy-king reign? What had happened to the beautiful Temple which Solomon had built? How did the minister get enough money to rebuild the Temple? What happened to King Joash after the old minister died?

Story 136

The Death of Elisha

II Kings 13

Jehu, the man who killed all of King Ahab's family, was king in Israel for twenty-eight years. Then his son, Jehoahaz, was the king for seventeen years. Jehoahaz was a most wicked king. Under him the kingdom of Israel was almost destroyed. The Syrians made war with Israel and took away most of its army and weapons. The Syrians also took away many of Israel's cities.

When King Jehoahaz died, his son, Jehoash, was made king. He, too, was wicked. While Jehoash was the king, Elisha became sick. Elisha was now an old man and the people knew that he would not get better from his sickness. When the king heard that Elisha was going to die, he went down to visit him.

The king stood at Elisha's bed and wept over him. He knew that it was this man of God who had helped Israel so many times. He cried out, "My father, my father, you are worth more than all the chariots and horsemen of Israel!"

Then Elisha got up and went to the window with the king. He told the king to open the window toward the east. "Get your bow ready to shoot," Elisha commanded. The king drew his bow, ready to shoot, but Elisha held his hand over the king's hand until the window opened. Then Elisha took away his hand and said, "Shoot."

As the arrow left the king's bow and shot through the window towards the east, Elisha cried, "It is the arrow of God's victory! Victory over Aram! You shall defeat them and wipe them out!"

Now Elisha told the king to take some more arrows. The king obeyed. "Strike them into the ground," Elisha said. The king took three arrows and struck them down into the ground. Then he stopped.

"Why did you stop?" Elisha asked. "You should have struck five or six times. Then you would have completely destroyed Aram. Now you will defeat them only three times."

Not long after this, Elisha died and was buried. One day, after Elisha had been buried, some people were burying another dead man. They were walking down the road, carrying the dead man to his grave. Just then the people saw a band of robbers, and they all ran away. The men who were carrying the dead body noticed that they were passing the tomb of Elisha. They threw the dead man into Elisha's tomb. As soon as the man touched the bones of Elisha, he became alive again and stood on his feet. So Elisha, the great man of God, worked miracles even after he was dead!

Elisha reminds us of our Saviour, Jesus Christ, doesn't he? Jesus worked even greater miracles than Elisha. When He died, He worked the greatest miracle of all. He arose again from the dead and saved all His people from their sins!

After Elisha was dead, his words to the king came true. King Jehoash made war with the Syrians and took back the cities which his father had lost. He also made war with the Kingdom of Judah. He marched to Jerusalem and broke down a great part of the wall. Then he stole all the gold and silver and the beautiful treasures from the Temple. From there he went to the palace of the king and stole all his treasures. When he returned to Samaria he took many of the people back with him as captives.

King Jehoash reigned sixteen years. When he died, his son Jeroboam became king in his stead. This was the second Jeroboam to be king.

Were you listening? Why did King Jehoash go to visit Elisha? Why should the king have shot six arrows instead of three? In what way did Elisha remind us of Jesus?

Story 137

Jonah Disobeys God

Jonah 1 and 2

Jonah was a prophet who lived while the second Jeroboam was king of Israel. Assyria was the greatest world-empire at this time. This country was great for about three hundred years. It became a great nation about the time when King Solomon died. During all the years that followed, Assyria fought against God's people time and time again.

The Assyrians fought against both Israel and Judah. They gradually took over and completely destroyed the Kingdom of Israel. So the people of Israel did not like the Assyrians. The prophet Jonah did not like them either.

One day God came to Jonah and said, "Jonah, I want you to go to the great city of Nineveh and preach to the people. The people of Nineveh are extremely wicked. You tell those people that if they do not turn away from their wickedness, I shall destroy their city."

Nineveh was the capital of the Assyrian nation. Jonah did not want to preach to the Assyrian people. They were his enemies. He would rather have seen them destroyed. So, although Jonah was a man of God, he did not obey his Master. He did not go to Nineveh. He tried to run away from God. Instead of going towards Nineveh, he went in the opposite direction. He went down to Joppa which was on the sea shore. There he boarded a ship going to Tarshish.

But Jonah could not run away from God. God is everywhere. As soon as God saw what Jonah was trying to do, He sent a great wind storm on the sea. The little ship tossed about in the stormy sea. The sailors were terrified. They were afraid their ship was going to be broken in pieces. They threw all their baggage into the sea so that the ship would not be so heavy. But this did not help. Each one of the sailors prayed to his own god to save him. But that did not help, either, for the sailors did not know the true God. They worshiped idols.

All this while, Jonah was fast asleep in his room below. Finally the captain went to him. He shook him awake and said, "What are you doing asleep when we are having such a bad storm? Get up and pray to your god. Perhaps he can save us."

But Jonah was running away from his God. He couldn't ask Him for help. Then the sailors drew lots to see who was to blame for this terrible storm. The lot fell on Jonah.

The sailors all looked at Jonah. "Who are you?" they asked. "What did you do and where did you come from?"

Jonah told them that he was running away from his God. "I am a Hebrew," he explained. "I worship the Lord, the God of heaven who made the sea and the dry land."

The sailors were filled with fear when they heard Jonah's words. "What shall we do?" they cried.

"Throw me into the sea," Jonah said, "then the storm will stop. For I see that I am to blame for this storm."

The men did not like to drown Jonah. They all tried as hard as they could to bring their ship to land. But they couldn't. Then they prayed to Jonah's God. They cried, "O Eternal God, we pray Thee, do not let us die for taking this man's life. Do not punish us for drowning him. You, Yourself, have sent us this storm."

Then they picked up Jonah and threw him into the water. The storm stopped at once. The sailors were filled with fear of the Lord. They offered sacrifices to Him and promised to obey Him.

But God did not let His servant drown. As Jonah was thrown into the sea, God sent a big fish to swallow him up. Jonah was swallowed whole. He sat in the belly of this fish for three days and three nights. He was like a prisoner in a dungeon. But while Jonah was in this fish, he had time to think. He realized that it was sin to disobey God. So he prayed to God. He promised God that he would obey His commands and do His will. Jonah was drawn very close to God in those days.

Then God spoke to the fish. The fish swam to the shore and threw Jonah out on the dry land.

Were you listening? What did God want Jonah to do? Why didn't Jonah want to do it? What happened to Jonah? What miracle did God work for Jonah?

Story 138

Jonah Is Unhappy Because of God's Kindness

Jonah 3 and 4

After the fish had thrown Jonah on the shore, God came to him a second time. "Jonah," God said, "go to Nineveh, that great city, and preach to it what I shall tell you."

This time Jonah obeyed God. He went to Nineveh. Now Nineveh was a large city. It took three days to walk across it from one end to the other. Jonah began at one end of the city and walked for one day. As he walked, he shouted to the people, "Forty days more and God will destroy this city!" So Jonah warned the people to turn away from their wickedness lest they be killed.

The people of Nineveh knew that Jonah's God was a great God. They knew that He would be able to keep His threat. They stopped their work. They changed their clothing. They wore sackcloth and ashes instead to show they were sorry for their sins. They did not even eat. When the news reached the king, he left his royal throne, took off his beautiful robe, and covered himself with sackcloth, too. Then he sat down in ashes. He sent messengers to cry to all the people of his city. They cried, "By order of the king and his nobles! No one — not man or animal — must taste any food or drink. They must put on sackcloth and pray earnestly to God. Everyone must turn from his wicked ways. Who knows, perhaps God will be kind and turn away from His hot anger and save us!"

God was kind. He saw what the people of Nineveh were doing and decided not to punish them as He had said He would.

Jonah was greatly displeased. He was angry with God. He

said, "O God, didn't I tell you that this would happen when I
was still at home? That's why I ran away to Tarshish. I knew
you were a gracious and kind God. I knew you were rich in love
and wouldn't get angry very quickly. I knew you would forgive
them! Now then, O God, take my life away. I would rather die
than live!"

"Do you have any right to be angry?" God asked.

Then Jonah went outside of the city. He put up a little shelter
and sat down under it, in the shade, so that he could watch and
see what would happen to the city.

God saw Jonah sitting there. God was kind to Jonah. He made
a lovely plant, called a gourd, grow up beside Jonah. The plant
was tall and big. It had broad leaves which shaded Jonah from
the sun. Jonah was filled with joy because of the gourd.

But the next morning, just as the sun was coming up, God
sent a worm into the ground where the gourd was growing. The
worm gnawed at the roots of the plant until it withered and died.
When the sun came up, God sent a hot east wind. The sun beat
on Jonah's head and the wind blew across his face until he fainted
and wished he were dead. "It is better for me to die than to live,"
Jonah cried.

Then God said to Jonah, "Are you right to be angry over the
gourd?"

"Yes," Jonah answered, "I have a right to be angry — angry
enough to die."

"Well," God said, "if you are sorry about the gourd, shouldn't
I feel sorry for that great city, Nineveh? You had nothing to do
with the gourd. You did not make it grow. Besides, it was a plant
that sprang up in one night and died in one night. But Nineveh
is a great city which I have made. Should I not feel sorry for it with
its thousands of helpless little children and all its animals?"

So God showed Jonah that it was wrong for him to want to
have his enemies destroyed, even though they were wicked. God
loves all the people He has made. He wants all to turn away from
their sins and turn to Him.

> *Were you listening?* What happened in the city of Nineveh when
> Jonah began to preach there? Why was Jonah angry with God?
> What did God teach Jonah by sending him the gourd and then
> letting it die?

A King Who Became a Leper

II Kings 14 and 15; II Chronicles 26

PART ONE

Jeroboam the second reigned over Israel for forty-one years. He was not a good king. He and his people worshiped the golden calves. Jeroboam was a brave soldier, however. He won many great battles against the Syrians. The Israelites had suffered so much because of the Syrians that God felt sorry for them and helped Jeroboam with the fighting. With God's help Jeroboam won back many of the cities which the Syrians had taken. So, for a time, the Kingdom of Israel was almost as large as it had been when Solomon was king.

While Jeroboam was the king, God sent two great prophets to talk to His people. They were Amos and Hosea. Amos and Hosea both tried to lead the people back to God. They told the people that God would surely punish them for all their sins. If they kept on worshiping idols, God would surely do what He had threatened to do hundreds of years before when Moses was still their leader. God had told Moses that if they worshiped idols and forgot Him, He would some day send them away from their wonderful "land of promise." For years Israel had been worshiping idols. Amos and Hosea told them that God would soon keep His threat if they did not turn to Him.

A few of the common people listened to the prophets and turned to God. But the leaders and most of the people kept right on with their wicked ways. Jeroboam's son, Zachariah, followed his father as king. He was worse than his father had been. He was king for only a half year when his servant Shallum killed him. Then Shallum became the king. Shallum was king for only a month when a man named Menahem killed him. Menahem ruled for ten years. He was a most cruel king. He led his people into even greater wickedness and idol worship.

King Menahem died and his son, Pekahiah, reigned. Pekahiah was as bad as his father. He reigned for only two years. He was killed by his own general, a man named Pekah. Then Pekah reigned for twenty years.

PART TWO

During all this time, while Israel had six bad kings, Judah had only one king. He was the good king Uzziah. Uzziah was only sixteen years old when he became the king. He reigned for fifty-two years. Uzziah loved the Lord and worshiped Him. He taught his people to worship the Lord, too. So good King Uzziah and his people were living in peace and happiness while the Kingdom of Israel was going from bad to worse.

Whenever King Uzziah went out to fight against his enemies, he always won the battle. He built strong walls and towers around Jerusalem to protect his people. He even had engines on the top of his towers to shoot arrows and stones. People were amazed at his great invention.

King Uzziah was a good farmer, too. He owned many wonderful vineyards and large flocks of sheep and cattle. His fame soon spread to other countries, even as far away as Egypt. Everyone knew that King Uzziah's kingdom was unusually great.

It is most difficult to love and obey God when one becomes great. A great man is so apt to become proud of his greatness. King Uzziah, too, became proud. In his pride he thought he could do things which a king was not allowed to do. Only the priest was allowed to burn incense on the golden altar of incense in the Temple.

One day King Uzziah took a censer and went into the Holy of Holies in the Temple to burn incense. All the priests saw him go. Eighty of them went in after him. They said, "You may not burn incense, King Uzziah. Only the priests of Aaron's tribe may do that. God will be angry with you if you do this."

King Uzziah was angry with the priests for trying to stop him. He stood still for a moment in front of the altar, his censer in hand. God punished the king even as he stood there in front of His altar. Great white spots began to appear on his forehead. The king put his hand to his head. It was leprosy! The priests stared in horror at their king.

When the priests realized what was wrong, they rushed up to the king and began to push him out of the sacred place. But they did not have to force the king to leave the Temple. As soon as the king saw that he was a leper, he ran out as fast as he could. From that day on King Uzziah lived in a house by himself. His son Jotham ruled for him in the palace. Never again could the proud king stand before his people or go into the House of the Lord! He was a leper until he died.

Were you listening? How many bad kings did Israel have? Who was the good king in Judah? Why did Judah's good king become a leper?

Story 140

The Brave Prophet Isaiah

Isaiah 6, 7, 9 and 53

While Uzziah was still the king of Judah, there lived a prophet whose name was Isaiah. Isaiah was perhaps the greatest prophet who ever lived. He was not a farmer as the prophet Amos had been. He was an educated man. Isaiah wrote history books. He was the prophet during the reign of four kings of Judah — Uzziah, Jotham, Ahaz and Hezekiah.

God called Isaiah to be a prophet in the same year that Uzziah died. Isaiah tells us about that call in the book of the Bible which has his name. When God called Isaiah, He came to him in a wonderful vision. Isaiah saw the Lord sitting on a shining throne. The Lord's robes trailed around Him and spread over the temple floor. The throne was high and lifted up. A host of angels surrounded it. These angels were the greatest of all God's heavenly beings. They were called seraphim.

Each seraphim had six wings. Two wings covered his face and two covered his feet. The other two he used to fly with. The seraphim called back and forth to each other. They cried, "Holy, holy, holy, is the Lord of Hosts! The whole earth is full of His glory!"

At the sound of the chanting, the doors shook and the Temple began to fill with smoke. Isaiah was afraid. He cried, "Alas, I am undone! Man of unclean lips that I am, living among a people of unclean lips! I am undone, for my eyes have seen the King, the Lord of Hosts!"

But one of the seraphim flew to the altar. He took a pair of tongs and lifted a live coal from the fire. Then he flew to Isaiah

and touched his mouth with the live coal. He said, "Now that this has touched your lips, your guilt is gone, your sin is forgiven."

As Isaiah stood before the throne, he heard the voice of the Lord. The Lord said, "Whom shall I send? Who will go for us?"

"Here I am," Isaiah answered. "Send me."

"Go," the Lord said, "and tell this people, 'Listen and listen — but never understand! Look and look — but never see! Make the mind of this people dull, make their ears heavy and close their eyes. Lest they see and hear and understand, and be made better.'"

Then Isaiah cried, "O Lord, how long?"

And God answered, "Until they are all ruined, till their towns are empty and their houses without people, and the land left desolate. Until the Lord sends His people far away, and much of the land lies bare."

So Isaiah became the prophet for the Lord. God gave Isaiah many messages for the people. The book of Isaiah is full of them. Isaiah has often been called the "Messiah-prophet" because he spoke so often about the coming of the great Messiah, the Son of God who was to be our Saviour. He talked about a young woman (a virgin) who would have a son. He wrote:

> "Unto us a child is born,
> Unto us a son is given.
> And his name shall be called
> Wonderful, Counselor, Mighty God,
> Everlasting Father, Prince of Peace."

He talked about the things that would happen to Jesus while He lived on this earth. He told how men would hate Jesus and make Him suffer. He called Him "a man of sorrows." He said He would suffer and die for our sins.

When Jesus lived on this earth, He knew all the things which Isaiah had said about Him. He often talked about Isaiah's words.

Although God's people did not understand all the things Isaiah told them, they knew that God was some day going to send them a Saviour. They were happy to hear these wonderful words of Isaiah. Isaiah helped them to look forward with eagerness to the day when God would fulfill His promises.

Were you listening? Who was the greatest prophet? How did God call him to be a prophet? Whom did Isaiah often tell about? What did Isaiah say about Him?

Story 141

The Ten Lost Tribes of Israel

II Kings 17; II Chronicles 28

PART ONE

Remember King Uzziah who became a leper? His son, Jotham, became the king of Judah when Uzziah left the throne. Jotham was also a good king, but his son, Ahaz, was one of the worst kings Judah ever had. He made idols for the heathen god, Baal. He sacrificed his children to Baal. Instead of sacrificing to God in His Temple, he sacrificed to heathen gods on hills and under green trees. He taught many of his people to worship idols, too. Ahaz was making Judah to be like Israel in its wickedness.

Then God punished Judah for its sins. He sent two kings and their armies to fight the people of Judah. One was the king of Syria, the other was King Pekah of Israel. The Syrians won over Judah, and so did the Israelites. In one day Pekah's soldiers killed one hundred twenty thousand men of Judah. They carried two hundred thousand women and children of Judah back with them as slaves.

The soldiers of Israel came back to Samaria with all their slaves. There a prophet of God refused to let them into the city. He went out to meet the soldiers. "God is already angry with you for all your sins. Do not make Him more angry by taking all these women and children, who are also God's people, as slaves."

Some of the leaders of the Israelites came to the soldiers, too. "You shall not come into our city with your captives," they said. So the soldiers left all their captives outside of the city of Samaria. They left all the treasures they had taken, too. Then the leaders gave these captives food and drink. They also gave them the clothing which the soldiers had brought with them. They gave the weak people donkeys to ride on. They sent them all back to their homes.

But the wicked King Ahaz still had not learned his lesson. Instead of asking God to help him against his enemies, he sent to the king of Assyria for help. He took all the gold and silver out of the Temple to pay the king of Assyria for his help.

The Assyrians came as far as Damascus and fought against it. King Ahaz went to help. While in Damascus, he sacrificed at a heathen altar. He liked that altar so much that he built one like it in Jerusalem when he came back home. Then he closed the doors of the Temple of the Lord and worshiped the heathen gods instead. He even cut up the gold and silver dishes of the Temple and used parts of them for the heathen altar which he had built.

King Ahaz was very foolish to ask the Assyrians to destroy Damascus. Now there was no city between him and the Assyrians. The Assyrians could come any time and destroy his country. Not too many years later, that is exactly what happened.

PART TWO

King Pekah of Israel had reigned for twenty years. Then Hoshea killed him and became the king. After Hoshea had reigned nine years, a new king of Assyria came and made war against Israel. He took the city of Samaria where the king lived. He made King Hoshea his servant. Hoshea had to pay him tribute money.

Soon King Hoshea refused to pay the tribute money. He tried to get the king of Egypt to help him fight against Assyria. But as soon as the king of Assyria heard about it, he marched against Samaria once more. He fought against Samaria for three years.

Finally he won. He took King Hoshea captive. And he carried most of the people of Israel back to Assyria with him.

Finally, after all those many years of warning, God carried out His threat. For the last time these people of Israel saw their lovely promised land. The land would have been theirs forever if they had remembered to worship the God who had given it to them. Now they were carried to the far-away land of Assyria. Soon they were scattered among the heathen nations.

After many years these Israelites married the heathen people and became a part of them. They were no longer a separate people. They were no longer God's special people. No one knows what has become of them. They are called "the lost tribes of the children of Israel." The Bible never tells of them again. All the rest of the stories of the Bible are about the Kingdom of Judah.

After the Israelites were gone from their country, people from Babylon were brought to live in the land. They were heathen people who did not know God. They worshiped their idols instead. At one time God sent lions to kill some of them. The king of Assyria heard about the lions. He sent one of the captive priests of the Israelites back to teach the heathen people how to worship God.

Although the priest taught the people about the true God, it did not work too well. For the people would not give up their idols. They worshiped God and their heathen idols, too. In later years these people were called Samaritans. The people of Judah always looked down on the Samaritans because they were not true Israelites.

> *Were you listening?* What happened to Judah when their king made them sin? What happened to the Kingdom of Israel? Where are the Ten Tribes of Israel today? Who are the Samaritans?

Story 142
Hezekiah Brings His People Back to God

II Kings 18; II Chronicles 29 and 30

There was only one Kingdom in Israel now. It was the Kingdom of Judah. The rest of the tribes of Israel (the ten lost tribes) had been completely destroyed because of their wickedness. The

Kingdom of Judah had been good when Uzziah was the king. His son, Jotham, had also been a good king and Judah had been happy during his reign. But Jotham's son, Ahaz, had turned his people away from God. He had brought idol worship into Judah. He had brought great trouble to his people because of it.

After wicked King Ahaz died, his son, Hezekiah, became the king. Hezekiah was twenty-five years old when he began to reign. He was not like his father Ahaz. He was like the great king David who loved to serve God. Hezekiah stopped his people from serving the heathen gods. He broke down their altars and cut down the trees in the parks where the people worshiped.

King Hezekiah trusted in God. He obeyed Him and did everything God wanted him to do. And God was with King Hezekiah wherever he went. God blessed him in whatever he did. When he went out to battle, God went before him and gave him the victory.

When Hezekiah had finished breaking down the heathen altars, he began to repair the House of God. The people had not taken good care of God's House. They had not kept the doors of the Temple open, nor had they kept the lamps burning. They had forgotten to offer incense and burnt-offerings in the Holy Place. They had been burning their sacrifices on the heathen altar which King Ahaz had built.

In the very first year of his reign King Hezekiah opened the doors of God's House. He called the priests and the Levites. Together they took out all the things which did not belong in the Temple. They lit lamps and burned incense and offered sacrifices. Then they called all the people to come to God's House to worship there and to keep the feast of the Passover. The Israelites were supposed to keep the Passover every year in the spring, but they had not kept it for a long time.

"Be not like your fathers," King Hezekiah said, "but come to Jehovah and serve your God." Many people heard the king's call. They came to God's House and worshiped Him there. And there was great joy among the people.

Were you listening? In what way was King Hezekiah like King David? What did King Hezekiah do for God's House? Why was there great joy in Judah?

God Destroys Israel's Enemy

II Kings 18 and 19; II Chronicles 32; Isaiah 36 and 37

Hezekiah had been the king of Judah for fourteen years. One day King Sennacherib of Assyria came with his army and took several of the strong cities of Judah away from King Hezekiah. Then he sent one of his officers to Jerusalem with a great army. The army came and stood by the upper pool near the highway. King Hezekiah sent his servants to meet the army.

Rabshakeh, the Assyrian officer, made fun of King Hezekiah because he trusted in God. King Hezekiah had only a few soldiers and the Assyrian army was extremely large. When the Assyrian captain began to mock Hezekiah, the servants of the king said, "Don't talk to us in our own language. We can understand your language. We do not want all of our people who are on the wall to hear you."

But Rabshakeh would not listen to the king's servants. He wanted all the people to understand him. He began to shout to all the Jews, "Don't let King Hezekiah fool you! He won't be able to deliver you! And don't trust in Hezekiah's God! He won't be able to help you against our army. Come and make peace with us, and we'll take care of you. We'll give you everything you want. Your God can't save you. Did any of the other countries' gods save them? Then why should your God save you?"

But the men of Judah did not answer the captain. Soon King Hezekiah heard about the wicked words which the Assyrian captain had shouted. He tore his clothes and covered himself with sackcloth. Then he sent his servants to tell Isaiah, the man of God, about it. "This is a day of trouble," he said, "and we do not know what to do. Please pray for us and ask God to help us."

Isaiah answered, "Jehovah says, 'Don't be afraid of the words of this wicked man. I will send these people back to their own land.'"

Not long after this, King Sennacherib sent a letter to Hezekiah. He wrote many bad things about God in his letter. He said, "Don't let your God fool you, King Hezekiah. He can't save you from my army. Don't you remember what happened to all the other nations when we came into their countries? Where are all the kings of those countries?"

King Hezekiah took this letter into God's House and spread it out before the Lord. "O Lord of Hosts," he prayed, "the God of Israel, Thou who sittest in the heavens. Thou art the only God of all the kingdoms of the earth, for Thou hast made them all. Hear my prayer, O God. Look and see this letter. Read the words which this wicked king has written. I know, O God, that the Assyrians have taken all the other countries and have thrown their gods in the fire. But they were no gods. Therefore, O God, save us from this wicked king so that all the earth may know that you are the only true God!"

The Lord heard the words of good King Hezekiah. He went into the Assyrian camp one night and killed a hundred and eighty-five thousand soldiers. When the other soldiers rose up in the morning and saw all those who had been killed, they broke camp and went back to their own country. So once more the Lord saved His people.

> *Were you listening?* What did King Sennacherib do in Judah? To whom did King Hezekiah send for help? What did King Hezekiah do with the letter he received? How did God help His people?

Story 144

God Answers Hezekiah's Prayer

II Kings 20; II Chronicles 32; Isaiah 38 and 39

Hezekiah was a good king who always prayed to God. He ruled over Judah for many years. One day Hezekiah became sick. While he was sick, God sent His servant Isaiah to visit the king. Isaiah said to Hezekiah, "Jehovah says you must get your house in order, for you are not going to get better from your sickness. You are going to die."

King Hezekiah was still a young man. He was not ready to die. He wanted to be king a while longer so he could help his people serve the Lord. The prophet's words made the king sad. As he lay in his bed, he turned his face to the wall and began to cry. He cried and cried. The prophet left the king and started back to his home.

While King Hezekiah was crying, he prayed to God. He said, "Remember me, O God. You know how I have always tried to obey You, and have led Your people in the right way. Please do not let me die now!"

As the prophet Isaiah was walking home, before he had gone through the middle of the city, God stopped him and said, "Turn back and go again to King Hezekiah. Tell him that I have heard his prayer."

So Isaiah went back to the king's palace. He went into the king's bedroom and said, "God has heard your prayer, King Hezekiah. He has seen your tears. He will make you better. In three days you will be well enough to go into God's House. And God will add fifteen years to your life."

King Hezekiah said to Isaiah, "How shall I know that God is going to heal me and that I shall be able to go into God's House in three days?"

Isaiah answered, "This is the sign from God to show you that He will do what He has promised. He will make the sun go backwards for a little while, so that the shadow will go back ten steps." Then Isaiah cried to God and God brought the shadow ten steps backward.

The servants of King Hezekiah made a plaster of figs and put it on the king's sore. The prophet Isaiah had told them to do this. Soon the king was healed. He went up to God's House to thank Him for His care.

Not long after that, the king of Babylon sent letters and a present to King Hezekiah. He had heard that the king had been sick and was now better. This made King Hezekiah happy. He invited the king of Babylon into his palace. He showed him all the wonderful things he had. He showed him his silver and gold, his spices, his armor, and his jewels. There was nothing in his palace that he did not show.

But God did not like what the king had done. The king was proud of all his fine things instead of giving God the honor. So

God sent Isaiah to the palace. "Who are these men? Where did they come from?" Isaiah asked.

"All the way from Babylon are they come," answered the king.

"And what have they seen in your house?" Isaiah continued.

"I have shown them everything," the king said.

Then Isaiah answered, "Hear the words of Jehovah, O king. Because of your pride, the day is coming when all your things shall be carried into Babylon. And your people shall go into Babylon, too!"

Were you listening? Why did King Hezekiah cry? How did God answer his prayer? What sign did God give the king? Why were the king's treasures and his people going to be carried away to Babylon?

Story 145

Wicked Manasseh Turns to God

II Kings 21; II Chronicles 33

When the good King Hezekiah finally died, his son Manasseh became the king. Manasseh was only twelve years old when he began to reign. He reigned longer than any other king. He reigned for fifty-five years. But Manasseh was not a good king like his father Hezekiah or like the great King David. He was wicked like his grandfather Ahaz.

Young King Manasseh went back to the wicked idol worship which his father had destroyed. All the high places which Hezekiah had broken down, he rebuilt. He made groves where his people could worship their idols. He worshiped the stars as if they were gods, even making altars for his idols inside the House of God. He broke down the real altar where the people were supposed to worship the Lord, their God and took the holy, golden Ark of the Lord out of the Temple. No longer did he and his people remember to keep the Sabbath Day holy as God had commanded.

God sent His prophets to warn the wicked King Manasseh again and again. They tried to get the king and his people to turn away from their wicked ways. But they would not listen. Then God punished King Manasseh. He sent the armies of Assyria back into Judah. The Assyrians captured Manasseh, and took him with them in chains to Babylon.

When Manasseh was in trouble, then he remembered his God and the things his father had taught him. He prayed to God and asked Him to forgive him for all the wicked things he had done. He promised that he would serve God for the rest of his life.

God heard Manasseh's prayer. He brought him back to Jerusalem and let him be king again. Then Manasseh knew that the Lord was the only true God.

After Manasseh came back from Babylon, he became a good king like his father. No longer did he listen to the wicked men in his kingdom. He built a huge wall around Jerusalem to protect the city of David against its enemies. And he kept soldiers in all the strong cities of Judah.

Now Manasseh broke down the altars to the heathen gods. He took away all the strange gods which he had made. He took the idols out of God's House, too. He threw them all outside the city. Then he built up the altar of the Lord and offered sacrifices of peace-offerings and thanksgiving to God. He commanded his people to serve the true God and not to worship idols any more. Then God blessed Manasseh, the king of Judah. The king and his people were happy once more.

Were you listening? How old was Manasseh when he became king? What did he do when he was first king? How did God punish him? What happened when Manasseh showed God he was sorry for his sins?

Story 146

Josiah and God's Lost Book

II Kings 22 and 23; II Chronicles 34 and 35

When King Manasseh died, his son Amon became the king. Amon did not follow his father's good ways. He was wicked like his father had been at first. He did not humble himself before God as his father had done. He kept right on being wicked. So God did not let him be king very long. After only two years Amon's own servants came into his house and killed him.

Then the people of Judah killed all the servants who had been against their king. They took the king's little son Josiah and made him their king. Josiah was just eight years old when be began to reign. He reigned for thirty-one years in Jerusalem. Josiah was a good king like the great King David. He always tried to do what was good, and he taught his people to serve the Lord.

One day, after Josiah had been king for eighteen years, he sent his servant, Shaphan, to the House of the Lord. "Go to the high priest, Hilkiah," he said, "and see how much money the door-keepers have collected from the people. Take the money and hire workers — carpenters, builders, masons — to buy wood and stone so that they may rebuild the House of the Lord."

So Shaphan went to Hilkiah and did as King Josiah had commanded him. While they were working together, Hilkiah suddenly said, "Look, Shaphan, see what I have found!" And he held up a big book. "I have found the Book of the Law in the House of the Lord." This book was a part of the Bible. It had been lost for a long time. The people had served idols for so long they did not even remember all the laws which God had given to Moses hundreds of years before. Moses had written all those laws in books. It was this book which the priest found hidden with some other things from the temple.

The priest gave the Book to Shaphan. Shaphan read it. Then he took it back to King Josiah. When Shaphan came before the king, he said, "We collected the money and hired the workers to repair the Temple, as you commanded. And Hilkiah gave me a book for you. He found it in the House of the Lord. Here it is."

Shaphan showed the Book to the king. Then he began to read all the words of the Book for his king. King Josiah grew more and more excited as Shaphan read. When the Book was finished, the king tore his clothing. He was greatly troubled, for the Book told about the laws which God wanted His people to obey. Israel had not been keeping those laws.

King Josiah sent Shaphan back to Hilkiah, the high priest. "Ask Hilkiah to pray for me and for all the people," he said. "Let him ask God what we should do."

Shaphan and several other men went to Hilkiah. Hilkiah took

them all to a woman who was a prophetess. Her name was Huldah. When Huldah heard about the Book which had been found in God's House, she said, "This is what the Lord God of Israel says, 'Behold, I shall send evil on this place and on all the people who live here, just as it is written in the Book which the king has read. I shall send this evil because the people have turned away from Me and have worshiped other gods. But tell the king of Judah, who sent you to Me: because your heart was kind, and because you humbled yourself before Me when you read the Book, and tore your clothes and wept, I shall not send all this trouble to your people while you are living. You shall die in peace and shall not see all the evil which is going to happen.'"

When King Josiah heard the words of the prophetess, Huldah, he gathered all his people together in God's House. He read to them all the words of the Book which had been found. And he commanded his people to throw away their idols. He burned their groves and killed their wicked prophets. So King Josiah turned his people to the Lord. And he celebrated with them the Passover Feast, which had not been celebrated for a long time.

Were you listening? How old was Josiah when he became king? What did the priest find in God's House? Why did the king tear his clothes when he heard the words of the Book? What did the prophetess tell the king? What did the king do about it?

Story 147

God Chooses a New Prophet

Jeremiah 1, 2, 36 through 40; II Chronicles 36

When Josiah had been king for thirteen years, there was a young man living in the land of Benjamin, in the city of Anathoth. His name was Jeremiah. One day Jeremiah heard the Voice of God calling him. God said to Jeremiah, "Before I made you, even before you were born, I chose you to be a prophet."

But Jeremiah did not think he would make a good prophet. He was shy and timid. He was afraid to be a leader. He said, "O Lord God, I cannot speak. I am only a child."

God answered, "Do not say, 'I am a child,' for I am going to send you to all the nations. And whatever I tell you to say, that you will say." Then the Lord put out His hand and touched Jeremiah's mouth, and said, "See, I have put My words in your mouth. This day I have set you over the nations to preach and to warn."

So Jeremiah became a prophet for the Lord. He taught the people to serve the Lord. He warned them about their sins. Jeremiah was the head prophet for many, many years. During that time Judah had several kings. King Josiah reigned for eighteen more years. Then his son, Jehoahaz, reigned for only three months. Then the king of Egypt took the kingdom away from Jehoahaz and gave it to his brother, Jehoiakim. Jehoiakim had reigned for eleven years when King Nebuchadnezzar bound him with chains and carried him off to Babylon.

King Nebuchadnezzar then chose an eight-year-old boy to be the next king. He was Jehoiakim's son, Jehoiachin. But when Jehoiachin had reigned for only three months he was carried off to Babylon, too. Then Nebuchadnezzar made his brother Zedekiah, the king. Each time the king of Babylon came to Jerusalem, he took some of the beautiful silver and gold treasures out of the Temple of the Lord. And he put them in his temple in Babylon.

When Zedekiah was the king, he and his people would not listen to the words of Jeremiah. They turned away from God and served idols instead. Then God sent the Chaldeans to make war against Jerusalem. King Zedekiah asked Pharaoh and his Egyptian army to help him chase away the Chaldeans.

One day King Zedekiah sent his servant to Jeremiah to ask him to pray for him and his people. When Jeremiah talked with God, God gave him this message, "Tell the king of Judah that Pharaoh's army is going back to Egypt. Then the Chaldeans will come back and burn your city with fire."

When the men of Judah heard Jeremiah's words, they said he was a traitor.

"It's a lie," Jeremiah answered. "I am not siding in with the Chaldeans."

But the men would not listen. They beat him and threw him into prison. After several days King Zedekiah took him out of prison and brought him secretly to his own house. "Is there any word from the Lord?" he asked.

"There is," Jeremiah answered. "You shall be delivered into the hands of the king of Babylon." Then Jeremiah pleaded with the king not to send him back to the dungeon. "I never did anything against you," he said. "Please don't send me back lest I die there." So the king put Jeremiah in the court of the prison-house, instead of the dungeon. And they gave him a piece of bread each day.

But when the leaders of Judah heard that Jeremiah had said their city would be destroyed by the king of Babylon, they persuaded the king to kill Jeremiah. The king was afraid of his leaders, so he said, "He is in your hands, do as you like."

Then the men of Judah let Jeremiah down into a dungeon. They let him down with ropes. There was no water in the hole, but it was filled with soft mud. So Jeremiah sank into the mud.

Now there was a black man who worked for the king. When he heard what had happened, he went to the king. "My lord," he said, "these men have done a wicked thing in throwing Jeremiah into this muddy hole. He will die there from hunger."

Then the king commanded the black man to take thirty men and go rescue Jeremiah. The black man and his helpers took some old rags from the king's palace and went to the dungeon. They let the rags down into the dungeon on the end of a rope. The black man called down to Jeremiah, "Put these old rags under your armpits, under the ropes, so the ropes will not cut you." Then the men pulled the ropes and pulled Jeremiah up from the dungeon.

Were you listening? Who was Jeremiah? What did the men of Judah do to Jeremiah? Who rescued him?

Story 148

God's People Taken to Babylon

II Kings 25; II Chronicles 36; Jeremiah 39

Not long after Jeremiah was rescued from the dungeon, King Nebuchadnezzar came again from Babylon to make war against God's people. He came with all his army, just as Jeremiah had said.

The king and his soldiers put up their tents outside the walls of Jerusalem. Then they tried to break down the walls. But the walls were strong and it took a long time. Finally, after almost two years, they broke the wall in one place. Then they came into the city.

When King Zedekiah and all his soldiers saw what had happened, they tried to run away. As soon as it was dark, they sneaked out through the king's garden and through the gate between the two walls. Then they ran out into the country. But King Nebuchadnezzar's army chased after them. They caught Zedekiah in the plains of Jericho and brought him back to their king.

King Nebuchadnezzar took Judah's king and made him watch while he killed all his sons and all the princes of Judah. Then he put out both of King Zedekiah's eyes. He was bound with chains and carried off to Babylon.

After that the soldiers from Babylon burned the king's palace and all the houses of the people. They broke down all the walls of Jerusalem. They carried away all the people who had not been killed. They brought them down to Babylon. But they left the poor people in Jerusalem. They gave them vineyards and fields so that they could earn a living.

While the Babylonians were destroying Jerusalem, they came into the House of the Lord, too. They took away all the rest of the beautiful gold and silver treasures and dishes which the people used when they worshiped God. Then they took everything out of the Temple which was worth anything — all the gold and silver and brass and iron. And they burned the Temple.

But Nebuchadnezzar, the king of Babylon, told his captain, "Take good care of Jeremiah, the prophet. Let him do as he pleases. Do not harm him." So the captain took Jeremiah out of prison and said to him, "What would you like to do? If you would like to come with me to Babylon, I shall take good care of you. But if you would rather stay here in the land of Judah, go where you like."

Jeremiah chose to stay with the poor people in Judah. So the captain gave him food and a present and let him go. Then God came to Jeremiah. He said, "Go to the black man who saved you from the dungeon. Tell him that he shall not be killed nor hurt. I shall deliver him because he put his trust in Me."

So Jerusalem was destroyed and the people of Judah taken captive to Babylon. But Jeremiah and the black slave were saved because they served the Lord.

> *Were you listening?* What did the king of Babylon do? What happened to King Zedekiah? What happened to God's House and to Jerusalem? Why were Jeremiah and the black slave saved?

Story 149

Daniel Refuses the King's Food

Daniel 1

One day King Nebuchadnezzar, the king of Babylon, needed some new men to work in his palace. He decided to take some of the best young men among his captives to be his helpers. He sent his head-servant to choose a great many young Jewish men who had come from the land of Judah. The servant chose all those who had belonged to the best families and who were handsome and bright. Among those who were chosen was a young man whose name was Daniel. Daniel had three friends who were also chosen.

All these young Jews had to live in one of the king's houses. They were taught all the things that a king's helper should know. They were also taught to speak the king's language, which was Chaldean. It took three years to prepare these young men. During all that time, the king gave them food and wine from his own table.

Now Daniel was a good young man. He loved God with all his heart, and he served God in all that he did. When Daniel found out that the food came from the king's table, he would not eat it. For he knew that the king ate the food which his people sacrificed to their idols. And the Lord, Daniel's God, had forbidden His people to eat food which had been sacrificed to idols. So Daniel begged the prince who was in charge of them not to make him and his friends eat that food.

The prince loved Daniel, but he was afraid to disobey the king.

"If I do not feed you the king's food," he said, "you four men will look thin and sickly when the king comes to choose his servants. Then I may get killed."

Daniel answered, "Please let us try it for just ten days. Let us eat vegetables and drink water. At the end of the ten days, if we do not look as well as the other men, then we shall eat the king's food."

So the prince tried them out for ten days. At the end of that time, Daniel and his three friends looked better than all the other men who ate the king's food. Then the prince allowed them to eat as they pleased.

When the three years were over, the prince brought all the young men in to see the king. The king questioned them and talked with them. Among all the men the king found none so wise and good as Daniel and his three friends. So he chose them to be his new helpers. And the king soon found that Daniel and his three friends were ten times wiser and better than all the wise men and workers in his kingdom.

> *Were you listening?* How did God's people get to Babylon? Why wouldn't Daniel and his three friends eat the king's food? Why did the king choose these four men to be his new helpers? What did the king think of them?

Story 150

Daniel Explains the King's Dream

Daniel 2

One day King Nebuchadnezzar had a bad dream. It made him wake up in fear. He couldn't get back to sleep again. In those days dreams always meant something. So the king was worried.

He called in all his wise men. "Tell me," he commanded, "what I dreamed last night. And then tell me what my dream means!"

The wise men could sometimes tell what dreams meant, but, of course, they first had to know what the dream was. "You tell us the dream, O King, and then we'll tell you what the dream means," they answered.

The king said, "If you do not tell me what my dream means at once, I shall have you cut in pieces and your houses destroyed!

But if you tell me the dream and what it means, I shall give you wonderful gifts and great honors. So, come, tell me the dream."

The wise men were terribly afraid. "O king," they answered again, "we cannot tell you the dream. No man on earth could do that. Only the gods could do what the king asks, and they do not live on this earth!"

Then the king became furious. "Kill all my wise men!" he commanded.

The king's guard quickly obeyed their master. They set out at once to kill all the wise men and to destroy their houses. They went first to the home of Daniel and his three friends. Now Daniel and his friends knew nothing about what had happened. They had not been called to see the king. "Why is the king in such a hurry to kill all his wise men?"Daniel asked.

The captain of the king's guard told Daniel about the king's dream. Daniel went at once to see the king. "If you will give me a little time, O king," he said, "I shall try to find out your dream and tell you what it means." The king listened to Daniel and gave him a certain length of time to find out the dream.

Then Daniel went home. He told his three friends all about the king's trouble. Together they prayed to God. They asked God to tell them what the dream was and what it meant. They prayed for a long time. And God heard their prayer. While Daniel was asleep that night, God showed him the dream. Then Daniel praised God and thanked Him for His kindness. "Blessed be the name of God for ever and ever," he said, "for wisdom and might are His. He shows the deep and secret things. He knows what is in the darkness, and light lives with Him. I thank Thee and praise Thee, O God of my fathers, for telling me the king's dream."

The very next morning Daniel went to see the captain of the guard. "Do not kill all the wise men," he said. "Bring me in to see the king and I will tell the king his dream."

So the captain brought Daniel before the king. "I have found a man among the captives of Judah," he said. "He will tell the king his dream."

The king looked at Daniel. "Can you tell me my dream and what it means?" he asked.

308   *The Fiery Furnace*

"No man could ever tell you your dream," Daniel answered. "But there is a God in heaven who can. He has sent you this dream to tell you what is going to happen in the days to come. This is your dream, O king. You saw a huge image like a man. This man was bright and strong and terrible. His head was of gold, his chest and arms were of silver. The rest of his body was of brass, his legs were of iron, and his feet were of iron and clay.

"And while you were looking at the image, you saw a stone which no man had cut. This stone crashed into the clay feet of the image. The whole image smashed to pieces, and the wind blew it away. But the stone grew and grew until it became so large that it filled the whole earth.

"This is what your dream means. You, O king, are a great king. You are the head of gold. The king who will come after you will not be as great as you. He is the chest and arms of silver. The other parts of the image are kings, too. And the stone which broke the image is God's kingdom. It will some day fill the whole earth and will break to pieces all the other kingdoms."

When King Nebuchadnezzar heard Daniel's words, he fell on his face and worshiped Daniel. And he commanded that they should offer sacrifices to him. Then he made Daniel a great man in his kingdom. He gave him many great gifts and made him the chief ruler in Babylon and the head man over all the wise men. And when Daniel asked the king, he made his three friends rulers, too. But Daniel was the greatest of all.

> *Were you listening?* Why did the king want to kill his wise men? How did Daniel find out the dream? Who was the head of gold? What was the stone?

The Fiery Furnace

At one time, when Daniel was not at home, King Nebuchadnezzar made a golden image. It was a huge image. It stood ninety feet high and was nine feet wide. The king set up his golden image in a big open space in the country, in a valley between two mountains. Then he gathered together all his princes and rulers who helped him in his entire kingdom. He invited them to come to a feast for his new image.

When the feast began, all the men came into the plain and stood before the golden image. Daniel was not there, but his three friends were. Suddenly a herald cried out, "To you it is commanded, O people and nations and languages, when you hear the sound of the music (the king had his band at the feast), you must all fall down and worship the king's golden image. Anyone who does not bow down and worship this image will be thrown into the fiery furnace at once."

So the band began to play. The people all fell down and worshiped the golden image which the king had made. But Daniel's three friends did not bow down and worship the golden image. They never worshiped images. They worshiped only God.

Now it happened that there were several Chaldean men standing near Daniel's three friends. They saw that these Jews did not worship the image. They did not like it that these Jews were rulers in their king's court. So they hurried to the king. "O king," they said, "these Jews whom you have made rulers in Babylon, they do not obey you. They do not worship your gods. They did not bow down to your golden image!"

The king was angry. "Bring these men to me!" he commanded. So they brought the three Jews before the king. "Is it true," the king asked, "O Shadrach, Meshach, and Abednego, that you won't serve my gods, or worship the golden image which I set up? Now I shall give you one more chance. If, when you hear the music this time, you bow down, fine. But if you don't, you will be thrown into a burning, fiery furnace. And who is that God who would be able to save you out of my hands?"

The three men answered, "O king, we will not serve your gods nor bow down before your image. And our God, whom we serve, is able to save us from the fiery furnace. He will deliver us out of your hand, O king. But even if He wants us to die in the furnace, we will not worship your image!"

Then the king was filled with rage. He commanded that the furnace be heated seven times hotter than usual. And he ordered his bravest soldiers to bind Daniel's three friends and throw them into the furnace.

The soldiers obeyed their king at once. They bound the three Jews and carried them to the furnace. But as they threw the three men into the burning furnace, the flames leaped out and killed them. The three Jews fell down, bound, into the middle of the furnace. Suddenly, as the king and all his men were watching, four men stood up and walked around in the midst of the fire.

The king was filled with fear. "Didn't we throw just three men in the furnace?" he cried.

"True, O king," the people answered.

"But I see four men," the king shouted, "and one looks like the Son of God."

Then the king went close to the furnace and called, "O Shadrach, Meshach, and Abednego, you servants of the Most High God, come out of that furnace!" And the three men came out of the fire. The king and all his people gathered round the three men. They saw that the fire had not even touched them, nor did they smell like smoke.

The king was amazed. He cried out, "Blessed be the God of Shadrach, Meshach, and Abednego, who sent His angel to save His servants who trusted in Him. Now I shall make a new rule. Anyone who says anything against the God of these men shall be cut in pieces and their house destroyed. Because there is no other God who can do such things."

Then the king gave the three friends of Daniel a higher position in his kingdom.

> *Were you listening?* What did King Nebuchadnezzar make? Did everyone bow down to the king's image? What did the king do to Daniel's three friends? What happened to the three men?

Story 152

A Proud King Humbled

Daniel 4

One night as King Nebuchadnezzar was sleeping in his palace, God sent him another dream. This time the king did not forget his dream. But it was a strange dream and it bothered him. In the morning he sent for all his wise men to tell him the meaning of his dream. But the wise men did not know the meaning of the dream. Finally, Daniel was brought to the king. The king said to him, "O Daniel, master of my wise men, I know that the spirit of the holy gods is in you. Tell me what my dream means!"

Then the king told Daniel his dream. He said, "I saw a huge tree which reached up to heaven and was as wide as the whole earth. It had beautiful leaves on it and it was filled with good fruit. All the people of the earth used the fruit for food. All the animals in the world rested in the shade of this tree, and all the birds of the heavens built their nests in it.

"Suddenly, I saw an angel come down from heaven. The angel cried with a loud voice, 'Cut down that tree! Cut off its branches, shake off its leaves, and scatter its fruit! Chase away the animals from under it, and the birds from its branches. But leave the stump of the tree in the ground. Tie it with a chain of iron and brass. Let it be wet with the dew of heaven, and let it live with the animals. And let his heart be changed from a man's to an animal's, until seven times pass over him. God wants this to happen so that everyone may know that God is the ruler of this world!'

When Daniel heard the words of the king, he could not talk for a whole hour. His thoughts troubled him. Daniel loved his king and didn't want to tell him what the dream meant. The king noticed that Daniel was troubled. "Do not let the dream bother you. Tell me what it means," he said.

Then Daniel answered, "My lord, I wish this would happen to your enemies and to those who hate you, rather than to you. The wonderful tree which you saw is you, O king. Your kingdom reaches to the end of the earth. But you are proud, and God is going to punish you. He is going to change you into an animal. Men will chase you away from the palace and tie you in the field with the animals. You will have to eat grass like the oxen. You will be wet with dew for seven years until you learn that God is the ruler of men. For it is God who has made you great!

"Now, O king, listen to me. Stop being wicked. Do not sin any more. Be kind to the poor. Then, perhaps, God will not let this dreadful thing happen to you."

King Nebuchadnezzer listened to Daniel. For some time he remembered God and tried to obey Him. But after a year he forgot all about his dream. He became filled with pride again. One day he was walking around in his beautiful palace, looking at all his wonderful things. He puffed out his chest, threw back his head, and cried, "Is not this the great Babylon which I have built!"

All at once the king heard a voice from heaven. It said, "O King Nebuchadnezzar, to you it is spoken, Now your dream is going to come true."

In that same hour the king became like an animal. Men chased him out of the palace. They drove him into the fields with the animals. He ate grass with the oxen. And he was wet with the dew. His hair grew long like eagle's feathers, and his nails grew sharp like birds' claws.

When the seven years were over, God gave the king his own mind back again. Then he went back to live in his palace once more. From that day on the king remembered to bless God and to praise Him for all His wonderful gifts. He was no longer proud. He honored God instead of himself.

Were you listening? Why did God send King Nebuchadnezzar a dream? Why was Daniel troubled about the dream? Why did the dream come true?

Story 153

The Writing on the Wall

Daniel 5

When Daniel was an older man, he still lived in Babylon. King Nebuchadnezzar died, and his son, Belshazzar, became the king. Belshazzar was not a great king like his father. He was a most wicked king. He forgot all about God and did just as he pleased.

One day King Belshazzar made a great feast for a thousand of his lords. It was a wonderful feast and the men were having a fine time. The king served wine at his feast, too. While the king was drinking wine at his table, he happened to think about the beautiful gold and silver cups which belonged in God's House in Jerusalem. His father, King Nebuchadnezzar, had stolen them out of the Temple when he had taken the Jews away as captives.

"Bring me those gold and silver cups," he cried, "so that we may drink wine out of them."

The servants hurried to obey their king. They quickly brought the gold and silver cups and set them in front of the king. Then the king and his lords and all his wives drank wine from these cups which belonged to God. And while they drank they praised their own gods of gold and silver and brass and iron and wood and stone.

In heaven, God saw what the wicked king was doing. He was filled with anger. Suddenly, while the men and women were still drinking, the fingers of a man's hand were seen on the wall next to the candlestick. And the fingers were writing something on the wall.

The king saw the fingers as they wrote. He became extremely frightened. He had never seen such a thing before. His legs shook. His knees knocked against each other. He cried out in a loud voice, "Bring in all my wise men! Let them read the handwriting for me!"

Soon the wise men were brought in. The king said, "If any of you can read this writing and tell me what it means, I will give him my royal purple coat and a chain of gold around his neck. And I will make him the third ruler in my kingdom."

All the wise men looked at the handwriting, but they could not read it. Then the king became still more afraid. Everyone in the room was worried and troubled.

Then the queen came in to see the king. "Don't be afraid," she said. "There is a man in your kingdom in whom is the spirit of the living God. He was the wisest man in your father's kingdom. He could tell the meaning of dreams. Now why don't you call this man, Daniel?"

So Daniel was brought in before the king. The king promised Daniel the same reward he had promised his wise men, if he could read the handwriting. Then Daniel said, "Let the king keep his gifts. And give your rewards to someone else. But I will read the writing for you. O king, my God wrote on your wall. When your father was king, he forgot about God and became proud. Then God punished him by changing him into an animal for seven years.

You knew all this, but you, too, have forgotten God. You were using God's gold and silver cups. You were praising your own gods which are no gods.

"This is what it says on your wall, 'Mene, Mene, Tekel, Upharsin.' And this is what it means. The first two words mean that God has counted the days that you will be king, and they are finished. The third word means that you are weighed on God's scale. Your bad works weigh more than your good works. The last word means that your kingdom has been divided and is going to be given to the Medes and the Persians."

Then the king gave Daniel his gifts as he had promised. He made him third ruler in his kingdom. But that very night King Belshazzar was killed. His kingdom was taken by the Medes. And Darius, the Median, became king.

> *Were you listening?* What wicked thing did King Belshazzar do? What did the people see on the wall? What did the writing mean? What happened that very night?

Story 154

Daniel Safe in the Lions' Den

Daniel 6

When Darius became the king of Babylon, he chose one hundred and twenty princes to rule over his kingdom. Although Daniel was an old man by this time, King Darius also chose him to be one of his princes. More than that, Darius chose three of his princes to be presidents over all the others. He made Daniel the first of the presidents. The king liked Daniel better than all his men because he was such a good man. The king even thought about making him the chief ruler over all his kingdom.

But the rest of the princes were jealous of Daniel. They didn't want him to be their ruler. So they watched him closely every day, trying to find some wrong in him. Then they would be able to report it to their king and have Daniel's high position taken away from him. But Daniel was faithful in all his work, so they could find no wrong in him.

Finally these princes thought of a clever plan to get rid of Daniel. They knew that Daniel would always be true to his God.

So they went to the king and said, "O king, wouldn't it be a fine idea to make a royal law stating that no one in your kingdom should pray to any God or man except you for thirty days? And if any man disobeys the new rule, he should be thrown into the lions' den."

The king did not know why these men wanted this new rule, so he was pleased to have his people treat him as a god for thirty days. He wrote out the new rule, signed it and sealed it with the seal of his kingdom, which meant that the rule could not be broken.

As soon as the new rule had been read to all the people, these wicked princes went to Daniel's home to spy on him. If they could prove that Daniel disobeyed the new rule, they would have him thrown to the lions.

Even though Daniel heard about the new rule, he went up to his room to pray as he always did. Three times that day he knelt before his open window, which faced toward Jerusalem, and prayed to his God.

Then the princes hurried to the king. "O king," they said, "didn't you make a new rule that any man who prays to any one but you for thirty days shall be thrown into the lions' den?"

The king answered, "The thing is true, according to our laws which cannot be changed."

Then these wicked men said, "This Daniel, whom you have made our ruler, pays no attention to you or your rule, O king. Three times a day he prays to his own God!"

The king now saw why these men had wanted this new rule. He was disgusted with himself for having fallen into their trap. He loved Daniel and tried all day to think of a plan to save him. But the princes kept after him until finally, as the sun went down, he commanded to have Daniel brought. And Daniel was thrown into the lions' den.

But the king said to Daniel, "Your God, whom you serve continually, He will save you." Then they brought a stone and put it in front of the mouth of the den. The king put his seal on it so that no one would be able to touch it. Then he went home and spent the whole night without eating. He would not listen to music, nor could he sleep.

As soon as it was light, he hurried to the lions' den. He called out, "O Daniel, servant of the living God, was your God, whom you always serve, able to deliver you from the lions?"

The king listened. Soon he heard Daniel's voice coming from among the lions. "O king," Daniel said, "live forever. My God has sent His angel and has shut the lions' mouths so they could not hurt me. For I did nothing wrong, O king, to you nor to my God."

The king was filled with joy. He commanded that Daniel be taken out of the lions' den. Then he commanded his men to get all those wicked princes who had plotted against Daniel. They with their wives and their children were thrown into the den of lions. And the lions caught them and tore them to pieces before they ever reached the bottom of the den. After that Daniel became the king's chief ruler again.

Were you listening? Whom did Darius choose to be head over all his princes? How did some of the other princes feel about that? What did they try to do to Daniel? What did God do for Daniel?

Story 155

God Brings Back His People

Ezra 1 through 8

God's people, from the Kingdom of Judah, lived in Babylon for many years. For seventy years they were a people without a country. During all that time the land of Judah was almost empty. The houses had been burned and the walls around Jerusalem had been broken down. The people who had remained in Jerusalem had turned away to idols and had forgotten the God of their fathers. It made God's people in Babylon extremely sad to think of their beautiful country lying in ruins.

By this time Darius was no longer king in Babylon. There was now a king whose name was Cyrus, the Persian. Cyrus was a good king. He loved God and was kind to the Jews in his country. One day he sent his servants throughout all his land with this message. He said, "The Lord, the God of heaven, has given me all the kingdoms of the earth. And He wants me to build Him a House in Jerusalem, in the land of Judah.

"Now who is there among all you Jews who would like to go back to your own country? You may go and rebuild the Temple of your God. Let all those who do not go, help those who go by giving them gold and silver and other gifts."

Then the leaders of the people of Judah and of Benjamin, and many of the priests and Levites, with a great many of the people, made ready to go back to their own home-land. Their friends took up a collection for them so they would have money to rebuild the House of the Lord. They gave them all sorts of fine gifts. And King Cyrus gave back the gold and silver cups and dishes stolen from the Temple by King Nebuchadnezzar. There were 5,400 of these treasures which belonged in the Lord's House.

It was a long way from Babylon to Jerusalem — more than 500 miles. Most of the people had to walk all the way, for the animals were needed to carry their household goods besides all the Temple treasures. It must have taken more than a month for the long journey. There were 50,000 people who left Babylon that day.

Although the journey was difficult, the men and women were filled with joy to think they were going back home after all those years. As they walked they sang. They sang the old songs of Zion which their fathers had taught them. Each day of their journey they became more excited.

Finally, they reached their homeland. Everything was in ruins just as they had expected. The Temple was nothing but a heap of rubbish. They quickly cleared away some of the rubbish and built an altar. Here they offered sacrifices to God every morning and every evening.

Each family looked around among the ruins until they found the piece of land which had been given to them hundreds of years before by Joshua. They had always kept a record so they would know where they were supposed to live. Each family put up tents on the land which had once belonged to their fathers.

It took a whole year to clear away all the rubbish and to make places to live. Then the people began to work on the new Temple. Before they began the work, they gathered together and sang the old songs of David, praising God for His mercy and kindness.

There were tears that day, too. For many of the older priests and Levites remembered the beautiful Temple which King Solomon had built. They knew that this Temple would never be as wonderful as that one. So there was weeping and shouting and there was much excitement as the first stones were laid for the new Temple.

> *Were you listening?* What did King Cyrus do? What did the king give the Jews? How many people went back to Jerusalem? Why were there tears mixed with their joy?

Story 156

Jerusalem Rebuilt

Ezra 4, 5 and 6

Although there had been much joyful excitement in Jerusalem when God's people first came back to rebuild their city, their joy did not last. The work was not as easy as they had thought. No sooner did they have the walls of their city finished than trouble began.

You remember that the Ten Tribes of Israel were also taken into captivity and were lost among the other nations. At that time the king of Assyria had brought people from other nations into Samaria to fill up that land. These people did not believe in God. They worshiped idols instead of the God of Israel. God punished them by sending lions to kill some of them. Then the king of Assyria sent a priest of Israel back to Samaria to teach those people how to worship the Lord.

During all those seventy years that Judah was in Babylon these people in Samaria worshiped both the Lord and their idols. When these Samaritans, as they were called, saw that the Jews were rebuilding their city and their Temple, they came to the high priest and offered their help. "We have worshiped your God ever since we came to this country," they said. "Let us help you build His Temple."

The leaders of Judah did not want the Samaritans to help them. "You have nothing to do with us in building a House for our God," they answered. "We shall build it ourselves, as King Cyrus commanded."

Then the Samaritans were angry. Since they could not help, they tried to stop the Jews from building. At this time King Cyrus was no longer living. Another king had ruled for a short time and now there was a third king. His name was Artaxerxes. These Samaritans sent a letter to the new Persian king. They wrote, "Let it be known to the king that the Jews who have come to Jerusalem are rebuilding that bad city. They have already finished the walls and joined the foundations. If this city is rebuilt, the people will not pay their taxes to the king. Look up the records of the earlier kings and you will find that this city has always been a bad city. That is why it was destroyed."

When the king received the Samaritans' letter, he did look up the records and found that the words of the letter were true. He wrote to the Samaritans at once, commanding them to stop the work in Jerusalem until he gave permission for it to begin again.

The Samaritans quickly hurried to Jerusalem with their letter. In great disappointment the Jews laid down their tools and stopped their building. For sixteen years the Jews did nothing to their unfinished Temple. *They looked after their own houses* Then the king of Persia died. The new king was another Darius. He was called Darius the Great.

During this time God sent two prophets to His people to encourage them to work again on their Temple. They were Haggai and Zechariah. The prophets told the people that even though this Temple would not be as great as Solomon's, some day God would fill the new Temple with His glory so that the glory would be greater than that of Solomon's Temple. The prophets were thinking about the time when God would send His own Son into that Temple to fill it with glory. "It will not be long," the prophets said, "and this promised Saviour will come." *Zerubbabel & Joshua*

So the Jews went eagerly to work once more. The work on the *led the work* Temple went on. But soon the troublesome Samaritans were back. "Who told you to work on that Temple?" they asked. "We shall tell the king if you do not stop."

When the Jews did not stop, the Samaritans sent a letter to King Darius. They told the king all about the trouble. They also wrote, "The Jews say that King Cyrus sent them back to build the

Temple. So let the king's servants search in the king's treasure-house to see if King Cyrus ever did such a thing."

King Darius soon found a roll in which was written King Cyrus' command to the Jews to rebuild their Temple. Right away he wrote to the Samaritans, "Let the work on the Jews' Temple go on. Do not stop them, but help them instead. Give them money and goods and anything they need. Take the money out of the king's treasury. Also give them animals and wheat and salt and wine and oil, and whatever else they need for their sacrifices each day. So they may offer their sacrifices to their God and pray for the life of the king and his sons."

Then King Darius added, "If anyone changes this law, wood shall be torn from his own house. A gallows shall be made from the wood, and he shall be hanged on it."

The Samaritans were afraid of the King's command, so now they helped the Jews. Soon the Temple was finished. It had taken twenty years to build it. As soon as it was finished, the people had a great feast. They offered hundreds of sacrifices. They set up the work of the priests and the Levites, just as in the days of Moses. Last of all, they celebrated the Passover Feast. Now they were truly filled with joy, for the Lord had sent them great King Darius who saw to it that their new Temple was finished.

> *Were you listening?* Who stopped the Jews from rebuilding their Temple? Who helped the Jews to finish the Temple? How long did it take?

Story 157

Beautiful Queen Esther

Esther 1 and 2

While the Jews in Jerusalem were rebuilding their Temple, many other Jews had remained in Babylon. After the first King Darius died, there was a king in Babylon whose name was Ahasuerus. He had a beautiful queen whose name was Vashti.

King Ahasuerus was a powerful king. He was known everywhere for his glory and riches. One day this king decided to give a great feast for all his princes and workers in his palace. He wanted them to see how rich and glorious he was. This feast lasted for a hundred and eighty days.

When that feast was ended, the king gave another feast for all the people in his royal city. This feast was held in the king's garden. It lasted for seven days. There were beautiful marble pillars in the garden. Lovely blue and white and green curtains were hung from the pillars. They were fastened to silver rings with purple cords. The ground was covered with red, white, yellow and black marble. There were davenports of gold and silver to sit on. The king served the people as much wine as they wanted in all sorts of different gold cups.

On the last day of the feast, when the king and his guests were almost drunken with too much wine, he called for his beautiful Queen Vashti to come. He wanted her to wear her royal crown and show the people her beauty. Now Queen Vashti was having a feast in her palace, too, for all the women of the palace. When the king sent for her, Queen Vashti would not come.

The king was filled with anger when he found out that his queen would not obey him. "What shall I do to my queen for not obeying me?" the king asked his wise men.

"O king," they answered, "you should punish the queen for not obeying you. If you do not, all the women in our homes will hear about it and will refuse to obey us. Do not let Vashti be queen any more. Send her away and get a new queen."

The king listened to his men. He sent Queen Vashti away. But now the king had no queen. When he was no longer angry, he was lonesome for Vashti. So his servants said, "Let the king send his servants to find all the pretty girls in his kingdom. Then let these girls be taken care of by the keeper of the women for one year, so that they will be as lovely as possible. Then let the king choose the most beautiful one for his queen." The king liked this idea, so he sent his servants to find all the pretty girls.

There was in the royal city at that time, a Jew whose name was Mordecai. His father had been taken captive many years before by King Nebuchadnezzar. There was a beautiful young girl living with Mordecai. Her name was Esther. Esther's father and mother were both dead, so Mordecai, her cousin, had adopted her.

When Mordecai heard about the king's plan to get a new

queen, he allowed Esther to go to the palace, too. The keeper of the women liked Esther and was kind to her. He gave her all the things she needed and the best place in the house. Esther did not tell the keeper of the women that she was a Jewish captive girl. Her cousin had told her to keep that a secret. Every day of that year, while Esther was in the house of the women, Mordecai walked in the yard to make sure that Esther was all right.

When the year was over, the girls went in to see the king, one at a time. They went in the evening and came back the next day. When the king had seen all the girls, he chose Esther to be his queen instead of Vashti. Then the king gave another feast for all his men. He called it Esther's Feast. The king loved his new queen, Esther, with all his heart. But he did not know that she was a Jewish captive girl from the land of Judah.

Were you listening? Why did King Ahasuerus need a new queen? Whom did he choose to be his new queen? What didn't he know about his new queen?

Story 158

Esther Saves God's People

Esther 3 through 10

Esther, the beautiful new queen of King Ahasuerus, lived in the royal palace. Her foster-father, Mordecai, who was also her cousin, sat each day at the king's gate. One day Mordecai found out that two men were planning to kill the king. Mordecai told Esther to warn the king. When Esther told the king, he had the two men caught and put to death. Then the king had Mordecai's name written in his big book, telling how he had saved the king's life.

There was at this time a proud man in the king's palace. His name was Haman. Haman was one of the king's most important servants. All the people of the kingdom had to bow down to Haman when they met him.

Mordecai would not bow down to Haman. This made Haman angry. He was so angry that he decided to hurt Mordecai and all his people. He asked the king to make a new rule saying that on a certain day his own people could kill all the Jews. "There is a certain people, the Jews," he told the king, "who live in your land, who do not obey your rules. They are of no good to you. Why don't you have them all killed?" Then he promised the king ten thousand pieces of silver if he made the new rule.

So the king gave Haman his wish. And Haman sent servants to tell all the people of the kingdom about the new rule. Mordecai soon heard about the rule, too. He was filled with sadness. He changed his clothing and wore sackcloth instead. And he put ashes on his head.

When Queen Esther saw her father in sackcloth and ashes, she sent clothing down to him. But he would not wear it. Then she asked him why he was so sad. Mordecai then told the queen about Haman's new rule to kill all the Jews. "You had better go to the king to ask him to save your people," he added.

But Queen Esther sent this answer, "I cannot go to the king unless he calls me. If he does not want to see me, he will kill me."

Her father insisted, "Go to the king just the same, and plead for your people. Perhaps this is why God let you be queen, so that you can save your people."

Then Queen Esther answered, "Tell all my people to pray with me for three days. Then I shall go to the king, even though he kill me."

On the third day, Queen Esther dressed herself as beautifully as she could. Then she went to see the king. The king was pleased to see his beautiful queen. He held out his golden sceptre to her. She came close and touched the top of the sceptre. Then she asked the king to come with Haman to a banquet in her palace that evening.

The king promised to come. Naturally Haman was proud to think that he was going to the queen's banquet. That night at the banquet, the king said to Queen Esther, "Now tell me what you want. I will give you anything you ask, even if you want the half of my kingdom." But Esther was afraid to tell the king. So she invited her two guests to come to another banquet the next night. She would tell them then.

That night the king could not sleep. He asked his servant to read to him from the big record book. His servant read about how

Mordecai had saved the king's life. "What was done for this man?" the king asked.

"Nothing," the servant answered.

At that very moment Haman came into the king's palace to ask if he might hang Mordecai. But instead, the king commanded him to take Mordecai through the streets on the king's own horse. Mordecai was dressed in the king's royal robe and he wore the king's crown. So Haman had to honor the man he wanted to kill.

At the queen's second banquet, she finally told the king what she wanted. "Please save me and my people," she said. "For we are all going to be killed."

"Who dares to do such a thing?" the king asked.

Queen Esther pointed to Haman. "That wicked Haman," she answered.

The king was filled with rage. He commanded that they hang Haman on his own gallows, which he had made for Mordecai. Then the king gave Haman's place of honor to Mordecai. And he made a new rule which would save the Jews from being killed. So beautiful Queen Esther saved her people from death.

Were you listening? How did Mordecai save the king's life? Why were the Jews going to be killed? Who saved the Jews from death? What happened to Haman?

Ezra Helps God's People

There was in the city of Babylon a man of God whose name was Ezra. Ezra was a scribe. He took care of the Books of the Law (which was the people's Bible in those days). He taught the people from these Law Books. Ezra was a good scribe. The Lord was pleased with him.

Ezra knew about God's people who had gone back to Jerusalem. He wished he could go to his people there and teach them the holy Law of God. So one day he asked the king of Babylon if he might go to his people in Jerusalem. King Artaxerxes gave Ezra permission to go.

The king sent Ezra a letter. He told him to take with him any of the Jews living in Babylon who would like to go. He gave Ezra a great deal of silver and gold which he and his princes had gathered together as an offering for Ezra's God. He also gave Ezra permission to take up a collection among all the Jews in his kingdom, to be used for the new Temple in Jerusalem. "If you need any more money," the king wrote in his letter, "ask the treasurer of my house. He will give you all you need."

Ezra was filled with joy when he read the king's letter. He thanked God and praised Him for the king's kindness. As soon as he could, Ezra sent word to all his people, inviting them to go back to Jerusalem with him. He gathered them all together at the river's edge. For three days they lived in tents.

Ezra counted the people and took note of those who had come. He found that there were no ministers in the group. So he sent word to Iddo, who was a chief Levite, to send some ministers. Iddo sent him two hundred and fifty-eight ministers. Everyone prayed for God's help on their journey.

Ezra knew that it would be a dangerous journey to take all those people through enemy country to get to Jerusalem. But he did not want to ask the king for soldiers to help them against the enemy. He had told the king that he did not need soldiers since God always takes care of those who trust in Him. So they prayed to God and asked Him to be their guide. And God heard their prayer.

Then Ezra set the ministers in charge of all the gold and silver which the king had given them. They also took care of all the money which the Jews had given as an offering. And Ezra gave them some golden bowls to be used in God's House.

When everything was ready, they left the river and began their journey. There were about seven thousand people in Ezra's group. They traveled for four months, and God took care of them all the way. Finally, they reached Jerusalem. Once more Ezra gathered the people together. They thanked God for a safe journey. And they offered a great many sacrifices to God to show their thankfulness.

> *Were you listening?* Why did Ezra want to go to Jerusalem? What did the king do for Ezra? What did the people do at the river's edge for three days? Why did they not need soldiers for their journey?

Story 160

Nehemiah Goes to Help Ezra

Nehemiah 1 through 6

Ezra worked in Jerusalem for thirteen years. Not only did he teach his people God's Word, he also helped them rebuild their city. Many years before, the Temple had been finished. But the walls of the city were still broken down. As fast as the people tried to build up the walls, enemies came and broke them down. Then they burned them with fire.

Back in Babylon, there still remained many of God's people, the Jews. One of them, whose name was Nehemiah, worked in the palace of King Artaxerxes. He was the cup-bearer for the king. That means that he served the king his wine each day.

One day Nehemiah's brother, Hanani, came with some other men from Jerusalem. Nehemiah talked with his brother and heard about all the troubles the people were having in Jerusalem.

When Nehemiah heard this sad news, he sat down and cried. He mourned and fasted and prayed to God for several days. Not long after this Nehemiah was again serving the king. The king noticed that Nehemiah was filled with sadness. Now no servant was allowed to be sad in the king's presence.

"Why are you so sad," the king asked, "seeing you are not sick?"

Then Nehemiah told the king about his brother's visit. "What would you like to have me do about it?" the king asked.

"If it please the king," Nehemiah answered, "please send me back to the city of my fathers. Let me help them build it."

"When you have finished, will you come back?" the king asked.

"Yes," Nehemiah promised.

So the king gave Nehemiah permission to go to Jerusalem to help Ezra and his men. And Nehemiah promised to return on a certain day.

Nehemiah took many of his own people with him and hurried to Jerusalem. The king appointed him to be the governor of Jerusalem, so he would be able to rule the people while he was there.

After Nehemiah had been in Jerusalem for three days, he took a few men with him and went out secretly one night to examine the broken walls of the city. Then, the next day, he called the people together and told them that he was now their governor. He gave them a good plan for the rebuilding of the walls.

"Every man," he said, "will build the part of the wall that is closest to his own house. And every man must have a sword as well as a trowel to build with. On the first day half of the men will work, and the other half will stand guard with their swords. On the next day, the men will change places."

So the work was begun. Although they had a great deal of difficulty with the enemy, in an amazingly short time the wall was finished. The entire wall was completed in just fifty-two days! The enemies were surprised and disappointed. Now they knew that Nehemiah's God had helped him finish the wall. And the Jews were filled with thanksgiving to God for sending them the great leader, Nehemiah.

Were you listening? Who was Nehemiah? Why was he sad? What were Nehemiah's plans for rebuilding the walls? How long did it take to finish the walls?

"If I Forget Thee, O Jerusalem"

Nehemiah 8 through 13

Nehemiah, the cup-bearer of the king of Babylon, and Ezra, the scribe, were still in Jerusalem. They had brought a great many people with them to Jerusalem. Together they had rebuilt the ruined city. Together they had taught the people to turn away from their evil ways and to worship the God of their fathers.

One day the people came together at the water gate. They asked Ezra to bring the Book of the Law of Moses, which was their Bible. They wanted Ezra to read from the Book, so that they might hear the words of God.

Ezra did as his people asked. He made a pulpit of wood and set it in the street in front of the water gate. He stood on the pulpit in front of all the people. Then he opened the Bible and held it up so everyone could see. The people all stood up. Ezra blessed God and all the people answered, "Amen, Amen." The people lifted up their hands and bowed their heads to the ground, and worshiped the Lord their God.

Then Ezra began to read. He read for a long time, from morning until noon. The people listened eagerly. While they listened, the tears ran down their faces. It had been so long since they had heard God's Word that it made them cry. But Nehemiah and Ezra said to the people, "This day is holy unto your God. You must not cry and be sad. Go home and eat and drink, and have a feast. And don't forget to send some food to the poor, so that they may feast with you. Don't be sad. Be happy and enjoy yourselves. For the Lord has brought you back into your own country. He has been extremely kind to you."

The people listened to Ezra and Nehemiah. They went home to get ready for a feast. They feasted for a whole week. On the second day, Ezra read again from God's holy Book. This time he read about the Feast of Tabernacles, which God's people celebrated in the days long ago. He read about how the people went into the hills to find large tree-branches, from which they built tents to live in during the feast days.

God wanted them to live in tents during the Feast of Tabernacles so they would remember the days when they had lived in the wilderness for so many years. When the people heard Ezra's words, they went out and found themselves branches so they could live in tents, too.

So all the people lived in tents for seven days. They feasted each day and everyone was happy. On each of the seven days Ezra read from God's Book, and the people listened gladly. Never again did the people forget that Jerusalem was the city of their God. Never again did they worship idols.

During the time that Nehemiah was the governor and Ezra was the teacher in Jerusalem, God sent His last prophet to His people. The Jews had been back in their own land for many years, but they were often discouraged. Life was not as it had been in the days gone by when the great kings, David and Solomon, reigned in Jerusalem. Life was hard, they were often poor, and there were enemies who came again and again to bother them.

Then God sent His prophet Malachi to comfort His people. Malachi told the people about God's great love for them. He promised them that God would soon send the Saviour, who would be the Sun of righteousness. He told about the coming of John the Baptist, too.

Malachi also talked about the great Memory Book which God has. He said that God would write in His book the names of all those who love Him and obey Him. "They shall be mine," God says, "in that day when I make up my jewels." What a wonderful thought for God's children! They are like shining jewels in a king's crown. And with this wonderful thought the Old Testament ends.

Were you listening? Why did the people cry when they heard God's Word? Why did they have a feast? Of what did the tree-branch tents remind them? What wonderful things did Malachi tell God's people?

THE NEW TESTAMENT

The Promise God Had Made

The Bible is God's Book. Many hundreds of years ago God directed a great many men to write down all the things He wanted to have in His Book. The Bible is divided into two large parts. The first part is called *The Old Testament*. It tells about the world when it was first made, and about God's special people, the children of Israel. The second part is called *The New Testament*. It tells more about the people, but it tells mostly about Jesus Christ, our Saviour.

The stories of the New Testament did not begin to happen as soon as the Old Testament times were finished. For more than four hundred years nothing was added to the Bible. The Bible does not tell us what happened to God's people during all those years. A great many history books were written about those years, however, and they tell us that most of the Jews still lived in Palestine.

The people who lived in Palestine when the New Testament begins were quite different from those who lived there four hundred years before. The Old Testament Israelites were always forgetting to serve the "real" God. They liked to serve idols instead. Again and again God punished them for serving idols. Finally, He sent them away to other countries as slaves. When they came back to Palestine once more, they had learned their lesson. Never again did they worship idols.

This new Palestine was different from the old in another way, too. Although the people were no longer slaves, they were not exactly free. During all those many years, kings of different countries ruled over them. The people always had to obey these kings and pay their taxes to them. At the beginning of The New Testament, the kings of Rome ruled Palestine. The great Caesar Augustus in Rome sent one of his men, King Herod, to Jerusalem to rule there. The people were not happy under the Romans. They longed for the day when God would set them free.

God's people were also waiting for something else. They were waiting for God to keep a wonderful promise He had made. When sin first came into the world and God drove Adam and Eve out of Paradise, this promise was given. God promised Eve that someday one of her children would win over Satan, that wicked angel, who had tempted her to sin. Satan had brought death into this world.

About two thousand years later, God gave the promise again. This time He told Abraham that this promised Child would come from one of his descendants, and through Him all the nations of the world would be blessed.

From that time on, the promise was given again and again. It was given to Jacob, and to his son, Judah. King David wrote of it often in his beautiful Book of Psalms. Many prophets, like Isaiah, Daniel and Micah told of this wonderful Child. They said He would be born in Bethlehem. They said He would be a prophet and a priest and a king. They said He would do many wonderful things. They said He would give His life to save His people from their sins.

And so the people waited and longed for the great day to come. Every mother in Israel hoped that she might be the one to receive this wonderful Child as her baby. Finally, after another two thousand years (since Abraham), it was time for God to fulfill His promise.

Were you listening? What are the two large parts of the Bible called? What lesson did the people learn while they were slaves? For what were the people waiting? How long was it before God kept His promise?

Story 163

An Angel Visits Zacharias

Luke 1

When Herod was king of Judea, an old man was a priest (minister) in God's House. His name was Zacharias. His wife's name was Elisabeth. Zacharias and Elisabeth were good people. They loved God and always tried to do what was right. These two old people were often lonely, for they had no children. They had asked God many times for a baby, but He had never sent them one. Now they were too old to have children.

Sometimes Zacharias stayed in God's House for many days. It was his work to burn incense on the altar in the inner room. One day Zacharias was burning incense to God. All the people were in the outer room praying. Then an angel came and stood on the right side of the altar beside the old priest. When Zacharias noticed the angel, he was afraid.

The angel said, "Don't be afraid, Zacharias, for God has heard your prayers. Your wife, Elisabeth, is going to have a son. Soon God will send you a baby boy, and you must call his name John. You shall be very happy with this baby, and many people will be glad at his birth. For he shall be great in the sight of God. You must not let him drink any wine or strong drink. And he shall be filled with the Holy Spirit, even from the time he is a baby.

"This baby," the angel went on, "will turn many people to the Lord, and he will teach them how to be good. Soon God is going to send His own Son into the world as a Saviour. Your son will be His herald. He will go ahead of Him, to make the way ready for Him."

It was hard for Zacharias to believe what the angel told him. "How shall I know," he asked, "that this is true? I am an old man and my wife is old, too. People don't have babies when they are old. Give me a sign so that I shall know that it is true."

The angel answered, "I am Gabriel. I live with God. He sent me down to you to tell you this happy news. I shall give you a sign. Because you did not believe me, you will not be able to speak until the baby is born."

All this while the people were waiting for Zacharias. They wondered why he did not come out. Finally, when he did come, he could not talk. He motioned to them and tried to tell them with motions what had happened. Soon the people understood that he had seen an angel.

When Zacharias' work in God's House was finished, he went home to Elisabeth. He could not tell Elisabeth what had happened, so he wrote it for her to read. Zacharias and Elisabeth were full of joy while they waited for their new baby to come.

Were you listening? Who was Zacharias? Why were Zacharias and his wife lonely? What message did the angel give Zacharias? Why couldn't Zacharias talk?

Story 164

Mary and the Angel

Luke 1

In the little city of Nazareth there lived a lovely young woman. Her name was Mary. Mary was soon going to be married to a carpenter, whose name was Joseph. One day Mary was sitting alone in her home. All of a sudden an angel stood before her. His name was Gabriel. It was the same angel who, about six months before, had visited Zacharias. Now God had sent him to Mary.

The angel said, "Hail Mary, you who are highly favored among women, the Lord is with you." Mary did not know what the angel meant. She was afraid. Gabriel said, "Do not be afraid, Mary. You have found favor with God. You are going to have a baby. You must call His name Jesus. He is to be a wonderful baby, Mary. He shall be called the Son of the Most High God. And the Lord God shall give Him the throne of His father, David. He shall be a king forever. There will be no end to His kingdom."

Mary did not understand. She said to Gabriel, "How can this be? I am not married." Gabriel answered, "Everything will be all right. God will be the baby's Father. Your baby will be the Son of God." So this was the Baby God had promised, and all God's people had waited for all those many years!

Gabriel had more news for Mary. He said, "Your cousin, Elisabeth, is also going to have a baby, even though she is old. When God promises something, He will see to it that it happens."

Then Mary was satisfied. She bowed her head and softly answered, "Behold, I am the servant of the Lord. Let it happen to me as you have said." Then Gabriel returned to heaven.

Not long after this, Mary went to visit her cousin, Elisabeth, in the hill country of Judah. When Elisabeth opened the door for Mary, God told her Mary's secret. She cried out, "Blessed art thou among women, and blessed is the baby you are going to have!

Who am I that the mother of my Lord should come to visit me?"

Mary was filled with joy. She was so happy, she praised God by singing a most beautiful song. Mary made up the song herself. She sang, "My soul praises God, and my spirit is happy in God, my Saviour. After this, everyone will call me blessed. For He that is mighty has done great things for me. God has kept His promise! He has not forgotten His people!" Mary stayed with Elisabeth for about three months. Then she went back home to Nazareth to get ready for her Baby to come.

As soon as Mary reached home, she went to find her friend, Joseph, so that she might share her wonderful secret with him. But Joseph had not seen the angel. It was hard for him to believe Mary's words. He did not see how such a thing could happen. He thought perhaps it might be better not to take Mary as his wife after all.

Joseph was troubled and worried. Then one night he had an unusual dream. An angel came to him and said, "Joseph, don't be afraid to take Mary as your wife. Her Baby is going to be the Son of God. You must call His name Jesus, because He is going to save His people from their sins."

Then Joseph was happy, too. He remembered the angel's words. He took Mary into his home as his wife. Together they waited for this wonderful Child to be born.

> *Were you listening?* What good news did the angel, Gabriel, bring Mary? What did Mary do to show her happiness? How did Joseph find happiness, too?

Story 165

John the Baptist Is Born

Luke 1

It was busy in the little country home of Zacharias and Elisabeth. They were making ready for the little baby the angel had promised them. Zacharias could not talk, you remember, because he had not believed the angel's message.

Not long after Elisabeth's young cousin, Mary, had returned to her home in Nazareth, God gave Elisabeth a little son, just as He had promised. All the neighbors and all their relatives heard how God had been so kind to them in giving them a little baby.

When the baby was eight days old, it was time to choose a name for him. Many people gathered in Elisabeth's home to help with the name-choosing. That was the way it was always done in those days. The people wanted to call him Zacharias after his father. But Elisabeth said, "That is not right. His name is John."

In those days people always named their children after their parents or other relatives. So the people said, "There isn't anyone in your relation by the name of John. Why don't you call him Zacharias?"

"Ask his father what his name is to be," Elisabeth said. Then they made signs to Zacharias asking him what he wanted to call the baby. Zacharias took his writing tablet and wrote, "His name is John." The people were all amazed.

Then, all of a sudden, Zacharias could speak again. He praised God and told everyone about the angel's visit. Just as Mary had done, he made up a beautiful song of praise and thanksgiving to God. First he thanked God for keeping His promise and bringing salvation to His people. Then he turned to his baby and said, "And thou, child, shall be called the prophet of the Highest. For it will be your work to go on ahead and make ready the way for the Son of God."

Soon the news of this unusual baby was spread over all the hill country of Judea. And the people said, "What kind of a boy will this be?" The little boy grew and God was with him. God helped him to get ready for his great work.

Were you listening? What did Elisabeth call her baby? Why didn't she call him Zacharias? What kind of work was John going to do when he grew up?

The Saviour Is Born

Mary and Joseph were still waiting for the baby the angel had promised them. One day, the Roman king, Caesar Augustus, sent out a messenger. He told the people about a new law which the king had made. Everyone was to go to the city where his parents and grandparents had been born, to pay taxes to the king.

Even though Joseph and Mary were expecting their baby to come soon, they, too, had to leave Nazareth and go to Bethlehem. Bethlehem was where the great King David had been born. He was a forefather of both Mary and Joseph.

It took many days to travel from Nazareth to Bethlehem. Day after day Mary sat on the back of the little donkey, while Joseph walked beside her. When they finally arrived in Bethlehem, it was too late to find a place to sleep. The city was crowded. There was no room for them anywhere. All the room they could find was a stable. The innkeeper owned it. He said they might sleep there. So Joseph made a bed for Mary on a pile of warm straw right there in the barn.

That night, while the little town of Bethlehem lay fast asleep, God sent Mary her Baby. She wrapped Him in some soft rags (called "swaddling" clothes) which mothers always used in those days to dress their babies. There was no cradle or basket in the stable for Mary's new Baby. So Mary laid Him in the manger where the cows usually ate.

That same night, there were shepherds in the fields near Bethlehem. They were taking care of their sheep. Suddenly they saw a great light. It blinded them. They hid their faces. An angel of the Lord stood in the midst of the light. The glory of God shone all around them. The shepherds trembled with fear.

But the angel said, "Don't be afraid. Behold, I bring you good tidings of great joy, which shall be to all people. For unto you is born this day in the city of David a Saviour, which is Christ the Lord. And this is the sign unto you, you shall find the Babe wrapped in swaddling clothes, and lying in a manger."

Suddenly, there were many angels above them. They all began

to sing, "Glory to God in the highest, and on earth peace among men, in whom He is well pleased." Then all the angels went back to heaven.

The shepherds looked at each other in amazement. Never before had they heard or seen anything like this. "Come," they said, "let us go at once to Bethlehem to see this strange thing which has happened." They left their sheep on the hillsides and hurried to Bethlehem. They went to the stable behind the inn.

"Is there a new baby here?" they asked, as soon as Joseph opened the door. "A bright, shining angel from heaven told us the news," they explained. "He is to be our Saviour and Lord. And we shall find Him wrapped in swaddling clothes and lying in a manger."

Joseph led these husky shepherds to the manger. Mary was sitting close by. The shepherds knelt in adoration. As they watched the tiny Boy, asleep so peacefully, their hearts leaped for joy. Their Saviour had finally come! God had kept His promise!

The shepherds told Mary and Joseph all about the angel's visit, and the wonderful song of the angelic hosts. When morning came, they went back to their sheep, shouting and praising God. They spread the good news to all they met.

That was how Jesus came into the world. What a wonderful day that was! As Mary watched her new-born Son, she thought about all the things which had happened. Surely this Child must be the most important child ever born, for no son of an earthly king was ever announced so royally! And yet no king ever placed his son in so humble a cradle! God's ways are too wonderful for us!

Were you listening? Why did Joseph and Mary go to Bethlehem? Where did they sleep in Bethlehem? Why was that the most important night of all history? Who were the first visitors to come to see the Baby Jesus?

Story 167

Anna and Simeon Meet Jesus

Luke 2

When Jesus was a tiny baby, Mary and Joseph took Him to God's House. God's House was then called a Temple. It was customary for parents in those days to do this. Jesus was about forty days old when He was brought to the Temple.

Mary and Joseph wanted to dedicate Jesus to God. Some parents, who had enough money, would sacrifice a lamb and a turtle-dove. But if they were poor, they might bring two turtle-doves. Mary and Joseph were poor, so they bought two turtle-doves.

Now it happened that when the Baby-Jesus was brought to the Temple that day, there were two very old people in the Temple. They were an old man named Simeon, and an old lady named Anna. Simeon was a good man. He had been waiting many years for God to send His promised Son. And God told him that he would not die until he had seen the Baby-Jesus.

When Simeon saw Mary and Joseph bringing their Baby into the Temple, he came up to Mary and took the Baby in his arms. He blessed God and said, "Now, Lord, let Thy servant die, for I have seen Thy salvation. This Baby shall be a light to lighten all the peoples of the world, and the glory of Thy people, Israel."

Then Simeon gave the Baby back to Mary. He blessed them both and said, "Some people are going to believe that your Baby is God's Son, and some people are not. Many people will be against Him. And a sword will pierce your heart. You will be sad because of the way they will treat your Son."

The old lady, Anna, came into the Temple about the same time. Anna was more than a hundred years old. She was a good woman. For many years she lived in God's House day and night. She had been married for seven years, but she had been a widow for eighty-four years.

Anna quickly came over to Mary to see her Baby. She looked at the dear little Boy in His mother's arms. And then she gave thanks to God. She told everyone about this Baby, that He was God's promised Son who would bring salvation to His people.

Joseph and Mary were amazed. They marveled at the words which Simeon and Anna had spoken. They never forgot this important day.

Were you listening? Why did Mary bring her Baby to the Temple? What did Simeon say about the Baby-Jesus? What did Anna do?

A Wonderful Star

Far, far away from Bethlehem, the little village where Jesus was born, there lived some wise men. These wise men liked to study the stars. Every night they looked up at the stars and tried to learn all about the beautiful, twinkling lights. One night, as they were watching the stars, they saw a new star. It was a beautiful star. It shone brightly in the dark eastern sky. They hurried to their books to find the meaning of this new star. They soon learned that it was a most unusual star. It was sent to tell them that a new King was born.

"This must be a great King," the wise men said, "to have such a beautiful new star to tell of His coming!"

"We must go find this new King," they decided. "We must bring Him presents, too."

So they made ready and rode away on their camels to find the new King. In their saddles they carried lovely gifts — gifts fit for a king — gold, frankincense, and myrrh. The men rode for many days. The days became weeks, and the weeks became months before they finished their journey. They had learned from their books that this King would be a king of the Jews. Since Jerusalem was the greatest city of the Jews, it was into this city that the wise men finally rode.

The people of Jerusalem looked with surprise at the stately visitors riding through their streets on such tall camels. "Where is the new Baby-King?" the men asked. "We have seen His star in the East and have come to worship Him." The people did not know about the new King. They had not heard the wonderful news of Mary and her Baby.

King Herod, whose beautiful palace was in Jerusalem, heard about these strange visitors. They worried him. He gathered all his leaders together. He asked them if they knew where this King was to be born. And they told him that the prophets had written in the Old Testament that this King would be born in Bethlehem.

Then King Herod secretly called the wise men to his palace.

He asked them many questions. He told them they should go to Bethlehem. "Go find the Baby-King," he said, "and when you find Him, come back to tell me so that I may worship Him, too."

Then the wise men started toward Bethlehem. The sun had already gone down behind the hills of Judea. Imagine their joy when they saw that same star which they had seen in the East. It seemed to be leading them. The star led them right into Bethlehem. Presently, it stopped above the very house where Joseph and Mary were living at that time. The wise men went into the house. They found Mary and her Baby. He was the new King! They had found Him at last. The wise men fell down at His feet and worshiped Him. They gave Him their gifts — the gold, the frankincense, and the myrrh.

> *Were you listening?* What led the wise men to Bethlehem? What were the wise men seeking? What did they give the new King? Why did they worship Him?

Story 169

God Takes Care of His Son

Matthew 2

God warned the wise men in a dream not to go back to King Herod. They went home another way. The king was a dreadfully wicked man, one of the most wicked kings who ever lived. He really wanted to kill Jesus, not worship Him. He was afraid that Jesus would grow up to be a king.

King Herod waited and waited, but the wise men did not

come. The king was filled with rage when he realized that the wise men had disobeyed him. He made his own plans. Even though he did not know where He lived, he would see to it that this Baby-King was killed! He sent his soldiers down to Bethlehem. "Kill every baby boy," he commanded, "two years old and younger!"

The soldiers hurried to Bethlehem to carry out their wicked master's orders. From house to house they went, putting to death every baby boy in Bethlehem. Not one was spared! But did the Baby-Jesus get killed? No, no! Just in time, God sent His angel to warn Joseph as he slept. Joseph jumped out of bed. He put Mary and her Baby on the little donkey's back. Staff in hand, Joseph quietly led his little family away from Bethlehem and the cruel king.

For many, many days the little family traveled, up and down the hillsides and through desert lands. Finally they came to the land of Egypt, where God's people had once lived for so many years.

Mary and Joseph made their home in Egypt for quite a long time. Here the Baby-Jesus grew to be a little boy. Here Mary began to teach her little Son about God. One night the angel of God came again to Joseph. "You may go back now to the land of Israel," the angel said. "Those who tried to kill the Boy are no longer alive."

The very next day the little family began their long trip home. Back again through the desert sands they went. At first they thought they would like to go back to Bethlehem, where Jesus was born. But then they learned that the man who was now king in Jerusalem was a son of the wicked King Herod. So they were afraid to go back there. Instead they traveled on to their home in Nazareth.

Here the little Boy-Jesus grew up. He ran and played with the other little boys of Nazareth. He played with His own brothers and sisters, too.

Jesus loved to stand and watch Joseph as he worked at his carpenter bench. It was not long before Jesus could handle the heavy tools all by Himself. Soon He was a great help to Joseph.

Jesus was always happy as He went about His work. When He was asked to run an errand or do some work, He always did it cheerfully and well. Jesus was the only little boy in Nazareth who was never cross or disobedient. In fact, Jesus was the only child who ever lived who was always good. For Jesus was not only Mary's Boy, He was also the Son of God.

> *Were you listening?* Why didn't the wise men go back to King Herod? Why didn't the Baby-Jesus get killed by the king's soldiers? Where did Joseph and Mary take Jesus? In what town did Jesus grow up?

Story 170

A Visit to the Temple

Luke 2

The Boy-Jesus loved His little country home in Nazareth. He liked to look at the flowers and the trees. He watched the birds and the animals around His home. Everything around Him, He knew, was all a part of the beautiful world His Father had made.

Jesus went to school, too. His school was quite different from our schools today. Only boys went to school in Jesus' day. Their school was the church. And their teacher was the minister. Each morning Jesus and the other little boys of Nazareth sat on the floor at the feet of the Rabbi, as their teacher was called. They learned to read the Old Testament and the other books of their church. Jesus did well in school. He always knew His lessons and He always understood what He learned.

Every year, in the spring, Mary and Joseph went to the big city of Jerusalem. They went to worship God and to take part in a wonderful feast called the Passover. This feast was held in the Temple, the same church where Jesus was taken as a Baby. The Passover feast was a remembering feast. Then at this feast God's people remembered how God had helped them to escape from Egypt.

Jesus was now twelve years old. His parents knew that He was now old enough to go with them to celebrate the Passover in Jerusalem. Jesus was happy and excited as He walked beside Mary and Joseph that fine spring morning.

Soon they left the hills of Nazareth far behind. They joined many other families as they moved slowly along the main highway which led to Jerusalem. Each night they camped under the stars and cooked their meals at an open fire.

Many days later they reached the hills of Judea. Below them in the valley lay the great city of Jerusalem. Tall mountains surrounded it on every side. There was Mount Moriah, where King Solomon had built God's Temple. The new temple which now stood on Mount Moriah was built by wicked King Herod to please the Jews. This temple looked rich and magnificent in the glow of the morning sun. The white marble pillars, the red cedar doors, and the splendid gold decorations dazzled the eyes of the Boy-Jesus. The group slowly descended into the valley.

Soon the travelers from Nazareth were mingling with the crowds as they entered the temple courts. There were thousands of priests milling about in their long, white-fringed, purple robes. There were stalls and booths where doves and lambs could be bought for the offerings.

It was an exciting week for Joseph and Mary. It was even more exciting for their twelve-year-old Son, Jesus. Day after day He went among the people, eyes bright with eagerness as He tried to watch everything at once.

The week finally over, Joseph and Mary set out once more on their homeward journey. They thought that Jesus was following with His friends. But when night came, and the people all gathered around the campfire, Mary missed her Son. No matter where they looked or whom they asked, they could not find Jesus. Immediately Mary and Joseph started back to Jerusalem.

Back in Jerusalem, they looked everywhere for Jesus. For three long days they searched. Up and down the narrow streets of Jerusalem they looked. They looked carefully among the crowds at the busy market place. They asked at many homes. And where do you think they found Him? They found Him in the Temple! And what do you think He was doing? He was standing among the doctors and the teachers, listening to them and asking them questions!

Mary rushed up to Jesus and threw her arms around Him. "Son, why did you frighten us so?" she asked. "Joseph and I have looked everywhere for you."

Jesus looked up. He knew He was where He belonged — in the Temple. "How is it that you looked for Me?" He asked. "Didn't you know I would be in My Father's House, doing My Father's work?"

Then Mary remembered that Jesus was not only her Boy. He was God's Son, too, and He had work to do. But Jesus was a good boy. Although He would have loved to have stayed in Jerusalem in His Father's House, He went home with His mother and obeyed her as before. But Mary never forgot the words of her Son. Nor did she forget what the men had said in the Temple. "That boy of yours," they had said, "why, He knows more than we do!"

Were you listening? In which way was Jesus different from other boys? Why did Jesus enjoy the Passover Feast so much? Why did not Jesus stay in the Temple at Jerusalem?

Story 171

Jesus Is Baptized by John

Matthew 3; Mark 1; Luke 3; John 1

For many more years Jesus lived quietly with His parents in the little town of Nazareth. He helped Joseph in the carpenter shop. Later, when Joseph died, Jesus took over his work. He was happy in His little home with Mary. But He knew that some day He would have to leave His home and friends in Nazareth to begin His great life's work. So as He worked, He waited — waited for His heavenly Father to tell Him when to begin.

Then, one day, He knew. The time had come. He said goodbye to His mother, Mary, and started down the road that led to Jerusalem. The Boy of Nazareth was now a man. A man who was also God. A man who was sent from God to save His people from their sins.

Jesus was thirty years old when He left Nazareth. He knew where He wanted to go. He was on His way to find His cousin,

John. Jesus had never seen John, but Mary had often told Him about John's father. She told how Zacharias did not believe the angel's message telling of the birth of his son. Jesus had heard, too, how Zacharias could not talk until the baby came, because of his unbelief.

News of this man, John, had come all the way to Nazareth. People said he walked in the desert hills of Judea. He was a strange man, this John. He wore a belt made from the skins of wild beasts and a coat of camel's hair. His hair and beard were long and tangled. His only food was locusts (a kind of grasshopper) and wild honey.

John's great work was to be the "herald" or "announcer" of Jesus' coming. Day after day he stood near the shores of the river Jordan preaching to the crowds who came to see him. He told them that the time had come for the people to repent of their sins. "You must turn from your wicked ways, and be kind and loving," he told them. "Get ready, for your Saviour is coming soon. When Jesus, the Son of God, comes, He will gather the good wheat into His barns, but He will burn the chaff in a fire that will never go out!" He meant that the people who love God and obey Him are like the good wheat. They will go to live with Jesus in heaven. But the wicked people are like the chaff. The chaff is the part of the wheat that isn't any good. These people will be burned in the fire of hell.

Many who listened to John were sorry for their sins. They believed John's message. God forgave their sins. Then John baptized them in the river Jordan. John baptized many people. Soon he came to be known as John the Baptist. The people wondered who John was. "Are you the Saviour?" they asked.

"No," John answered, "I am just a voice, telling you to make your hearts ready because the Saviour is coming soon. I can baptize you with water, but He will baptize you with the Spirit of God. He is much greater than I am. I am not even worthy to stoop down and undo the lace of His shoe!"

One day, as John was preaching, Jesus came to the desert where John was. He walked up the path along the river's edge. John saw

Him coming. His heart leaped for joy! Although he had never seen his cousin, John knew at once that it was Jesus. God told him. John stopped preaching. Pointing to Jesus as He was coming, he said, "Behold the Lamb of God which taketh away the sin of the world! This is the Man I have been telling you about!"

Jesus went up to John. He wanted to be baptized, too. At first John did not want to baptize Jesus because He was the Son of God. John had baptized only sinful people. Jesus had no sin. "No," John said, "You are the Son of God, You should baptize me." But Jesus wanted to be baptized because His Father in heaven had told Him that He should.

So John went with Jesus down into the river Jordan. There he baptized Him. As they were coming up out of the water, a wonderful thing happened. The sky opened up. The Holy Spirit, like a dove, came down and rested on Jesus' head. And the heavenly Father's voice was heard from heaven, saying, "Thou art my beloved Son. In Thee I am well pleased." Then everyone knew that Jesus was truly the Son of God.

Were you listening? Why did Jesus leave His home in Nazareth? What was John doing at the river Jordan? Why didn't John want to baptize Jesus? What did God say about His Son?

Story 172

Jesus Is Tempted by Satan

Matthew 4; Mark 1; Luke 4

After Jesus had been baptized by John, He went far into the desert to be alone. It was cold and lonely in the desert. For forty days and nights Jesus wandered about. He had no bed, not even a pillow on which to lay His weary head. At night He could hear the wild beasts howling as they left their dens in search of food. But there was no food for Jesus. During all that time He went hungry and thirsty.

Jesus was not alone in the desert, however. That wicked angel, Satan, was there, too. He is the one who hated God and was cast out of heaven. He was the one who led Adam and Eve to sin in Paradise. Now he wanted Jesus to sin. Satan knew that Jesus was the Son of God. He knew that Jesus had come into the world to save His people from their sins. Satan did not want Jesus to be our Saviour. So he tried to make Jesus sin, just as he had made Adam sin. If Jesus sinned Satan knew He could not save others from sin.

When Satan saw that Jesus was hungry, he said to Him, "If you are the Son of God, why don't you turn these stones into bread?" Jesus could have made bread out of the stones, but then He would have been obeying Satan. So He answered, "It is written (in the Bible) that man shall not live by bread alone, but by every word of God."

Satan would not give up that easily. He tried again. This time he and Jesus went into Jerusalem. Satan took Jesus to the top of the steeple of the Temple, where God's people came to worship every day. There they stood, high up on the top of the Temple. They could see all the people on the streets below. Satan said to Jesus, "If you are the Son of God, throw yourself down to the ground, and show the people that God will take care of you. For the Bible says (Satan knew what was written in the Bible, too),

He shall give His angels charge over Thee:
On their hands they shall bear Thee up,
Lest haply Thou dash Thy foot against a stone."

Satan was telling Jesus that God would send His angels to catch Him so He would not get hurt. But Jesus would not listen to Satan. He answered, "I will not do as you tell Me. The Bible says that we may not tempt God."

Once more Satan tried to make Jesus obey him. This time he took Jesus to a high mountain. From this mountain-top they could see all the countries of the world. Satan showed Jesus all the beautiful things in the world—the wonderful kingdoms, the riches, and the beauty. Then he said to Jesus, "I will give you all these things if you will just fall down and worship me."

But Jesus would not listen to Satan. He said, "Go away, Satan. God's Holy Word tells us that we must worship God alone. We may not worship anyone else."

Satan could not make Jesus sin. He saw that Jesus would not

obey him, so he went away. Then God sent His angels into the desert to be with Jesus. They took care of Jesus and gave Him all that He needed.

Were you listening? What happened to Jesus in the desert? Why was it wrong for Jesus to make the stones into bread? What would have happened if Jesus had obeyed Satan?

Story 173

Followers of Jesus

Matthew 9; Mark 3; John 1

On the day after he had baptized Jesus, John was again standing by the river Jordan with two of his disciples. They saw Jesus walking along. John pointed to Jesus and said again, "Behold the Lamb of God." The two disciples left John and ran after Jesus.

Jesus turned and saw the two men following Him. "What are you looking for?" He asked. The two men answered, "Master, where do you live?" And Jesus said, "Come and see." So the two men went with Jesus and stayed with Him that night. Now one of the two young men was Andrew, the brother of Simon Peter. As soon as Andrew found his brother, Peter, he said to him, "Peter, we have found the Christ."

Andrew brought Peter to Jesus. Jesus looked at Peter and said, "You are Simon, the son of Jona, but I am going to call you Peter, which means a rock." On another day Jesus met Peter and Andrew as they were washing their fishing nets on the shore of the Sea of Galilee. Jesus called to them, "Follow Me and I will make you fishers of men." Peter and Andrew left their nets and followed Jesus. A little farther along the shore, two other brothers, James and John, were sitting with their father in his boat, mending a hole in their net. Jesus called to them, too. So these two brothers also followed Jesus.

Now Jesus had four helpers. Later He met Philip walking down a street in Galilee. "Follow Me," was all Jesus said, and Philip came. Soon Philip told his friend, Nathanael, about Jesus. "We have found Him, whom Moses and the prophets promised, even Jesus of Nazareth," Philip said. But Nathanael asked, "Can any good thing come out of Nazareth?" "Come and see," Philip answered. So Nathanael went with Philip to find Jesus.

When Jesus saw Nathanael coming, He said, "Here comes an honest Israelite." Nathanael was surprised. "How did you know me?" he asked. Jesus answered, "I saw you, Nathanael, even before Philip called you, when you were still sitting under the fig tree." Nathanael answered, "Teacher, you are the Son of God! You are the King of Israel!" Then Jesus said, "You believed, Nathanael, because of what I told you. You will see greater things than these. You will even see the heavens open, and the angels of God coming down on the Son of Man."

On another day Jesus found Matthew sitting at a tax-collector's table. Jesus went up to him and said, "Follow Me." Matthew left his tax table at once and followed Jesus. Matthew was so happy to be chosen by Jesus that he gave a banquet for Jesus. He invited all his friends. But some of the leaders found fault with Jesus for eating with such common people. "Why do you eat and drink with publicans and sinners?" they asked. Jesus answered, "Those who are well don't need a doctor; it is the sick people who need him. I did not come into this world to help good people. I came to help sinners."

One day Jesus went up into a mountain and called several people to come to Him. Then He chose twelve men to be His special helpers. Besides Peter and Andrew, and James and John, and Philip and Nathanael and Matthew, He also chose Thomas, and another James, and another Simon, and Thaddaeus, and Judas Iscariot. He called these men His twelve disciples. They followed Him wherever He went.

Were you listening? Who were the first men to follow Jesus? What new name did Jesus give Simon? What two words did Jesus use to call His friends? How many of the twelve disciples can you name?

Story 174

Jesus Helps at a Wedding Feast

John 2

Not long after Jesus began His work, He went back to Nazareth to visit His mother. Five of His new friends came with Him. Mary was happy to see her Son again. She was happy to meet His new friends, too. But Mary was very busy that day. There was to be a wedding at the home of one of her friends, in the nearby town of Cana. So Jesus and His friends went along with Mary to the wedding.

Everything at the wedding feast seemed to be going along nicely, when suddenly something happened. Mary hurried to Jesus. "There isn't enough wine for all the guests," she said. If the wine was all gone there would be nothing for the people to drink.

"Why do you tell Me?" Jesus asked. "My hour is not yet come." He was really saying, "Do you realize what you are asking? If I make wine for these people, then everyone will know that I am not only your son, but that I am the Son of God."

Mary knew what Jesus meant. She turned to the servants and said, "Do whatever Jesus says. He will help you."

In the kitchen Jesus found six water pots. The family used them when they washed themselves at their feasts. "Fill these water pots with water," Jesus said. The servants filled them to the brim. "Now pour some of this water into a wine glass and take it to the master of the feast."

When the servants obeyed Jesus, they found that all the water in the pots had turned to wine! The servants brought some of this new wine to the leader of the feast. He was surprised when he tasted the wine. He called the bridegroom. "People usually serve their best wine first," he said, "but you have saved your best wine for the last." The bridegroom was surprised, too. He did not know where this good wine had come from. But the servants knew, and they told what had happened.

This was the first time Jesus had shown His great power by working a miracle. A miracle is a wonderful act which only God can do. Now Jesus' friends truly believed that He was the Son of God. They believed that He was their Saviour.

Were you listening? What happened at the wedding in Cana? How could Jesus turn water into wine? What did Jesus' friends learn from this miracle?

My Father's House

Jesus and His friends did not stay long in Nazareth. They soon made their way back to Jerusalem. It was spring and time for the people to celebrate the Passover Feast. Great throngs of people were crowding into the Temple when Jesus and His disciples arrived. The Temple was a noisy place that day. It did not seem like God's House where men should come to pray quietly to God.

The people had turned the Temple into a market place instead of a House of Prayer. Men had brought live oxen, sheep, and doves into the Temple to sell for sacrifices.

All those who came to the Temple for the Passover Feast had to give a piece of silver money, called a half shekel, to the priests. If the people did not have a half shekel, they had to change their money for one. And so there were money changers sitting at their tables in the Temple, too.

When Jesus heard all the noise, and saw all the confusion, it made Him angry. This was His Father's House. Men should come here to worship and to pray, not to buy and sell and do business! He looked around and found some small ropes, or cords. He tied them together to make a whip. Then He chased the men and their sheep and oxen out of the Temple. He upset the tables of the money changers and poured out their money on the floor. And He said to the men who owned the doves, "Take these doves out of here. Don't make My Father's House a place of business!"

When the disciples saw what Jesus had done, they remembered that it was written in God's Word about Jesus' love for His Father's House. The Bible says, "The zeal (love) of thine house hath eaten me up."

Many of the people did not like what Jesus had done. They said, "Who gave you the right to do this? Show us a sign." Jesus said, "Destroy this temple, and in three days I will raise it up." Jesus meant His own body. He knew that some day the people would help to kill Him. He meant that in three days He would rise again from the dead.

But the people thought He meant their beautiful Temple. They sneered at Jesus. "What!" they said. "It took King Herod forty-six years to build this Temple. Do you think you can rebuild it in three days?"

While Jesus was in Jerusalem during the week of the Feast, He taught the people and did many wonderful things. Many of the people believed that Jesus was the promised Messiah, who would save His people from their sins.

> *Were you listening?* Why did Jesus become angry when He entered the Temple? What did Jesus do? What temple would Jesus rebuild in three days?

Story 176

A Ruler Visits Jesus

John 3

Jesus was a great teacher. Wherever He went, He taught people many things. He told them about the Kingdom of God. He wanted them to know how to please God and obey Him.

Many of the leaders did not like Jesus' teachings. They did not like it that Jesus scolded them for being proud, and selfish, and unkind. When the people followed Jesus, instead of coming to them, it made them angry.

There were a few leaders who liked what Jesus taught. They wished they could follow Him, too, and listen to His wonderful words. But they were afraid of the rest of the leaders. Nicodemus was one of these men. He wanted to see Jesus, but he didn't want his friends to know about it. So, one night, after dark, Nicodemus went to the home where Jesus was staying.

Jesus was happy to talk with Nicodemus and to listen to his questions. Nicodemus said, "Rabbi (which means teacher), we know You are a teacher come from God. No man could do all these wonderful miracles which You do, unless God were with him."

Jesus gave Nicodemus a strange answer. He said, "If you want to see the Kingdom of God, you must be born again." Nicodemus knew that God was going to have a great new kingdom, and that God's Son would be the King. But Nicodemus thought that every

Jew would have a place in that kingdom. He was surprised at Jesus' words.

"How can that be?" he asked. "Can a man be born again when he is old? Can he become a baby again?"

Jesus answered, "You must be born of the Holy Spirit. You must become a child of God. Don't be surprised that I say you must be born again. You can not understand it, but you can know that it has happened. You can't see the wind, either. You don't know where the wind comes from or where it goes, but you can feel the wind and see what it does."

Nicodemus asked many more questions, for he did not know how to become a child of God. "Are you a teacher in Israel, and don't you know these things?" Jesus asked. "Don't you remember what happened to the Israelites in the wilderness?"

The people in the wilderness had sinned. God had sent snakes to bite them. Those who were bitten became very sick and some died. Then the people cried to God for help. God told Moses to make a shiny, brass snake. Moses was to lift this brass snake high on a pole for all to see. And all who looked at the brass snake were made better.

"Just as that brass snake was lifted up in the wilderness," Jesus explained, "even so must the Son of man be lifted up. Whosoever believes in Him may have eternal life."

Jesus was lifted up on the Cross. Everyone who looks to Him in faith shall live. We may have life in Christ because God loved the world so much that He gave His only Son to die for sinners! If we believe that Jesus died for us, then we, too, are born again.

Nicodemus talked with Jesus for a long time. He never forgot the words of Jesus. After a while, he, too, believed that Jesus was the Saviour.

Were you listening? Why didn't the Jewish leaders like Jesus? Why did Nicodemus go to Jesus at night? What did Jesus tell Nicodemus? How can you be born again?

Story 177

"No, Never Thirst Again"

John 4

One day Jesus and His friends were traveling to Galilee. They had to go through a country called Samaria. Soon they came to a little town called Sychar. Sychar was not far from the piece of land which Jacob had once given to his favorite son, Joseph. And Jacob's well was there.

It was noon-time. Jesus stopped at the well to rest. The disciples went on into the city to buy food. Presently, a woman came to the well to draw water. She was carrying a water jug on her shoulders. She paid no attention to Jesus. She tied a rope to the handles of her jug and lowered it into the deep well.

"Give me a drink," Jesus said, suddenly. The woman was surprised. She quickly pulled up her heavy jug and set it on the stone.

She turned and looked at Jesus. "How is it," she asked, "that you, a Jew, would ask *me*, a Samaritan, for a drink of water?"

"If you knew the gift of God," Jesus answered, "and if you knew who I was, you would ask *Me* for a drink."

"Ask you for a drink?"

"Yes," Jesus nodded, "and I would give you living water."

The woman didn't understand Jesus at all. "Sir, you have nothing to draw water with, and the well is deep," she marveled. "Where would you get this living water?"

Jesus answered, "If you drink of the water from this well, you will thirst again. But whoever drinks of the water I give him, he shall never thirst. The water will become in him a fountain of water, springing up into eternal life."

"Sir," the woman quickly said, "give me this water, that I may not thirst, nor come here every day to draw water."

Then Jesus began to tell her many things about herself. She was really surprised that He knew so much about her. She realized that He was no ordinary Man.

The woman leaned against the well. "Sir," she gasped, "I see you are a prophet." Then Jesus taught her about the Kingdom of God. And when she asked about the Messiah who was someday going to come, Jesus said, "I am the Messiah."

She stared at Him without saying a word. Jesus had told her His great secret! He had not even told that to His disciples. At that very moment the disciples came back. They were surprised to see Jesus talking with this woman, but they said nothing. The woman left her water jug and ran back to the city. She told everyone that the Messiah was at Jacob's well.

Jesus was no longer hungry or tired. He was happy to be doing His Father's work. He explained this to the disciples. Soon the woman came back with a crowd of Samaritans. They listened gladly to Jesus' words. They liked what He said. They pleaded with Him not to leave. So Jesus and His disciples stayed in Samaria for two days. And many of them believed that Jesus was the Christ, the Saviour of the world.

> *Were you listening?* Why was Jesus visiting Samaria? How could Jesus give living water to this woman at the well? Why was Jesus no longer hungry when His disciples brought Him food?

Story 178

Jesus Helps a Believing Father

John 4

Wherever Jesus went, a crowd of people always followed Him. Jesus went up to Jerusalem for the Passover Feast. There many people believed in Him because they saw all the wonderful things He did.

After the feast, Jesus left Jerusalem and went to Galilee, the place where He had lived as a boy. Although the people of Galilee had known Him for thirty years, they did not think He was the Son of God. They did not think that Mary's son could also be the Son of God. But when Jesus came back to His home town to visit that day, His own people were glad to see Him. They, too, had been to the feast in Jerusalem and had seen His wonderful works.

Jesus stopped in the little town of Cana. Remember, He had made water into wine at the wedding feast there. In the city of Capernaum there lived a certain nobleman. This nobleman was an important man. He probably worked in King Herod's court. At home in Capernaum he had a son whom he loved a great deal. This son was very sick. The doctors could not make him well.

When this nobleman heard that Jesus was in Cana, he hurried down to see Him. He knelt in front of Jesus and said, "Please come to my home and heal my son. He is so sick, I am afraid he is going to die."

"Unless you see signs and wonders, you don't believe," Jesus answered, looking down at the rich nobleman.

"Please, Lord, come down before my son dies," begged the father, breaking into tears.

Jesus felt sorry for the poor father. "Go your way," He said softly, "your son is well."

The nobleman turned away at once. He believed what Jesus told him. He knew that Jesus could make his little boy better even without seeing him.

It took many hours for the nobleman to reach his home. On the next day, when he was almost home, his servants came running to meet him. "Your son is well again," they shouted.

"Praise God!" the father exclaimed. "When did it happen?"

"At one o'clock yesterday afternoon his fever left him."

Then the father knew that it was Jesus who had made his boy better, for that was the exact time when Jesus had said, "Go your way, your son is well." Then the father and his family, and all those who lived in his house, believed in Jesus. They believed that He was more than a man who could do wonderful things. He was the Son of God who came into this world to save His people from their sins. This was the second miracle that Jesus did in His own country of Galilee.

> *Were you listening?* Why were the people of Cana glad to see Jesus? Who came to see Jesus in Cana? How did Jesus help this man? How did the father know that it was Jesus who had healed his son?

Story 179

The Cripple at the Pool of Bethesda

John 5

It was feast-time again in Jerusalem. Jesus and His disciples went up to celebrate the feast. On the Sabbath afternoon, they took a walk to a place not far outside the city. It was called the Pool of Bethesda. There were five porches around this pool. These porches were filled with sick people. There were blind people there, and deaf, and lame, and people with all kinds of sicknesses.

The sick people stayed on these porches day after day, from one year to the next. For this was not just an ordinary pool. These sick people were waiting for a miracle to happen. Once every year an angel came down from heaven to stir the water in this pool. As soon as the water had been stirred, the people tried to get into the pool. The first person in the water would be cured. Then the rest of the people would have to wait until the angel came again. They all tried to be first. It was because of the angel's healing that this pool was called Bethesda. Bethesda means "House of Mercy."

There was a man on one of these porches who had been sick for thirty-eight years. What a long time! During all that time he had been lying on his mat because he could not walk. Jesus noticed the lame man. Jesus knew all about him, of course. He felt sorry for the poor man. "Would you like to be made whole?" He asked, as He stopped beside the sick man.

The lame man thought Jesus was talking about the angel and the pool. He answered, "Sir, I don't have any one to help me get into the pool. While I am trying to get in, someone always gets in ahead of me."

Jesus smiled at the poor man. He had not understood Jesus at all. So Jesus said, "Rise, take up your bed, and walk!"

At that very moment the man was healed! He stood up, took up his bed, which was really just a mat, and walked away. He walked toward the Temple. He soon met some of the leaders. "You must not carry your bed on the Sabbath Day," they said. "That's against the law."

The healed man answered, "The One who made me better told me to take up my bed and walk."

"Who made you better?" the men asked.

But the man did not know who it was, for Jesus had not told him. When He saw a crowd of people gathering, He had quickly disappeared.

A little while later, Jesus met the man in the Temple. "Look," He said, "you are better. Don't sin any more, or a worse thing will happen to you." Then the man knew who Jesus was. He left the

Temple and went to find the leaders. He told them that it was Jesus who had healed him.

This made the men still more angry. Jesus had told this man to carry his bed on the Sabbath. He had also healed him on the Sabbath! They thought it more important to keep the Law than to heal the poor lame man. They tried right then to hurt Jesus. Then they began to make plans to kill Him.

But Jesus was not afraid of them. He said, "My Father works, and so I work."

Now the men were furious. It was bad enough for Jesus to work on the Sabbath, but now He was claiming that God was His Father. They tried still harder to kill Jesus. But Jesus went His way, teaching and preaching. "Those who do not honor the Son of God, are not honoring the Father who sent Him," He said. "The time is coming when even the dead shall hear the voice of the Son of God. And they that hear shall live!"

Were you listening? What does Bethesda mean? What did Jesus do for the lame man at Bethesda? Why were the Jews angry? What did Jesus tell them?

Not Wanted by His Own People

Jesus and His disciples were traveling through Galilee. One day they came to Nazareth, the little town where Jesus had lived as a boy. The news of His return spread quickly through the town. The people had heard about all the wonderful things Jesus had been doing in other cities. Now they would be able to hear and see for themselves what Jesus would say and do.

On the Sabbath, Jesus and His disciples went with Mary to the little church, called a synagogue, where He had gone so often as a little boy. The little church was crowded, for all the people wanted to see Jesus.

Jesus stood up to show that He wanted to read from the Bible. In those days the books of the Old Testament were all separate. They were written on long strips of paper, which were rolled up on a scroll. When Jesus stood up, the man who had charge of the scrolls handed Jesus the roll which the prophet Isaiah had written. Jesus unrolled the scroll and found the place where He wanted to read. He read these words, which told about the promised Saviour:

> The Spirit of the Lord is upon me,
> Because he has anointed me to preach the gospel to the poor;
> He has sent me to heal the brokenhearted,
> To preach deliverance to the captives,
> And recovering of sight to the blind,
> To preach the acceptable year of the Lord.

When Jesus finished reading, He rolled up the scroll, handed it back, and sat down. In those days the minister always stood up to read God's Word. Then he sat down to explain what it meant. Everyone waited eagerly to hear what Jesus was going to say.

"Today," Jesus began, "you are seeing these words, which I just read, happening before your very eyes. I am the One whom Isaiah promised would come. I am the One who must preach and heal and help. I am the Messiah you are looking for."

The people were amazed at the way Jesus spoke. "Is not this Joseph's son?" they asked. Jesus was only the son of a poor carpenter, they thought. How could he preach like this? And how could he be the Messiah they were looking for?

Jesus knew that they would not believe Him. "Oh, I know what you are going to say," He went on. "You would like to have Me do some wonderful works here as I did in Capernaum. But you wouldn't believe Me anyway. No prophet is accepted in his own country. You remember, there were many widows in Israel in the days of Elijah, when it did not rain for three and a half years. There was a great famine in the land. But God did not send Elijah to any of them. He sent him to a widow in the land of Zarephath, instead. And there were many lepers in Israel in the time of Elisha. But God did not let Elisha heal any of them. He healed Naaman, the Syrian, instead."

When the people heard Jesus' words, they were filled with anger. What was Jesus trying to tell them? That God cared for other people besides children of Israel? They would not listen to such words! The leaders rushed up to Jesus and pulled Him out of their little synagogue. They dragged Him to the top of the hill on which Nazareth was built. They were going to throw Him headlong over the cliff so that He would be killed. But their terrible plans were not carried out. God was protecting His Son. Jesus simply walked through the angry mob and went His way. No one touched Him.

Then Jesus and His mother moved away from Nazareth. They went to live in the city of Capernaum. Capernaum was on the shores of the Sea of Galilee. Here Jesus taught the people about God, His Father. And they were glad to listen to Him.

> *Were you listening?* Why were the people of Nazareth glad to have Jesus visit them? Why did they turn against Jesus? Why did they not kill Jesus as they planned?

Story 181

A Wonderful Catch of Fish

Luke 5

Although Jesus now lived in Capernaum, He was not often at home. He spent most of His time walking about from city to city. Wherever Jesus went, crowds of people followed Him.

One day Jesus was walking along beside the Sea of Galilee. The crowds were following Him as usual. The people crowded so close, they almost pushed Jesus into the water. Jesus looked about and noticed two boats tied at the water's edge. The fishermen were close by, washing their nets. These fishermen were two of Jesus' disciples — Peter and Andrew. "Peter," Jesus called, "may I use your boat?" "Yes," Peter quickly answered.

Jesus and Peter got into the boat. "Row a little way away from the shore," Jesus said. So Peter rowed the boat away from the shore. When he had gone a little way, he dropped the anchor. Now the people could not crowd around Jesus. So Jesus sat down in Peter's boat and taught the people.

When Jesus finished preaching, the people went away. "Let's go fishing," Jesus said to Peter. "Take your boat out into the middle of the lake. Then drop your nets for some fish."

Peter and his friends had been fishing all night. They had caught nothing. So Peter said to Jesus, "We fished all night without catching anything, but if You want us to, we'll try again."

Jesus wanted them to try, so Peter and Andrew rowed their boat into the deep water. James and John brought their boat, too. Peter and Andrew let down their nets. In a short time their nets were filled with fish. The nets were so full of fish that they began to tear. And they were so heavy that Peter and Andrew could not lift them out of the water. They called James and John to pull up their boat alongside, so that they could help. Together the men pulled in the heavy nets. Both of the boats were filled with fish. The boats were so full that they began to sink. The fishermen had to row them to shore at once.

Peter and his friends wondered at the great power of Jesus. They became afraid. Peter fell down at Jesus' feet, and said, "Go away from me, Lord, for I am a sinful man." Peter felt that Jesus was too great to be with sinful men.

But Jesus spoke kindly to Peter and his friends. "Don't be afraid," He said. "From now on you won't be fishermen any more. You will catch men instead." Jesus meant that from then on they wouldn't have time to go into their boats and catch fish. They would have a greater work to do. They would be preachers like Jesus. They would go to tell people everywhere about Jesus, the wonderful Saviour.

The four friends were amazed at their Master. Quietly they rowed their boats to shore and tied them up. As soon as they could take care of the many fish which Jesus had helped them to catch, they left their boats and their fishing. They were fishermen no more. From that day on they traveled with Jesus.

Were you listening? Why did Jesus use Peter's boat? Who wanted to go fishing? Why didn't the disciples want to go fishing? How did Peter and Andrew catch so many fish? How could Peter catch men?

Story 182

A Busy Sabbath Day for Jesus
Matthew 8; Mark 1; Luke 4

Jesus was a great teacher. Wherever He went, crowds of people followed Him and listened to His words. Jesus was a great doctor, too. When sick people came to Him, He always made them better. He could cure any kind of sickness without using any medicine. If He just spoke a word, He could make the sickness go away.

One Sabbath Day Jesus was visiting in Capernaum. This was the city where his mother now lived. Peter lived in this city, too. When it was church time, Jesus went with His friends to the little synagogue in Capernaum. He preached to the people. They were all amazed at His words.

There was a wild man in the synagogue that day. Evil spirits lived in his heart. When this wild man heard the words of Jesus, the evil spirits in him began to shout. "What have we to do with you, Jesus of Nazareth?" they cried. "Did you come here to kill us? We know who you are are. You are the Holy One of God!"

Jesus stopped preaching. "Be quiet," He said to the evil spirits, "and come out of the man." The man became even more wild for a few moments. The evil spirits threw him on the floor. They continued to cry out with a loud voice. Then they came out of the man.

"What is this!" the astonished people cried. "He commands evil spirits, and they obey!"

On the way home that day, the people told everyone they met what had happened. Soon the fame of Jesus spread all over the region of Galilee.

When the church services were over, Jesus went home with Simon Peter. Peter's wife's mother was very sick. She was in bed with a high fever. Peter and his wife begged Jesus to help the sick woman. Jesus went into the bedroom. He stood at her side and scolded the fever. Then He took her by the hand and helped her get up. At once the fever was gone! The woman was well. She got out of bed and waited on her visitors. She prepared their supper and served them.

The sun began to sink behind the lovely hills of Galilee. It was a busy evening for Jesus. The people came from miles around. They had heard what had happened in the synagogue that morning. Now they brought their sick loved ones to Peter's door. Jesus went out to them. He laid His hands on every one — a sick baby here, a blind father there, a crippled child, a deaf boy — and He healed them all! He chased away the evil spirits out of the hearts of many people, too. The evil spirits all cried out and said, "Thou art the Son of God!" But Jesus told them to keep quiet and not to tell anyone that He was the Christ.

That night Jesus stayed at Peter's home. Long before it was morning, Jesus slipped away into the desert to be alone. He wanted to talk with His Heavenly Father. But soon Peter and his friends found Him there. "All the people are looking for you," they said.

"I cannot spend all My time in Capernaum," Jesus answered. "I must preach the Good News in other cities, too. I must go everywhere. That is why God sent Me here."

So they traveled on, teaching and preaching in all the cities and little towns of Galilee.

Were you listening? Where did Jesus go on the Sabbath Day? Why were the people in the synagogue astonished at Jesus? What made this Sabbath Day such a busy day for Jesus? Why couldn't Jesus stay in Capernaum?

Jesus Heals a Leper

Matthew 8; Mark 1; Luke 5

The news about the miracles Jesus was doing spread all over the country. The crowds following Jesus became larger and larger. People came from as far away as Jerusalem and even beyond the Jordan River.

One day Jesus and the people were approaching another city. A man came and fell on his face in front of Jesus. This man had a terrible sickness called leprosy. His body was just covered with sores which would not heal.

No one would touch a leper. People were afraid they might get leprosy, too. A leper had to live all by himself, out in the country. Lepers often lived together in the caves or among the rocks.

When this leper knelt at Jesus' feet, the people backed away. No one would come near him. The leper had heard about Jesus. He knew that Jesus made sick people well. He believed that Jesus could heal him, too. "Lord, if You want to, You can make me clean," he said.

Jesus felt sorry for the poor man. He was not afraid of leprosy. He put out His hand and touched the man's dirty sores. "I do want to," Jesus said. "Be clean!" The leper looked at himself. His leprosy was all gone!

"Go show yourself to the priest in God's House," Jesus added. "And say thank you to God for making you better. But don't tell anyone that I did it."

The leper was too happy that Jesus had healed him to keep still about it. He told everyone. Soon the crowds which followed Jesus became so large that He could no longer walk through the cities. He had to go out into the desert where there was more room. And the people came to Him from everywhere.

Were you listening? What did the leper say to Jesus? What did Jesus answer him? Why did Jesus go into the desert to do His work?

Through the Roof

Matthew 9; Mark 2; Luke 5

One day Jesus went home to Capernaum. When the people of Capernaum heard about it, they came crowding to see Him and to hear Him preach. So many people came that there wasn't room in the little house. They even crowded around outside the door.

There was a man in Capernaum who couldn't walk. He trembled and shook all over. When this man heard that Jesus was home, he, too, wanted to see Him. But how could he get there? He had four kind friends, however, who loved him. "We'll take you to see Jesus," they said. They put him on a bed, or mat, and carried him through the streets.

When they came to the house where Jesus was, they could not even get near the door because of the crowd. The poor sick man was sadly disappointed. He was afraid he would have to go back home without even seeing Jesus. But his four friends did not give up so easily. They had faith in Jesus. So they looked for a way to get their sick friend in to see Him.

All of a sudden they had a wonderful idea. Up to the roof they carried their friend. Carefully they moved away some of the tile. They made a big hole in the roof, just above where Jesus stood. Slowly they let down the sick man on his mat until he lay at Jesus' feet.

How surprised the people were! They watched the roof open up and saw the man come down. But Jesus wasn't surprised. He knew the man (He knows every one). He also knew that the man and his four friends believed that Jesus could make the sick man better.

Jesus looked down at him. "Son," He said, "your sins are forgiven you."

There were men listening to Jesus that day who had not come because they loved Him. In fact, they hated Him. They had come to find fault with Him. "How can He forgive sins?" they mumbled to themselves. "Only God can do that!" They did not believe that Jesus was God.

Jesus knew what they were thinking. "It is just as easy for Me to forgive sins as it is to make this man walk," Jesus explained. "But, so that you may know that I have power to do both, listen!" He turned once more to the sick man. "Get up, take up your bed, and go home!" Jesus commanded.

The man obeyed. He got up, rolled up his mat, and walked out of the door. When the enemies of Jesus saw His great power, they hated Him still more. But Jesus' friends were amazed. They glorified God, saying, "We never saw such a thing before!"

> *Were you listening?* How did four friends help a sick man? How did Jesus prove that He was the Son of God? What did His friends say when they saw what had happened?

Story 185

The Lord of the Sabbath

Matthew 12; Mark 2 and 3; Luke 6

It was the Sabbath morning. Jesus and His disciples were on their way to church. They hadn't eaten any breakfast that morning and they were hungry. It so happened that they came through some cornfields. Ripe ears of corn were growing on the stalks. In those days it was all right to pick another man's crops to eat if one were hungry. But a man was not supposed to take more than he could eat at that time. The disciples pulled off some of the ears of corn. They rubbed the kernels in their hands, breaking off the shells. The corn tasted good.

Some Pharisees saw Jesus and His friends walking through the cornfields. The Pharisees were leaders of the Jews and prided themselves on keeping every law of God perfectly. They had made a great many extra rules about what a man might do and what he might not do on the Sabbath Day. But they forgot to be kind and loving to those in need. Jesus often helped those who were sick on the Sabbath Day, so these Pharisees had turned against Him. They were now His enemies.

The Pharisees called to Jesus. "Look, Jesus," they said, "your disciples are doing that which is not right to do on the Sabbath. Why do you let your disciples work on the Sabbath?"

"Didn't you ever read what David did?" Jesus answered.

"David and his men, when they were hungry, went into God's House (the tabernacle) and ate the shewbread, which was in the Holy Place. That bread was for the priests alone, but David ate it and gave some to his friends, too. The Sabbath was made for man, and not man for the Sabbath. You are particular about keeping all the rules. But you forget the most important rule. You forget to have mercy instead of bringing sacrifices. Yes, I, the Son of Man, am Lord also of the Sabbath Day."

When Jesus finished talking to His enemies, He went into the synagogue. Inside He noticed a man who had a withered hand. The man could not use his hand at all. It was all shrunken and dried up. Jesus' enemies saw the man, too. They wanted to see if Jesus would heal this man's hand on the Sabbath. They would also call that work. They would once more have something to say against Jesus. So they said to Jesus, "Is it right to make sick people better on the Sabbath Day?"

Jesus answered, "Which one of you men, if one of your sheep would fall into a deep hole on the Sabbath Day, would leave the sheep in the hole until the next day? You would all go quickly and pull the sheep out of the hole, wouldn't you, even though it were the Sabbath Day? And isn't a man much better than a sheep? So, I say, it is right to do good on the Sabbath Day!"

Jesus' enemies said nothing. Jesus looked at them in silence. Then he said to the man, "Hold out your hand." The man held out his hand, and immediately it was healed. As soon as the Pharisees saw this, they left the church and made further plans to kill Jesus.

Were you listening? Was it stealing for Jesus and His disciples to eat the corn from the cornfields? Why did the Pharisees say it was wrong? What happened in the synagogue that day? What did the Pharisees do when they saw Jesus' miracle?

Story 186
Jesus Teaches on the Mountain Side

Matthew 5; Luke 6
The friends of Jesus had been following Him for more than a year. One spring night, Jesus went up into a mountain to pray. His friends stayed down below. All night long, Jesus prayed to

His Heavenly Father there on the mountain top. When it was morning, He came down to His followers. He called them to come to Him. Then he chose the twelve (whom I have mentioned before in Story 173) to be His special helpers. He called them His disciples. Later He called them His apostles, because He sent them out to do His special work. He gave them power to heal the sick and to cast out evil spirits. And He told them to preach the Kingdom of God.

As Jesus and the disciples came down the mountainside, they were met by a huge crowd of people. The people came from near and far. Some came from as far away as Jerusalem and even from the seacoast beyond their own country. These people came to hear Jesus' word and to be healed from their many diseases. They all crowded around so that they might touch Jesus. For when they touched Him, they were healed. So Jesus touched them and healed them all.

Then, looking around at the great crowd of people, Jesus went back up the mountainside and sat down. His disciples sat around Him. The crowd sat at His feet and listened to the greatest sermon that was ever preached. Today we call it "The Sermon on the Mount."

Jesus began this famous sermon by talking about nine different kinds of people. He said that all these people were most happy, or blessed, because they will be rewarded by God for the way they live. God will give them the things they are longing for. We call this part of Jesus' sermon "The Beatitudes," because it tells about these blessings or "happinesses."

Jesus began by saying, "Blessed (happy) are they who hunger and thirst after righteousness, for they shall be filled." He meant the people who want to be good just as much as they want to eat or drink.

He went on, "Blessed are the merciful, for they shall obtain mercy." Jesus was talking about the people who are kind to other people. God will be good to such people.

Jesus also explained, "Blessed are the pure in heart, for they shall see God. Blessed are the peacemakers, for they shall be called the sons of God." Those whose hearts are clean and who try to be at peace and keep the peace will be happy because they are obeying God.

After Jesus had finished giving the Beatitudes, He went on with His sermon. He said, "You are the light of the world. You must let all the world see your light. You can't hide a city that is on a hilltop. And people don't put a lighted candle under a bushel. They put it on a candlestick, then it gives light to everyone in the house. So you must let your light shine, by doing the things I have taught you to do. Then people will see your good works, and will praise your Father, who is in heaven."

The things Jesus taught in His Sermon on the Mount were not only meant for those who were listening to Jesus that day. They were also meant for you. Jesus wants His children to let their light shine today, too. Each day you should pray,

> God make my life a little light
> Within the world to glow —
> A tiny flame that burneth bright
> Wherever I may go.

Were you listening? Where did Jesus go to preach? What are the Beatitudes? Why wouldn't you put a candle under a bushel? How can you be a light for Jesus?

Story 187

Jesus Teaches His People to Pray

Matthew 6

The Sermon on the Mount was a long, long sermon. In it Jesus taught the people many things. He said, "When you do kind things, don't do them in front of other people. Then you are doing good so that everyone will praise you. Don't blow a trumpet to get everyone to look at you, so that they may say what a wonderful person you are. But do your good deeds quietly when no one is looking. Your Heavenly Father can see what you are doing. He will reward you for your kindness."

Jesus also taught the people how to pray. Jesus knew how to pray. He often spent many long hours in prayer with His Heavenly Father. Sometimes His prayers were "Thank-you" prayers, thanking God for all His gifts. When Jesus was sad, He prayed to His Father for help. Often He prayed for His friends and for all people. At meal-time He asked God to bless His food, and He never forgot to thank God for His food. Jesus loved to pray. He was always happy when He could be alone with His Father.

His friends often heard Jesus pray. They saw that prayer helped Jesus and made Him happy. They wished they could pray as He did. "Lord, teach us to pray," they asked. And Jesus said, "When you pray, don't try to show off. Don't stand in the middle of the synagogue, or on the street corners, so everyone can hear you. When you pray, go to your own room. When you have shut the door, pray secretly to your Father. He will hear you. And don't try to show off by using a lot of big words over and over again. God doesn't hear your prayer because of the words you use. He knows what you need even before you ask Him."

Then Jesus taught them a beautiful prayer. We call it "The Lord's Prayer," because our Lord gave it to us. In this prayer, Jesus taught His friends to say, "Our Father who art in heaven." God *is* our Father. He loves us and cares for us as our earthly fathers do. But He is much greater than any earthly father.

"Hallowed be Thy name. Thy kingdom come." Since God is holy, His people should honor Him. They should pray that His kingdom may come, so that He will be King over all the earth.

"Thy will be done on earth, as it is in heaven." In heaven, the angels always do God's will. God's people on earth should obey Him, too.

"Give us this day our daily bread." Only God can give us each day the things we need.

"And forgive us our debts, as we forgive our debtors." We must ask God to forgive our sins. We must also forgive those who sin against us.

"And lead us not into temptation, but deliver us from evil." God will keep us from sin, if we serve Him and go the way He wants us to go.

"For Thine is the kingdom, and the power, and the glory, for ever. Amen." All praise and glory belong to God. We, His children, should never forget to praise Him!

Were you listening? How must we do our kind deeds? What must we not do when we pray? Why do we call the prayer Jesus taught us "The Lord's Prayer"?

Story 188

Jesus Shows the Way to Heaven

Matthew 7

Before finishing His Sermon on the Mount, Jesus talked about His heavenly home. "Not everyone is going to heaven," Jesus said. "Only those who know the way will get there. There are two roads which lead from this earth to eternity. The one road is broad, and the gate which opens on this road is wide. Many people walk this road for it is an easy road. But it does not lead to heaven. It leads to hell. The other road is narrow and its gate is hard to enter. It is difficult to walk this road. There are not many people on it. But it leads to heaven.

"When you come to My heavenly home, not everyone who knocks and calls will have the door opened to him. Not even if he calls, 'Lord, Lord, open the door for me, didn't I do many wonderful things in your name?' Only those who have obeyed My Heavenly Father will come in. To the rest, I shall say, 'Go away, I never knew you, you wicked people!'

"Now then," Jesus went on, "all you who hear My words and do them, are like the wise man who built his house on a rock. When the storm came, and the rain poured down, and the floods came, and the winds blew and beat upon that house, it did not fall because it was built upon a rock.

"But every one of you, who have heard these sayings of Mine and don't do them, you are like the foolish man who built his house upon the sand. When the storm came, and the rain poured down, and the floods came, and the winds blew and beat upon that house, it fell and was broken to pieces because it was built upon the sand."

With the story of the wise man and the foolish man Jesus ended His great Sermon on the Mount. The people who heard

Him were surprised at His teaching. "He isn't like our teachers," they said. "He teaches as one who knows all about God."

Jesus' words were spoken for you, too, even though you did not hear Him preach on the mountainside that day. Are you on your way to heaven? Jesus will lead you there if you ask Him. For He said, "Ask, and it shall be given you, seek and ye shall find, knock and it shall be opened unto you."

Were you listening? Where does the broad road lead? Why do not many walk on the narrow road? Who are like the wise builder? What happened to the foolish builder's house?

Story 189

Jesus Heals a Servant and Gives Life to a Son

Matthew 8; Luke 7

Jesus has often been called the "Great Physician." This is a good name for Jesus. For He was, and still is, the greatest doctor who ever lived. Almost every day of the three years of His ministry, He healed those who were sick. No wonder every one followed Him wherever He went!

One day Jesus was walking through the streets of Capernaum. There was a captain of the Roman army who lived there. His servant was so sick he was about to die. This captain loved his servant and did not want him to die. When the captain heard that Jesus was again in Capernaum, he sent some of his friends to ask Jesus to heal his servant.

The men came to Jesus. "Please help the captain," they pleaded. "He's a good man. Even though he is not a Jew, he loves our people and is kind to them. At one time he even built us a synagogue."

Jesus answered, "I will come and heal the servant."

Then Jesus turned and followed the men. They had almost reached the captain's house, when the captain sent some other friends to Jesus. "Lord," they said, "the captain doesn't want you to trouble yourself any further. He says that he is not worthy to have you come into his house. Nor did he think he was worthy to come to you. He says, 'Just say the word, and my servant shall be healed. For I am also a man who rules. If I say to my soldiers,

Go, they go; and if I say Come, they come; or if I say Do this, they do it. So, if I have power to make my soldiers obey me, I know you have power to speak and be obeyed, too!' "

When Jesus heard these words, He marveled at the captain. He turned to the people who were following Him and said, "I have never found such great faith, no, not in Israel." Then He turned back to the captain's friends and said, "Go and say to your captain, 'As you have believed in Me, so shall it happen to you.' "

The men went back to the captain's house. There they found that the servant was completely well.

The next day, Jesus and His disciples went into a city called Nain. Many people crowded around them. At the gate of the city, they met another crowd of people coming out of the city. Jesus and His friends waited for the people coming out of the gate. They noticed that it was a funeral procession. A widowed mother was walking beside a stretcher on which lay the body of her only son. The people were carrying him to the cemetery. A crowd from the city was following the procession.

When Jesus saw this poor widow, He felt sorry for her. He went up to her and said, "Don't cry." Then He went and touched the stretcher. Those who were carrying it stood still. Jesus looked at the dead man. "Young man," He said, "I say unto you, arise!" The dead man sat up and began to talk. Then Jesus gave him back to his mother.

Everyone who saw what had happened was filled with fear. They all glorified God, saying, "A great prophet is risen among us. God has visited His people!"

Were you listening? Why is Jesus called the "Great Physician"? Why did Jesus marvel at the captain? What did Jesus say to the sorrowing mother? What did He do for her?

Story 190

A Sinful Woman Shows Her Love for Jesus

Luke 7

There was once a Pharisee named Simon. He was not a friend of Jesus, but he invited Jesus to have dinner at his house. He wanted to see this man who was doing so many wonderful things.

He wanted to find fault with Him. Simon invited other men to his dinner, too.

Although Simon invited Jesus to his home, he wasn't very polite to Him. In those days, when a man went visiting, his host would greet him with a kiss. Then he would bring a basin of water and a towel, and would wash his visitor's feet. And, sometimes, he would pour oil on his head. But Simon didn't do any of these things for Jesus.

While they were eating, a woman came in to see Jesus. She carried a bottle of expensive perfume (ointment) with her. As she stood there, she began to cry. Her tears fell on Jesus' feet. She stooped and wiped them with her long hair. Then she kissed His feet and poured the perfume over them. Although she had been a wicked woman, she was filled with love for Jesus. And she was sorry she had been so wicked.

When Simon saw what the woman was doing, he didn't like it. He grumbled to himself, "If this Jesus were really a prophet, He'd know that this woman was a sinner, and He wouldn't let her touch Him."

Jesus knew what Simon was thinking. He said to him, "Simon, I want to tell you something."

"Go ahead," Simon answered.

Then Jesus told Simon a story. "There was once a man," He began, "who had two debtors. (A debtor is a man who owes you something.) The one owed him five hundred pieces of money (which would be about eighty-five dollars in our money), and the other owed him fifty pieces (which would be about eight dollars and fifty cents in our money). Neither of the two men could pay the money. When the lender found out that they could not pay, he felt sorry for the two men. He forgave them both. He said they did not have to pay him the money. Now, Simon, which of those two debtors, do you think, loved the lender the most?"

Simon answered, "I suppose the one who owed the most, for the lender forgave him the most."

"You are right," Jesus said. Then He nodded toward the woman at His feet. He said to Simon, "Do you see this woman,

Simon? When I came into your house, you didn't even wash My feet with water. But she has been washing them with her tears and wiping them with her hair. You didn't kiss Me, but she, since the very moment she came in, has been kissing My feet. You didn't anoint My head with oil, but she has poured perfume on My feet. I tell you, her sins, which are many, are forgiven because she loved much. But to those to whom little is forgiven, the same loveth little."

Then Jesus said to the woman, "Thy sins are forgiven." The other guests said to themselves, "Who is this that can forgive sins?" But Jesus said to the woman, "Your faith has saved you. Go in peace."

> *Were you listening?* Why wasn't Simon a good host? What did the woman do for Jesus that Simon had not done? Why did Jesus forgive her sins?

Story 191

The Farmer Who Planted His Seed

Matthew 13; Mark 4; Luke 8

Jesus and His friends were walking along the seashore one day. Since the crowds were so large, Jesus went into Peter's boat, as He had done before. It was easier to talk to the people from the boat. So Jesus sat down in the boat and began to teach.

Sometimes when Jesus taught the people, He told them stories. He called these stories "parables" because they always taught a lesson. A parable is an earthly story with a heavenly meaning.

Sitting there in Peter's boat, Jesus told a story about a farmer. He began: "Once there was a farmer who went into his fields to plant his seed. This farmer walked back and forth across his fields, scattering his seed over the ground. Some of the seed fell on the path where he was walking. The birds soon came and ate that seed. Some of the seed fell on stony ground. Since there wasn't much dirt on the stones, the roots couldn't get a good hold. This seed grew up into plants right away. Later when the hot sun shone down, the plants were scorched and withered away because they had no root.

"Some of the seed fell among thorns. When this seed began

to grow, the thorns grew, too. The thorns grew faster than the seed. Soon the little plants choked and died. The rest of the seed fell in good ground. It grew deep roots, it sprang up into good plants, and it had much good fruit on it."

When Jesus finished His story, He said, "Anyone who has ears to hear, let him listen to My story."

Later, Jesus was alone with His twelve disciples. They asked Him about the story, because they didn't understand it. Jesus said, "Don't you know the meaning of this parable? Listen, the farmer is the minister or teacher, who teaches God's Word. The seed is God's Word, and the soil (ground) is the hearts of men.

"Some people have hearts like the path. When they hear God's Word, they don't do anything with it. Then Satan comes and takes it away. Some people's hearts are like the stony ground. When they hear God's Word, they listen to it gladly and are happy. But soon they forget. When trouble comes they turn away from God. Other people have hearts that are like the ground which had thorns growing in it. They listen to God's Word, but all the things of this world — cares, money, fun — take up so much of their time, that the Word is choked out. Still other people have hearts which are like the good ground. When they hear God's Word, they listen to it gladly. And they do what God says."

Were you listening? What is a parable? Who was the farmer in Jesus' story? What was the seed? Which kind of ground is your heart like?

Story 192

Jesus Teaches About His Kingdom

Matthew 13

Jesus told another parable, or story, to His followers. He was talking about the Kingdom of Heaven. He said, "The Kingdom of Heaven is just like the farmer in my story. One spring morning this farmer gave his servants a bag full of good seed. The servants walked through the fields and planted the good seed in the farmer's land.

"When the seeds had all been planted, the servants waited for the rains to come and for the sun to shine so that the seeds would grow into little plants. But one night, while the farmer and his servants were asleep, an enemy came and sowed bad seeds in the fields. They were seeds which would grow weeds instead of food. The weeds were called tares.

"After many days, the field full of seeds began to grow. Deep roots grew down into the ground and fine plants grew up into the sunshine. But the tares began to grow, too. The servants could not understand where the tares had come from. They went to the farmer. 'Sir, did you not give us good seed to plant in your fields?' they asked.

" 'Yes,' the farmer answered. 'I gave you the best seed.'

" 'Then where did all those tares come from?' they asked.

"The farmer answered, 'An enemy must have done it. He must have come in the night and planted tares in my fields.'

" 'What shall we do then?' the servants asked. 'Shall we go and pull out all of the tares?'

" 'No,' the farmer said, 'that would not work. The tares are growing so close to the wheat that while you are pulling out the tares you might pull out the wheat, too. You had better let them both grow until the harvest. Then I shall tell the reapers to first gather the tares. They can bind them in bundles and burn them in a big bonfire. After that they can gather the wheat and store it in my barns.'

"So that is what happened. The tares and the wheat grew side by side until the harvest. Then the reapers came. They gathered the tares and burned them in the fire. Then they gathered the wheat into the farmer's barns."

When Jesus had sent the people away, His disciples asked, "Lord, tell us what the story of the wheat and the tares means."

Jesus answered, "I am the farmer who sowed the good seed. The field is the world. The good seed are the good people who belong to Me. The tares are the children of Satan. The enemy who planted the tares is Satan. The harvest time is the end of the world. The reapers who gathered in the wheat are the angels. Just as the tares were burned and the wheat was brought into the barns, so shall it be with the people at the end of the world. The Son of Man will send His angels and they will throw all the wicked ones into a furnace of fire. But the good people will shine like the sun in the Kingdom of their Father."

Were you listening? What did the farmer in this story do? Where did the weeds or tares come from? Who was the enemy in the story? Who will shine like the sun in heaven?

Story 193

More Stories Which Jesus Told

Matthew 13; Mark 4

When Jesus talked about the Kingdom of Heaven, He often told parables to help the people understand.

One time He said, "With what shall we compare the Kingdom of Heaven, or what shall we say it is like? It is like a grain of mustard seed, which is the smallest of all the seeds which can be planted. But when it is planted and grows up, it becomes taller than all the other plants. It shoots out great branches. It becomes a tree. The birds of the air come and make their nests in its branches."

Later He said, "The Kingdom of Heaven is like a wonderful treasure which was hidden in a field. When the man found the treasure, he sold everything that he had so that he could buy the field and own the great treasure."

Another time He said, "The Kingdom of Heaven is like a dealer who was looking for good pearls to buy. Finally, he found the greatest pearl in the whole world. He quickly went out and sold everything that he had, and bought the wonderful pearl."

Once more He said, "The Kingdom of Heaven is like the fishermen's net. When the fishermen threw their net out into the deep water of the sea, the net gathered many fish of every kind. When the net was full, the fishermen drew it to shore. Then they sat down and sorted out the fish. They put the good fish into their pails so that they could sell them, but they threw the bad fish away. So shall it be at the end of the world. The angels shall come. They will divide the wicked from the good. They will throw the wicked into the furnace of fire. There shall be wailing and gnashing of teeth."

So Jesus taught about His Kingdom. It will grow like a mustard seed, until it covers the whole earth. It is more wonderful than any treasure you could find on this earth. It is worth more to God's people than the greatest pearl you could buy. How happy we should be to know that children, too, may belong to that wonderful Kingdom. Are you a member of that Kingdom?

Were you listening? Why is the Kingdom of Heaven like a mustard seed? Why is it like the dealer who wanted to buy good pearls? Why is it like the fishermen's net?

Story 194

Jesus Rules the Wind and the Waves

Matthew 8; Mark 4; Luke 8

The people of Galilee were intensely interested in the stories Jesus told about the Kingdom of Heaven. As He sat by the seaside telling His stories, the crowd became larger and larger. Finally, Jesus noticed that the sun was going down. Jesus was preaching from Peter's boat, you remember. He turned to Peter and said, "Come, let's go over to the other side of the lake." So Peter began to pull in the anchor.

When the people saw that Jesus was getting ready to leave, one of them came to Jesus and said, "Master, I will follow you wherever you go."

Jesus answered, "The foxes have holes and the birds of the air have nests, but I, the Son of man, do not even have a place to lay my head."

Another man came to Jesus and said, "Lord, I'll follow you, but first let me go home to say goodbye to my family."

But Jesus said, "No man, after he has once put his hand on the plow, should look back; for then he is not fit for the Kingdom of God." Jesus meant to say that when you hear His call, you must follow Him at once. There is nothing as important as following Jesus.

As soon as Jesus succeeded in sending the crowds away, Peter began to row his boat across the lake. Jesus was tired after His busy day of work. He went to the back of the boat and lay down on a pillow. Soon He was fast asleep.

The disciples kept on rowing their little boat. There were

other little boats crossing the lake, too. Suddenly, the sky became black with clouds. The winds began to blow. The disciples were afraid. Soon a great storm arose. The little boat tossed from side to side in the angry waves.

The disciples tried frantically to get the boat to the shore, but the wind was too strong. Every now and then great waves of swirling water splashed into the boat, nearly upsetting it. The disciples tried to scoop out the water as fast it came in, but they couldn't keep up with it. The boat soon filled with water. The disciples were good sailors. They were used to storms, but they were really frightened now.

During all this time Jesus was still asleep. Finally, the disciples called to Him and said, "Master, wake up! Don't you care if we all drown?"

Jesus sat up and looked around. He saw how the boat was being dashed about by the huge waves. How frightened the men were! Calmly, Jesus stood up and stretched His hands over the angry waves. He scolded the wind and said, "Peace, be still." At once, the wind stopped. Everything was very quiet.

Then Jesus turned to His friends. "Why are you so afraid?" He asked. "How is it that you do not have any faith?"

Although the disciples had seen Jesus do many wonderful things, they had never seen anything like this before. They were filled with great fear. They said one to another, "What sort of man is this, that even the wind and the sea obey Him?"

> *Were you listening?* Why were the foxes and the birds better off than Jesus? Why did Jesus fall asleep in Peter's boat? Why were the disciples terrified? What did Jesus do to amaze His friends?

Story 195

Jesus Heals a Wild Man

Matthew 8; Mark 5; Luke 8

When Jesus stopped the angry storm on the little Sea of Galilee that day, He and His disciples were on their way across the lake. Soon they came over to the other side of the lake, to the country of the Gadarenes. Along the shore there were huge rocks with caves among them. As they stepped out of their little boat, a wild man came running towards them.

This man lived in the caves because he was too wild to live with other people. No one could control him. If they tied him with chains, he broke the chains. If they tried to clothe him, he tore off the clothing. No one dared pass the cave where he lived. Night and day he roamed the mountains, crying out and cutting himself with stones.

When this wild man saw Jesus, he ran and worshiped Him. Jesus knew that this man was wild because evil spirits lived in his heart. So He said to these spirits, "Come out of the man, you unclean spirits."

But they shouted, "What have we to do with you, Jesus, thou Son of the Most High God? Please do not hurt us."

"What is your name?" Jesus asked.

"Our name is Legion, because there are many evil spirits in my heart."

The evil spirits kept begging Jesus not to send them away out of the country. Just then they noticed some herdsmen coming down the mountainside with a herd of swine. Now the evil spirits pleaded with Jesus to send them into the swine.

Jesus said, "All right, go into the swine." So the evil spirits went out of the man and into the swine. There were about two thousand swine. Now they all became wild. Down the mountainside they ran and into the sea. There they all drowned.

When the herdsmen saw what had happened, they ran into the city and told everyone they met. Soon a crowd of people came out to the seashore. When they saw the man who had been wild sitting at Jesus' feet, completely clothed and quietly listening, how surprised they were. They were afraid of Jesus. They begged Him to go away from their country.

So Jesus went back into Peter's boat. The man who had been wild wanted to come along, too. He wanted to go with Jesus. But Jesus said, "No, you go back home to your friends and tell them about the great things the Lord has done for you." The man obeyed Jesus and everyone marveled at his words.

Were you listening? Who met Jesus when He got out of Peter's boat in the Gadarenes' country? Why was this man called Legion? Why did the Gadarenes ask Jesus to leave their country? Why did the man called Legion want to go with Jesus?

Jesus Gives Life to the Dead

Matthew 9; Mark 5; Luke 8

After the Gadarenes asked Jesus to go away from their country, He and His disciples went back across the lake. As soon as He came ashore, a crowd of people gathered around Him again.

While Jesus was talking to the people, Jairus, a ruler of one of the synagogues, came and fell down at Jesus' feet. He worshiped Jesus and said, "My little daughter is very sick. She is going to die. Please come and put your hands on her and make her well." So Jesus went along with Jairus.

Jairus was most eager to have Jesus hurry to his little girl. He and his wife loved their twelve-year-old daughter dearly. They could not bear to stand beside her bed and watch her suffer so. Now Jairus was afraid she would die before Jesus got there. Then it would be too late. But Jesus couldn't hurry at all, for the crowds came, too. There just wasn't enough room to walk fast.

As they were walking, a woman joined the crowd. For twelve long years she had been very ill. There was something wrong with her blood. She had tried everything to make herself better. All her money had gone to the doctors, but she grew worse instead of better.

When this woman heard about Jesus, and about all the wonderful things He could do, she believed in Him. She believed that Jesus could heal her, too. "If I could just get close enough to Jesus to touch His clothing, I know I would be cured," she told herself. So she pushed through the crowd, put out her hand, and touched the hem of Jesus' coat. At once she was cured.

Jesus turned around and said, "Who touched me?"

The people all said, "We didn't touch you."

Then Peter and the other disciples said, "Master, there is such a big crowd of people around you, how can you ask, 'Who touched me?' Many people are touching you."

But Jesus didn't mean that. He knew that someone had touched Him to be healed. So He said again, "Someone touched me, for I felt power to heal go out of me."

Then the woman was afraid. She came to Jesus, trembling, and knelt at His feet. She told Him all about herself. Jesus was not angry with her. He said, "Daughter, your faith has made you whole. Go in peace."

But all the while that Jesus was healing this woman, Jairus was getting more and more anxious. Before Jesus had finished talking with the woman, a servant came up. He said to Jairus, "Don't bother the Master any more. It is too late. Your little girl is dead." Jairus was filled with sadness. Why had Jesus taken so long? Jesus turned to Jairus and said, "Do not be afraid, only believe."

They went on to Jairus' house. When they arrived, they found many people there, crying and weeping. With Him Jesus took His three best friends — Peter, James, and John — and went inside. As He passed the noisy people, He said, "Why are you making such a fuss, and why are you weeping so? The little girl isn't dead, she's only sleeping." They laughed at Jesus because they knew she was dead. Jesus meant to say that He could make her better just as easily as if she were sleeping.

Jesus went into the bedroom. There lay the girl on the bed. Jesus took her by the hand and said, "Young girl, I say to you, arise!" The girl opened her eyes. She was alive again! Leaving her bed, she walked about the room. She was well again.

Jesus said, "Give her something to eat."

Her parents, and all that were in the house, were astonished at what Jesus had done. But Jesus commanded them not to tell anyone what had happened.

> *Were you listening?* What did Jesus promise to do for Jairus? Why did it take so long to get to Jairus' house? How did Jesus make the girl alive? How will Jesus make you live after you die?

Story 197

The Death of John the Baptist

Matthew 14; Mark 6; Luke 3

After Jesus began to preach, John still kept on with his work for a time. But one day King Herod became very angry with him. John had scolded King Herod because he had stolen his brother Philip's wife. He told King Herod that it was a sin to do what he had done. King Herod did not like to be scolded, so he threw John into prison. Now John could not preach any more. Day after day he lay in the prison. The king did not dare to kill John. He knew that the people loved John and believed him to be their prophet.

It was lonely and sad for John in the prison. He even began to wonder whether Jesus was really the King, whose "herald" he had been. So John sent two of his friends to Jesus. "Go ask Jesus," John said, "if He is the one we have been looking for, or must we look for another?"

John's friends came to Jesus with their question. Jesus answered, "Go and tell John again about all the things you have heard and seen. Tell how the blind see, and the lame walk, the deaf hear, the lepers are cleansed, the dead are raised up, and the poor have the Gospel preached to them." So John was assured that Jesus was the King he had been looking for.

Herodias, King Herod's new wife, hated John. She wanted to have John killed, but King Herod would not listen to her. He knew that John was a good man and a holy man. So he kept John safe in prison. At times, Herod even went to the prison to talk with John. He liked to listen to John's teachings, but he was puzzled at his words.

It was the king's birthday. There was to be a party for King Herod. All the captains and the lords were there. The chief men of Galilee were invited. They all sat down to supper. The young daughter of Herodias (her name was Salome), came in to dance for her new father at his party. King Herod was pleased with her. "I will give you anything you want," he said, "even if it is half of my kingdom."

Salome did not know what to ask for. She had everything she wanted. So she went to her mother. "What shall I ask for?" she said. Her mother answered at once. "Ask for the head of John the Baptist," she said. "Tell him to have it brought to you on a platter," she added.

Salome hurried back to the king. "I want the head of John

the Baptist brought to me on a platter," she said. How sorry King Herod was to hear those words! He did not want to kill John. But because all his guests at his supper had heard him make the promise, he felt that he had to keep it. So he sent one of his soldiers to the prison to carry out the promise. Soon the soldier returned with the head of John the Baptist on a platter. He gave it to Salome and she brought it to her mother.

When John's friends heard what had happened, they came and buried John's body. Then they went to tell Jesus.

Were you listening? Why did King Herod put John the Baptist in prison? What did Jesus tell John's friends? What did Salome ask for?

Story 198

Jesus Feeds Five Thousand People

Matthew 14; Mark 6; Luke 9; John 6

Jesus and His twelve disciples had been working hard. So many people were coming and going, wanting help from Jesus, that they couldn't even find time to eat.

Finally Jesus said, "Come, let us go away for a little while and rest in a desert place." So they went into their boat and rowed across the lake. They found a quiet spot where they all sat down to rest.

The disciples looked forward to a lovely quiet time with their Master. But many people had seen them go into their boat. They, too, wanted to be with Jesus and hear His words. Many of the people wanted Jesus to heal them or their loved ones. So they followed Him. Since they had no boat, they walked all the way around the lake.

Jesus saw the crowds coming. The disciples didn't want to be bothered when they were resting. They wanted to be alone with Jesus. But Jesus felt sorry for all the people who needed Him so badly. He talked to them, teaching them many things and healing those who were sick. The people kept Him busy until evening.

It was getting late. The disciples said to Jesus, "This is a desert place. Send the people home so they can buy some supper."

But Jesus said, "Why can't we feed them?"

"How could we feed all these people?" the disciples asked. "We'd need a thousand loaves of bread!" There were more than five thousand people in the crowd.

"Go and see how much food you can find," Jesus commanded.

The disciples went among the people. After a while, Andrew came back to Jesus. He said, "There is a little boy here who has brought his lunch. He has five small loaves of barley bread (they were flat and round like our large cookies), and two small fishes. But what are they among so many?"

"Let me have the bread and the fish," Jesus answered. So the little boy gave his lunch to Jesus. Then Jesus told the people to sit down on the grass. He made them sit in groups of fifty and a hundred. He took the bread and the fish. He looked up to heaven and asked God, His Father, to bless the food. Then He broke the bread and the fish into pieces. He gave each disciple a basket of the broken food, and they passed it among the people. When the baskets were empty, the disciples came back to Jesus to have them filled. And Jesus made more and more bread, and more and more fish, until there was enough for everyone. All the people ate and were filled. After supper, the disciples gathered what was left in their baskets. They had twelve baskets full!

The people were amazed. They said, "This must surely be the prophet who was to come!" They tried to make Jesus their king. But Jesus did not want to be made king at that time. He quietly slipped away into the mountain to be alone with His Heavenly Father.

> *Were you listening?* Why did Jesus and His disciples go across the lake? Why couldn't they rest, after all? What miracle did Jesus perform at supper time? How could Jesus feed so many people with one little boy's lunch?

Story 199

Jesus Walks on the Water

Matthew 14; Mark 6; John 6

After Jesus had finished feeding the five thousand people, they wanted to make Him king, you remember. But when Jesus saw what they were trying to do, He told His disciples to go away

in their boat. "Go back across the lake," He said, "while I send these people home." So the disciples left Jesus, and He sent the thousands of people home.

As soon as the people had all gone, Jesus went up into a mountain to pray. He wanted to be alone with His Heavenly Father. All night long Jesus prayed. He was so busy talking with His Father that He didn't even notice that a storm had come up on the lake.

The disciples were still in their boat. They were trying as hard as they could to row the boat across the lake. But the wind was so strong that they could get nowhere. They were still in the middle of the lake. And they were afraid that their boat would soon be covered by the huge waves. Then they would all drown.

About three o'clock in the morning, Jesus finished talking with His Heavenly Father and came down from the mountain. He went at once to the water. He could see the boat in the middle of the lake, tossing about among the rough waves. He stepped right out on the water and walked on top of the waves toward the boat. No man had ever done that before!

When the disciples saw Jesus coming, they were filled with fear. "It is a spirit!" they cried.

But Jesus called to them, "Be of good cheer. It is I, don't be afraid."

Then Peter called, "Lord, if it is you, let me come to you on the water."

"Come," Jesus called back.

So Peter stepped out of the boat and walked on the stormy waves, just as Jesus was doing. But then Peter looked down at the rough water under his feet. He forgot to look at Jesus. Then he was filled with fear and he began to sink. "Lord, save me!" he cried.

Jesus stretched out His hand and caught Peter. He lifted him back to the top of the waves. "Why were you afraid, oh, you of little faith?" Jesus asked.

Together they walked to the boat and stepped inside. As soon as Jesus came into the boat, the storm stopped. The disciples fell down at Jesus' feet, and worshiped Him. "Surely, You are the Son of God!" they said.

> *Were you listening?* Why didn't Jesus know that His friends were in trouble? Why were the disciples afraid when Jesus came to them on the water? Why did Peter begin to sink?

Story 200

Jesus Answers Prayer

Matthew 15; Mark 7

Some of Jesus' friends were leaving Him, and His enemies were becoming stronger, too. Wherever Jesus went there were always Pharisees and Scribes in the crowd. They did not come to learn from Jesus. Rather, they came to find fault. "He does not teach as we do," they said, "so His teachings cannot be true. Besides, He heals people on the Sabbath Day, so He disobeys our laws. We ought to stop Him from stirring up the people."

One day the Pharisees came to Jesus with another complaint. "Why do your disciples eat without washing their hands?" they asked. "They are bad because they do not obey our rules."

Jesus answered, "Eating without washing his hands does not make a man wicked. It is not what goes into a man that makes him bad. It is that which comes out of his mouth that makes him bad. The things that come from his heart — such as stealing, and killing, and lying — those are the things that are sinful."

The Pharisees went away angry.

"Master, you have offended the Pharisees," the disciples said.

"Let them alone," Jesus answered. "They are blind leaders of the blind. And if the blind lead the blind, they'll both fall into the ditch."

Soon after that Jesus left the city where the Pharisees were. First He went to Galilee and then beyond Galilee to the heathen cities of Tyre and Sidon. He did not want His own people to know where He was, for the Jews were trying to kill Him.

One day as Jesus was walking along in this strange city, a Greek woman came behind Him and called after Him, "Have mercy on me, O Lord, Thou Son of David. My daughter is most unhappy because a devil lives in her heart."

But Jesus kept on walking and paid no attention to the woman. The woman, however, kept on following Jesus and calling after Him. The disciples finally said to Jesus, "Lord, send her away. She keeps on crying after us."

Jesus answered, "I have not come to help the Greeks. I came only to help the Israelites."

The woman heard Jesus' words. She came and fell down at Jesus' feet and worshiped Him. "Please help me, Lord," she begged.

Jesus answered, "I shouldn't take the children's bread and throw it to the dogs." He meant to say, "I'm supposed to help My own people, not you."

The woman answered, "Yes, Lord, that's right. But the dogs eat the crumbs that fall from their masters' tables."

Jesus was amazed at the woman's faith. "Oh, woman," He said, "great is your faith! Let it happen to you as you wish." Jesus was saying to the woman, "I'll do what you want Me to do. I'll make your girl better."

So the woman went home. She found that the devil had left her little girl. Her daughter was lying on her bed, cured.

Soon Jesus returned to Galilee. Some people came to Him, bringing a man. This man was deaf and dumb. He could not hear, and he could not talk. His friends wanted Jesus to put His hands on the man and make him better. Jesus took the man away from the crowd. He put His fingers in the man's ears. And He touched the man's tongue. Then Jesus looked up to heaven. He sighed and said, "Be opened!"

At that very moment the man's ears were opened and his tongue was loosed. He could hear and he could speak plainly.

Jesus asked the people not to tell anyone what He had done, but the more He asked them not to tell, the more they told it to everyone. And all who heard about it were astonished. "He has done all things well," they said, "for He makes both the deaf to hear and the dumb to speak."

> *Were you listening?* Why did a Greek woman follow Jesus? What did Jesus mean when He said, "I must not throw the children's bread to the dogs"? What did the woman mean when she said, "The dogs eat the crumbs"? What did Jesus do for the man in our story?

Story 201

Jesus Feeds the Hungry People Again

Matthew 15; Mark 8

The news of Jesus and His wonderful works was spreading all over Galilee. It spread even beyond Galilee into other countries. Sick people everywhere came seeking Jesus. Some were lame, or blind, or deaf. Others were covered with leprosy. Many were sick with fevers. And some had hearts which were filled with evil spirits. They all found their way to the Great Physician who was so willing and able to heal them.

One by one they came, waiting their turn, eager to have Jesus listen to their troubles, lay His hands on them, and heal them. And one by one Jesus healed them. What a busy time it was for Jesus! What a happy time it was for the crowds who stood by. As each one was healed, the people shouted and praised God.

It took a long time for Jesus to heal all the people who came. When night came there were still sick folk waiting. So eager were they to be healed, that they did not want to go home to eat and sleep. They went without food and slept on the grass under the starry sky. For three whole days Jesus worked to heal all these people. For three whole days the people went without food, more eager to be healed than to satisfy their hunger.

But Jesus knew how hungry they were. He felt sorry for all those poor people who had waited so patiently. He called His disciples to Him and said, "I feel sorry for these people. They have been with Me for three days and have had nothing to eat. If I send them away now, they will faint on the way, for some of them have come a long way."

The disciples answered, "How could we feed all these people here in this wilderness? There is no bread to be bought here."

"How many loaves of bread do you have?" Jesus asked.

"We have seven," they answered, "and a few little fishes."

Jesus turned to the people and said, "Come, sit on the ground."

The people sat. Then Jesus took the seven loaves of bread and the little fishes. He thanked God for the food. Then He broke it into pieces and asked His disciples to pass it out among the people. The people took all the bread and fish they wanted. They all ate until they were filled. And the disciples filled seven baskets with the food that was left!

This time Jesus fed about four thousand people with the bread and fish. And when they had eaten, He sent them home. How happy those people must have been!

> *Were you listening?* What did Jesus do for the people who fol-
> lowed Him for three days? How much food did He have this
> time? How many people did He feed?

Story 202

The Blind Man of Bethsaida

Mark 8

Not far from the town of Bethsaida, which is on the Sea of Galilee, lived a blind man. He had never been with the crowds of people who had followed Jesus. But he had heard about all the people who had been healed by His wonderful power. When this blind man heard that Jesus was in Bethsaida, he wanted to go at once to see Him, too.

He asked his friends to take him to Jesus, for he could not see to go by himself. The friends soon found Jesus. They led the blind man to Him. "Please touch him, Jesus, and make him see," they said.

Jesus did not want the people to crowd around Him at that time. He wanted to spend some time with His disciples alone. So He took the blind man by the hand and led him outside of the town. When the two were alone, Jesus touched the blind man's eyes. "What do you see?" Jesus asked.

The blind man looked up. He saw something, but it all seemed to be blurred. "I see men walking," he said, "but they look like trees."

Jesus touched his eyes again. "Now look up," He said.

The man looked up. Now he could see clearly. He was no longer blind. His eyesight was restored.

"Go home quietly," Jesus said. "Don't go into the town, and don't tell any of the people in the town what I have done."

The man went home full of joy and happiness because of the wonderful gift of sight which Jesus had given him.

> *Were you listening?* How did Jesus heal the blind man? How many times did Jesus touch his eyes? What happened the first time?

Story 203

Jesus Asks, "Who Am I?"

Matthew 16; Mark 8; Luke 9

One day Jesus took His disciples with Him on a journey to a country where they had never been before. They went about thirty miles north to Caesarea Philippi. As they were walking through this country, Jesus turned to His disciples, "Whom do the people say that I am?" He asked.

"Some people say you are John the Baptist," they answered.

"Some say you are Elijah."

"Some say you are Jeremiah or one of the prophets."

Then Jesus asked, "But whom do you say that I am?"

Quick as a flash, Peter answered, "Thou art the Christ, the Son of the living God!"

Jesus liked Peter's answer. "Happy are you, Simon Barjona," Jesus said. "You didn't get that answer from any man. You learned this from My Father in heaven. I have called you Peter, which means rock, and on this rock I will build My church. And the gates of hell will never destroy it. I will give you the keys of the Kingdom of Heaven. Those whom you let in, will be in, and those whom you lock out, will be out."

Then Jesus said to them all, "Don't tell anyone that I am the Christ."

From that time on, Jesus began to tell His disciples about all the things that were going to happen to Him. "The rulers of My people will turn against Me," He said. "I will be put in prison. After that they will kill Me; but after three days I will rise again."

Peter did not like to hear Jesus say such things. He did not want these things to happen to Him. "Be it far from Thee, Lord," Peter said. "These things will never happen to You!"

Jesus turned to look at Peter. "Get thee behind Me, Satan!" He said. "You do not know the things that are of God. You are tempting Me. God wants Me to suffer and die and be raised again!" Jesus meant that Peter was saying the kind of things Satan would say. Peter did not understand. He did not know that if Jesus did not die, He could not be our Saviour.

Then Jesus called all the people to Him. He told them and His disciples, "If you want to be My followers, you must not do what you want to do, you must take up your cross and follow Me. If you want to live to please yourself and always do what you want to do, you'll lose your own soul. What good would it be to you to gain the whole world for your own, if you lost your own soul?

"If any of you shall be ashamed of Me and My words in this world, I will be ashamed of you in heaven before My Father and His holy angels."

Were you listening? Whom did the people think Jesus was? Who is Jesus? Why did Jesus later call Peter "Satan"? Should we ever be ashamed of Jesus?

Story 204

Jesus' Face Shines As the Sun

Matthew 17; Mark 9; Luke 9

One day Jesus called His three best friends — Peter, James, and John — and led them up a high mountain. There they were all alone. Suddenly, the three men noticed that Jesus' face had changed. He was shining like the sun. And His clothes were white, white as snow. Jesus shone from head to foot and glistened like the sunlight.

Then, as the disciples watched, they noticed two men talking with Jesus. These two men, Moses and Elijah, had come from heaven to talk with Jesus about how He must go to Jerusalem and die for His people.

Peter, James and John were filled with fear. They tried to watch what was happening, but their eyes soon became heavy and they fell asleep. When they awoke, Moses and Elijah were about ready to go back to heaven. The disciples could still see the glory which was all around them and wanted that glory to remain. Abruptly Peter called out, "Lord, let's always stay up here. Let us make three tents, one for You, one for Moses, and one for Elijah." But Peter didn't realize what he was saying.

While Peter was still talking, a big bright cloud came and covered them. God's voice was heard in the cloud, saying, "This is My beloved Son in whom I am well pleased. Hear ye Him."

The three disciples were so afraid when they heard God's voice that they fell on their faces. A little later, Jesus came and touched them. "Get up," He said, "don't be afraid." The disciples lifted their eyes. Everything had changed again. The cloud was gone. Moses and Elijah were gone, too. Jesus wasn't bright and shining any more. Then they came down from the mountain.

As they walked down the mountainside, Jesus said, "Don't tell anyone what you saw today. Wait until I have died and have been raised from the dead again. Then you may tell everyone."

When they reached the bottom of the mountain, a great crowd had gathered around the waiting disciples. As soon as the people noticed Jesus, they ran to Him.

"What is the trouble?" Jesus asked.

A man came and knelt at Jesus' feet. "Master," he cried, "have mercy on my son, for he is insane. He acts very wild. He gnashes his teeth and foams at the mouth. Sometimes he falls into the fire or into the water. I asked your disciples to help him, but they couldn't."

Jesus said, "O faithless people, how long shall I be with you? Bring the boy to Me!"

They brought the boy to Jesus. There was no question that he acted like a wild man. He foamed at the mouth and crawled on the ground. Jesus said to the father, "How long has your boy been this way?"

"Since he was a small boy," the father answered. "We're afraid he is going to kill himself some day. If you can do anything for him, please have pity on him and help us."

Jesus said, "*If* I can! All things are possible to those who believe."

The father began to cry. He shouted, "Lord, I believe. Please help my unbelief!"

Then Jesus scolded the evil spirit in the boy telling it to come out. Crying out, the evil spirit tore the boy and then came out of him. The boy dropped on the ground as if he were dead.

The people who were watching said, "Look, he's dead."

But Jesus took him by the hand and lifted him up. And the boy was healed.

As they left the mountainside, the disciples said to Jesus, "Lord, why couldn't we heal the boy?"

Jesus answered, "Because you didn't have enough faith. Faith can do wonderful things. If you had faith which was no bigger than a grain of mustard seed, and would say to this mountain, 'Move over there to that place,' it would be moved. Nothing is impossible, if you have faith. But it would have taken much prayer to cure that wild boy."

> *Were you listening?* Who was with Jesus on the mountain? What happened to Jesus? Who came to talk with Jesus? Why couldn't Jesus' disciples make the wild boy better?

Story 205

Who Is First with Jesus?

Matthew 17 and 18; Mark 9; Luke 9

The second summer of Jesus' ministry was almost over. With His disciples He returned once more to the Sea of Galilee. After they arrived in Capernaum, the tax-collector came to Peter. He asked, "Doesn't your Master pay the church tax?" This was a tax which all the men of the church had to pay. Jesus did not really have to pay it because He was the Lord of the church.

Peter answered, "Yes, He pays it."

When they came into the house, Jesus said to Peter, "What do you think, Peter? Do the kings get their money from their own children or from strangers?"

"From strangers," Peter answered.

"That's right," Jesus said. "But lest the people misunderstand, go to the lake and throw in your fish hook. Take the first fish you catch and cut it open. You'll find a piece of money in its mouth. Take it and go pay your tax and mine."

Peter did as Jesus commanded. He found the money in the fish's mouth and paid their tax.

On the journey to Capernaum, the disciples had begun to quarrel among themselves, arguing about Jesus' Kingdom. They thought Jesus was going to be a king on earth, that He was going to have a beautiful palace and sit on a king's throne. They expected that when Jesus lived in His palace and sat on His throne, He would give them all an important place in His Kingdom. Each of the disciples wanted to sit at Jesus' side, next to the throne, and be the greatest in the Kingdom. And so they quarreled about it.

Now that they were in the house, Jesus said, "What were you quarreling about on the way?" The disciples were ashamed to tell Jesus about their quarrel, so they kept still. But Jesus knew what they had been saying. He sat down and called His friends to come sit around Him. "If you want to be first in My Kingdom," He said, "you must take the last place, and you must be the servant of the others."

Jesus' Kingdom is not of this earth. His Kingdom is heavenly. His throne is in heaven. And if anyone wants to be great in Jesus' Kingdom, he must be a servant, he must be willing to help others.

It happened that there was a little child playing nearby as Jesus was talking. Jesus called the little one to come to Him. Jesus took the child in His arms. Then He looked at His friends and said, "Unless you are changed, and become as little children, you will never enter into the Kingdom of Heaven. Whoever, therefore, will be humble as this little child, he will be the greatest in the Kingdom of Heaven."

Jesus went on, "Whoever shall receive such a little child in My name receives Me. And if you receive Me, you are receiving My Father, who sent Me."

Later, John said to Jesus, "Master, we saw someone chasing away evil spirits from people's hearts, in Thy name, and he wasn't one of our followers. So we told him to stop."

"Don't do that!" Jesus exclaimed. "If he was doing it in My name, he was My friend. For if anyone gives you a cup of cold water in My name, because you belong to Me, he shall have his reward. But if anyone should hurt one of these who love Me and are Mine, it would be better for him if a stone were hung around his neck and he were thrown into the sea."

> *Were you listening?* Where did Peter get the money to pay the tax for himself and Jesus? What were the disciples quarreling about? In what way must men be like little children if they want to be great in Jesus' kingdom?

Story 206

Jesus Teaches About Forgiveness

Matthew 18

One day Peter came to Jesus and asked, "Lord, how many times should I forgive my brother if he sins against me? Should I forgive him seven times?"

Jesus answered, "You must forgive him seventy times seven."

Peter was surprised. How could he forgive anyone that many times! Jesus could see that Peter didn't understand. So He told him this story:

"The Kingdom of Heaven is like the king in my story. This king had several servants. Oftentimes this king would lend his servants money. One day the king checked his books to see how much money his servants owed him. Then he had his servants come in to pay what they owed.

"One servant, who owed the king a huge sum of money, was brought in. 'Pay me the money you owe me,' the king demanded.

10,000 talents = 1 million pounds

But the servant had no money. So the king said, 'Sell this man, and his wife, and his children, and all that he has, so that I may get my money.'

"The poor servant shook with fear. He fell down on his knees and worshiped the king. 'Lord, have patience with me,' he begged. 'Give me a little time, and I will pay you all of it.'

"The king felt sorry for the poor man. 'All right,' he said, 'you may go. You do not have to pay me any of the money. I forgive you your debt. You are free.'

"Not long after, this same servant was walking along the street. He met one of the other servants who owed him some money — just a little, about fifty dollars. Going up to his fellow-servant and taking him by the throat, he said, 'Pay me what you owe me!' *One denarii equalled a days wage for a labourer*

"His fellow-servant fell down at the other servant's feet and cried, 'Have patience with me, and I will pay you all!'

"But the servant was not kind as his king had been. He had his fellow-servant thrown into prison and kept there until he could pay what he owed.

"When the other servants saw what had happened, they were sorry and came to tell the king about it. The king was most angry when he heard what his servant had done. He sent for him right away. 'You wicked servant,' he began, 'I forgave you all your debt because you asked me. Then shouldn't you have felt sorry for your fellow-servant and have forgiven him, as I had pity on you?'

"Then the king sent the wicked servant to prison, too, until he should pay all that he owed."

When Jesus finished His story, He turned to Peter and explained, "Just as the king treated his servant, even so will My Heavenly Father treat you if you do not forgive those who sin against you."

Were you listening? What question did Peter ask Jesus? What kind thing did the king in Jesus' story do? What unkind thing did the servant do?

I Am the Light of the World

While Jesus was in Jerusalem for the Feast of Tabernacles, He taught in the Temple every day. On one of these days, Jesus sat among the people and cried, "I am the Light of the world. He that followeth Me shall not walk in darkness, but shall have the light of life!"

The Pharisees did not believe His words. They said, "You are speaking for Yourself. Your words are not true."

Jesus answered, "It is written in your law that the testimony of two men is true. What I say is true, for I witness for Myself, and My Father who sent Me, witnesses for Me."

"Where is Your Father?" they asked. They knew about Joseph, and they knew that he was no longer living.

"You don't know Me, and you don't know My Father," Jesus answered. "If you knew Me, you would know my Father also."

The Pharisees did not like to hear Jesus say such things. They would have liked to arrest Him, but they did not dare lay hands on Him.

At another time Jesus said, "I go my way, and you will look for Me. You will die in your sins, but where I go, you cannot come."

Again the Jews did not understand His words. They whispered to each other, "Does He plan to kill Himself? He says where He goes we cannot come."

Jesus knew what they were saying. He said, "You are from below; I am from above. You are of this world; I am not of this world."

Jesus told them many things about Himself and His Heavenly Father. He also said, "If any of you believe in Me and obey My teachings, you shall not die in your sins. You shall have eternal life."

This made the Jews angry. "Now we know You have an evil spirit in You," they said. "Abraham is dead and so are all the prophets. Yet you say that anyone who obeys Your teachings shall never die. Are You greater than our father Abraham? Who do You think You are, anyway?"

Jesus answered, "I am not honoring Myself. It is My Father in heaven who gives Me honor. You say that He is your Father, but you do not know Him. But I know Him, and I obey His words. Your father Abraham was glad to see My day."

"How could you have seen our father Abraham?" the Jews cried. "You are not even fifty years old!"

"Truly, truly, I tell you," Jesus said, "before Abraham was, *I am.*"

In the olden days, when Moses lived, God called Himself by the name of Jehovah which means "I AM THAT I AM." When the Jews heard Jesus use that sacred name for Himself, they were horrified. They picked up stones to kill Jesus, but He hid Himself and was soon lost in the crowds.

Were you listening? Who is the Light of the world? How can Jesus give His followers eternal life? What does Jehovah mean?

Story 208

The Man Born Blind

John 9

It was the Sabbath Day. Jesus and His disciples went for a walk along the narrow streets of Jerusalem. They passed a man who had been blind all his life. And because he was blind he couldn't work. So he had become a beggar.

As they passed the poor blind beggar, one of the disciples asked, "Master, why is this man blind? Did his parents sin, or did he?"

"It is not his parents' fault, nor is it his fault that he was born blind," Jesus answered. "He is blind so that the power of God may be shown through him. I must do the work of My Father who sent Me while it is day. Soon the night will come when no man can work. As long as I am in the world, I am the Light of the world."

When Jesus finished answering the disciples, he spit on the ground and made some clay. He covered the blind man's eyes with clay. "Go wash," He said, "go wash in the pool of Siloam."

Off went the blind beggar, thump, thump, thump, with his cane. Jesus went on with His walk. But soon there was a great commotion behind Him. Here was the beggar back again, and he could see! For the first time in all his life he saw the blue sky, the trees, the birds, the flowers. He saw the people, and the happy, smiling children. He shouted for joy. And the people said, "Isn't that the blind man who always sat and begged?"

"Yes, I am the blind beggar," the man said.

"How were your eyes opened?" the people asked.

"A man called Jesus covered my eyes with clay and told me to wash in the pool of Siloam. I went, and I washed, and now I can see!"

"Where is the man?" they asked.

"I do not know," the beggar answered.

Then the people brought the beggar to the Pharisees. As soon as the Pharisees heard what had happened, they made a big fuss. "It is sin to heal on the Sabbath," they said. They questioned the beggar again and again. Then they found his parents and questioned them, too. But his parents were afraid of the Pharisees. They said, "Ask him. He's old enough to know. Let him speak for himself."

"Don't you know that this man, Jesus, is a sinner?" the Pharisees asked the beggar.

The beggar answered, "I don't know if He is a sinner or not. But this I know: once I was blind but now I can see!"

Then they asked him again, "What did He do to you? How did He open your eyes?"

The beggar was tired of their questions, so he asked, "Why do you keep questioning me? Do you want to be His disciples, too?" Then the Pharisees threw the beggar out of their church.

When Jesus heard what had happened, He went to find the poor man. "Do you believe on the Son of God?" He asked.

"Who is He, Lord, that I may believe in Him?" the beggar asked.

"You have seen Him, and you are talking to Him right now!" Jesus answered.

The beggar fell down at Jesus' feet, and worshiped Him. "Lord, I believe," he said.

Were you listening? What did Jesus do for the blind beggar? Why were the Pharisees excited? Why did the beggar worship Jesus?

Story 209

"I Am the Good Shepherd"

John 10

While Jesus was talking with the beggar, whose eyes He had opened, a crowd of people began to gather around. Many Pharisees were in the crowd, too. Jesus turned to the people and told them a story.

"A shepherd," He said, "is a man who takes care of his sheep. He keeps them in a sheepfold (which is a barn without a roof). In the morning, when the shepherd goes to get his sheep, he goes into the sheepfold through the door. The shepherd knows all his sheep. He gives them names. And when he comes for them at the door, he calls them by their names. The sheep hear the shepherd's voice. They know his voice, and they know their names, so they follow him.

"If a thief or a robber comes to the sheepfold, he does not come in at the door. He climbs over the wall. And when a robber calls the sheep, he doesn't know their names, and they don't know his voice, so they won't follow him. They run away instead.

"At noon time the shepherd stands by the door of his fold. The sheep may go in or out as they please. They may rest in the fold, or they may go out into the pasture to find food. The shepherd takes good care of his sheep so that they may live and be happy. The robber is not interested in the sheep. He comes to steal the sheep. He will hurt the sheep, and perhaps he will kill them.

"In the evening, when the shepherd is leading his sheep back to the fold, he stays close to them so no wolf will get them. He chases the wolf away. He will even risk his own life to save his sheep. The man who is hired to care for the sheep, and who is not a shepherd, does not love the sheep because they are not his. When this man sees a wolf coming, he runs away and leaves his sheep. Then the wolf eats some of the sheep and scatters the others."

Then Jesus explained, "I am the Door of the sheepfold. By Me, if any man enter in, he shall be saved. You Pharisees are like the robbers, but the sheep won't follow you.

"I am the Good Shepherd. I know My people and they know Me. And they follow Me. I will not let anyone hurt My people (who are my sheep). I will lay down My life to save My sheep. I will die for My people. I have many sheep. Some are of this fold, and others are of other folds far away. But I shall bring them all together. They will hear My voice and will follow Me. They will all be one flock and I shall be their shepherd."

Were you listening? Why do the sheep follow the shepherd? Who is the Door of the sheepfold? Who is the Good Shepherd?

Story 210

The Good Samaritan

Luke 10

One day Jesus was teaching the people. A certain lawyer was among those listening. Suddenly, the lawyer stood up and asked, "Teacher, what must I do to go to heaven?" He did not ask this question because he really wanted to know the answer. Rather, he asked it because he wanted to see if he could trap Jesus into saying something wrong.

No one could trap Jesus. He always knew what to say. He answered the lawyer, "What does the Bible tell you to do?"

The lawyer said, "The Bible says we must love God with all our heart, and with all our soul, and with all our strength, and with all our mind. And we must love our neighbor as ourselves."

"That is right," Jesus said. "Do what the Bible says and you will go to heaven."

"But who is my neighbor?" the lawyer asked.

Jesus answered this question by telling a story. He said, "A certain man was going down from Jerusalem to Jericho.(17 M The road led through lonely hills where there were rocks and caves. Sometimes robbers hid in those hills. They watched for lonely travelers. When this man came through those hills, the robbers caught him and beat him. They took all his money, tore off his clothes, and left him lying on the road, half dead.

THE INJURED MAN IN LACE WOULD HAVE MADE THE PRIEST CERMONIALLY UNCLEAN. THE PRIEST MAY NOT HAVE TOUCHED HE WAS ACTUALLY DEAD. THAT

"After the robbers had gone away, one of the man's own people came along. He was a priest (a minister) who worked in the Temple. He saw the poor man lying in the road, so sick he might die; but he didn't even try to help him. He walked on the other side of the road and hurried away.

A LEVITE POLICED THE TEMPLE RESPONSIBLE FOR THE MUSIC - PERHAPS THEY WERE TEACHERS AS WELL

"Soon after, another man came down the road. He was a Levite who also worked in God's House. When he saw the poor sick man, he, too, crossed the road, and hurried away.

"The sick man still lay in the road. After a while a man came riding along the road on a donkey. This man was a Samaritan. His people and the injured man's people were not very friendly toward one another. They would not speak to each other. But this Samaritan, when he saw the sick man lying in the road, did not turn away as the others had done. The Samaritan felt sorry for the sick man. He gave him a drink. He got some medicine /WINE & OIL from his saddle and put it on the sick man's sores. Then he bandaged them. He lifted the man gently and set him on his donkey. Then he walked beside the donkey and held the man up. They went along this way until they came to an inn.

"The good Samaritan carried the sick man into the inn. He put him to bed and stayed with him all night. The next morning he paid the inn-keeper some money. 'Take care of the sick man,' he said. 'And if you need more money, I shall pay you the next time I come.'"

When Jesus finished the story, he turned to the lawyer. "Which of these three men was a good neighbor to the sick man?" He asked.

WINE WAS AN ANTISEPTIC OIL WOULD HAVE SOOTHED

"The one who was kind to him," the lawyer answered.

"That's right," Jesus answered. "You go, now, and be like the good Samaritan."

Were you listening? Who asked Jesus a question? What story did Jesus tell him? Why was the Samaritan called the "good" Samaritan?

Story 211

Jesus in the Home of Friends

Luke 10 and 11

Not far from Jerusalem was the little town of Bethany. Jesus often went to Bethany, for He had friends there. There were two sisters and a brother who loved Jesus very much. Mary and Martha, the sisters, and Lazarus, the brother, were always happy to have Jesus visit them.

One day Jesus and His disciples came to Bethany to rest. Mary and Martha invited them into their home. Martha went at once into the kitchen. She wanted to show her love for Jesus by making Him a lovely dinner. She hurried about, working as fast as she could.

Mary did not help her sister. She was sitting at Jesus' feet, listening to His wonderful words. Martha was too busy to sit at Jesus' feet, and it made her cross to have her sister do so. She wanted Mary to help in the kitchen. Finally, she went to Jesus and said, "Lord, don't you care that my sister leaves me to do the work all alone? Tell her to come and help me."

Jesus looked at Martha. He quietly shook His head. "Martha, Martha," He chided. "You make yourself so busy and worried about so many things. There is just one thing that is needful, to sit at My feet and learn about God. Mary has chosen this good part and it shall not be taken away from her."

Not long after this, Jesus told His friends a story. He said,

"Which of you would have a friend who would not help you if you came to him? If you went to your friend at midnight and said, 'Friend, let me have three loaves of bread, for a friend of mine has come to my house unexpectedly, and I have nothing to give him to eat,' would your friend let you stand outside the locked door, and would he call out to you, 'Don't bother me. The door is now shut and everyone is in bed. I can't get up and give you bread now'? No, I tell you, even though he wouldn't help you as a friend, because you kept on calling and asking, he would finally get up and give you as much as you needed.

"But my Father in heaven is not like your friend. For, if you ask God for something He will give it to you. And if you look, you shall find. And if you knock, the door will be opened to you. For everyone that asks shall receive, and he that seeks will find, and he that knocks will have the door opened.

"If a son asks his father for some bread, would the father give him a stone instead? Or if he asks for a fish, will his father give him a snake? Or if he asks for an egg, will his father offer him a scorpion (something like a spider)? Well then, if you who are sinful know how to give good gifts to your children, how much more shall your Heavenly Father give the Holy Spirit to those who ask Him?"

Were you listening? How did Martha show her love for Jesus? How did Mary show her love for Jesus? Who chose the better part? How do we know that God hears us when we ask Him for something?

Story 212

The Rich Fool

Luke 12

One day such a great crowd of people had gathered around Jesus that they were almost stepping on each other. Jesus sat down and began to teach about His Heavenly Father. After a while, one of the men in the crowd said, "Master, speak to my brother and tell him to divide the inheritance with me." The inheritance was the money his brother had received from their father.

Jesus answered, "Man, who made me a judge over you? Be careful and do not long for that which is your brother's. A man's life is made up of more than just his money and his possessions."

Then Jesus told this story:

"There was once a very rich farmer. He had a large farm, and in the spring he planted much seed in his farm. The seed grew and grew until his farm was filled with golden grain. In the fall, when the grain was cut down, the farmer did not have enough room in his barns for all his food. When his barns were full, he could have given away the rest for he would never need it. But no, the farmer said to himself, 'I know what I shall do. I shall pull down my barns and build bigger ones. Then I shall have room for all my food!'

"When the new barns were built, and the food was all stored away, the farmer said, 'Now I have enough food laid away for many years. I will not have to work any more. I will take it easy: I will eat and drink and be merry. I will enjoy myself.'

"But God said to this rich farmer, 'You fool, this night I shall take your soul. Then who will own all the food in your huge barns?'"

This rich man had thought only about his food and all the things he owned. He had forgotten all about God, and he forgot all about his neighbors. When Jesus finished the story, He added, "What good would it do a man if he owned the whole world, and lost his own soul?"

Then Jesus turned to His disciples and said, "Therefore, don't worry about your life, what you shall eat or what you shall wear. Look at the black birds (ravens), they do not plant seeds and cut down grain, or store it in barns. But God feeds them. How much better are you than the birds!

"You should not worry about things. Which one of you could make yourself grow even one cubit? Look at the lilies, how they grow. They do not work hard every day. They do not make their own clothes. And yet, I say to you, even Solomon with all his wonderful things, was not as beautiful as one of these lilies. So, if God takes care of the grass of the field, which grows for a few days and then is burned, how much more will He take care of you, O you of little faith? Therefore, seek first the kingdom of God and all these things shall be added unto you."

Were you listening? Why was the rich farmer a fool? Is it sin to worry? What can we learn from the birds and the lilies?

Story 213

The Lost Is Found

Luke 15

We all like to hear a good story, don't we? When Jesus was on earth, everyone loved to listen to His stories, for He was a wonderful story-teller. And Jesus' stories always taught a good lesson. One day Jesus told two stories.

He told one story about a kind shepherd and his sheep. He said, "There was once a shepherd who had a hundred sheep. This shepherd loved all of his sheep and cared for them each day. He knew exactly which sheep were his. He gave them names, and called them by their names. The sheep knew his voice and came running when he called.

"But one evening, when the long day's work was over, the shepherd brought his sheep back to the sheepfold. As he counted his sheep to make sure they were all there, he found that he had only ninety-nine, instead of one hundred. One sheep was not there.

"The shepherd still had ninety-nine sheep. Surely that would be enough for him. But no, the kind shepherd loved all his sheep. He left his ninety-nine sheep and went back to the desert to find the sheep that was lost. Up and down the mountains he walked, calling and looking everywhere for the sheep that was lost. Finally, after a long time, he found him. Quickly the shepherd picked up his little lost sheep and laid it on his shoulders. How happy he was as he hurried back to his other sheep. He did not care how long it had taken, or how rough the way had been, or how tired he was. When he came home, he called his friends and his neighbors and said, 'Be happy with me, for I have found my sheep that was lost!' "

When Jesus had finished this story, He added, "I tell you, that is exactly the way it is with Me and My people. There is more joy in heaven over the one sinner who is sorry for his sins, than for the ninety-nine."

The second story was about a farmer who had two sons. Jesus began,

"A certain man had two sons. What a loving father he was. He was kind to his sons and shared everything he had with them. The sons worked for their father. But the younger son was not happy in his father's house.

"Finally, the son went to his father and said, 'Father, give me my share of your money now.' The father was sad, but he gave his boy the money. In a few days, the younger son took his possessions and went away to a far-off country. There he wasted his money spending it for wicked things. As long as he had money, he had many friends who were happy to share his money with him. But when his money was gone, his friends left him, too. Soon he was poor and hungry and tired. There was a famine in that country, so there was no work and no food for the people. The only work the young son could find was to feed a farmer's swine (pigs). He was so hungry he would have liked to eat the garbage they fed the pigs, but no one gave him any food.

"One day, as the boy sat there with the pigs, he suddenly realized how wrong he had been. He said to himself, 'My father's hired servants have more than enough to eat, and here I am starving! I am going to get up right now, and go to my father. I shall say to my father, "Father, I have sinned against God and against you. I am not good enough to be your son any longer. Let me be one of your servants."'

"So the boy started for home. His shoes were worn and his clothes were in rags. He looked like a tramp. Would his father refuse to open the gate? Would he send him away in anger? No, the father still loved his boy, even though he had been bad. Each day the father had been watching for his son to come back. As soon as he saw him coming, he ran to meet him. He threw his arms around the boy and kissed him.

"The son cried, 'Father, I have sinned against God and against you. I am not good enough to be your son. Let me be one of your hired servants.'

"But the father welcomed him home with joy. He gave him new clothes and new shoes, and a ring for his finger. And he said, 'Let's have a party. Let's celebrate, for I thought my boy was dead and he's alive again; I thought he was lost, and he's found!'

"So they celebrated with a wonderful feast. But the older brother was out in the field. When he came close to the house, he heard music and dancing. He asked one of the servants what was happening. When he heard that his brother was back, and that his father was so happy he was celebrating with a feast, he was jealous and would not go in. His father came out to him and begged him to come in.

"But the older brother said, 'Look, all these years I worked faithfully for you. I never disobeyed you, but you never gave me a party so that I could have a good time with my friends. But as soon as my bad brother comes home, after he has wasted all your money, you give him a party.'

"The father answered, 'Son, you are always with me and all that I have is yours. You can have a party any time you like. But it was fitting that we should celebrate and be glad. I thought your brother was dead and now he is alive again. I thought he was lost and now he is found!' "

"Just so," Jesus added, "there is joy in heaven over one sinner who comes back to God!"

> *Were you listening?* Why did the shepherd go back into the desert alone? What did the shepherd tell his friends when he came back? How was the younger son bad? How did the father treat him when he came back?

Story 214

The Rich Man and Lazarus

Luke 16

Jesus also told a story about two men, one who was very rich and one who was very poor. The rich man had everything he wanted. His beautiful home looked like a palace. His clothing was the best money could buy. And he ate the best food every day. He could have anything he wanted.

The poor man, whose name was Lazarus, had nothing at all. Lazarus had no money or home. He was dressed in rags and had to beg for food. Every day Lazarus lay at the rich man's gate, hoping to get the crumbs that fell from the rich man's table. Lazarus' body was full of sores. As he lay at the rich man's gate, the dogs would come and lick his sores.

Although the rich man had everything, he did not love God. He paid no attention to God. And he did not love his neighbor either. He lived only for himself. Lazarus, even though he was a poor beggar, was a child of God. He loved God and obeyed Him.

One day the poor beggar died. No one on earth paid any attention. No one cared. But God cared. He sent His angel to get Lazarus' soul. The angels carried Lazarus to heaven.

Not long after, the rich man also died. His friends had a big funeral for him. They buried him in a rich man's grave. But no angel came for his soul. Instead, he went to a place of great torment. There he was very thirsty. Then he looked up and saw Abraham in heaven. And he saw Lazarus in the place of honor next to Abraham.

The rich man cried out, "Father Abraham, have mercy on me. Please send Lazarus to me! Let him dip the tip of his finger in water and cool my tongue, for I am tormented in this flame!"

Abraham answered, "Son, remember when you were on earth you had everything, and Lazarus had nothing. Now things are just turned around. Now Lazarus has everything, and you are suffering. Besides, there is a great hole between us and you. No one can go from heaven to your place of torment, nor can anyone come from your place to heaven."

"Then," the rich man begged, "please send Lazarus to earth to my family. I have five brothers who are just as bad as I was. Let him warn them lest they come to this terrible place."

But Abraham said, "They have the Bible. Let them read the Bible. That will tell them how to live."

"No, Father Abraham," the rich man pleaded, "they don't believe the Bible. But if someone came to them from the dead, then they would listen."

Again Abraham answered, "If they won't listen to the Bible, they won't listen to Lazarus either, even though he should rise from the dead."

Were you listening? Why did the rich man go to hell? Why did the poor man go to heaven? Why would not Abraham do what the rich man wanted?

Jesus Makes Lazarus Live

One day Jesus was traveling in Perea, a country on the other side of the river Jordan. While Jesus was gone from Jerusalem, His friend Lazarus became sick. Mary and Martha wished that Jesus were there to help Lazarus. They believed that Jesus could make their brother well. So they sent a messenger to Jesus. The messenger told Jesus, "Your friend Lazarus, whom you love, is sick."

Usually when people asked Jesus to come to heal the sick, He went with them at once. In this case, although Lazarus was His special friend, Jesus did not hurry to Bethany to help him. Instead He waited. The disciples thought Jesus did not go because He was afraid of the Pharisees who wanted to kill Him. But that wasn't the reason Jesus stayed away. He wanted to show His friends what a wonderful Saviour He really was. He wanted to show His power.

Lazarus became worse and worse. Mary and Martha waited anxiously for Jesus, but He did not come. Finally Lazarus died. Kind neighbors came to help the sisters in their trouble. They wrapped the body of Lazarus in white linen cloth and buried him.

Some days after Jesus had received the message that Lazarus was sick, He said to His disciples, "Come, let's go back to Judea."

The disciples answered, "Master, why do you want to go there now? Don't you remember that the Jews want to stone you?"

Jesus replied, "Are there not twelve hours in a day? If a man walk in the day, he won't stumble because he can see." He meant, "They won't hurt Me until it is time." And then Jesus added, "Our friend Lazarus is sleeping. I want to go to wake him up."

"If Lazarus is sleeping, he will soon be well," the disciples answered.

Then Jesus told them what He really meant. "Lazarus is dead," He said.

So Jesus and His disciples went to Bethany. The home of Mary and Martha was filled with friends who had come to comfort them in their sorrow. Mary and Martha said to Jesus, "Lord, why didn't You come sooner? If You had been here, our brother would not have died."

Jesus answered, "Your brother shall live again."

"I know," Martha said, "he will live again in the last day, at the end of the world."

Jesus said, "I am the Life. Everyone who believes in Me, even though he were dead, yet shall he live."

Jesus felt sorry for Mary and Martha. "Where have you laid him?" He asked. They took Jesus to the grave. When Jesus saw his friends crying, He began to cry, too.

"See how Jesus loved Lazarus!" the people said.

Some people said, "Could not this man who could open the eyes of the blind keep his friend from dying?"

Jesus sighed. He went close to the grave. It was a cave with a big stone rolled in front of it. "Roll away the stone," Jesus said.

"Oh, no, Lord," Martha answered, "he has been in the grave too long! By this time his body has begun to smell, for he has been dead four days."

Jesus said, "Didn't I tell you, Martha, that if you would believe, you would see the glory of God?"

Then they took away the stone from the grave. Jesus looked up to His Heavenly Father and prayed. He said, "Father, I thank You that You always hear Me. I know that You always hear Me, but I said it so that these people may believe that You sent Me into this world."

Jesus stood at the opening of the cave and called with a loud voice, "Lazarus, come out!" Lazarus heard Jesus calling. He came out of the grave wrapped from head to foot in white grave clothes. He was alive again! Jesus said, "Loosen Lazarus and let him go."

They quickly took off the grave clothes. Mary and Martha and their friends were filled with joy. Many of the Jews who saw what happened believed in Jesus. But the Pharisees and the leaders hated Jesus all the more. They planned how to kill Him.

Were you listening? Why did Jesus often visit Bethany? Why didn't Jesus go to His friends when they needed Him? What happened at the grave of Lazarus?

A Lesson in Thankfulness

Everyone looks forward to Thanksgiving Day. It is a day when all of God's people may go to church to thank God for the many blessings He has given them during the past year. We must never forget to say "thank you" to God for all His care.

When Jesus was on earth, He expected the people to say "thank you," too. One day Jesus and His disciples were on their way to Jerusalem. They decided to take the road which led through the country of Samaria. As they came near to one of the villages of Samaria, Jesus sent men on ahead to find a place to spend the night.

The Samaritans did not want Jesus and His disciples to stay overnight in their town. James and his brother, John, were angry when they heard of the unkindness of the Samaritans. They said to Jesus, "Lord, why don't you call down fire from heaven and burn up their village like Elijah did?"

Jesus looked at His friends. He shook His head and said, "No, no, you do not understand at all! The Son of man is not come to destroy men's lives, but to save them." Then Jesus led His disciples to another village.

While they were coming to another village in Samaria, Jesus and His followers passed the caves in the rocks where the lepers lived. Lepers often had ugly, running sores all over their bodies. As time went on, a leper's skin would rot away, his fingers and toes would drop off. There was no cure for leprosy.

Lepers were not allowed to live with other people. Since leprosy was catching, people did not want to be near a leper. So the lepers lived together in the caves at the edge of their city. If the lepers came to the city well for water, they would have to call out, "Unclean! Unclean!" Then the people who were coming to the well for water would wait until the lepers had gone.

As Jesus and His friends passed the lepers' caves, ten lepers came out and looked at them. They cried out to Jesus, "Jesus, Master, have mercy on us!"

Jesus turned and looked at the lepers. He felt sorry for them.

He said, "Go and show yourselves to the priests." If it ever happened that a leper was cured from his leprosy, he had to show himself to the priest. If the priest could see that leprosy was all gone, he would allow the leper to go back to his family.

As soon as these ten lepers heard the words of Jesus, they went off to find the priest. And as they went, they looked at themselves and found that their leprosy was gone! Jesus had healed them all!

One of them, when he saw that his leprosy was gone, turned back. He fell on his face at Jesus' feet, praising Him with a loud voice. He thanked Jesus again and again.

Jesus said, "Were there not ten lepers that I healed? Where are the other nine? No one came back to say 'thank you' and to give glory to God, except this stranger."

Then Jesus turned to the Samaritan and said, "Arise, go thy way. Your faith has made you whole."

> *Were you listening?* What must we always remember to do? Why would not Jesus let the disciples call down fire to burn the unfriendly village? What was wrong with the nine lepers whom Jesus healed?

Story 217

Lessons on Prayer

Luke 18

Jesus is the greatest teacher who ever lived. He taught His people many important things. Many times, you remember, He taught others by telling a story. One day, when He was teaching about prayer, Jesus told two stories.

Jesus said, "There was once, in a certain city, a judge. He did not love God, and he did not love his neighbor. One day a widow came to him. She asked him to help her get rid of her enemies. This judge paid no attention to the poor widow. He would not help her.

"The widow, however, would not take 'No' for an answer. She came to the judge again and again, asking him for help. Finally the judge said, 'Though I do not fear God, and though I do not care for people, I shall help this widow. I shall help her because her constant coming tires me and I want to get rid of her.'"

When Jesus finished this story, He said, "If this unkind judge

would help the widow because she kept on asking him, don't you think God will help His own children who cry to Him day and night? I tell you, He will answer them in a hurry!"

Then Jesus also told this story:

"Two men went up in the Temple to pray. The one was a Pharisee (one of the proud leaders of the church) and the other was a publican (a tax collector, whom the people hated and called a 'sinner'). The Pharisee stood in the Temple where everyone could see him. He threw back his shoulders and raised his hands toward heaven. Then he prayed in a loud voice so that everyone could hear.

"The Pharisee said, 'God, I thank Thee that I am not wicked like other men who are unkind and selfish and evil. Or even like this publican. I fast twice a week, and I give one-tenth of all that I own to God.'

"The publican was quite different. He stood in a corner where no one could see him. He did not raise his hands to heaven, as the Pharisee had done. He did not even dare to raise his eyes toward heaven. He stood with bowed head. He beat himself upon his breast and said softly, 'God, be merciful to me, a sinner.'

"I tell you," Jesus went on, "this man, the publican, went home happier than the Pharisee, for everyone who is proud shall be brought low, and he that is humble shall be honored."

The Pharisee was not even praying. He was just telling God, and all those who could hear him, how wonderful he felt himself to be. He did not think he needed anything from God. The publican, on the other hand, knew he was a sinner. He knew he needed God's mercy. And God answered his prayer.

Were you listening? Why did the unkind judge finally help the poor widow? Why does God help us when we pray? Who really prayed, the publican or the Pharisee?

Story 218

Jesus Loves Little Children

Matthew 19; Mark 10; Luke 18

In the days when Jesus lived on this earth, life was quite different than it is today. Women and children were not considered important. Only the men were important. The women were supposed to stay at home with their children. And even the children were supposed to work most of the time.

One day Jesus was busy talking with the leaders of the people. The Pharisees had been asking Him many questions. Some mothers, with their little children, came up to the group. These mothers had heard that Jesus was kind and that He loved little children. The children loved Jesus, too. They wanted to see Him and be near Him.

There was a big crowd around Jesus so that the children could not see Him at all. Eagerly, some of the children began to push their way through the crowd to get to Jesus. The mothers tried to get closer, too.

Jesus' friends, the disciples, did not like to have the mothers and the children bother them. "Go away," they scolded. "Can't you see Jesus is busy?"

Jesus stopped talking. "What's the matter?" He asked.

"Oh, the mothers and their children are trying to push through the crowd to get to You," the disciples answered. "We told them to go away."

"Don't do that!" Jesus said. "Let the little children come unto Me. Don't stop them, for of such is the kingdom of heaven."

So the crowd stepped aside, and made way for the mothers and their children. The children gathered around Jesus. They climbed up on His lap. Jesus took them in His arms. He put His hands on them and blessed them.

The children went home happier than they had ever been. They never forgot the day they had been with Jesus. How kind He looked when He said, "Let the little children come unto Me."

Although we cannot meet Jesus like that now, we are His children, too. He loves us just as much as He loved those little ones long ago. Even though we cannot see Him, we may go to Him in prayer and receive His blessing.

> *Were you listening?* Why did the disciples stop the children from coming to Jesus? What did Jesus say? How can you receive Jesus' blessing today?

Story 219

The Rich Young Ruler

Matthew 19; Mark 10; Luke 18

Jesus was walking along the road from Galilee to Jerusalem. It was time to celebrate the Feast of the Passover. While He was on the way, a young man came running and knelt at His feet. "Good Master," he said, "what must I do so that I may have eternal life?"

Jesus answered, "Why do you call Me good? Don't you know that there is only One who is good, and that is God? (Jesus knew that the leaders of His people did not believe that He was God.) You know what you must do. You know what the Ten Commandments tell you. You must not steal, nor kill, nor lie about anyone, nor cheat anyone. You must honor your father and your mother. You must love your neighbor as much as you do yourself."

The young man answered, "Master, I have done all these things ever since I was a little boy. What else must I do? Isn't there something that I lack?"

Jesus could see that the young man really tried to do what was right. He was a ruler in the Temple and was careful to obey all the rules of the church. Jesus knew what was wrong with him.

This young man was very rich, and he loved his money more than he loved God. So Jesus said, "Yes, there is one thing you lack. Go your way, sell all that you have, and give to the poor. Then you will have treasure in heaven. Then come, take up your cross, and follow Me."

The rich young ruler was filled with sadness when he heard Jesus' words. He turned sorrowfully away. And he left. Jesus turned to His friends. "How hard it is," He said, "for those who are rich to enter into the kingdom of God."

The disciples were surprised at His words. But Jesus said a second time, "Children, how hard it is for those who trust in riches to enter into the kingdom of God! It is easier for a camel to go through the eye of a needle than for a rich man to enter into the kingdom of God."

The disciples looked at each other in amazement. "Who then can be saved?" they asked.

Jesus looked at them and said, "With men this is impossible, but not with God. For with God all things are possible."

Were you listening? Would you have liked the rich young ruler? Since this ruler was such a good man, why could he not go to heaven? What must we do to go to heaven?

Story 220

The Workers in the Vineyard

Matthew 20

Jesus was again talking about the kingdom of heaven. He said:

"The kingdom of heaven is like a farmer who owned a large vineyard. Early one morning this farmer went into the town to hire workers for his vineyard. He found several men who were willing to come to work for him that day. They agreed together that the men would work all day for a penny. This was not like our pennies. It was the amount of money that a man usually got for working one day. With it he could buy all the things he and his family would need for one day.

"So the workers went to work. Several hours later, at nine o'clock, the farmer went into the town again. He went to the market place where men usually gathered to wait for someone to hire them for work. The farmer saw several men standing idly around with nothing to do. 'Go, work in my vineyard,' the farmer said to these men, 'and I will pay you whatever I think is right.' So these men also went to work in the vineyard.

"About noon the farmer went back to the market place in the town. Once more he found men who had no work. 'Would you like to work in my vineyard?' he asked. And the men agreed to come and work for the rest of the day.

"About three o'clock in the afternoon, the farmer found still more idle men who needed work. Although there were only three hours left in which the men could work, the farmer sent them to his vineyard and promised to pay them what was right.

"When the day was almost over, at five o'clock, the farmer went back to the market place once more. There he found men standing idly by with nothing to do. 'Why do you stand here all day, doing nothing?' the farmer asked.

"The men answered, 'Because no man asked us to work.'

The farmer said, 'Then you had better go into my vineyard, too. There is still one hour left to work. You work and I will pay you what is right.'

"When the working day was over, at six o'clock, the farmer told his servant to call all the workers to come to him. They lined them up according to how long they had worked. Those who had worked but one hour came first. Then those who had worked three hours, then six hours, then nine hours, and last of all, those who had worked all day for twelve hours.

"And he gave those who had worked one hour, one penny. Those who had worked three hours received one penny, and so did those who had worked six hours and nine hours. When those who had worked all day came up for their pay, they expected to receive more since they had worked the longest. But they, too, received just one penny.

"These men were angry with the farmer. One of them said, 'That isn't fair! These men worked only one hour and you have made them equal to us, who have worked all day.'

"But the farmer answered, 'Friend, I didn't do you any wrong. Didn't you agree with me this morning to work for one penny?

Take what is yours and go your way. I will give just as much to those who came last, as I give to you. Is it not right for me to do what I want to with my own money? Are you jealous because I am good?'"

When Jesus had finished the story, He added, "So the last shall be first, and the first shall be last. For many are called, but few are chosen."

God's people are just like these workers in the vineyard. Some people have loved God and served Him ever since they were small children. They will go to heaven. Some people learned about God only after they were grown up. They will go to heaven, too. Some people never loved God until they were old, but they also will go to heaven. There are even some people who never gave their heart to Jesus until the very last day of their lives, like the thief on the cross. But even they will go to heaven.

> *Were you listening?* Did the workers in the vineyard all work equally long? Was it fair for the farmer to give them all the same amount of money? Why?

Story 221

Jesus Teaches His Friends to Be Humble

Matthew 20

Jesus is our King. We belong to His kingdom. But Jesus is not a king as King David was. When Jesus lived on this earth, He did not live in a palace and sit on a throne, as King David did. Jesus' throne is up in heaven. His kingdom is a heavenly one.

Jesus often tried to teach His friends, the disciples, about His kingdom. But they did not understand. They thought Jesus was going to be a king on earth and rule as King David had.

One day, two of Jesus' best friends, James and his brother John, came to Jesus. With them was their mother Salome. They worshiped Jesus. And then Salome said, "Lord, will You promise me something?"

"What do you want Me to promise?" Jesus asked.

"When You are in Your kingdom, and are sitting on Your throne," Salome answered, "will You let my two sons sit closest to You? May one of them sit on Your right and the other on Your left?"

Jesus said, "You don't know what you are asking, Salome. If your sons want to have an important place in My kingdom, they will have to be able to suffer with Me first. Besides, it is My Father's kingdom. It is My Father who will decide who will be the greatest in My kingdom, and who will sit on My right and on My left side."

The other disciples heard what Salome asked. They were angry with James and John for wanting the best place in Jesus' kingdom. Then Jesus said to all the disciples, "You know that in the world those who are in the highest place rule over the rest of the people. But in My kingdom, he who wants to be the greatest must serve the others. If he wants to have a high place, let him be a servant. For I, who am your King, came into this world, not to have people serve Me, but to serve others. I came to give My life to save others."

Were you listening? Who is our King? Why is Jesus' kingdom different from other kingdoms? Why couldn't James and John have what they asked for? Who is the greatest in Jesus' kingdom?

Story 222

Blind Bartimaeus

Matthew 20; Mark 10; Luke 18

Jesus was still traveling from Galilee to Jerusalem. He and His disciples walked from one village to the next. Whenever they came to a little village or town, the people would crowd around Jesus. They wanted to be near Jesus and hear Him speak. At one place, you remember, the rich young ruler asked Jesus about heaven.

After the rich man went away, Jesus began to walk on ahead. His disciples followed. They were afraid because of what Jesus had said to the young man.

Then Jesus gathered them close once more, and said, "We are on our way to Jerusalem. When we get there, they are going to capture Me, and turn Me over to the chief priests and the scribes. They will sentence Me to death. Then they will deliver Me to the heathen. They will mock Me and whip Me. They will spit on Me and kill Me. But on the third day I shall rise again." The disciples did not understand His words.

After that they came to Jericho. A great crowd of people began to follow them. When they were almost through the city, they came to a place in the road where a blind beggar was sitting. His name was Bartimaeus. Bartimaeus sat at the curb to beg from the people who passed by.

The blind man could hear the sound of many feet as Jesus and the crowd came along. "What do I hear?" he asked those who stood near him. "Why are all those people coming this way?"

"Jesus of Nazareth is passing by," was the answer.

When Bartimaeus heard that, he shouted, "Jesus, Thou Son of David, have mercy on me!"

"Be quiet!" the people said. "Don't bother Jesus."

But Bartimaeus shouted all the more, "Thou Son of David, have mercy on me!"

Then Jesus stood still. "Bring him to Me," He commanded.

So the people called to the blind man, "Be of good cheer. He is calling you." Bartimaeus threw off his robe, got up and went to Jesus.

"What do you want me to do for you?" Jesus asked.

"Lord, if You would only open my eyes and make me see!" Bartimaeus answered.

Jesus said, "I will. Go your way. Your faith has made you whole." When Jesus touched the man's eyes, at once Bartimaeus could see!

Bartimaeus glorified God and followed Jesus. And all the people, when they saw it, praised God.

Were you listening? Where was Jesus going? What was going to happen in Jerusalem? What did Jesus do for Bartimaeus?

Story 223

Zacchaeus

Luke 19

Jesus was on His way to Jerusalem. This would be the last time He would visit that great city before His death. It was almost time to celebrate the Passover Feast.

Many interesting things had happened on this long journey. Ten lepers had been cleansed in one village. In another, the rich young ruler had turned sadly away. In Jericho, Jesus had taken time to give sight to blind Bartimaeus.

Jesus and His followers were still in Jericho. In Jericho, a man, whose name was Zacchaeus, was the chief tax-collector. The people hated the tax-collectors. These men often asked for more money than the people were supposed to pay. The extra money they would keep for themselves. Zacchaeus did this, too, and he was very rich.

When Zacchaeus heard that Jesus was passing through Jericho, he wanted to see Him, too. But Zacchaeus was a small man, not much bigger than a boy. He couldn't see over the heads of crowds following Jesus. Besides, Zacchaeus didn't like to mix with the crowd because of the way the people felt about him.

Suddenly Zacchaeus had a good idea. He ran ahead of the crowd and climbed up into a small sycamore tree. No one would see him there, and he would be able to see Jesus as He passed. Zacchaeus sat very still, watching and listening, as the people came close. He almost held his breath as Jesus walked under the tree. He hoped no one would look up and spy him there!

To Zacchaeus' great surprise, Jesus stopped directly under his tree. He looked up into the tree and said, "Come, hurry down, Zacchaeus, for today I must visit at your house." Zacchaeus jumped down and joyfully walked along with Jesus.

Zacchaeus paid no attention, now, to the people who hated him. He was happy to be with Jesus. But the people did not like it. They sneered and said, "Jesus has gone to eat with sinners."

While Jesus visited with Zacchaeus, He taught him the right way to live. He showed him how wrong it was to take money which did not belong to him. Zacchaeus was sorry for what he had done. He said, "I'm sorry, Lord, that I took money which did not belong to me. Now I'm going to give half of all my possessions to the poor. And out of the rest, I am going to pay back four times as much as I took wrongfully from other people."

Jesus was happy to hear Zacchaeus' promise. He said, "This day salvation has come to your house, Zacchaeus."

The crowd was still gathered outside Zacchaeus' house. They were still finding fault because Jesus made friends with sinners. But Jesus said, "That is why I came into this world. The Son of man is come to seek and to save that which is lost."

Were you listening? Who was the chief tax-collector in Jericho? Why did he climb a sycamore tree? How did Zacchaeus make up for the wrong he had done?

Story 224

Mary Shows Her Love for Jesus

John 12

The Feast of the Passover was being celebrated. Jesus had still not arrived in Jerusalem. Everywhere people were saying, "Will Jesus come to Jerusalem for the Feast?" Those who loved Jesus were afraid to have Him come, for they knew that the leaders were trying to capture Him. The chief priests and the Pharisees had promised a reward for anyone who would help capture Jesus.

But Jesus did not go directly to Jerusalem. Six days before the Feast, He and His disciples went to Bethany instead. Mary, Martha and Lazarus lived in Bethany. Jesus usually stopped there to see His friends on the way to Jerusalem.

Jesus had other friends in Bethany, too. There was a man, named Simon, who had been a leper. He loved Jesus with all his heart, for Jesus had cured him of his leprosy. Simon invited Jesus and His helpers to have supper at his home. Martha wanted to show her love for Jesus, too. So she helped Simon get the supper ready.

When it was time to eat, there were many people gathered around Simon's table. Jesus and His twelve disciples were there. Mary and Martha and Lazarus were there, too. Martha served the food. While they were eating, Mary left her place and went quietly up to Jesus. She wanted to show her love for Jesus, too. She had with her a bottle filled with expensive perfume. She had saved her money a long time to buy the perfume. It was her gift to Jesus.

Mary removed the cover of the bottle and poured some of the

perfume on Jesus' head. Then she stooped and poured the rest of the perfume on His feet. After that she wiped Jesus' feet with her long hair.

As soon as the bottle was opened, the room was filled with the sweet smell of the perfume. Everyone at the table looked at Mary to see what she was doing. They knew that the perfume had cost a great deal of money.

Some of the disciples thought Mary had wasted the perfume by pouring it on Jesus. They whispered among themselves. Judas Iscariot, the disciple who later sold his Master for thirty pieces of silver, was also angry. He said, "Why is this expensive perfume wasted? It should have been sold and the money given to the poor." Judas didn't say this because he loved the poor so much. He took care of the money-bag for the disciples, and he loved money.

Jesus knew what the men were saying. He knew, too, that Mary had given Him the perfume because she loved Him. So He took Mary's part. "Leave her alone," He said. "The poor will always be with you. You can help them any time. But I will not always be with you. Mary has done a good deed. She has shown how much she loves Me. Instead of waiting until I was dead, she has poured perfume on My body while I am still alive. In years to come, whenever people talk about Me and My death, they will also remember the good deed which Mary has done today."

Were you listening? Why did Simon invite Jesus for supper? How did Martha show her love for Jesus? How did Mary show her love for Jesus? What did Jesus say about Mary's gift?

Story 225

Jesus, the King   JESUS WAS COMING FROM JERICHO

Matthew 21; Mark 11; Luke 19; John 12

Jesus and His disciples had slept at the home of Mary and Martha in Bethany. Now they continued on their way to Jerusalem to visit the beautiful House of God, the Temple. The Feast of the Passover ₐwas being celebrated. EXODUS FROM EGYPT As they began their short journey of about two miles, a great many people followed them.

Bethany was on the south-eastern slope of the Mount of Olives. So Jesus and His disciples had to cross over the mount and then go down into Jerusalem. About a mile from Bethany was another little village called Bethphage (which means House of Figs). As they neared Bethphage, Jesus asked two of His friends to go ahead into the little town. He told them that they would find a donkey there. They were to bring the donkey to Him. Kings often rode into their cities on donkeys when they wanted to show their people that they were coming peaceably. When they came for war they rode a great, charging horse. Jesus was coming to His people as a King of Peace, so He, too, wanted to ride the donkey. And He asked His men to get a young donkey, a colt on which no one had ever ridden.

"You will find a donkey," Jesus said, "tied to a pole. Loose him, and bring him to Me. If the owner asks what you are doing with his donkey, say, 'The Lord needs him,' and then he will let you use him."

The two men went and found the donkey, just as Jesus had said they would. And the owner was willing to let him go, when he knew it was for Jesus. The two men brought the donkey back to Jesus. The people were all excited when they saw that Jesus was going to ride into Jerusalem as a King of Peace. They laid their coats on the donkey's back, and set Jesus on the animal. Some took off their coats and spread them on the ground in front of Jesus. Others ran and cut down branches from the palm trees. They waved the green branches and spread them in the way. (Today, we call this day "Palm Sunday" because of the palm branches.)

They were now nearing Jerusalem. Slowly down the mountain they came. Below them lay the beautiful city. Jesus stopped His donkey for a moment and looked down. And as He looked, He wept over Jerusalem, the beloved city of His people. "If you had only known the things which bring about peace!" He cried. "But the day is coming when your enemies will destroy your city. They will not leave one stone upon another!" Jesus meant to say that Jerusalem would be completely destroyed because they would not accept Him. CITY DESTROYED 70 A.D. BY ROMANS

But the followers of Jesus did not know what was soon to

happen. They thought that Jesus was now going to have a kingdom for them on earth. How happy they were as they sang and shouted, "Blessed is he that cometh in the name of the Lord; Hosanna in the highest!" They wanted their Heavenly Father to bless the King who had come to save His people from their sins.

Jesus passed through the city gate, still riding on the donkey. Some of the people went ahead, others followed. They kept on shouting, "Hosanna, hosanna in the highest!" The streets were full of people. Some strangers asked, "Who is this man riding on a donkey? Why are the people singing to Him?" Others, who knew Jesus, answered, "This is Jesus, the Teacher of Nazareth."

The Pharisees said to Jesus, "Master, tell your disciples to keep still."

But Jesus answered, "If I did, the very stones would cry out."

The Pharisees said to each other, "See, we do not make any impression on Him. The whole world is gone after Him!"

Then Jesus went into the Temple. He preached to the people, and they listened to Him gladly. JESUS WANTS TO BE KING OVER YOUR LIFE TOO.

Were you listening? How far was Bethany from Jerusalem? Why did Jesus want to ride a donkey? Why did the people shout to Jesus? Why would Jerusalem be destroyed?

Story 226

Chasing the Wicked from the Temple
Matthew 21; Mark 11; Luke 19

When Jesus rode into Jerusalem on that Palm Sunday long ago, He spent the rest of the day in the Temple. At evening He led His twelve disciples back to Bethany. They stayed at the home of their friends, Mary, Martha and Lazarus.

On Monday morning they traveled once more to Jerusalem. This time they went by themselves. No crowd followed them. And Jesus walked all the way.

When they reached Jerusalem, they went straight to the Temple again. Jesus did not like what He saw there. You remember that in Jesus' day, animal sacrifices were made in the Temple. Some men had set up stalls and cages for the animals and doves right on the Temple grounds. They were selling them to the people for their sacrifices. Besides, each man was supposed to bring money to the priest when he came to sacrifice. This money had to be Jewish money, for no temple dues could be paid in foreign money. So the money changers brought their tables into the temple, too.

This buying and selling, and changing of money on the Temple grounds was not wrong in itself. But the people had turned the Temple court into a wicked market place. There was much noise and loud talking. The pilgrims, who had come from far countries, were shouting angrily at the sellers, who were cheating them and making them pay huge prices for their sacrifices. And the money-changers were cheating the people, too. Besides all this, men were using the Temple grounds as a short-cut through the city on the way to the Mount of Olives. Merchants, carrying their heavy boxes of goods on their heads, pushed their way through the crowds of worshipers. It did not sound at all like a quiet House of God, where people came to worship and pray.

Jesus moved quickly among the buyers and sellers. With some small pieces of rope, which He had found, He made a whip. Then He chased all the wicked men out of the Temple. He overturned the tables of the money-changers and poured the money out on the floor. Then He tipped over the seats of those who sold doves. The men hurriedly picked up their dove cages and led their animals away. Jesus also stopped the merchants from passing through the Temple grounds with their goods. He sent them all away. And He said, "Is it not written, My house shall be called of all nations the house of prayer? But you have made it a den of thieves!"

The scribes and the chief priests were angry with Jesus because the people loved Him. They were afraid of Him and wanted to get rid of Him. But Jesus went quietly into the Temple and began to preach. He healed the blind and the lame who came to Him. Even the children crowded around Him and shouted, "Hosanna to the Son of David!"

This made the leaders still more angry. They said, "Don't you hear what these children are saying?"

Jesus answered, "Yes, I hear them. Have you never read in

the Bible, 'Out of the mouth of children and babies God has made perfect His praise'?"

Were you listening? Why was Jesus unhappy when He came into the Temple? What did Jesus do? Were there children in the Temple? What did they do?

Story 227

A Day in the Last Week

Matthew 21; Mark 12; Luke 20

Jesus had less than a week to live. He knew that the leaders of His own people were getting ready to capture Him. He wanted to spend as much time as He could in His Father's House. So, that morning, He went once more to the Temple in Jerusalem.

When they reached the Temple, Jesus sat down and taught the people. He told them several stories. He said,

"A certain man had two sons. He went to his first son and said, 'Son, go work today in my vineyard.'

"The son answered, 'No, I don't want to.' But after a while, the son was sorry he had not obeyed his father. He changed his mind and went to work in the vineyard after all.

"The father also went to the second son. 'Son,' he said, 'go work today in my vineyard.'

"The son answered, 'All right, father, I will go to work in your vineyard.' But the second son didn't keep his promise. He didn't go to the vineyard at all.

"Which of those two sons," Jesus asked, "obeyed his father?"

"The first son," they answered.

"That's right," Jesus said. "And I tell you, leaders, some of the people you call sinners will go into the kingdom of God before you. For when John the Baptist came and preached, you would not believe him. But they believed him and were forgiven."

Jesus also told this story:

"There was once a farmer who carefully planted a lovely vineyard. To protect it from robbers, he planted a big hedge around it. He dug a winepress in it, so that his grapes could be made into wine. And he built a high tower at one end, where a watchman could sit to guard the vineyard from harm.

"After the vineyard was finished, the farmer hired some workers to take charge of it for him. Then he went away to a far country to live. When autumn came and the grapes were big and ripe, the farmer sent his servants to the vineyard to get the grapes for him.

"But the workers were not kind to the servants. They would not give them the grapes. They beat up one of the servants, they killed another, and they stoned still another.

"When the farmer heard what had happened to his servants, he sent another group of servants to try to get the grapes for him. But the workers treated them the same way. They beat them up or killed them.

"Finally, the farmer said, 'I know what I will do, I will send my son, my only son. Surely, they will be kind to him and give him the grapes.'

"But when the workers saw the son, they said to each other, 'Look, here comes the son. He will be the owner of this vineyard when his father is too old. Come, let us kill him, and steal the vineyard for ourselves!' So, when the son came near, they caught him and threw him out of the vineyard, and killed him."

When Jesus finished this story, He turned to the leaders and said, "And when the farmer hears about what happened to his son, what do you think he will do to the workers in his vineyard?"

And the people answered, "Why, he will quickly destroy those wicked workers and give his vineyard to other workers who will be glad to give him the fruit when it is ripe."

"That is right," Jesus said. "And you leaders did the same thing. You would not listen to God's prophets who came to teach you how to obey God. You cast them out and stoned them. And now you are about to kill His own Son. So the Kingdom of God will be taken away from you, too. It will be given to people from other countries who will accept Me and obey My teachings."

When the chief priests and the Pharisees heard these stories, they knew that Jesus was talking about them. But they did not dare to lay hands on Him there in the Temple. They were afraid of the crowd who believed that He was a prophet.

Were you listening? Where did Jesus spend Tuesday morning of His last week on earth before He died? Why will the publicans go into the kingdom of God before the Pharisees? Why were the Pharisees like the workers in the vineyard?

Story 228

The Wedding of the King's Son

Matthew 22

Later that same morning Jesus told another story. Still talking about the kingdom of heaven, He said,

"The kingdom of heaven is like a king who made ready a wedding for his son. He sent his servants to invite the guests.

"After all the guests had been invited, the day finally came when the wedding was to be held. So the king sent his servants to the homes of the guests to tell them to come. But they would not come.

"When the servants told the king, the king sent them back again. 'Go once more,' he said, 'and tell them I have my dinner all ready, and everything is set. Tell them to please come to the wedding.'

"So the servants went back again and urged the people to come. But the guests were not interested. They just shrugged their shoulders and said, 'I'm busy.' And they went about their own work, one to his farm, another to his business. And the rest of the guests were unkind to the servants. They beat them up and even killed some of them.

"When the king heard what had happened, he was angry. He sent out his armies to kill those murderers and burn their city. Then he said to his servants, 'The wedding is ready, but those who were invited were not worthy to come. Go out now, to the highways and the busy streets. Invite anyone you find to come to my son's wedding.'

"So the servants went out and gathered together as many people as they could find, both bad and good, until, finally, the wedding hall was filled with guests. As the people entered the room, they were given a beautiful wedding robe to wear.

"After a while, the king came in to see the guests. And he saw a man who did not have on a wedding robe. That man had not been invited. He had sneaked in by the back door. The king said to him, 'Friend, how did you get in here, without a wedding robe?' And the man had nothing to say. So the king said to his servants, 'Tie him up, hand and foot, and take him away. He must be punished!' "

The Pharisees understood what Jesus meant. For they, like the first guests, would not accept Jesus' invitation to belong to the kingdom of God. And they were like the man without the wedding robe, too. For they thought they could go to heaven without a "wedding robe," which meant their hearts washed clean in Jesus' blood.

> *Were you listening?* Why would not the guests come to the wedding? Who did finally come to the wedding? Why was one man thrown out?

Story 229

A Widow's Gift

Mark 12; Luke 21; John 12

During all that morning Jesus sat in the Temple and talked with the people. For a long time He talked with the leaders about many things. They would not agree with His teachings at all. Finally, He took His disciples and sat with them in a part of the Temple, called the Court of the Women.

The treasury of the Temple was in the Court of the Women. This court was surrounded by pillars. There were thirteen money-chests beside these pillars. The opening of each chest was shaped like a trumpet. The people were supposed to drop their offerings into the trumpet-opening.

Now Jesus and His disciples sat in this court and watched to see how the people brought their gifts to the Lord. Many rich men came into the treasury and threw a great amount of money into the chests.

As they watched, a poor widow came in all alone. Her clothing was old and ragged. She looked thin and tired. To provide food and clothing for herself and her children, she had to work very hard. All the money that she had was two mites. A mite was the smallest piece of money the Jews had. It would take eight mites to make one of our pennies.

Although this widow was poor, and needed all the money she had, she loved God and wanted to show her love by giving Him something. To show how much she loved God she gave Him all that she had. She dropped both of her mites into the chest.

When Jesus saw what the woman did, He said to His disciples, "Did you see what that poor widow did? She gave all that she had to the Lord. I tell you, this widow has given more than all those rich men who came in here this morning. For all the others, even though they gave a great deal of money, gave only a small part of all that they had. And she, even though she needed it herself, gave everything that she had."

After a while some strangers came into the Temple. They were men from the faraway land of Greece. These Greeks had heard about Jesus and wanted to see Him. They went to Philip and said, "Sir, we would like to see Jesus."

Philip told Andrew, and the two of them went to tell Jesus.

Jesus explained, "Now the time has come that I am going to be glorified. Truly, I tell you, unless a grain of wheat fall into the ground and die, nothing will ever happen to it. But if it die in the ground, it will grow up into much wheat."

Then Jesus began to think about Himself, how He must first die before He could save His people. It is not an easy thing to die. Naturally Jesus was concerned about it. He said, "Now my soul is troubled. But what shall I say? Shall I ask My Father in heaven to save Me from this hour? Shall I ask Him not to let Me die? But that is why I came into this world." Then He looked up to heaven, and said, "Father, glorify Thy name."

And there came a voice from heaven, saying, "I have glorified it, and I will glorify it again."

The people standing around heard it. They said, "It thundered." Others said, "An angel spoke to Him."

Jesus answered, "This voice didn't come for My sake, but for you. Now I must die. And I, when I am lifted up from the earth, will draw all men unto Me." Jesus was thinking about the Cross when He said this. Then Jesus left the Temple and hid Himself from the people.

Were you listening? What was the treasury of the Temple? Why did the widow give more than the rich men, when she gave only two mites? How will Jesus draw all men unto Him?

Story 230

Ten Girls and Their Lamps

Matthew 25

That afternoon, Jesus once more went back to the Temple. For the last time He taught the people by telling two more stories. He first told the story of ten girls, who were called virgins. He said,

"The kingdom of heaven is like ten girls, who were invited to a wedding. This wedding was to take place at night. When the wedding night arrived, the girls made ready to meet him.

"Now, the ten young girls went down the road to meet the bridegroom, as he would come back with his beautiful bride. Since it was dark, the girls had lamps with them, but five of them were foolish, for they forgot to bring extra oil for their lamps.

"The bridegroom was long in coming, so all the girls sat down to wait. They put their lamps beside them and soon fell asleep. And while they slept, their lamps kept on burning until all the oil in them had been burned up. Then the lamps went out.

"Suddenly, at midnight, there was a cry, 'Here comes the bridegroom. Go out to meet him!' The girls quickly awoke. They looked about them for their lamps, but they were no longer burning. The five wise girls, who had brought extra oil with them, hurriedly filled their lamps and lit them. Now they were ready to join the wedding party.

"But the five foolish girls had no oil. They said to their friends, 'Please give us some of your oil, for our lamps have gone out.'

" 'We can't do that,' the wise girls answered, for then we would not have enough for ourselves. You had better go back to the city to buy oil for yourselves.'

"The five foolish girls hurried back to the city to buy oil, but while they were gone the bridegroom came. He took his bride and all their friends with him into his home for the wedding feast. And he shut the door.

"After a while, the five foolish girls arrived at the closed door of the bridegroom's home. They called, 'Lord, Lord, open the door.'

"But the bridegroom called back, 'Go away! I do not know you!' So the five foolish girls were too late for the wedding feast."

And Jesus added, "You had better watch, therefore, for you do not know the day nor the hour when I shall come again. And if you are not ready when I come, you will not be able to go with Me to My heavenly home." Jesus is the heavenly bridegroom.

> *Were you listening?* What did the ten young girls have with them? Why were five of them foolish? What does this story teach us about heaven? How can you keep your lamps burning brightly until Jesus comes?

Story 231

The Story of the Talents

Matthew 25

When Jesus finished telling the story about the ten girls at the wedding, He told another story. He began,

"The kingdom is also like a man who was traveling to a far country. When he was ready to go, he called his servants to him. 'I am going away,' he said, 'and I want you to take care of my money while I am gone.' (His money was called talents. Each talent was worth, let us say, about one thousand dollars.) He gave his first servant five talents, or five thousand dollars. He gave his second servant two talents, or two thousand dollars. And he gave his third servant one talent, or one thousand dollars.

"Then the man went off on his journey. As soon as he was gone, the first servant took his five talents and traded with them. He worked hard until he had five more talents. That made ten talents, or ten thousand dollars.

"The second servant took his two talents and traded with them. He also worked hard until he had two more talents. Then he had four talents, or four thousand dollars.

"The third servant, who had received only one talent, was

lazy. Instead of working with it, he went out and dug a hole in the ground and buried his master's money.

"After a long time, the master returned home. He called his servants to him and asked for his talents. The first servant said, 'Lord, you gave me five talents. See, I have earned five more. Now I have ten talents.'

"And the master said, 'Well done, you good and faithful servant! You have been faithful over a few things, I will make you ruler over many things. Enter into the joy of your Lord!'

"Then the second servant came. He said, 'Lord, you gave me two talents. See, I have earned two more. Now I have four talents.'

"And the master said, 'Well done, you good and faithful servant! You have been faithful over a few things, I will make you ruler over many things. Enter into the joy of your Lord!'

"Then the third servant came. He stood before his master and said, 'Lord, I knew that you were a hard man and would be angry with me if something happened to your money. So I was afraid and went and hid your talent in the ground. See, here is the talent you gave me.'

"The master answered, 'You wicked and lazy servant! If you knew that I was a hard man, why didn't you work with my money? You could at least have put it in the bank. Then you would have received interest on it.' Then he turned to another servant and said, 'Take the one talent from him and give it to the one who has ten talents. For to those who have worked with my talents shall be given more, but to those who have not, shall be taken away even that which they do have. And take the wicked servant out and punish him.'" By this story Jesus taught the importance of being faithful in our Christian lives.

When evening came, Jesus went back to Bethany to be with His friends. That night all the rulers of the Jews met together at the palace of the high priest to decide how they could capture Jesus. "We must not do it on the main Feast Day," they said, "for the people will cause a riot if we do."

While the rulers were still meeting, one of Jesus' own friends,

Judas Iscariot, one of the twelve disciples, came to them. Judas loved money and honor more than he loved Jesus. He expected Jesus to become an earthly king and rule His people from an earthly throne in a beautiful palace. Judas thought that Jesus would give him an important place in His kingdom and would make him rich. When he saw that Jesus was not interested in an earthly kingdom, Judas turned against Him.

Judas said to the leaders, "What will you give me if I capture Jesus for you?"

The men talked it over and finally agreed to pay Judas thirty pieces of silver. And Judas promised to lead them to Jesus when the crowds of people were not with Him. Now the rulers were filled with joy because they had found a way to capture Jesus. And Judas went back to the disciples. No one knew what he had done.

> *Were you listening?* What is a talent? Why was it wrong for the servant to bury his talent? What did the Jewish leaders do on Tuesday night? What terrible thing did Judas do?

Story 232

The Last Supper

Matthew 26; Mark 14; Luke 22; John 13

It was the main feast day of the Passover. It was the day when God's people ate the roasted lamb and the bread without yeast, and drank bitter herbs. This was to remind them of the night, long ago, when God took them out of Egypt.

The disciples went to Jesus and said, "Lord, where do you want us to make ready the Passover Feast for you?"

Jesus answered, "Peter and John, you go into the city (Jerusalem) and you will see a man carrying a pitcher of water. Follow him into his house. And say to him, 'The Master wants to know where your guest room is, where He may eat the Passover with His disciples.' And the man will show you a large upper room, all furnished and ready. There you can make ready the Feast."

Peter and John quickly obeyed their Master. They found the man and his room, just as Jesus had said they would. And they made ready the Passover meal. In the evening, when everything was ready, they all came to the supper. It was the custom in those days for the man of the house to meet his guests at the door with a basin of water and a towel. People always left their shoes outside the door. Then the man of the house would wash the dust off their feet.

Since the man of the house was not there, there was no one to wash the dusty feet. None of the disciples wanted to do it. So they all sat down to supper without washing their feet. John sat next to Jesus. Peter was close to John. Judas Iscariot sat across the table.

As Jesus sat down, He said, "I have been very eager to eat this last supper with you before I die." But the disciples were arguing with each other about who was to be the greatest in Jesus' new Kingdom. Their arguing did not please Jesus. He suddenly left the table. He found a towel and a basin of water, and stooping down, began to wash their feet. Jesus knelt at Peter's feet, too. Now Peter was ashamed of himself.

"No, no, Jesus!" Peter cried. "You are not the servant. You are our Master. You shall never wash my feet!" And Peter tried to pull away from Jesus.

Jesus looked at Peter. "You do not understand, Peter," He said gently, "but some day you will know that the person who loves is the person who helps. I love you and am trying to help you now."

Then Peter said, "Then don't wash my feet only, wash my hands and my head, too."

But Jesus answered, "The feet are enough to make one clean." Then He added, "But you are not all clean." Jesus was thinking of Judas. He knew what Judas had done.

When Jesus finished washing the disciples' feet, He sat down again. He knew that His disciples were sorry and ashamed. He talked kindly to them. "If you love Me, you will try to be like Me," He said. "You will also help others, as I have helped you. If you want to be the greatest in My new Kingdom, you must be the servant, just as I came to serve you."

Then they all began to eat their supper. As they ate, Jesus talked to them. He said, "Soon I am going to be killed, but woe to that man who is going to sell me to the enemy! He is sitting here at the table with Me!"

His friends were surprised and filled with sadness. They wondered who it could be. They looked at each other. They looked at themselves, and said, "Lord, is it I?" Then Peter whispered to John, who was sitting next to Jesus, "Ask Jesus who it is."

John leaned toward Jesus and whispered, "Lord, who is it?"

Jesus answered, "The one to whom I give this bread after I have dipped it in the dish, he it is." Then Jesus dipped the bread and handed it to Judas. Judas ate the bread, and then Satan entered into his heart. Jesus said to him, "What you are going to do, do quickly!" The other disciples did not know what Jesus meant. They thought that since Judas took care of their money, Jesus wanted him to buy something for the Feast; or, perhaps, give something to the poor. But Judas knew what Jesus meant. He left the table and went out into the night.

> *Were you listening?* Who was sent to get the Passover supper ready? Why did Jesus wash the disciples' feet? Who is the greatest in Jesus' Kingdom? What did Jesus know about Judas?

Story 233

The Lord's Supper

Matthew 26; Mark 14; Luke 22; John 13; I Corinthians 11

As soon as Judas had left the room where the disciples were eating the Passover Feast with Jesus, Jesus said, "Now is the Son of man (He meant Himself) glorified. And God, the Father, is glorified in Him. Little children, I shall be with you just a little while longer, and where I go you can not come. So now I give you a new rule. Love one another, as I have loved you. All the world will know that you are My disciples, if you love one another."

They were now finished with the Passover supper. Then Jesus took a piece of bread in His hands. He blessed it, and broke it in pieces. As He gave each disciple a piece, He said, "Take, eat, this is My body, which is broken for you. This do in remembrance of Me." Jesus was thinking of His own body which would be broken on the Cross.

Then Jesus took a cup of wine. He prayed, giving thanks, and

then passed the cup to the disciples. He said, "This cup is the new covenant in My blood, which is poured out for many for the forgiveness of sins. Drink ye all of it (from it). This do as often as ye drink it in remembrance of Me. Remember and believe that My blood was shed for the forgiveness of your sins. For as often as ye eat this bread and drink this cup, you will be reminded of the Lord's death until He come."

The disciples never forgot His words. Whenever they came together, they ate the broken bread and drank the poured-out wine so that they would remember how Jesus had died for them. Today, Jesus' people are still obeying His words. Many times each year they celebrate the Lord's Supper, just as the disciples did. The broken bread reminds them of Jesus' body which was broken on the Cross, and the poured-out wine reminds them of Jesus' blood which was shed on the Cross. And then they remember and believe that Jesus died for them to save them from their sins.

Today, Jesus' followers do not celebrate the Passover Feast any more. They celebrate the Lord's Supper instead. The Passover lamb was killed to save the Israelites. Jesus is our Passover Lamb, who died to save us. So we do not have to celebrate the Passover any more.

When Jesus and His disciples had finished their supper, they sang a hymn together. Then they left the house and went to the Garden of Gethsemane.

Were you listening? What did Jesus do with the bread? What does it remind us of? What did He do with the wine? What does that remind us of? Why do we celebrate the Lord's Supper?

Jesus Prays in the Garden

Matthew 26; Mark 14; Luke 22; John 13 through 18

It was evening. Jesus and His friends had just finished supper in the upper room. Judas had gone away. "Come, let us go to the Garden of Gethsemane," Jesus said. He often went to this garden with His friends.

The Garden of Gethsemane was not far away. It was on the Mount of Olives road, just outside the city. As they walked to the garden, Jesus talked about His death. "You'll be afraid," He said, "and all run away from Me tonight."

Peter quickly answered, "Even if all the others run away, I won't, Lord. I am ready to go to prison and to death with you!"

Jesus shook His head. "Peter, Peter," He said, "before the cock crows tomorrow morning, you will have said three times that you do not even know Me!"

But Peter insisted that even though he should have to die for Jesus, he would never disown Him. All the others said the same thing.

Jesus told them many things on His way to the garden. He said, "I am going to leave you soon. But in My Father's house are many beautiful mansions. If it were not so, I would have told you. I am going to make a place ready for you, so that some day you can come to be with Me, too."

Jesus also prayed a wonderful prayer. He prayed for Himself, for His disciples, and for all those who will ever believe in Him. He said, "Father, I have finished the work You asked Me to do. I have glorified You on earth, now glorify Me in heaven, as I was before I came to this earth.

"I do not pray for the world, but for those whom Thou hast given Me, for they are Mine. I do not ask that You take them out of this world, but keep them, Father. Keep them from doing wrong. Help them to do My will. And bless all those who will believe on Me. Help them all to love one another and be one big family. And Father, I would like to have all My people be where I am, so that they may see My glory!"

Finally, they came to the garden. Jesus asked His disciples to sit near the gate to wait for Him, while He went farther into the garden to pray. He took His three best friends, James, Peter and John, with Him. "I am very sad tonight," He said. He was thinking of the terrible things which were going to happen to Him. He knew that His enemies were going to hang Him on a cross. He knew, too, that it was because the people had sinned against God that He had to suffer and die for them. Jesus loved His people and was willing to die for them, but it was going to be a hard thing to do.

Jesus left His three friends. He asked them to watch with Him while He went a little farther to pray. But the disciples were tired. They soon fell asleep. While they slept, Jesus dropped down to the ground. He fell on His face and prayed earnestly. "Father, it is hard to have to die this way," He prayed. "If it be possible, do not let Me have to do it. However, not My will, but Thine be done."

Then Jesus came to His disciples and found them sleeping. He said to Peter, "What, Peter, are you sleeping? Couldn't you watch with Me for just one hour? Watch and pray, lest you fall into sin. I know you want to pray with Me, but you are so weak."

Jesus went back to pray a second time. He prayed the same way. And when He returned to the disciples, they were again asleep. Then Jesus went back a third time. He prayed still more earnestly. His soul was filled with agony. He prayed so hard that His sweat was like great drops of blood falling down to the ground. And when He finished praying, an angel came from heaven to strengthen Him.

Jesus went back to His disciples a third time. They were still asleep. He awakened them. "It is enough," He said. "The hour is here when the Son of man (Jesus) is going to be given into the hands of sinners. Come, let us go. He that sold Me to the enemy is here." And they walked back to the other disciples at the gate.

Were you listening? Why did Jesus go into the garden to pray? Why didn't His three best friends pray for Him? Who came to help Jesus?

Jesus Sold by His Friend

Matthew 26; Mark 14; Luke 22; John 18

Do you remember how Judas Iscariot went to the leaders of the Jews and promised to lead them to Jesus? And do you remember how Jesus sent Judas away from the table at the Last Supper? When Judas left his friends that night, he went back to the rulers of the Jews. Judas knew that Jesus would go to the Garden of Gethsemane after supper. He also knew that Jesus and the disciples would be alone in the garden. So he thought this would be a good time to arrest Jesus.

Judas made plans with the chief priests and the Pharisees. They gave him his thirty pieces of silver and selected a group of men and officers to go with him to the garden.

It was now late at night. Jesus had just finished praying. He came with James and Peter and John to the rest of the disciples at the gate. Just then a crowd of men entered the garden, swinging torches and carrying sticks and clubs. Judas was at the head of the crowd. Before they reached the gate, the men had asked Judas how they would know which one was Jesus. Judas had said, "I'll go up to Him and kiss Him. Then you can take Him." So Judas went up to Jesus and kissed Him. "Hail, Master," he said.

Jesus looked at Judas. "Friend, what are you doing here?" He asked. "Are you trying to sell the Son of man with a kiss?"

Then Jesus went up to the men and said, "What man are you looking for?"

"Jesus of Nazareth," they answered.

"I am Jesus," Jesus said. The men were so afraid that they stepped back and fell to the ground. So Jesus asked again, "Whom are you looking for?"

And they said again, "Jesus of Nazareth."

Jesus said, "I told you that I was He. If you are looking for Me, take Me; but let these men go their way." And He pointed to His disciples.

Then Peter drew his sword and cut off the right ear of the high priest's servant.

Jesus said, "Peter, put back your sword. Don't you know that I must die for My people? Do you think that I couldn't stop these men if I wanted to? I could pray to My Father this very minute, and He would send Me about forty thousand angels to fight for Me." Then Jesus touched the servant's ear and healed him.

Jesus turned to the crowd. Among them were the chief priests and the elders and the rulers of the Temple. He said to them, "Do you think I am a thief or a robber, that you come after Me with swords and sticks? I was in the Temple every day with you, teaching. Why didn't you take Me then?"

Then they took Jesus, bound Him and led Him away. And just as Jesus had said, the disciples did not stay with Jesus to help Him. They turned their backs on Him and ran away.

As they led Jesus away, a young man, whose name was John Mark (he wrote one of the Gospels about Jesus, and it was in his home that Jesus ate the Passover supper), followed them. Having heard all the noise, and seeing the lights in the garden, he jumped out of bed and came to see. He had grabbed a linen cloth to wrap around his body. As he followed the crowd, one of the young officers laid hold on him. But Mark, leaving the linen cloth in the officer's hands, ran away.

> *Were you listening?* Why was Judas not in the garden with the disciples on Thursday night? Why did he come later with the Jews? Why didn't Jesus want Peter to use his sword? How did Jesus' warning to the disciples come true? What happened to young John Mark?

Story 236

Peter's Great Sin

Matthew 26; Mark 14; Luke 22; John 18

When Jesus was taken prisoner, all the disciples had run away. They were afraid that the Jews might take them prisoner, too. Even Peter had left Jesus. Peter was the one who had said, "Even if they all run away, I won't!" And then, you remember, Jesus had said, "Peter, Peter, before the cock crows to tell us that it is morning, you will have said three times that you do not even know Me!" But Peter did not believe what Jesus said. He still thought he was brave.

After running away, Peter turned back and followed the crowd far behind. He wanted to see what the men were going to do to Jesus. John was following, too. He was a little ahead of Peter.

The soldiers led Jesus to the house of the high priest. First they took Him to the high priest's father-in-law, Annas. After Annas had talked to Jesus a while, he sent Him to Caiaphas, the high priest. The enemies of Jesus then held a meeting in Caiaphas' house. They hated Jesus and wanted Him to die. Some wicked men told lies about Jesus. The soldiers whipped Jesus and hit Him in the face. They laughed at Him and made fun of Him.

While these wicked men were having their meeting, John came to the house. The servant-girl at the door was a friend of his, so she let him in. A little later, Peter came to the door, too. John asked the servant-girl to let him in also. The servants had made a fire in the fireplace on the porch, for the night was cold. Peter stood by the fire to warm himself. The servant-girl looked at Peter. "You were with Jesus," she said. "Aren't you one of His friends?"

Peter was afraid. "No," he lied, "I don't even know Jesus."

A little later the servant-girl again approached Peter. Turning to Peter she said, "Aren't you one of Jesus' friends?"

"No," Peter lied again, "I don't even know Jesus."

Sometime later Peter was standing with some men around the fireplace. As he was warming himself, he began to talk with the men. One of the men abruptly said, "You talk just like that man of Galilee. You must be a friend of Jesus." Then he looked closer, and added, "Aha, didn't I see you in the garden?"

Peter shook with fear. "I don't even know Jesus!" he shouted. And he cursed and swore. Just then Jesus walked past on the way to another room. Jesus looked right at Peter. And as He looked, a cock began to crow. Then Peter remembered Jesus' words and was deeply sorry for his sin. He went out into the early morning and cried bitterly!

That same night there was another man who was sorry for what he had done. It was Judas. When he saw the leaders take Jesus away, he knew he had done a terrible thing. He knew that Jesus had never done anything wrong. Now the thirty pieces of silver in his pocket bothered him. He didn't want to keep them any longer. He went back to the rulers of his people. "Here is your money," he said. "I do not want it. I have sinned in that I have sold a good man."

"What is that to us?" the men answered. "That's your business."

Then Judas threw the money on the floor and went out.

The rulers took the money and said, "What shall we do with it? It is against our rules to put it back in the treasury since it is the money we paid for someone's blood." So they talked it over and finally decided to buy a field with it. In it they could bury strangers and those who were too poor to buy their own grave. This cemetery was called a potter's field, but the people always called it "the field of blood" because it was bought with the money given for Jesus' blood.

After leaving the high priests, Judas found himself a rope and hung himself on a tree. When the rope broke, his dead body was dashed headlong down a hill and his body broken into many pieces.

Were you listening? What was Peter's great sin? Why did he go out into the early morning and cry bitterly? What was the "field of blood"? What happened to Judas?

Story 237

Jesus Must Die

Matthew 27; Mark 15; Luke 23; John 18

Jesus lived on this earth for about thirty-three years. During all that time He went about helping others. He was kind to all who came to Him. But there were many who hated Jesus. They didn't like to have the people follow Him. They wanted to be the leaders. So they paid Judas Iscariot thirty pieces of silver to capture Him. All night long the rulers questioned Jesus to see if they could find something which He had done that they could say was wrong.

When morning came, as soon as it was light, they took Jesus to the Roman governor, Pilate. Jesus stood before Pilate. Pilate asked, "Are you the King of the Jews?"

Jesus answered, "Yes, I am, but My kingdom is not of this world."

Then the men told Pilate many bad things about Jesus which

were not true. But Jesus never said a word. Pilate turned to Jesus. "Don't you hear all the things these men are saying against you?" he asked. Still Jesus said nothing. Usually, prisoners gave Pilate many excuses, so he was amazed at Jesus.

When Pilate heard that Jesus was from Galilee, he sent Jesus to King Herod, who happened to be at Jerusalem that day. Herod was the king of Galilee. He was glad to see Jesus. Having heard about all the wonderful things Jesus had done, he hoped Jesus would perform a miracle for him. So he questioned Jesus, and the leaders again said many bad things about Him. But Jesus said nothing. Then King Herod sent Him back to Pilate.

Pilate stood before the leaders and said, "Neither Herod nor I have found anything wrong with this man. So I shall whip him and let him go."

But the people did not want to let Jesus go. Then Pilate said, "You have a custom that at the time of your Passover Feast I let one of your prisoners go. Now you have a prisoner whose name is Barabbas. (Barabbas was a robber and a murderer.) Which one shall I let go, Barabbas or Jesus?" Pilate thought this was a good way to get them to free Jesus, for Barabbas was too dangerous a man to free.

And all the people shouted, "Barabbas!"

"Then what shall I do with Jesus?" Pilate said.

The people shouted, "Let Him be crucified!"

"Why, what wrong has He done?" Pilate asked.

But the people kept on shouting, "Crucify Him! Crucify Him!"

Pilate saw that he could not persuade the people. So he took a basin of water and washed his hands in front of all the people. He said, "I am innocent of the blood of this good man. It will be your fault."

The people answered, "We don't care, let His blood be on us and our children."

Pilate was afraid to sentence Jesus to death. He knew Jesus was a good man. Pilate's wife had just sent him word telling him not to have anything to do with Jesus, "that just man." She had had a terrible dream about Him. But Pilate freed Barabbas, and had Jesus whipped with a scourge. A scourge was a leather whip loaded with pieces of metal. Such a whipping was most cruel. Men often died of it.

Pilate tried once more to see if he could get the people to free Jesus. He had his soldiers take Jesus out into the common hall. The whole band of soldiers gathered around Him. They took off His clothes and put an old, purple robe on Him. Then they made a crown of thorns and put it on His head. And they put an old stick in His right hand, as if it were a king's golden sceptre. Bowing before Jesus, they mocked Him. They cried, "Hail, King of the Jews!" They even spit on Him and hit Him on the head with the stick.

Then Pilate brought Jesus back in front of the people. Pilate pointed at Jesus. Jesus was still wearing the purple robe and the crown of thorns. Pilate said, "Behold the man!"

But the people shouted, "Crucify Him! Crucify Him!"

Pilate said, "Behold your King!"

But they answered, "Away with Him! Away with Him! Crucify Him!"

And Pilate said, "What, shall I crucify your King?"

"We have no king but Caesar," they answered.

Finally Pilate gave Jesus to be crucified. And He was led away from the judgment hall.

> *Were you listening?* Why did Pilate marvel at Jesus? Who was to be freed—Barabbas or Jesus? Why did Pilate wash his hands? Why did they put a crown of thorns on Jesus' head? What did Pilate finally do?

Story 238

Jesus Dies on the Cross

Matthew 27; Mark 15; Luke 23; John 19

PART ONE

The enemies of Jesus were happy now. They were finally going to get rid of Jesus, they thought. Then the people would forget about Jesus and follow their old leaders.

The soldiers laid a heavy wooden Cross on Jesus' shoulders. Then they led Him through the streets of Jerusalem, out into the country. But the Cross was too heavy for Jesus. He had suffered all night. His back was bleeding from the whipping. He was so weak, He stumbled and fell. A man named Simon, who came from the country of Cyrene, happened to come along. The soldiers made him carry the Cross for Jesus.

A great many people followed Jesus. There were women in the crowd, too. They felt sorry for Jesus. They cried and wept for Him. But Jesus turned to them and said, "Daughters of Jerusalem, don't weep for Me, but weep for yourselves and your children. Because this city is doing this to Me, the day will come when it will be destroyed, and the people will call on the mountains to fall on them, and the hills to cover them."

When they came to the hill of Calvary, they nailed Jesus to the Cross. Pilate put a sign above His head. It said, "Jesus of Nazareth, the King of the Jews." The words were written in three different languages. Then the Cross was raised high into the air. When the people saw the sign, they objected. They said to Pilate, "Don't write 'The King of the Jews.' Write 'He said, I am the King of the Jews.'" But Pilate would not change it.

Two other crosses were raised on Calvary that morning. Two robbers were to be crucified, too. Jesus' Cross stood in the middle, the robbers' crosses were on each side. The soldiers offered the three men a drink of wine mixed with myrrh. This was supposed to help deaden the pain. But when Jesus tasted it, He would not drink it.

Jesus was on the Cross a long time. It was nine o'clock in the morning when the Cross was raised, and it was three o'clock in the afternoon when He finally died. As Jesus looked down from the Cross, He noticed the soldiers. They were dividing His clothes among them. Each of the four soldiers got his share. But when they came to Jesus' coat, it was too good to cut up. So they cast lots (as we draw straws) to see who would get it. So one of the soldiers got the coat. Jesus was suffering great pain, but He was still thinking about others. He prayed for the soldiers and for all His enemies. He said, "Father, forgive them, for they do not know what they are doing."

PART TWO

The people, who stood watching, mocked Jesus. They said,
"If you're the Son of God, come down from the Cross." And the
rulers said, "He saved others, but He can't save Himself. If He is
the King of Israel, let Him come down from the Cross now, and
then we'll believe Him! He said He's the Son of God, He trusted
in God, then let God deliver Him." One of the robbers mocked
Him, too. "If you are the Christ, save yourself and us," he said.
But the other robber said, "Aren't you afraid of God, seeing we
are about to die? We are hanging here because we are wicked,
but this Man never did anything wrong!" Then he turned to Jesus
and added, "Lord, remember me when You get into Your kingdom." And Jesus promised, "Today, I'll take you with Me to
paradise."

Jesus' friends were also at the Cross. They wept bitterly. Oh,
how badly they felt! Jesus noticed them there. There was His
mother and His best friend, John. "John," He said, "take care
of My mother for me." After that Mary always lived with John.

At noon, it suddenly grew dark. Everyone was afraid. For
three hours Jesus suffered there alone in the darkness. Even God,
the Father, left Him. The people heard Him cry, "My God, my
God, why hast thou forsaken me?" Jesus actually suffered the tor-
tures of hell for His people.

At three o'clock it became light again. Jesus cried, "I thirst!"
The soldiers filled a sponge with vinegar and put it on a long pole.
They held the sponge to His lips and Jesus drank.

Then Jesus cried with a loud voice, "It is finished!" He cried
out once more, saying, "Father, into Thy hands I give my soul!"
Then Jesus bowed His head and died. His great suffering was
over. His work was finished. He had done what He had come
into this world to do. He had died to save His people from their
sins.

As Jesus died, God sent an earthquake. The ground trembled
and shook. The rocks were torn apart. In the cemetery, graves
were opened and many dead people came to life again. Something
happened in the Temple at Jerusalem. The veil which separated

the Holy of Holies, the holiest place, from the rest of the Temple, was torn from the top to the bottom. Now everyone could look in and see what only the high priest had ever seen before. And he had gone in only once a year. The altar and all the sacrifices would no longer be needed. Jesus was the sacrifice. He was the Lamb of God who had taken away the sins of the world!

When the captain of the soldiers saw what had happened, he was filled with fear. He said, "Surely, this was the Son of God!" The Roman captain was right, it *was* the Son of God who died on Calvary's Cross! He died for the sins of His people. He died for you and me! We now call this day *Good Friday*, and what a good Friday it was!

> *Were you listening?* Why did Jesus come into this world as a man? Why did He let the soldiers hang Him on the Cross? What would have happened to you and me if Jesus had refused the Cross? Can you name the seven sentences Jesus spoke on the Cross?

Story 239

Jesus Is Buried

Matthew 27; Mark 15; Luke 23; John 19

One of the rulers of the Jews, Joseph of Arimathaea, loved Jesus. He did not like what the rest of the rulers had done. He now went boldly to Pilate and asked if he could have the body of Jesus.

"What, is Jesus dead already?" Pilate asked. He was surprised that Jesus had died so quickly. So he called the captain of the soldiers to make sure Jesus was dead. When the captain assured Pilate that Jesus was dead, Pilate gave Joseph permission to take down the body of Jesus and bury it.

Joseph bought some fine linen cloth. Then he wrapped the body of Jesus in it.

There was another friend to help Joseph. It was Nicodemus, the one who had visited Jesus at night when it was dark. He was one of the Jewish rulers, too. He also loved Jesus and wanted to show that he was sorry for what had been done. He brought about a hundred pounds of spices and perfume to wrap inside the linen cloth around Jesus' body.

Joseph was a rich man. He owned a lovely garden which was just below the hill of Calvary. In this garden, he had a tomb (a grave) which he was saving for his own body and for the other members of his family. He now carried Jesus' body to this tomb. It was a sort of cave, cut out of the rock wall which surrounded his garden. It was a new tomb, never used before. Joseph carefully laid Jesus' body inside his tomb. In front of the mouth of the cave was a groove. There was a huge, round stone, like a wheel, standing in this groove. Joseph rolled this stone in front of the opening of the cave. Then he went home.

The women friends of Jesus, who had come with Him from Galilee, were also at the tomb. They had followed Joseph and Nicodemus as the two men carried Jesus' body down from Calvary's hill. They watched closely as Joseph buried their Lord. Then they, too, went home.

The next day was Saturday. It was the Jews' Sabbath Day. The friends of Jesus were filled with sadness. They spent the day together in the home of John Mark, where they had eaten the last supper with their Lord. How disappointed and unhappy they were. Their Lord who was going to be their King and Saviour, was dead. A dead king could not help them! They had not understood when Jesus had told them that He was going to die and then come alive again. His death was the end of everything for them. They did not even remember that Jesus had said, "And in three days I shall rise again." So they just sat in the house and wept and mourned for their lost Friend.

But the chief priests and the Pharisees did not forget Jesus' words. On that same Saturday they went to Pilate and said, "Sir, we remember that Jesus said, while He was yet alive, 'After three days I will rise again.' So, please put a guard at Jesus' tomb until the three days are past, lest His disciples come by night and steal His body away, and tell the people that He is risen from the dead. Then we would have more trouble than we had while He was alive!"

Pilate said, "You may have a guard. Go your way, make the tomb as safe as you can." So they hurried back to the tomb. They put Pilate's seal on the stone, which meant that no one was allowed to roll it away. And they commanded soldiers to sit at the tomb and watch. They wanted to make sure that this was the end of Jesus of Nazareth. They wanted to hear no more of Him!

Although they were the leaders of the Jews, how little they understood the teachings which God had given them in His Holy Word! How wrong they were!

> *Were you listening?* When did Jesus die? Why were the Jews in a hurry to take down His body? Who buried Jesus? What had the friends of Jesus forgotten? Why did the leaders of the Jews put a guard at the tomb?

Story 240

Jesus Is Alive Again

Matthew 28; Mark 16; Luke 24; John 20

The Saturday after the darkest day of their lives for Jesus' friends, finally came to an end. As the early morning light began to streak the eastern sky, things began to happen. First of all, the women made ready some sweet spices for the body of Jesus and started out for the garden. They wanted to go into the tomb where Jesus' body lay and anoint His body with the spices. The women had not had time to do this on the day Jesus died, so they wanted to do it now.

As they walked along in the early dawn they remembered that they had seen Joseph roll the heavy stone in front of the tomb. "Who will roll away the stone for us?" they asked.

But they need not have worried about the stone. God took care of that. Before the women arrived at the tomb, there was a great earthquake at the garden. The whole garden shook. Huge cracks appeared in the garden wall. And the angel of the Lord came down from heaven. He rolled the stone back into the groove, away from the door of the tomb. Then he sat on the stone. He was bright and shining. His face was like lightning, and he was dressed in clothing as white as the snow.

When the soldiers felt the earthquake, they were filled with fear. And when they saw the angel, they dropped to the ground as if they were dead. As soon as they dared, they left the tomb and ran back to the city. They went to the chief priests and told them all

456 Jesus Is Alive Again

that had happened. When the angel had opened the tomb, the soldiers had seen that the grave was empty. Jesus was not in the tomb. He had risen and gone away without anyone seeing Him!

The chief priests talked things over. They finally decided to bribe the soldiers to lie for them. Giving them large sums of money, they instructed the soldiers to say that they had fallen asleep at the tomb. While they slept the disciples had come and taken away the dead body of Jesus. "And if Pilate hears of it," the leaders promised, "we'll buy him off, so you won't be punished for sleeping while on guard." So the soldiers took the money, and spread that story around to all the people. And many believed it.

As the soldiers were running from the tomb in terror, the women entered the garden. They knew at once that something had happened. As soon as they came in sight of the tomb, they saw that the stone was rolled away. Quickly they ran to the tomb and went in. The body of Jesus was not there, but there were two angels in the tomb, sitting beside the slab of marble on which Jesus' body had lain.

When the women saw the bright, shining angels, they bowed their faces to the earth and trembled with fear. "Do not be afraid," one of the angels said. "I know that you came here looking for Jesus who was crucified. Don't look for the living in a place where the dead are supposed to be. Jesus is not here. He is risen, as He said. Don't you remember, when you were still in Galilee, how He told you that sinful men were going to crucify Him, and that on the third day He would rise again?" Then the women remembered the words of Jesus.

"Come, see the place where your Lord lay," the angel went on. "And then go quickly and tell His disciples and Peter that He is risen from the dead. Tell them that He will lead them again in Galilee. There they will see Him."

The women quickly obeyed the angel's words. Leaving the tomb with fear and great joy, they hurried to tell the disciples. But before they reached the city, while they were still on the way, Jesus met them. He greeted them with the words, "All hail!" (That is the same as if we would say, "Good morning!" or "Hello!") The women fell down at Jesus' feet and worshiped Him.

Jesus said, "Don't be afraid. Go, tell My brethren to go into Galilee. I'll see them there."

We call that wonderful day Easter because the word Easter means "new life." The ancient peoples had a god they called "Easter." She was the goddess of spring who was supposed to bring new life to the flowers and trees in the spring. We use the word "Easter" because Jesus, by dying and living again, brought new life to all His people.

> *Were you listening?* Why did the women go to the tomb? What happened in the garden at the early dawn? How did the chief priests bribe the soldiers? What was the angel's message?

Story 241

Mary Magdalene

John 20

Mary Magdalene was a special friend of Jesus. At one time Mary had been a most unhappy woman. Seven evil spirits lived in her heart. But Jesus had felt sorry for Mary. He had chased the evil spirits away. Since that wonderful day Mary had been one of Jesus' disciples. She had followed Him everywhere. She was happiest when she could be where Jesus was, and when she could be helping Him in some way.

On that first Easter morning Mary had been one of the women who had made their way to Joseph's garden. The other women were Mary, the sister of Jesus' mother; Salome, the mother of James and John; and Joanna, the wife of one of the servants of King Herod. Mary Magdalene, too, had carried spices for the body of her Friend.

When the women came into the garden and found the stone rolled away from the grave, Mary did not wait to see what had happened. She did not see the angels, nor did she hear their wonderful message. When she saw that empty grave, she was filled with sorrow and grief. She thought someone had stolen the body of her Lord. So she turned away and ran back to the city to find Jesus' friends.

As Mary Magdalene ran back toward the city, she met Peter and John, who were also on their way to the garden tomb. "Someone has taken away our Lord from the grave," she cried, "and we do not know where they have laid Him!"

Peter and John hurried to the garden. John got there first. He stooped down and looked into the tomb. By this time the women had already gone to obey the angel's words. The tomb was empty. The angels were no longer there, either. But John saw the marble slab where Jesus had lain. And he saw the linen cloths which had been wrapped around Jesus' body. Then Peter came. He went into the tomb. He too saw the linen cloths lying on the burial slab. Just as Jesus had left them, they lay still stiff with the spices. They were wrapped round and round, but the inside was hollow. Peter also saw the napkin which had been wrapped around Jesus' head. It was carefully folded and lying in a place by itself. Then John came in, too. When he saw the empty cloths, he believed that Jesus was no longer dead, but alive again. The two men went back to their home.

But Mary Magdalene came again to the garden. She stood at the empty tomb and wept, for she still believed that someone had stolen her Lord's body. As Mary wept, she stooped down and looked into the tomb. All of a sudden she saw the two shining angels. One was sitting where Jesus' head had been, the other where His feet had been. "Why are you weeping?" they asked.

"Because they have taken away my Lord, and I don't know where they have laid Him," Mary answered. As she spoke, Mary turned and noticed a man standing behind her.

"Woman, why are you weeping?" the man asked. "For whom are you looking?"

Mary, thinking the man was a gardener, answered, "Sir, if you took Him away, please tell me where you laid Him, so I can bring Him back."

But it wasn't the gardener. It was Jesus! He said just one word. He said, "Mary!"

Mary knew His kind voice at once. "Master!" she called, and fell down at Jesus' feet. She threw her arms around Jesus' feet and worshiped Him.

"Don't hold on to Me, Mary," Jesus said, "for I have not yet gone up to My Father in heaven. But go find My brethren, and tell them that I am going to go up to My Father and your Father, to My God and your God." Mary got up and joyfully ran to obey Him.

> *Were you listening?* Why did Mary Magdalene love Jesus so much? Why hadn't she seen the angels early on Easter morning? What made John believe that Jesus was no longer dead? Why must Mary no longer touch Jesus?

Story 242

Jesus Comes to His Friends

Mark 16; Luke 24; John 20; I Corinthians 15

It was late afternoon on the first Easter Sunday. Strange things had happened on that Easter Sunday. Just as it was getting light, an angel had come from heaven and had rolled away the stone from Jesus' tomb. The tomb was empty! Jesus had risen from the dead, even while the soldiers were still guarding the grave with great care.

Besides all that, the women who had gone to the garden early that morning had reported that they had seen angels who told them they must not look for Jesus among the dead, for He was alive again. Then Mary Magdalene had seen Jesus in the garden, and the women had later met Him on the road. The disciples of Jesus were troubled about all these things.

When the day was almost over, two of Jesus' friends, one whose name was Cleopas, were walking down the road. They had been in Jerusalem and were now going to their home in the little town of Emmaus, about seven miles from Jerusalem. As they walked, they talked about the strange things which had happened. They were sad and worried.

As they were walking along, a man joined them. It was Jesus, but they did not recognize Him. He said to them, "What are you talking about that makes you so sad?"

Cleopas answered, "Are you a stranger in Jerusalem? Haven't you heard what has happened these last few days?"

"What things?" Jesus asked.

Then Cleopas told Jesus all about the Cross and the empty

tomb and the angel's message. Cleopas and some of the others could not believe the women's story.

"O, you foolish men!" Jesus said. "How slow you are to believe what the prophets told you in the Bible. Didn't Christ have to suffer these things in order to enter into His glory?" Then Jesus went on to explain what the Bible tells about Himself and His death and resurrection.

Finally, the men reached their home. Jesus acted as if He were going to walk on, but the men said, "Come, stay with us. The day is almost gone, and the night will soon be here." So Jesus went in with them. Soon they sat down to supper. Jesus asked the blessing. While Jesus was praying, God made it known to the two men that their guest was Jesus. But just that quickly Jesus was gone! He disappeared out of their sight. With His new body He could come and go without having to use doors or streets. He could move about without being seen.

The men left their supper uneaten. They hurried back to Jerusalem at once. They found Jesus' friends together in the upper room of John Mark's house. "Jesus is alive again!" they shouted. "He walked with us, and ate with us!"

"Yes," the disciples answered, "He is truly risen. Peter has seen Him, too." No one knows what happened when Jesus met Peter. The last time they had seen each other, you remember, was in the home of the high priest. Then Peter had lied about Jesus and said he never knew Him. Now Jesus lovingly went to Peter alone, so He could forgive him for his great sin.

There were ten of Jesus' disciples in the upper room that Easter Sunday night. Judas was dead, and Thomas had stayed at home. The doors of the house were locked, because they were afraid the enemies of Jesus would try to arrest them as they had their Master.

All at once, Jesus was with them in the room. He had come in, even though the doors had not opened. The men were afraid when they saw Jesus. They thought He must be a ghost. Jesus did not want them to be afraid. He stretched out His hands over them and said, "Peace be unto you!" But they were still afraid. They could not believe that Jesus was real.

Jesus said, "Why are you so afraid? Don't you believe it is I?"

Then He showed them His hands and His feet. They could see the holes where the nails had gone through. He showed them the place in His side where the soldier had pierced Him with his sword. "See My hands and feet," Jesus said. "Come, touch Me, and see for yourselves that I am alive again."

The disciples came and touched their Lord. Their eyes grew big with wonder. It was hard to believe what they saw! So Jesus asked, "Have you anything to eat?" They gave Him a piece of broiled fish. Jesus ate it in front of them all, so they could be certain that He was truly alive. A ghost would not eat. Then the disciples believed and were filled with joy.

Jesus blessed them again and talked with them a long time. He told them many things. "As My Father sent Me into the world, even so send I you," He said. Jesus came into the world to die for His people. Now He was going to send His disciples to all the world to tell them how He died and rose again, so that others, too, could learn to love Him.

"I am going back to My Father in heaven," Jesus went on. "My work here is finished. You wait here until I send My Spirit to live in your hearts, then go and teach all nations. Lo, I will be with you always, even to the end of the world!"

When Jesus finished talking to His friends, He disappeared again. He did not use the doors or windows. He went without being seen. What a wonderful Saviour He is!

Were you listening? Who was the first person to see Jesus alive again? Who saw Him at supper in Emmaus? Who saw Him still later in the upper room?

Story 243

Thomas

John 21

When Jesus showed Himself to His disciples that first Easter night, Thomas was not there. He hadn't heard the women's message. He didn't see his Lord. Thinking that Jesus was still dead, Thomas was filled with sadness and despair. He thought the Kingdom of God would never come now.

Not long after that Easter Sunday, Thomas met some of the

disciples. They were happy and joyful. "We have seen the Lord," they shouted, "He is alive again!" But Thomas would not believe them. Sadly he shook his head.

"No," Thomas said, "I don't believe you. Jesus is dead. Unless I can see the nail-prints in His hands and feet, and touch them with my fingers; and unless I can see the hole in His side, and can put my hand in the hole, I won't believe!"

A week later, it was now eight days since Easter, the disciples were once more in the upper room. This time Thomas was there, too. The doors were again shut to keep out any enemies. All at once, Jesus stood in the midst of them. He held His hands over them and blessed them. "Peace be unto you," He said.

Then Jesus looked at Thomas. "Come here, Thomas," He said. Thomas went to Jesus. Jesus held up His hands. There were the nail-prints. "Reach out your fingers, Thomas, and touch the nail-prints," Jesus said. Then He opened His coat. There was the hole the sword had made. "Put your hand in My side, Thomas," Jesus went on. "And don't doubt any more, just believe."

Then Thomas was ashamed of himself. He knelt at Jesus' feet and said, "My Lord and my God!"

Jesus said, "Because you have seen Me, Thomas, you believe. Blessed are they who have not seen and yet have believed!"

The Bible gives us this story of Thomas so that we, too, may believe that Jesus is alive. So that we, too, may serve a risen Saviour! Jesus was thinking of you and me when He said those words. We cannot see the holes in Jesus' hands and feet, nor the hole in His side, but we can know that Jesus is alive and is our Saviour.

> *Were you listening?* Why were the doors of the upper room closed? How did Jesus get in? What made Thomas believe that Jesus was alive again? Why do you believe that Jesus is alive?

Story 244

By the Sea of Galilee

John 21

One day, several of Jesus' friends were together by the Sea of Galilee. Peter was there, and Thomas, and Nathanael, and James and John, and two other disciples. They were wandering

about aimlessly, wondering what to do. Peter noticed his boat tied near the shore. "I think I shall go fishing," he said.

"We'll go with you," the other men answered. So they all got into Peter's boat. They rowed to a good spot out on the lake and began to fish. They stayed there all night, but they caught nothing.

When it began to get light, they noticed a man standing on the shore. "Children," the man called, "did you catch any fish?"

"No," they called in answer.

"Throw your nets on the right side of the boat," the Stranger called back, "and then you'll find some fish."

The men hurried to obey. At once their net was so full of fishes they couldn't pull it up. When the men saw all the fish, John said to Peter, "It must be Jesus!" Peter quickly pulled his fisher's coat about him and swam to shore. The other men followed with the boat, dragging the net of fishes behind them.

When they came to the land, they noticed that Jesus had breakfast all ready for them. There were fish frying on the fire, and there was bread. "Bring some of the fish you caught," Jesus said.

Peter went to the boat and dragged the net ashore. He counted the fish. There were one hundred and fifty-three large fish! And the net had not even broken!

Then Jesus said, "Come and eat." The men all came and had breakfast with Jesus. He gave them bread and fish. This was now the third time that Jesus had shown Himself to His disciples. And none of them dared ask Him, "Who are you?" For they knew it was the Lord.

After breakfast, while they were still sitting around the fire, Jesus turned to Peter and said, "Simon Peter, do you love Me more than these other friends?"

Now Peter was the man, you remember, who had denied Jesus that night in the house of the high priest. Three times Peter had been ashamed to show his love for his Lord. Three times he had lied about it. And so, in front of all these friends, Jesus asked Peter this question.

Peter was sorry for what he had done. He answered, "Yes, Lord, You know that I love You."

Jesus said, "Feed my lambs."

A second time Jesus asked, "Simon Peter, do you love Me?"

Again Peter answered, "Yes, Lord, You know that I love You."

Jesus said, "Feed my sheep."

Once more, for the third time, Jesus asked, "Simon Peter, do you love Me?"

Peter was sad because Jesus had asked him this question three times. He said, "Yes, Lord, You know everything. You know that I love You."

Again Jesus said, "Feed my sheep."

Three times Peter had denied his Lord. Three times now he said that he loved his Saviour. Now he could be Jesus' helper again. Never again was Peter ashamed of Jesus. He worked for Him all his life. He even died for Him!

When Jesus worked with His disciples, He had called them "fishers of men." It was their task to draw men to Jesus just as fishermen drew fish to themselves in their nets. Now that Jesus' work was finished and He was ready to go back to His heavenly home, He gave His disciples a new task. From now on, they must not only be "fishers of men," getting people to come to Jesus, they must also be "shepherds," and take care of the people who come to Jesus, just as a shepherd takes care of the sheep.

> *Were you listening?* Where did Jesus meet with His disciples one day? How many times had the disciples seen Jesus since He was alive again? Who helped the disciples catch fish? Why did Jesus ask Peter about his love?

Story 245

Jesus Goes Back to Heaven

Mark 16; Luke 24; Acts 1

Jesus is God. His home is up in heaven with God, the Father. Jesus is also man. He came into this world to save His people from their sins. He died on the Cross and rose again on Easter morning. He then stayed on the earth for forty more days. He showed Himself to all His friends — to Mary Magdalene who couldn't find His body on Easter morning, to Peter who had been ashamed of his Lord, to Thomas who wouldn't believe that

He was alive. He ate breakfast with them one morning by the seashore and helped them catch fish. But Jesus did not live with His friends any more. Sometimes they saw Him, sometimes they didn't know where He was.

When it was time for Jesus to go back home to His Heavenly Father, He led His friends out of Jerusalem to the top of the Mount of Olives. Not far from Bethany, this was the same hill over which He had ridden on His donkey on Palm Sunday. Here Jesus talked with His friends for the last time. He told them many things.

Jesus said, "All power is given Me in heaven and on earth. Go ye, therefore, and teach all nations, baptizing them in the name of the Father, and of the Son, and of the Holy Spirit. Lo, I am with you alway, even unto the end of the world!"

Then Jesus promised to send the Holy Spirit to live in their hearts. "You wait in Jerusalem," He said, "until the Holy Spirit comes into your hearts. Then you must go to all the world and tell everyone about Me, so that men may turn away from their sins and love Me."

When Jesus finished talking, He held His hands over His friends and blessed them. As He was blessing them, He began to rise slowly into the air. His feet left the ground, and He went up, up into the sky. The disciples kept their eyes on Jesus and watched Him go up. He rose higher and higher until a bright cloud came and hid Him from sight. They kept on looking, but they couldn't see Jesus any more.

While the disciples were still looking up into the sky, two angels in shining white came and stood by them. "Ye men of Galilee," they said, "why are you standing there looking up into heaven? This same Jesus, whom you saw going up to heaven, shall come again some day, on the clouds of heaven, as you saw Him go up."

Although the disciples could no longer see their Saviour, they were filled with great joy. They worshiped Jesus. He was now their King! He was sitting on His throne at the right hand of God, the Father! No longer was He a lowly, humble man who had walked the streets of Galilee as a poor carpenter's son. He was now a mighty King who had gone out to do battle against His great enemy, Satan. And He had come home a victor!

No wonder the disciples were filled with joy. They went back to Jerusalem to wait for the coming of the Holy Spirit, as Jesus had commanded. They knew that Jesus would be with them as He had promised, even though they could not see Him. And they knew, too, that He would some day come again to take them with Him to His happy home in heaven.

> *Were you listening?* Who is your King? Where is He now? What is He doing in heaven? Why is He a victor? Can He see you at this very moment?

Story 246

Jesus Sends His Spirit

Acts 1 and 2

Jesus had gone to heaven. His twelve disciples were still waiting in Jerusalem. Now they were to be called apostles because they were going out to preach about Jesus. They were waiting for Jesus to send His Holy Spirit as He had promised. While they waited they had chosen Matthias to be the twelfth apostle in the place of Judas. They spent most of their time in the upper room of John Mark's house, where they had eaten the last supper with Jesus.

Ten days had passed since Jesus had gone to heaven. It was Sunday morning. A great many people were gathered together with the apostles in the upper room. There were one hundred and twenty people in all, including the women who had been friends of Jesus — Mary Magdalene, Salome, and Mary the mother of Jesus.

Suddenly, there came a sound from heaven. It sounded like a strong, rushing wind. The noise filled the house. And there came little tongues, as of fire, from heaven, and rested on the head of each one in the room. This was a sign to show that the Holy Spirit had come into their hearts. At once, they all began to preach about Jesus. They talked in different tongues, which they had never been able to do before. The Holy Spirit was telling them what to say.

It was a feast day in Jerusalem that day, and there were Jews from all the different nations of the world there. When they heard what was happening in that upper room, they all came to see. They were amazed to hear these men talking their own language. "Are not all these men from Galilee?" they asked. "What does this mean?"

Some of the men mocked. They said, "Oh, these men are filled with new wine, they are drunken!"

But Peter stood up and said, "Listen to me! We are not drunken. We are filled with the Holy Spirit! God told you this would happen in His Holy Word.

"This Jesus of Nazareth, whom you hung on a cross and killed, is the Son of God. You saw all the wonderful things He did when He was with you. When you killed Him with your wicked hands, God raised Him up. Death could not hold Him, He became alive again! This same Jesus is now Lord and Christ. And it is His Spirit which is in our hearts!"

When the people heard Peter's words, they were afraid. "Men and brethren, what shall we do?" they asked.

Peter answered, "Repent, tell God you are sorry for what you did. Then be baptized, every one of you, in the name of Jesus Christ. Then He will forgive your sins, and you will also receive the Holy Spirit."

All those who believed Peter's words were baptized. They became members of Jesus' new church. There were about three thousand people who were baptized that day.

Were you listening? What did Jesus tell His disciples to do at Jerusalem? What were the disciples now called? What did the rushing wind and the tongues of fire mean? How many people joined Jesus' new church that day?

Story 247

The Lame Man Healed

Acts 3

Jesus' own work on earth was now finished. He had gone back to His heavenly home to sit at the right hand of His Father forever. But His work on earth went on, for Jesus was still present with

His apostles, even though they could not see Him. His Spirit was in their hearts. With the Spirit's help, the apostles obeyed Jesus' last words to them. They went out into all the world to preach the Gospel. Jesus had said they should begin at Jerusalem. Then they should go to Samaria, and then farther and farther away, until all the nations of the world had heard the wonderful story.

Each day the apostles went into the Temple at Jerusalem and preached about Jesus. One day, as Peter and John were going into the Temple, they passed through the gate called "Beautiful." A lame beggar was lying at the gate. This beggar had been lame ever since he was a baby. Every day his friends carried him to the Temple and laid him at the Beautiful Gate. Here the poor man would sit from morning until night, begging money from those who passed the gate to go into the Temple.

As Peter and John walked by, the lame beggar called to them, asking for money. The two men stopped. "Look at us," Peter said. The lame man held out his little cup, expecting them to give him some money. Peter shook his head. "I do not have any silver or gold (money)," he said, "but what I do have I will give you. In the name of Jesus Christ of Nazareth, rise up and walk."

Peter took the lame beggar by the right hand and lifted him up. At once the beggar's feet and ankles became strong. He leaped up, and stood, and walked! He came into the Temple with Peter and John, walking, leaping and praising God!

When the people saw them, they all crowded around. They were filled with wonder and surprise. Peter said, "Why are you so surprised at this? Why do you look at us as if we, ourselves, made this man to walk? God, our Father, hath glorified His Son, Jesus, whom you killed. You chose a murderer instead of Jesus. You killed the Prince of Life, but God raised Him up. It is this Jesus who made this lame man strong."

Then Peter went on, saying, "I see you didn't know that Jesus was the Son of God. Tell God you are sorry. Ask Jesus to wash away your sins and believe on Him. He will save you!"

Many who heard Peter's words, believed. But the rulers in the Temple didn't want to believe in Jesus. They put Peter and

John in prison over night. The next morning they brought them to a meeting. "Where did you get your power to heal this lame man?" they asked.

Peter told them again about his wonderful Saviour. "There is no other name under heaven, given among men, whereby we must be saved," he said.

The rulers were surprised at the boldness of Peter and John. They knew that Peter and John had been only poor, ignorant fishermen. "You can see that they have been with Jesus," the rulers said. But when they saw the lame man walking, they could say nothing against it. They could see that it was a miracle.

Then the rulers held a meeting to decide what they should do with Peter and John. They realized now that killing Jesus hadn't solved their problem. Now there were twelve men doing the work that just one (Jesus) had done before! So they called Peter and John and commanded them never to speak or teach in the name of Jesus again.

But Peter and John answered, "Whether it be right for us to listen to you rather than to God, you decide. But we cannot help but talk about the things we have seen and heard."

After threatening Peter and John again, the rulers finally let them go. They were afraid to punish Peter and John since the people were all glorifying God because of the miracle. Then Peter and John went back to the other apostles and told them what had happened. They all praised God and asked Him to give them courage to speak in Jesus' Name and to work miracles for Him. When they finished praying, the whole room shook. The Holy Spirit filled them all again. And they went out unafraid, speaking with boldness.

Were you listening? Who sat each day at the gate Beautiful? What did Peter give him? What did Peter tell the people? Why did the leaders put Peter and John in prison?

"Thou Shalt Not Lie"

The new church, which started after Jesus went back to heaven, grew rapidly. Thousands of people met with the apostles every week. They were all filled with joy and showed it by being kind to each other. Those who had plenty shared with those who were in need. Many who owned land or houses sold their property and brought the money to the apostles. One rich man, Barnabas, sold all his land and brought the money to the apostles.

But there was another man whose name was Ananias. He and his wife, Sapphira, owned some land, too. They wanted the people of the church to think that they were as kind as Barnabas. But they loved their money and really wanted to keep it for themselves. What a time they had deciding what to do. Finally they sold the land and gave only part of the money to Peter, keeping the rest of it for themselves. But they did not tell Peter that it was only part of the money. He must think that they were kind enough to give all of their money.

When Ananias laid half of the money at Peter's feet, Peter just looked at the selfish man. The Holy Spirit had told him what Ananias had done. "Is this all the money you received for your land?" Peter asked.

"Yes, that is all the money," Ananias answered.

"Ananias," Peter said, "why did you listen to Satan and lie to the Holy Spirit? Why did you keep back part of the money? It was all your own money. You could have done as you pleased with it. Why did you lie about it? You didn't lie against me, you lied against God!"

When Ananias heard Peter's words, he fell dead at Peter's feet. Some young men came, wrapped him up and carried him out of the church to bury him. Everyone who heard about it was filled with fear.

That afternoon Sapphira came into the church. She didn't know anything about what had happened to her husband. Perhaps she came to look for him. As soon as Peter saw her, he said, "Tell me, Sapphira, how much money did you get for your land? Was it so much?" And Peter mentioned the amount of money Ananias had brought.

"Yes," Sapphira answered, "that's how much money we got for our land."

Peter shook his head. "How is it," he said, "that you agreed together to cheat the Lord? Listen and you can hear the footsteps of the men who just buried your husband. The young men are at the door, and they will bury you, too."

When Sapphira heard Peter's words, she also fell dead at Peter's feet. The young men carried her out and buried her next to her husband.

All the people who heard about what happened to Ananias and Sapphira were filled with great fear. They never forgot what happens to people who try to cheat God by trying to make themselves look better than they really are. God wants His people to be honest and truthful.

> *Were you listening?* Why was Barnabas a good man? What did Ananias and Sapphira want to do? What did they do that was wrong and why did God punish them the way He did?

Story 249

The Apostles Persecuted for Doing Good

Acts 5

The new Christian church kept growing and growing. Hundreds of men and women were added to the church each day. The apostles went about among the people working many signs and wonders, as Jesus had done. Peter was very busy healing the sick. The people finally brought their sick friends on beds and laid them along the streets. They hoped that as Peter walked down the street his shadow would fall on some of them and they would be healed. And they were not disappointed. God helped Peter to heal every one!

But the high priest, and all the leaders of the Temple, were jealous of the apostles. They did not like it that the apostles were carrying on Jesus' work. Finally they succeeded in putting them all in prison. During the night, however, the angel of the Lord opened the doors of the prison and brought the apostles out. "Go back to the Temple tomorrow morning," the angel said, "and preach to the people the Words of Life."

Early the next morning, the apostles went back to the Temple and began to preach. The high priest thought the apostles were still in prison. He sent for the prisoners.

The officers came back and said, "We found the prison all safely locked. The keepers were standing outside the doors. But when the doors were opened, there was no one inside."

The leaders wondered what had happened. Then a man came into the room. He said, "The men whom ye put in prison are standing in the Temple, teaching the people."

The soldiers went to the Temple to get the apostles. They did not dare take the apostles by force, however. They were afraid the people would stone them. So the soldiers asked the apostles to come along. And the apostles came.

The high priest said to the followers of Jesus, "Didn't we command you not to teach in Jesus' Name? Now you have filled Jerusalem with your teaching!"

Peter answered for himself and the other apostles, "We ought to obey God rather than men. The God of our fathers raised up Jesus, whom ye slew and hanged on a tree. But God exalted Him to be a prince and a Saviour to give forgiveness of sins to Israel. We are His witnesses, and so is the Holy Spirit, whom God has given to those who obey Him."

When the leaders heard these words, they were filled with anger and wanted to kill the apostles. But Gamaliel, one of their great lawyers and teachers, stood up and said, "Be careful what you do with these men! Leave them alone. For, if their work is only of men, it will soon be forgotten. But if it is of God, you won't be able to stop it. You cannot fight against God."

The leaders listened to Gamaliel. They agreed to do as he said. But they warned the apostles not to preach in Jesus' Name. Then they beat the men and let them go. The apostles went away happy to be able to suffer for Jesus' sake.

> *Were you listening?* Why were the apostles so busy? What could
> Peter do with his shadow? Why were the apostles put into prison?
> Why were the apostles happy?

Stephen Gives His Life for Jesus

Acts 7

Taking care of all the people who were members of the new church kept the apostles busy all day long. It took so much time to do all the work for the church that there was little time left for preaching. So Peter called the people together.

"We need help," he said. "We must have someone to visit the sick and to take care of the poor. Jesus told us, His apostles, to preach and pray." So they chose seven good men to be the apostles' helpers. These men were called deacons.

One of these deacons was Stephen. Stephen was a good man who worked hard for Jesus. He helped take care of the poor and visited the sick. Jesus gave Stephen the power to pray for the sick and make them better. Stephen did many wonderful things. He also found time to preach about Jesus. Many people believed in Jesus after they had listened to Stephen.

But the leaders became angry at Stephen for teaching the people to believe in Jesus. They caught him and put him on trial. Some men stood up and lied about Stephen. "He is a wicked man," they said. "He says wicked things about God's House and about God's Holy Word." While the men were telling these lies, the people looked at Stephen. His face was bright and shining like an angel's.

Then the high priest asked Stephen, "Are these things true?" And Stephen stood up before his enemies and began to preach about Jesus.

"God loved your fathers," Stephen began, "but they would not obey His Word. They even killed the ministers God sent them. Now you men are just as bad as your fathers were. You would not listen to God's ministers, either. And when God sent His own Son, you hanged Him on the Cross!"

When the men heard Stephen's words, they were filled with rage. They gnashed their teeth. But Stephen wasn't afraid. Looking up into heaven, he saw God in all His glory, sitting on His throne. He saw Jesus Christ standing at God's right hand.

Stephen cried out, "Behold, I see the heavens opened. And I see Jesus, the Son of man, standing on the right hand of God!"

This made his enemies even more angry. Shouting loudly, they stopped up their ears so they could not hear what Stephen was saying. They dragged Stephen down from the platform and out into the street. Outside the city, they began to throw stones at him. A young man named Saul took charge of their coats which they took off so that they could better throw the stones.

Stephen fell on his knees, praying to God. He prayed the same prayer Jesus had prayed for His enemies. "Lord," he said, "do not blame these men for stoning me." Even as he was praying, "Lord Jesus, receive my spirit," he died. Stephen gave his life for the Lord whom he loved and served. He was the first person to die for Jesus. We call him the first Christian martyr. Most of the apostles became martyrs, and, throughout the ages, many other Christians have been martyrs for Jesus. But Stephen was the first one.

Were you listening? Why did the apostles choose deacons? Why didn't the Jewish leaders like Stephen? What did they do to him? Who held their coats? What is a Christian martyr?

Story 251

The Magician Who Tried to Buy God's Power

Acts 8

The Pharisees hated the followers of Jesus. After they had killed Stephen, they tried with all their power to stop the apostles from preaching. Saul, the young man who had held the leaders' coats, was one of the worst persecutors. He went into every house where he thought there might be people worshiping and praying to Jesus. And he put many in prison.

Although the apostles stayed in Jerusalem, many of the people fled to other cities. And it was a good thing they did, for wherever they went, they brought the story of Jesus. In that way many more people were brought into Jesus' new church.

The apostles had chosen seven deacons, you remember, to help them with their work. Stephen, the first martyr, was one of the deacons. Philip was another. When many of Jesus' followers had fled to Samaria, Philip went down there to be their minister. He also preached to the Samaritans. God helped Philip to heal many sick people and work miracles, as Jesus had done. He brought great joy to Samaria.

A few years earlier Jesus had visited Samaria. He had talked to the woman at the well and she had brought the people of the city to Him. The people had been interested in His teachings and had asked Him to stay for a few days. Most likely these people remembered the kind of Man who had visited their city. Now they listened gladly to Philip as he taught them about this same Jesus. They believed that Jesus was the Messiah who had come to save them from their sins. After being baptized, they became a part of Jesus' new church.

But there was a certain magician in Samaria, a man named Simon. His many tricks fooled the people. He had pretended that he was a great man sent from God. For many years the people had believed that this man was a man of God who could do wonderful things. They honored him, and said, "This man has great power of God."

But when Philip came into their city and taught them about Jesus Christ, they no longer believed in Simon's magic. They believed in Jesus instead. And even Simon himself, when he heard Philip and saw him heal the sick, believed in Jesus, too. After he was baptized, Simon followed Philip wherever he went. All the things Philip said and did amazed him.

Back in Jerusalem, the apostles heard the good news that the people of Samaria were believing in Jesus, too. They sent Peter and John to visit the Samaritans. Now the Samaritans had been baptized in Jesus' Name, but they had not received the Holy Spirit in their hearts. So, when Peter and John came, they prayed for the new Christians and asked God to give them the Holy Spirit. The two apostles laid their hands on the people. Then God sent the Holy Spirit into their hearts.

Simon the magician watched all this with interest. He wondered as he saw these people receive the Holy Spirit when Peter and John laid their hands on them. Never had he been able to do anything like this! Thinking it was just magic, he wished he could do it, too. He went to Peter and John and offered them money to teach him how to do it.

"Let me buy this power, too," he said, "so that when I lay hands on people they will receive the Holy Spirit."

Peter frowned on Simon. "May you and your money perish!" he cried. "You cannot buy the Holy Spirit! It is a gift of God. You are not a follower of Jesus, if that is what you think. Your heart is not right with God. Be sorry for your wickedness and ask God to forgive your sin."

Simon was filled with fear. "Pray God for me," he begged, "so that I shall not perish, as you said." He saw now that God's power was not magic as his tricks had been.

Were you listening? Who was Philip? Why did he go to Samaria? Who was Simon? What terrible thing did he do?

Story 252

Philip Helps the Ethiopian

Acts 8

After Peter and John had left Samaria to go back to Jerusalem, Philip remained in Samaria to take care of the new church there. One day an angel visited him. The angel said, "Go, Philip, and walk on the road to Gaza." That was all.

The road to Gaza runs through a desert, a dry, sandy place where few people lived. Philip must have wondered why God was sending him away from busy Samaria, where he could do so much good, to the lonely desert. But he obeyed the angel, for he knew Jesus had sent him.

So Philip walked along the desert road as the angel had commanded. Ahead of him he noticed a fine chariot in the road. A man was riding in the chariot. He was a leader in a country called Ethiopia, where black people lived. His queen, Candace, had put him in charge of everything belonging to her. From his far-away home he had come to the Temple in Jerusalem to pray and to worship the true God. Now he was on his way home.

As he rode along, he was reading from God's Holy Word, the Bible. His Bible did not look like ours today. It was a scroll —a long piece of paper, rolled up on a wooden roller. When a person read from a scroll he unrolled the paper as he went along.

God's Spirit said to Philip, "Go near this chariot." So Philip ran and caught up with the chariot. He listened to the man reading aloud from the Bible. "Do you understand what you are reading?" Philip asked.

"How can I understand," the man answered, "if no one tells me what it means?" And he begged Philip to come up and sit with him in the chariot.

The man was reading about Jesus, our Saviour. He was reading what Isaiah, a prophet, said about how the enemies of Jesus would hurt Him when they killed Him. Isaiah had written, "He was led like a sheep to be killed; and like a lamb who does not cry out when they cut his wool, so he opened not his mouth."

"Who is this man the prophet is writing about?" he asked. "Is the prophet talking about himself or someone else?"

So Philip told the man all about Jesus. He told how God had sent His own Son to die on the Cross to save His people from their sins. The man listened to every word and God helped him to believe in Jesus.

The chariot had been moving along all the while Philip was talking. Just then they rode past some water. The man said, "See, here is water. Why can't I be baptized?"

"You may," Philip answered, "if you believe in Jesus with all your heart."

"I do believe that Jesus is the Son of God," the man said.

So the man told his servants to stop the chariot. Then he and Philip went down into the water. Philip baptized the man. When they came up out of the water, Philip was gone. The Holy Spirit had caught him away, and brought him to another city to preach. But the Ethiopian went home with a happy heart, for Philip had taught him to believe in Jesus, the Saviour.

Were you listening? Why did Philip leave Samaria? Who was riding in the chariot? What did Philip teach him? What happened at the water?

Saul Turns to Jesus

Do you remember the young man, Saul, who held the coats for the men who stoned Stephen? Saul had become one of the worst enemies of the Christians. All day long he was out capturing the followers of Jesus and locking them up in prison. He wanted to make all the Christians stop loving Jesus. If the Christians would not forget Jesus, then he wanted to kill them. Saul wanted to destroy the church of Jesus.

Saul thought he was doing a good work for God. He thought that God would be pleased if Jesus' followers were captured. Saul did not believe that Jesus was God's Son. When he heard that there were Christians far away in the city of Damascus, Saul went to the high priest.

"Give me a letter which says I may catch the Christians in Damascus," he said. "I shall bind them with chains and bring them back to Jerusalem."

So the high priest gave Saul the letter. Soon he rode away with his servants. Day after day they traveled until they came near to the big city of Damascus. Suddenly a bright light began to shine around Saul. He fell to the ground and covered his face with his hands. The light was too bright to look at. Then he heard a voice saying, "Saul, Saul, why are you fighting against Me?"

"Who are you, Lord?" Saul cried in fear.

"I am Jesus, whom you are trying to hurt."

Saul began to tremble and shake. "Lord, what do you want me to do?" he asked.

Jesus answered, "Get up and go into the city. You will be told what you must do."

The men who were with Saul were terribly afraid. They heard Jesus' voice, but they could not see Him. When Saul arose and opened his eyes, he found that he was blind. His servants had to lead him by the hand and bring him into Damascus.

Saul's servants took him to a house belonging to a man named Judas. Here Saul stayed for three days. All that time he could not see nor did he eat or drink. He spent all his time in prayer, asking Jesus to guide him.

There lived in Damascus a Christian whose name was Ananias. One day God came to him and called, "Ananias."

"Here I am, Lord," he answered.

"Go, Ananias," God said, "and find the house in Straight Street, where Saul is staying. I have shown him in a dream that you will lay your hands on him so that he may see again. Behold, he is praying."

But Ananias was afraid of Saul. He had heard about Saul and he knew why he had come to Damascus. So Ananias said, "Lord, I have heard many bad things about this man. I have heard of all the wicked things he has done to Your people in Jerusalem. And I know that now he has come here with chains to capture all those who worship You."

But Jesus answered, "Don't be afraid, Ananias. Go ahead and do as I said. For Saul is now a changed man. He is going to be a great missionary for Me to all the countries of the world and even to kings. He will now suffer, too, for My name's sake."

So Ananias went to find Saul. When he found Saul at Judas' house, he went in and laid his hands on him. He said to him, "Brother Saul, Jesus has sent me so that I may make you see again, and so that His Spirit may live in your heart."

And at his words something like scales fell from Saul's eyes. He could see again! Saul got to his feet and was baptized. Now he loved Jesus with all his heart. He began at once to preach about Jesus in the churches of the Jews in Damascus, telling everyone that Jesus was the Son of God.

How surprised the people were! They said, "Is not this the man who killed the Christians in Jerusalem and came here for that same purpose?"

Some of the Jews in Damascus made plans to kill Saul. They set a guard to watch for him at the gates of their city day and night. But the Christians heard about it and helped Saul escape. Putting Saul in a big basket, they let him down outside the city wall. As soon as he reached the ground, Saul hurried toward Jerusalem. He tried to join himself to the Christians there, but they were afraid of him. They would not believe that he was now one of Jesus' followers. But finally, one of the leaders, Barnabas, took Saul and brought him to Peter. He told Peter how Jesus had changed Saul. That is how Saul, too, became one of Jesus' disciples.

Were you listening? What was Saul going to do in Damascus? What happened on the way? What great work did Jesus have for Saul?

Story 254

Peter Works Miracles for Jesus

Acts 9

The new church of Jesus Christ grew and grew. Many people in Jerusalem learned to love the Lord, and people became Christians in all parts of Judea, Galilee and Samaria. In all these places those who loved the Lord gathered together to form a new church. Peter moved here and there among them, visiting the new churches.

It so happened on one of his visits that Peter came to the church at Lydda, which was not far from the Mediterranean Sea. There he found a man called Aeneas, who had been paralyzed for eight years. Aeneas could not walk.

"Aeneas," Peter said, as he stood beside the man's bed, "Jesus Christ makes you better! Get up and make your bed!"

Aeneas believed Peter's words. He stood right up. Just that quickly he was cured. Jesus had made him well! When the people of Lydda heard about Aeneas, they believed in the Lord, too.

Not far from Lydda was a place called Joppa. Joppa was right on the seacoast. In Joppa there lived a lady whose name was Dorcas. Dorcas loved God and was always showing her love for God by doing kind things for people. She spent much of her time sewing dresses and coats and other clothing for the poor people.

While Peter was in Lydda, Dorcas became sick and died. Her friends were all filled with sadness.

When these people heard that Peter was in Lydda, they sent two men to him, begging him to come at once. Peter returned to Joppa with the two men. When he reached the home of Dorcas, the people took Peter up to the room where Dorcas was lying.

The room was filled with people. When the widows and the other poor people whom Dorcas had helped saw Peter, they showed him all the things Dorcas had made for them. They cried as they talked about her.

Then Peter sent all the people out of the room. He knelt down and prayed that God would give Dorcas her life back again. Then Peter stood up, his prayer finished. Turning toward the dead body he said, "Tabitha, arise."

At once, Dorcas opened her eyes. When she saw Peter, she sat up. Then Peter gave her his hand and helped her up. Calling all the people into the room, he gave Dorcas back to them alive.

Soon everyone in Joppa heard what Peter had done for Dorcas. And many people believed in Jesus.

> *Were you listening?* What did Peter do in Lydda? What miracle did he work in Joppa? How could Peter work miracles?

Story 255

Peter Is Sent to Help the Roman Soldier

Acts 10

Peter lived in Joppa for some time. He stayed at the home of a man named Simon. Simon lived right next to the sea. Because of the work he did, Simon was called a tanner. He made leather out of the skins of animals.

Up the coast of the Mediterranean from Joppa, was a town called Caesarea. There lived a man named Cornelius. Cornelius was a captain of a hundred Roman soldiers. Although he was not a Jew, Cornelius loved God and prayed to Him every day.

One afternoon an angel came to Cornelius. "Cornelius," the angel said, "God has heard your prayers. He knows that you give much to the poor. In Joppa lives a man named Peter. God wants you to send for him. Peter is living with Simon, the tanner, in his house by the sea. Peter will tell you what to do." When the angel was gone, Cornelius sent two of his servants and a soldier to find Peter.

On the next day, even while the men were traveling toward Joppa, Peter was up on the roof praying. It was noon and Peter was hungry. While he was waiting for his lunch, Peter fell into a strange sleep and dreamed. He saw heaven open up and a large sheet being let down toward the earth. It was filled with all kinds of wild animals, creeping animals, and birds. As Peter looked, he heard God's voice.

"Rise up, Peter, kill, and eat," the Voice said.

But Peter answered, "Not so, Lord. For I have never eaten anything which was common and unclean."

Then God said, "What God has made clean, you must not call unclean."

Three times Peter saw the sheet and heard God's words. He wondered what God was trying to tell him in this dream. While he was thinking about it, the servants of Cornelius arrived. They stood at the door, asking for Peter.

God said to Peter, "See, three men are asking for you. Go home with them, for I have sent them."

Peter went down to meet the men. He invited them to stay at Simon's house over night. In the morning, Peter and several friends from Joppa went along with Cornelius' servants.

Back in Caesarea Cornelius was waiting. Many of his friends and relatives were waiting, too. Cornelius ran out to meet Peter. He fell at his feet and worshiped him.

"Stand up," Peter said. "Don't worship me. I am only a man like you."

All the people gathered around Peter. He told them about his vision. Then Cornelius told Peter about the angel's visit. "I always thought," Peter explained, "that God cared only for my people, the Jews. But now I know that God wants all people to love Jesus."

Then Peter taught Cornelius and all his house about Jesus. He told them the wonderful story of Jesus' death and how He came to life again. And while Peter was talking, the Holy Spirit suddenly came into the hearts of all those who listened. Peter and his friends from Joppa were amazed to see these strangers filled with the Holy Spirit.

The men from Joppa said to Peter, "How can you refuse to baptize these people, when God has already given them the Holy

Spirit?" Then Peter baptized all those who were in the house. And so a new church was started in Caesarea.

When the people in Jerusalem heard what Peter had done, some of them were angry. As soon as Peter came back to Jerusalem, they scolded him for letting people who weren't Jews into Jesus' church. Then Peter told them what had happened, about his dream, and his stay with Cornelius. When the others realized that it was God who had sent Peter to the heathen city, they kept still. They glorified God and said, "It must be that God wants the heathen to be saved, too."

> *Were you listening?* What did Peter see in his vision? What did the vision mean? Did Jesus die only for the Jews?

Story 256

An Angel Saves Peter

Acts 11 and 12

Things were not going so well in Jerusalem. The wicked King Herod, who ruled the land of Israel, came to Jerusalem. He was the nephew of the Herod who had killed John the Baptist, and he was also cruel.

King Herod made friends with the leaders of the people. When he saw that the leaders hated the Christians, he tried to hurt them, too. One day he killed James, the brother of John, with a sword. This greatly pleased those leaders. When King Herod saw that they were pleased, he caught Peter, too, and put him in prison. It was springtime, the time of the Passover Feast. "After the Passover, I'll kill Peter, too," King Herod said.

All the while Peter was in prison, his friends prayed for him. They met together in that same upper room of John Mark's, where they had met so often before. They asked God to show His great power and save Peter. And God heard their prayer!

It was the last day of the feast, the night before Peter was to be killed. Peter was sleeping between two soldiers, his hands fastened with chains. Other soldiers were watching at the door. Suddenly an angel stood next to Peter. And the room was filled with light. The angel touched Peter on the side and awakened him. "Get up quickly," he said. The chains fell from Peter's hands.

484 An Angel Saves Peter

"Get dressed," the angel went on. "Put on your coat and shoes and follow me."

Peter did what the angel told him, but he thought he was dreaming. The angel led Peter out of the room, past the sleeping soldiers. They passed the first group of soldiers at the first door. And they passed the second group of soldiers at the second door. Finally, they reached the great iron gate, which opened into the street. As they neared the gate, it swung open by itself. Peter and the angel walked out into the street. Then the angel was gone.

When Peter saw that he was free, he said, "Now I know that Jesus sent His angel to save me from the hand of the wicked king."

Peter went at once to John Mark's house. The house was filled with people. They were still praying for Peter. Peter knocked at the door. Rhoda, a servant girl, came to the door. "Who's there?" she called.

"It is I, Peter," Peter answered. "Let me in."

Rhoda was so excited when she heard Peter's voice, that she ran back upstairs without opening the door. "Peter is at the door!" she cried.

"You must be out of your mind!" they said.

But Rhoda insisted that it was Peter.

"Perhaps it is his angel," they said.

All this while, Peter kept on knocking. Finally, they opened the door. How surprised they were to see Peter standing there. Peter's friends had been praying for a long time, asking Jesus to save Peter. Still they did not have enough faith to believe that Jesus would actually save him. How joyful they were when Peter told them how the angel had saved him.

That same night, Peter went away to another place where the wicked King Herod could not find him. As soon as it was morning, King Herod sent to the prison for Peter. The soldiers were very much upset when they found Peter gone. And when King Herod learned of it, he had all the soldiers put to death instead.

But the wicked King Herod did not live much longer himself. One day he dressed himself in his beautiful robe and sat upon his throne. He gave a speech to his people. When the people heard the words of their king, they shouted, "It is the voice of a god, and not of a man!"

King Herod liked such praise. He liked to have the people think he was a god and did not tell them they were wrong. As soon as he took the glory to himself, instead of giving it to God, the angel of the Lord sent him a terrible sickness. In five days he died.

So this enemy of the Christians died, and the church of Jesus Christ continued to grow!

> *Were you listening?* What happened to James? What happened to Peter? What happened to King Herod?

Story 257

Paul Goes on a Missionary Journey

Acts 13

Saul and Barnabas were working in Antioch. By this time there were several other teachers working in Antioch, too. One day, as they were all working together, they heard the Holy Spirit calling them.

"Separate me Barnabas and Saul," the Holy Spirit said. "I have a special work I want them to do."

The men quickly obeyed. They met together to pray and to fast. (When people fast, they do not eat food for many hours.) After praying and fasting for a long time, they laid their hands on Barnabas and Saul and blessed them. Then they sent them away.

Jesus did not want all His workers (apostles) to stay in His own country and preach to His own people, the Jews. He wanted Saul and Barnabas to go out and tell the "good news" to all the people of the world, so that men everywhere might learn to love Jesus. So Saul and Barnabas started out on their trip.

Now Saul became a missionary to the Gentiles. (All the people who were not Jews were called Gentiles.) His name was changed to Paul. Soon he became known everywhere as Paul, the great missionary for Jesus.

When Paul and Barnabas started out that first day, they took a boat and sailed to Cyprus. Young John Mark went with them to be their helper. They stopped at a place called Salamis and preached about Jesus in the churches there.

Soon they went on to Paphos. There they visited one of the rulers of the country, a man named Sergius Paulus. This ruler had heard about the three missionaries of Jesus and wanted to hear them preach. There was a magician or wise man who worked for Sergius Paulus. He had two names, sometimes he was called Bar-Jesus, and sometimes, Elymas. He was a wicked man who said he was a prophet. Elymas taught the people wicked things. He did not want the ruler, Sergius Paulus, to listen to Paul and to believe in Jesus. He knew that then Paulus and the people would no longer listen to him. So he said bad things about Paul and his teachings.

Elymas was standing beside the ruler's chair as Paul was preaching. He kept whispering to the ruler not to believe what Paul said. Then Paul looked up at him sternly and said, "You wicked man! You child of the devil! You enemy of everything that's good! When are you going to stop your wicked works? See, the hand of the Lord is upon you. He is going to make you blind! You will not be able to see for a while." At once the magician became blind. He had to be led away by the hand.

When Sergius Paulus saw what had happened, he was amazed. He believed Paul's words and became a Christian. Then Paul and Barnabas continued their journey and John Mark went back to Jerusalem.

Were you listening? What special work did the Holy Spirit have for Saul and Barnabas? When was Saul's name changed to Paul? Why was Paul sent to the Gentiles? What happened to the magician in Paphos?

Story 258

Paul Stoned at Lystra

Acts 14

After John Mark left them, Paul and Barnabas continued their journey to a Roman city which was also called Antioch. When it was the Sabbath Day, they went into the synagogue of the Jews and preached about Jesus. When Paul had finished preaching, the people in the church were divided. Half of them followed

Paul and Barnabas and believed their teaching. But the other half would not believe that Jesus was the Saviour.

As soon as the two missionaries had left the synagogue, the Gentiles came to them and asked if they would preach the same words to them on the next Sabbath Day. So, when the next Sabbath Day came, all the people of the city, both Jews and Gentiles, came to hear Paul preach.

But when the leaders who were against Paul saw the crowd, they were jealous of Paul. They told the people not to listen to Paul because he was telling lies. Paul and Barnabas were not afraid. They stood up in front of the people and said, "God wanted us to first bring the Gospel to you. But seeing you would not believe, we turn to the Gentiles. That is what God told us to do. For God said, 'I have sent you to be a light to the Gentiles, so that all the people of the world may be saved, even to the end of the earth.'"

When the Gentiles heard these words, they were filled with joy. Many believed and were baptized. But Paul's enemies stirred up trouble and chased Paul and Barnabas out of their city.

Then the two missionaries went to the city called Iconium, which was not far away. Here they stayed for quite a long time. They preached to great crowds of people, both Jews and Gentiles. And just as it was in Antioch, so it was in Iconium. The people were divided — half of them believed Paul and half did not.

Finally, those who were against Paul and Barnabas made plans to hurt them and to stone them. As soon as the two missionaries heard about it, they fled to the next city, called Lystra.

They preached in Lystra for many days. As they were preaching one day, a man, who had been lame ever since he was born and had never walked, sat at Paul's feet. He listened closely to everything Paul said. Paul could see that he believed that Jesus could heal him. Stopping right in the middle of his sermon, Paul pointed to the lame man and shouted, "Stand up on your feet!" The lame man stood up at once and walked!

The people were amazed. They began to shout, "The gods have come down to us!" They believed that Barnabas was Jupiter, and Paul, Mercurius. (These were heathen gods which they once worshiped.) The priest of Jupiter (Jupiter's temple was in Lystra) brought sacrifices to be burned to Paul and Barnabas.

As soon as Paul and Barnabas noticed what was going on, they ran among the people and shouted, "Don't worship us! We're not gods! We're only men as you are!" Then Paul began again to tell them about his wonderful Saviour. When he finished, the people still wanted to burn sacrifices to them.

One day the men who had stirred up trouble in Iconium heard about the great success Paul and Barnabas were having in Lystra. So they came down to Lystra to turn the people against Paul. When enough people were won over, they captured Paul and threw stones at him until they thought he was dead. Then they dragged his body outside the city and left him lying there.

The friends of Paul had followed the crowd. Now when Paul was left alone, they gathered around him. They were making plans to bury him. But, to their great surprise, Paul suddenly stood up. He was not dead at all. Jesus had kept him from being killed. Paul went back to the city with them. The next day Paul and Barnabas went on to another city called Derbe.

Paul and Barnabas preached in Derbe for a while. They won many new disciples for Jesus. Then they went back and visited all the places where they had preached before. In each one of these cities a church had been started. Now, on their second visit, Paul and Barnabas appointed elders to take care of the new churches for them.

Finally, the first missionary journey was over. Paul and Barnabas got into a ship and sailed back to Antioch, to the church that had sent them out. All the followers of Jesus in Antioch came together to listen to Paul and Barnabas, as they told about all the exciting things that had happened on their trip. The people were filled with joy to hear that so many people had turned to the Lord.

Were you listening? Why were the Gentiles in the Roman city of Antioch filled with joy? Why did Paul and Barnabas flee to Lystra? Why didn't Paul die when the Jews stoned him?

Paul's Second Missionary Journey

After they had been in Antioch for a year or so, Paul said to Barnabas, "Let's go on another missionary journey and visit all the new churches to see how they are getting along."

Barnabas thought this would be a good idea. "Let's take my cousin, John Mark, with us again," he said.

"No," Paul answered, "I don't think we should take Mark with us this time. Mark does not make a very good missionary. Last time, we had just got started when he left us and went back home."

Paul and Barnabas could not agree about Mark. Finally, they decided to have two missionary teams instead of one. Barnabas took his cousin Mark and went by boat to the island of Cyprus. Paul chose Silas to go with him. They did not take a boat. They traveled on land across the mountains.

One day Paul and Silas came to Derbe and Lystra, where churches had been started on Paul's first visit. Here they found a young man whose name was Timothy. Timothy's father was a Greek, but his mother, Eunice, and his grandmother, Lois, were both Jews. Timothy's mother and grandmother were good women. Ever since Timothy was a little boy, they had taught him to love God and to know the Bible. Paul learned to love Timothy as his own son. He invited Timothy to join him on his journey. Timothy was happy to join Paul and Silas.

Soon the three missionaries set out again. They traveled from one city to another, preaching wherever they went. One day they came to Troas, a city on the seashore. One night while they were in Troas, Paul had a dream. In the dream Paul saw a man from a country called Macedonia. The man was beckoning to Paul and calling, "Come over into Macedonia and help us!" Paul knew at once that Jesus had sent him the dream. He felt that Jesus wanted him to go to the country of Macedonia where no one had ever heard about Jesus.

Macedonia was a large country across the sea from Troas. Paul and his helpers made plans to set sail for Macedonia. They were on the boat for several days. Finally they came to one of the big cities of Macedonia. It was called Philippi. Here they stayed for a few days.

Now there were four men in Paul's group. Before they had reached Troas, a doctor named Luke had joined them. He was one of Paul's best friends. When the Sabbath day came, the four men went out to find a place where they could worship God. There was no synagogue in Philippi, for there were not enough Jews there. So Paul and his friends went out of the city to the river side, where they had heard people gathered for prayer. They found several women gathered together at the water's edge.

Paul and his friends sat down with the women and preached to them. One of the women, Lydia, already believed in God. She had heard about God and came each week to the river's edge to pray and worship Him. Lydia was a business woman — she sold purple dye. When Paul had finished preaching, Lydia believed his words about Jesus. She gave her heart to Jesus and was baptized. Her family and all those who lived in her house were baptized, too. Then Lydia said to Paul and his party, "Please live at my house while you are in our city." So Paul, Silas, Timothy and Luke all went to live at Lydia's home.

> *Were you listening?* Why did Paul want to go on another missionary journey? Why did Paul and Barnabas quarrel? Who went with Paul when he started out? Who joined him later? Why did Paul and his friends go to Macedonia?

Story 260

Paul Suffers for Jesus

Acts 16

In the city of Philippi, where Paul and his three friends were working, there lived a young girl who was a fortune-teller. An evil spirit lived in her heart. Through the working of this evil spirit, she could tell what was going to happen in the future.

This poor girl was a slave. Some evil men were her masters. They were glad that she could tell fortunes. The money she made telling fortunes went into their pockets. In that way they had become rich, for many people came each day to have their fortunes told. The people believed that what the girl said was sure to happen.

Whenever this poor slave-girl saw Paul and Silas and the others walking down the street, she would follow them shouting, "These men are the servants of the Most High God, and they have come to show us the way of salvation."

This went on for several days. Paul knew that it was the evil spirit in her heart that was making her do this. He felt sorry for the poor girl, and he did not like to hear what the spirit said. One day, as the girl was following them again, Paul turned around and said to the evil spirit, "I command you in the name of Jesus Christ, come out of her!" The evil spirit left her at once.

How angry her masters were! When they saw that their slave girl was now just like any other girl, they knew that they could not earn any more money through her. They caught hold of Paul and Silas and dragged them into the marketplace before the rulers. "These men are troubling our city and teaching wrong things," they said.

The crowd which had gathered joined them against Paul and Silas. The rulers stripped off the clothing of Paul and Silas and had them beaten. Then they threw them into prison. The jailor was warned to keep them safely. So he put them in the inner prison, which was the worst place of all. He locked their feet in a wooden frame called stocks.

Paul and Silas suffered greatly in that prison. Their backs were swollen and bleeding from the cruel whipping. The stocks caused them great pain, too. It was impossible for them to move even one inch. But when they remembered that they were suffering for Jesus, who had suffered the cruel death of the Cross for them, their hearts were happy even though their bodies were in pain. All night long they prayed and sang songs of praise to God. Everyone could hear them.

Suddenly, about midnight, there was a great earthquake. The prison shook. All the doors were opened and the chains of all the prisoners fell off. When the jailor awoke and saw what had happened, he thought all his prisoners had escaped. He drew his sword and was ready to kill himself.

But none of the prisoners had escaped. When Paul saw what the jailor was about to do, he called, "Don't hurt yourself! We are all here!"

The jailor called for a light. He came in and fell at Paul's feet, trembling. "Sirs," he cried, "what must I do to be saved?"

"Believe on the Lord Jesus Christ, and you shall be saved — you and your whole family," Paul answered.

Right away the jailor brought Paul and Silas out of the prison. He washed their sore backs and took care of them. Then he took Paul and Silas to his house. There Paul taught him and his family about Jesus. They all believed and were baptized. There was great rejoicing in the jailor's house that night.

The next morning the ruler sent his soldiers to the jailor saying, "Let those men go." The jailor said to Paul, "The ruler has sent word to let you go. So now you may go in peace."

But Paul answered, "Yesterday they beat us openly in front of all the people, without giving us a trial. Then they threw us into jail. And now they want us to go away quietly, without anyone seeing us. I am a Roman. You cannot treat a Roman that way. Tell the rulers to come themselves and get us out."

When the soldiers told the rulers what Paul had said, the men were afraid. They did not know that Paul and Silas were Romans. (Although Paul and Silas were Jewish, they had both been born in Roman cities. So they were also Romans.) So the rulers came themselves and brought Paul and Silas out of prison. They begged Paul and Silas to leave their city.

Paul and Silas went first to the home of Lydia. Here they met with all the believers. Then they said good-bye and continued their journey.

Were you listening? Where did Paul and his friends stay in Philippi? Why were they thrown into prison? What happened at midnight? Which three people in Philippi felt the power of Jesus?

"The Unknown God"

After leaving Philippi, Paul and Silas visited several other cities in Macedonia. While they were in a city called Thessalonica, Paul preached in the Jewish synagogue on three Sabbath days. He told the people there the whole story of Jesus Christ, how He suffered and died to save sinners. Some of the Jews believed Paul's teaching, and a great number of Greeks were filled with joy to learn of the Saviour.

But the rest of the people did not believe Paul's words and were jealous of him. They gathered together a mob of rough men and tried to capture Paul and his friends. The missionaries were staying in the home of Jason. But the mob did not find them there. So they took Jason to the rulers instead. The rulers made Jason promise not to cause any trouble in the city and then let him go.

Seeing it was no longer safe for the missionaries to stay in Thessalonica, the Christians brought them by night to the next town of Berea. Here the people were glad to have Paul visit them. They listened to Paul and tried to understand his teachings. Many of them believed after studying their Bibles every day to see if Paul were teaching the truth.

Soon the Jews of Thessalonica heard where Paul had gone. They came down to Berea to stir up the people there, too. But a group of Christians helped Paul get to a town on the seashore. Here Paul took passage on a ship, sailing to the city of Athens in Greece. Silas and Timothy stayed in Berea, but Luke, the doctor, went with Paul.

Athens was one of the greatest cities of the world in those days. All the important men of Greece lived in Athens. There was a big university in Athens, too. Each day the learned men of the city met together in the marketplace to talk. They liked to learn about new things and think about new ideas.

Most of the people of Athens had never heard about God, although there was a small church there. The Greeks worshiped idols. They had made their city very beautiful by making lovely marble statues of their idol-gods. And there were many beautiful temples throughout the city, where the people came to worship their idols.

As Paul waited in Athens for Silas and Timothy, he wandered through the streets and noticed all the marble statues. There were idols and altars to every god imaginable. Paul even saw an altar with these words, "To the Unknown God." The people wanted to be sure they did not miss any god. If there were a god they did not know, they made an altar for him, too!

Paul was angry when he saw this great city so filled with idols. He preached to the Jews in their synagogue and argued with them about the true God and His Son, Jesus Christ. Each day he went into the marketplace and talked with the learned men also. He preached to them about Jesus Christ and the resurrection (how Jesus was raised from the dead). The men were interested in what Paul had to say. Some said, "What is this babbler trying to say?" Others said, "He seems to teach about strange gods." They brought Paul to their court of learning, which was on top of Mars Hill. This was an ancient place where the learned men often gathered to hear people speak.

So Paul stood up on Mars Hill. "Tell us," the Greek men said, "about this new teaching of yours, for it sounds strange in our ears."

Then Paul answered, "Ye men of Athens, I see that you are most religious. As I passed through your city, I saw that you worship many gods. And I noticed that you even worship at an altar on which is written 'To the Unknown God.' Now, this God, whom you worship without knowing, He is the One I bring to you. For He is the only true God. He is the One who made this world and everything in it. And, since He is the Lord of heaven and earth, He does not have to live in temples made with hands. He does not need to have you give Him food or any of the things you give to your gods when you sacrifice to them. He is the God who gives life to everything. And He wants people to seek Him and find Him, for He is not far from any of us.

"Some of your poets have said, 'We are the children of God.'

If we are the children of God, we ought not to think that God is an idol which men can make out of silver or gold or stone. Before this you did not know about the true God, but now you know, for God hath sent His Son, Jesus Christ, whom He raised from the dead, to be your Saviour."

When the men heard Paul speak about Jesus being raised from the dead, some of them mocked for they did not believe that was possible. Others said, "We would like to hear about this again." But a few of them believed and followed Paul.

Were you listening? Why didn't Paul stay in Thessalonica? How did Paul know that the people of Athens did not believe in the true God? About what did Paul preach to them?

Story 262

A Great Bonfire

Acts 19

After Paul left Athens, he went on to Corinth. For about two years he lived there with a tent-maker named Aquila. Paul helped Aquila make tents. And every week, on the Sabbath Day, he preached to the people about Jesus.

From Corinth, Paul went to Ephesus, but he did not stay there very long. He wanted to go to Jerusalem to celebrate a feast. But he promised he would come back to Ephesus if it was God's will. So he sailed from Ephesus and once more headed for home. He stopped many places on the way, however, to visit all the little churches which had been started by the apostles. Finally he reached Jerusalem and so brought to an end his second missionary journey.

Paul did not stay in Jerusalem very long. By fall he was ready to start on his third missionary journey. He returned at once to Ephesus, as he had promised. There he preached to the people and taught them more about Jesus. After about two years everyone had heard about Jesus.

While Paul was in Ephesus, he did many wonderful things. Everyone round about heard about the miracles God helped Paul perform. So they brought sick people to Paul to be healed. Some took handkerchiefs and towels which Paul had used and brought them to their sick ones at home. When the sick people touched

Paul's handkerchiefs or towels, they were made better. Their sicknesses left them and the evil spirits went out of them.

There were some wicked magicians in Ephesus. They often fooled people with their tricks. When these magicians saw Paul chase the evil spirits from men's hearts, they tried to do it, too. They used the name of Jesus, just as they had heard Paul do.

A Jewish high priest named Sceva also lived in Ephesus. He had seven sons who were magicians. One day they tried to chase away an evil spirit out of a man. They said, "We command you to get out in the name of Jesus, whom Paul preaches."

But the evil spirit in the man said, "Jesus I know, and Paul I know, but who are you?" And then the man who had the spirit jumped on those wicked men and almost tore them to pieces. Finally they ran out of the house in great fear and terribly wounded.

Soon everyone in Ephesus had heard about what had happened. They all became afraid and glorified God. Many magicians believed in Jesus, too. Coming to Paul they confessed their sins and told Paul all the wicked things they had done. Then they brought all their bad magic books, from which they had learned their wicked tricks, and burned them in a big bonfire. The price of these books was fifty thousand pieces of silver!

Thus, because of Paul's teachings, the church of Jesus Christ grew steadfastly in Ephesus.

> *Were you listening?* How many missionary journeys did Paul make? What did Paul do for the sick people in Ephesus? What did the magicians try to do? Why did they burn all their magic books?

Story 263

A Riot in Ephesus

Acts 19

Paul was planning to leave Ephesus and go back to Jerusalem. On his way back he wanted to visit all the churches in Macedonia again. He sent Timothy and Erastus, two of his helpers, on ahead.

While Paul was still in Ephesus, there was a great riot one day because of him. There was a silversmith in Ephesus whose name was Demetrius. He made things out of silver. Much of his time he spent making little silver images of Diana, their god, which he would put in a small silver shrine.

The Ephesians believed that their god, Diana, had fallen from heaven. She was, they said, the god who gave life to plants and to babies. Some worshiped her as a huntress and a moon-goddess. The temple of Diana in Ephesus was gorgeous. It was one of the seven wonders of the world. Made of pure marble, it had taken two hundred and twenty years to build. Whenever people came to worship Diana in her wonderful temple (and people came from all over the world to see it), Demetrius would sell them his little silver shrines of Diana.

As long as Paul was in Ephesus he tried to teach the people that it was sin to worship Diana. Those who worshiped Diana did many wicked things. So Paul preached against Diana every day. He told the people that gods made with hands are not gods. There is only one God, and He was not made by man. Paul told the people to worship the true God and to throw away their silver Dianas.

That was why Demetrius did not like Paul. He knew that if the people listened to Paul they would no longer buy his silver shrines. So he called all the silversmiths together. "What shall we do?" he asked. "We earn our money by selling these little shrines of Diana. And now Paul is telling people everywhere, not only in Ephesus but in all the cities of our country, that they are not gods which are made with hands. So, not only are we in danger of losing our work, but even the wonderful temple of our great goddess, Diana, is in danger. What will happen to Diana if people no longer come here to worship her? They might even destroy her magnificent temple!"

When the silversmiths heard Demetrius' words, they were filled with anger. They shouted, "Great is Diana of the Ephesians!" Soon the whole city was in a terrible uproar. They caught Paul's two helpers and rushed them to the center of the crowd. Paul wanted to go into the crowd, too, but his friends stopped him. The people all shouted at one another. Many did not even know why they had come together.

Alexander, one of the Jews, tried to quiet the mob, but the people wouldn't listen to him. For two hours they shouted, one louder than another, "Great is Diana of the Ephesians!" Finally, the town clerk managed to get them quiet enough to listen to him.

"Men of Ephesus," he said, "who doesn't know that the temple of Diana is in Ephesus, and that the great goddess, Diana, fell down from the stars? Seeing everyone knows this, why get so excited? These men have not done anything harmful. If Demetrius has something against them, let him go to court with it. But don't start a riot. We are in danger of being sent to prison for this uproar, since there was no cause for it."

The town clerk then sent the people home. And Paul met with all the Christians in Ephesus to say goodbye to them. Then he went on with his journey.

> *Were you listening?* Where did Paul stay on his third missionary journey? What happened just before he was ready to leave? Who finally quieted the riot?

Story 264

Eutychus Falls From a Window

Acts 20

After leaving Ephesus, Paul went first to Macedonia where he had started several churches on his second missionary journey. He visited all these churches and then went on into Greece, to the city of Corinth where he had been a tent-maker for two years. Paul stayed in Corinth for about three months, but when he heard that his enemies there were planning to capture him, he decided to go back by way of Macedonia once more.

On his way back, Paul stopped at Philippi, where he and Silas had been thrown into prison on his second journey. He visited the Christians in Philippi and then went on to Troas. Troas was the city on the seacoast. It was in Troas, you remember, that Paul had received the call, in a dream, to go over into Macedonia.

When Paul reached Troas, there were seven men waiting for him. They wanted to travel with him to Jerusalem. Whenever Paul had started a new church in one of the heathen (Gentile) cities, he had suggested that these new Christians take up collections for the poor Christians in the Jerusalem church. These churches had followed Paul's suggestion. Now they had chosen seven men to go with Paul to bring their gifts to Jerusalem.

Paul and these seven men stayed in Troas for seven days. The last day of Paul's visit in Troas came on Sunday. On Sunday evening all the Christians in Troas gathered together at the home of a friend. In those early days the Christians often met together for their evening meal. When they had finished their supper, they would celebrate the Lord's Supper by eating the broken bread and drinking the poured-out wine. This was to remind them of the broken body and the shed blood of their Lord when He died for them on the Cross.

When they had finished their supper that evening in Troas, and had celebrated the Lord's Supper, Paul began to preach to them for the last time. Now it happened that the room where the people had gathered was on the third floor of a building. It was a large room, lit up with many bright lights. The room was crowded. People were even sitting in the open windows.

Paul had many things he wanted to tell these people before he left them. He preached to them for a long, long time. A young man named Eutychus had come to hear Paul preach that night, too. Eutychus sat in one of the open windows to listen. But as Paul kept on preaching, Eutychus became sleepy. The smoke from all the oil lamps made him still more sleepy. And the longer Paul preached, the more sleepy Eutychus became. Finally, he fell fast asleep. Backward he went out of the window and down to the ground below.

When the people went downstairs, they found Eutychus lying dead on the ground. Paul took the body of the dead man in his arms, and God gave life back to the young man. "Don't trouble yourself," Paul said to the people. "Look, his life is still in him."

Then the people all followed Paul to the upstairs room again. Paul went on with his preaching. He preached all night. When morning came, everyone finally went home. Paul and the seven men from the Gentile churches continued their journey. Luke was with Paul again. He had met Paul at Philippi, just before Paul came to Troas. Luke went back to Jerusalem with Paul and stayed with him most of the time for the rest of his life. It was Luke who later wrote down all the things that happened to the followers of Jesus after Jesus went back to heaven. Although Luke was a Greek, and was not one of Jesus' disciples when Jesus was on earth, he was one of the great leaders of the early church. His writings are a part of our Bible. He wrote the story of Jesus — the Gospel According to St. Luke, and the story of the early church — The Acts of the Apostles.

> *Were you listening?* What happened to Eutychus? What did Paul do for him? Who went back to Jerusalem with Paul? What do we know about Luke?

Story 265

Paul a Prisoner in Jerusalem

Acts 23

Paul was finishing his third missionary journey. He wanted to be back in Jerusalem by Pentecost Sunday. On his way he stopped at a town called Miletus, which was about thirty miles from Ephesus. Paul sent for the elders of the church at Ephesus to come to see him. He talked to them for a long time and warned them about all the things which would happen to them if they were not true to Jesus.

Paul knew that this would be the last time he would see his friends from Ephesus. And the elders knew, too, that there were enemies in Jerusalem who would try to kill Paul. They were sorry to let him go. But Paul was not afraid. He knew Jesus would be with him. He and his friends knelt together and prayed. Filled with sadness, the elders wept and wept. They threw their arms around Paul and kissed him. Finally they went with him to the ship and watched him sail away toward Jerusalem.

Paul also stopped for several days in Caesarea. Paul and the men with him stayed at the home of Philip, the preacher. Philip had taught the Ethiopian in his chariot, you remember. While they were staying with Philip, a prophet named Agabus came to see Paul. He took Paul's belt and tied up his own hands and feet with it. Then he said, "This is what the Holy Spirit says, 'So shall the Jews at Jerusalem tie up the man who owns this belt, and give him into the hands of the Gentiles.' "

When Paul's friends heard the prophet's words, they tried to persuade Paul not to go to Jerusalem. But Paul said, "What do you mean, weeping and trying to break my heart? I am ready not only to be bound, but to die for Jesus' sake!"

The friends of Paul stopped trying to persuade him then, and said, "The will of the Lord be done." And they sent several men to go with Paul to Jerusalem.

Soon Paul and those traveling with him left Caesarea and went on. Finally they came to Jerusalem. The Christians were happy to see them. They rejoiced with Paul for all the great things God had done among the Gentiles.

But the men who hated the Christians soon heard that Paul had come. They laid hands on him in the Temple one day. They dragged him outside and began to beat Paul. He would have been killed, but the captain of the Roman army heard about the excitement. He came with his soldiers and took Paul away. The soldiers bound Paul with two chains and asked who he was and what he had done. Shouting loudly, the people tried to tell the soldiers what they had against Paul. There was so much confusion that the soldiers didn't know what to make of it. Finally, the captain commanded the soldiers to carry Paul into the castle.

When they carried Paul up the steps of the castle, Paul said to the captain, "May I say something?" Paul spoke in the Greek language.

The captain was surprised. "Can you speak Greek?" he asked. "I thought you were that Egyptian who has been causing trouble with his four thousand wicked men."

"No," Paul answered, "I am a Jew. Please let me speak to these people."

When the captain had given permission, Paul stood on the stairs and preached to the people. He told them all about his whole life, how first he had hated the Christians and later had become a missionary for Jesus.

At first the Jews listened, but finally they shouted, "Away with such a fellow from the earth, he is not fit to live!" And as they cried, they tore off their clothing and threw dust into the air.

Then the captain commanded his men to bring Paul into the castle and whip him with a scourge (as they had once done to Jesus). They took Paul into the castle and began to tie him with leather cords. Paul looked at one of the soldiers and said, "May you scourge a man that is a Roman without first proving that he is guilty?"

The soldier quickly went to the captain. "Be careful what you do," he said, "for this man is a Roman."

The captain hurried over to Paul and said, "Tell me, are you a Roman?"

"I am," Paul answered.

"I had to pay a great sum of money to become a Roman," the captain said.

"But I was born a Roman," Paul answered.

Then they took off Paul's chains and left him in the castle over night.

> *Were you listening?* Why didn't Paul's friends want him to go to Jerusalem? What did Agabus do and say? Why did the soldiers take Paul into the castle? Why didn't the captain scourge Paul?

Story 266

Paul Saved by His Nephew

Acts 23

All night Paul stayed in the castle where the Roman soldiers had brought him. In the morning, the captain called the Jews together and brought Paul to them. Paul looked at the men and said, "Brethren, I have tried to live rightly before God until this very day."

When the high priest heard Paul's words, he told the man standing near him to slap him on the mouth. But Paul said, "God will slap you, you wicked one! Do you, the judge, break the law yourself?"

After Paul had talked a while longer, the Jews began to quarrel among themselves. They became so excited that the captain was afraid they would tear Paul to pieces. So he ordered his soldiers to take Paul back into the castle. That night, while Paul slept, Jesus stood by him and said, "Be of good cheer, Paul. Just as you have preached about Me here in Jerusalem, so must you also do in Rome." Paul was happy to hear this. Although he had brought the Gospel to a great many cities, he had never been to the greatest city of all, Rome. The great emperor, Caesar, lived in Rome, and Paul had planned several times to visit Rome. How happy he was to know that he was to carry the Gospel to the Roman emperor, too.

When morning came, some men got together and made plans to kill Paul. They swore to each other that they would neither eat nor drink until Paul was dead. "We'll tell the captain we want to talk to Paul again and ask him some questions," they said. "Then when the captain brings him down, we'll quickly kill him."

But Paul's sister's young son heard about their wicked plan. He went into the castle to tell Paul. When Paul heard about the plan, he sent his nephew to the captain. The captain took the boy by the hand and led him aside. "What is it you have to tell me?" he whispered. The boy told the captain all about the wicked plan. "You may go now," the captain said, "but don't tell anyone that you told me these things."

So the boy went away without being seen. The captain called for two hundred soldiers, and seventy horsemen, and two hundred spearmen. When it was late at night, they took Paul and brought him safely to another city, Caesarea, where Felix was the governor. The governor kept Paul safe until it could be decided what should be done.

> *Were you listening?* What happened to Paul when he tried to argue with his enemies? Who spoke to him in the night? Who saved him from being killed?

Story 267

Paul on Trial

Acts 24, 25 and 26

After the governor put Paul in prison, he waited until the Jewish rulers came to tell him what Paul had done. When the high priest and elders came, they told the governor that Paul was a troublesome fellow and had done many wrong things. The governor then let Paul answer them. Paul tried to prove to his enemies that he had done nothing wrong. But Felix, the governor, said, "Let's wait until the chief captain comes. Then I'll find out more about it." He commanded a soldier to take charge of Paul.

For some time Paul was allowed more freedom. A soldier guarded him, but his friends were allowed to visit him at any time. Several times Felix had Paul brought to his home so that he and his wife, Drusilla (who was a Jewess), could hear more about Paul's teachings. Paul talked to them again and again about the things of God. He warned them that God would some day come to punish all those who were wicked. Felix was often afraid of Paul's words, but he never gave his heart to Jesus.

Felix hoped that Paul would pay money to get his freedom back, so he sent for him often. But when Paul gave him no money, he left Paul in prison for two years. Then Felix was sent to another city and a new governor came to Caesarea.

Festus, the new governor, soon visited Jerusalem. The people there tried to trick him into bringing Paul back to Jerusalem, so they might kill him. But Festus insisted that they should come with him to Caesarea. As soon as Festus arrived at Caesarea, he had Paul brought to trial once more.

While Paul was pleading his cause, he said, "I have not done anything wrong, not against the laws of the Jews, nor against their Temple, nor even against Caesar, the great emperor."

Then Festus, trying to please the Jews, said, "Would you like to go to Jerusalem and be judged there?"

"You know very well that I have done no wrong to the Jews," Paul said. "I would like to take my case to the great emperor, Caesar, in Rome. If I have done anything worthy of death, I am willing to die. But if I haven't done anything wrong, no man may sentence me to death but Caesar. I want to go to Caesar."

Festus answered, "If you want to go to Caesar you shall go!"

Not long after this, King Agrippa and Queen Bernice came to visit Festus. Festus told them all about Paul. "I should like to hear this man, myself," King Agrippa said. So the next day the king and queen dressed themselves in their fine clothing and went with Festus to the judgment hall. Paul was brought in and Festus introduced him to the king. King Agrippa turned to Paul. "You may speak for yourself," he said.

Once more Paul told his story. "I am happy, O King," he began, "to be able to tell you my story." Then he told the king all about his life and about the wonderful Gospel of Jesus Christ. He spoke for a long time. Finally, Festus shouted, "Paul, you are beside yourself! Too much learning has made you insane!"

"I am not insane, most noble Festus," Paul answered. "I am speaking the words of truth. I think the king knows what I am talking about." Then he turned to the king and said, "King Agrippa, do you believe what the prophets have written in the Bible? Yes, I know you believe!"

King Agrippa was much upset. "Paul," he said, "you almost persuade me to be a Christian."

"Would to God," Paul answered, "that not only you, but everyone in this room, might be as I am, except for these chains!"

Then the king and those with him left the room. "This man might have been set free," the king added, "if he had not asked to go to Caesar."

Were you listening? How long did Felix keep Paul in prison? Where did Paul ask to go? What did King Agrippa say about Paul's teachings? Why could the king not free Paul?

Story 268

Paul Shipwrecked

Acts 27

Paul was going to Rome. Although he would have to go as a prisoner, Paul waited eagerly for the day when he should set sail. Soon everything was ready. A Roman captain named Julius took Paul and several other prisoners aboard the ship. Two of Paul's friends also went along. Luke, the doctor, and one of his former helpers, Aristarchus, were allowed to accompany him. Paul soon made friends with the captain. The ship stopped at several different ports along the seacoast. At Sidon Julius allowed Paul the freedom to go visit his friends for a short time. Then Paul returned to the ship. After several days of sailing, they came to Myra. Here Julius found another ship which was going to Rome. This ship was one of the boats which carried corn from Alexandria, in Egypt, to Rome.

In those days it was dangerous to sail on the Mediterranean Sea after September 14. Sailing stopped altogether for the winter after November 11. By the time Julius took his prisoners on the Egyptian ship it was already nearly fall. The winds were no longer favorable for sailing. The ship moved along slowly for several days. Finally, with much difficulty, they reached a place called the Fair Havens. It was now well into October, and since it was getting pretty late for safe sailing, the captain of the ship called a meeting of his crew (and other important men on the ship) to decide what should be done. Since Paul was a great missionary and had much experience as a traveler, they asked him to attend the meeting, too.

Paul strongly urged the men to stay at Fair Havens for the winter. "Sirs," he said, "it will be much too dangerous to go on now. Not only could you lose your ship, but many of the people on your ship could be killed."

But the shipowner and his crew thought they would be able to make another port, called Phoenix, which was farther west along the coast of Crete. Phoenix was a much better port and would be a more pleasant place to stay for the winter. Julius, the Roman captain, had to decide what they should do. He accepted the advice of the sailors rather than of Paul, and so they set out for Phoenix.

All went well at first. The south wind blew gently and the ship sailed smoothly along. They stayed close to the shores of Crete. But soon they ran into a bad storm. A strong wind, called a typhoon, blew down from the mountains in Crete and forced the ship away from the shore out into the angry sea. With great difficulty they finally succeeded in bringing the lifeboat, which was usually tied to the back of the ship, on board the ship. As they came along the north coast of Africa they were in danger of being driven onto the quicksands along the shore. That would have killed them all. Quickly they threw overboard all the heavy boxes and freight to lighten the ship. Then they threw out the ship's furniture. Thus they finally succeeded in escaping the quicksand.

For fourteen days the storm raged. The sky was black with clouds all the time. No sun nor moon, nor even tiny stars, appeared to show them the way. Day after day the helpless ship tossed back and forth on the raging sea like a huge plaything of an angry monster. All hope of being saved was gone. The 276 people on board huddled together in fear. No one dared eat or sleep.

Paul was the only one on board that helpless ship who was not afraid. He trusted in God and knew that God would take care of him. One night God sent His angel to Paul. "Do not be afraid, Paul," the angel said. "God wants you to stand before the great Caesar in Rome, so He will see to it that you get there. And for your sake He will save all the men who are traveling with you on this boat."

The next morning Paul gathered all the men together and said, "You should have listened to me when we were in Fair Havens. But don't be afraid. Although the ship is going to be lost, no one will be killed. An angel told me last night that God wants me to stand before Caesar. And He will save all of you for my sake."

On the fourteenth night the sailors noticed that they were approaching land. It was too dark to see, but by dropping their anchor they could tell that the sea was not as deep as it had been. Since they could not see where they were going, the sailors were afraid the ship would be dashed to pieces against a rock. A few of them made plans to quietly escape in the little lifeboat, but Paul saw them and reported it to the captain. Paul said, "Unless these men remain, you cannot be saved." The captain quickly ordered the soldiers to cut the ropes and the lifeboat fell into the water.

When morning finally came Paul ate breakfast and urged the others to eat, too, so they would have strength to save themselves. They had not eaten for many days. Then they threw the rest of the food, and all the corn, overboard to lighten the ship. As they drew near to land, they noticed a little bay with a sandy beach. Hoisting the main sail, they headed for shore. But they went aground between two islands and the front end of the ship stuck fast. The waves continued to beat against the back of the ship and it soon broke in half.

As the ship began to sink, the men jumped into the water and swam to shore. The soldiers wanted to kill the prisoners lest they escape, but the captain liked Paul and wanted to save him. So he ordered the prisoners to jump into the water, too. Everyone made for the beach, some swam, some came in on boards, and some were helped by others. But they all reached shore in safety, just as Paul had promised.

> *Were you listening?* Where did Paul want to go? Why did Paul think they should wait until spring? What happened on the sea? Why were all the men saved?
>
> *Story 269*

Paul Reaches Rome

PART ONE

Acts 28

When the men reached land, they found that they were on a little island called Melita. The people of the island soon learned of the shipwreck. They hurried to the shore to meet those who came from the ship.

The people from the ship were wet and cold. The natives quickly built a big bonfire. The men all stood around the fire to dry their clothing and to warm themselves. Paul hunted around for more wood to help the natives with the fire. As he was placing a bundle of sticks on the fire, a poisonous snake jumped out of the wood and clung to Paul's hand. Paul must have mistaken the snake for a stick since it was asleep and still from the cold. As soon as the snake felt the heat of the fire, it awoke and curled around Paul's hand.

When the natives saw the poisonous snake hanging from Paul's hand, they said to each other, "This man must be a murderer. Even though he didn't drown in the sea, he'll surely die now!" And they watched to see what would happen. They thought Paul's body would swell until he would drop dead. But nothing happened. Paul just shook the snake from his hand into the fire and went on with his work.

Then the natives changed their minds. They decided Paul must be a god.

The chief of the people on the island was a man named Publius. He invited Paul and his friends to stay in his home until they could find a place to live. They stayed with Publius for three days. When they first arrived at Publius' house, they found that his father was very sick with a bad fever. Paul laid his hands on the sick man and prayed to Jesus. At once the sick man was healed. It wasn't long before all the sick of the island were brought to Paul. And he healed them all.

When spring finally came, Paul set out once more for Rome. This time there was no storm, and after many days the ship arrived in Italy. First it stopped at Syracuse for three days. The next day it landed at Puteoli. Here Paul and his friends were entertained by several Christians. They stayed with the Christians for one week. From here they walked up the Appian Way towards Rome. While they were still forty miles from Rome, they were met by a group of Christians from Rome. These Christians had walked all the way to greet the great Apostle and to escort him to their city. When Paul saw the Roman Christians he was filled with joy and courage. He thanked God for finally fulfilling his great desire.

PART TWO

After arriving in Rome Paul was turned over to an officer of Caesar's court. He was not sent to prison but was allowed to live in his own house with a soldier to guard him. A light chain at his wrist kept Paul close to this soldier. Each day friends came in to see Paul and to hear him preach. And each day a different soldier heard the Gospel, too. For two years Paul lived in Rome, boldly preaching and teaching about Jesus Christ. And many who heard, believed.

In the Acts of the Apostles Luke, the author, does not tell us what happened to Paul. But Paul writes about it himself in his letters to the different churches. And the history books of that time also tell us about Paul's last days. It was in the year 60 (60 years after the birth of Christ) that Paul was sent to Caesarea as a prisoner. In the spring of 61 he reached Rome. In the spring of 63 he was released. Once more he went on a missionary journey. This time he visited another country which he had always wanted to visit — Spain. He also spent some time in Ephesus. Stopping off at Crete, he left Titus there to start new churches. After visiting Miletus and Corinth again, he went on to Troas, where he left some of his belongings. He intended to spend the winter of 64 in Nicopolis, which was a Roman colony. It was during that winter that there was a terrible fire in Rome. The emperor, Nero, blamed the Christians for the fire. Since Paul was considered the leader of the Christians in Rome, he was arrested and sent to prison in Rome. This time he was not treated with kindness. He was thrown into a dungeon where he was cold and miserable.

During all of Paul's missionary journeys he wrote letters to the different churches which he had started. During his first stay in Rome, he wrote the letters to the Ephesians, Philippians, Colossians, Philemon and, possibly, Hebrews. The letters to Timothy and to Titus were written while he was again traveling. The second letter to Timothy was written while he was in the Roman dungeon. It was in this letter that he asked for his belongings to be sent to him.

Paul was brought to trial and was condemned to death. Since he had many followers, Paul was taken outside the city of Rome to be killed. Since he was a Roman Paul could not be tortured or crucified. Thus, a Roman soldier killed him with a sword. Later a Roman emperor, Constantine, built a church in Paul's honor at the place where he was killed. It is still in Rome today, as is the dungeon where Paul was held prisoner. And so the greatest missionary who ever lived became a martyr and was happy to give his life for his King.

Were you listening? Why did the natives of Melita think Paul was a murderer? Why did they later think he was a god? What did Paul do in Rome? What finally happened to Paul?

Story 270

Jesus Shows Himself to John

Revelation 1

The apostles of Jesus Christ were all faithful to the very end. We know that James was killed by King Herod and that Paul was killed near Rome. The Bible does not tell us what happened to Peter. King Herod tried to kill him, but he was rescued by an angel, you remember. Many history books claim that Peter was crucified as his Lord had been.

John, the brother of James, was the youngest of the apostles. He was still living after all the other apostles had died. John, too, had to suffer for Jesus' sake. About thirty years after the death of Paul, about the year 95, John was captured and sent to a lonely island called Patmos. John stayed on the island for about a year. In 96 he was released and allowed to go back to his home in Ephesus. While in Ephesus John had charge of the seven churches in Asia. It was then that he wrote the Gospel of John, his three letters, and the last book of the Bible, the Revelation. John lived to be very old, and as far as people know, he did not die a martyr.

When John was captured and sent to Patmos, he had to live all alone on the island. But John was not lonely, for God was with him. One Sunday morning, while John was thinking about God, he suddenly heard a loud voice behind him. It sounded like a trumpet.

The Voice said, "I am the first and the last. I want you to write in a book all the things I am going to show you. Send the book to the seven churches in Asia."

John turned to see who was talking to him. He saw seven golden candlesticks or lampstands. And Jesus was walking among the lamps. He wore a beautiful robe which hung down to His feet and a gorgeous golden belt around His waist.

Jesus' head and hair were as white as wool or snow. His eyes were like a flame of fire. His feet were like brass which had been burned in a furnace. And His voice was rich and full and deep. It sounded like the voice of many waters. Jesus held seven stars in His right hand. His face was shining as bright as the noon-day sun. And a sharp, two-edged sword came out of His mouth.

When John saw Jesus, he fell at His feet as if he were dead. But Jesus laid His right hand on John and said, "Don't be afraid, John. I am the first and the last. I am He that liveth and was dead, but now I am alive forever more. And I have the keys of hell and of death. I want you to write all the things you have seen, and all the things I am going to show you."

Then Jesus explained to John the mystery of the things he had seen. "The seven golden candlesticks," Jesus said, "are the seven churches. And the seven stars which I am holding in My hand, are the ministers of the seven churches."

John obeyed Jesus' words. He wrote all that he saw and heard. And after he left the island, he sent those letters to the seven churches. Today John's letters are at the very end of God's Holy Bible. They are called "The Revelation of Saint John, the Divine." They were written for us, too. In those letters John blesses God's people with the peace of Jesus Christ, who loved us and washed us from our sins by His blood. John also wrote, "He is coming again on the clouds, and every eye shall see Him!"

After John had seen and heard all these wonderful things, he fell down and worshiped the angel who showed them to him. But the angel said, "Don't do that, for I am only one of God's servants, like you are, who obey God. Worship God!" And then he added, "Don't lock up the writings of the things you saw, for the time is getting closer. For Jesus says, 'Behold, I come quickly and I will bring my reward with me.' "

Won't that be a wonderful day when Jesus comes again to take us to His beautiful new home in heaven? Let us never forget Jesus' words. Let us remember to obey His teachings so that we shall be ready to meet Him when He comes!

Were you listening? Who got to be the oldest of all the apostles? What did John hear on the island one day? What did John see? Where can we read about these things?